The Jews of Germany

The Jews of Germany

A Story of Sixteen Centuries

by Marvin Lowenthal

PHILADELPHIA

The Jewish Publication Society of America

1936

PRINTED IN THE UNITED STATES OF AMERICA

In memory of
Henry and Diana L. Gitterman.

CONTENTS

CONTENTS

PREFACE

LIKE most histories the present book tells more than its title is likely to suggest. For one thing the experience of the Jews in Germany was, until recent years, largely a counterpart of their experience elsewhere. Except for dates, personalities, and local circumstance, its story is the story of all Jewry.

Moreover the history of Germany itself is less familiar to the English-speaking world than that of England, France, or even Italy. Henry IV of England means something to everyone, if only the title of a play; so too Henry IV of France, if only a plume and a pointed beard. But Henry IV of Germany? To relieve the embarrassment of meeting strange names and faces and in order, naturally, to make our story intelligible, many strands of purely German history—perhaps superfluous to the student but an act of helpfulness, we hope, to the layman—have been woven into the Jewish narrative.

Again, in an endeavor to furnish an adequate background for the German Jews who are a portion of all Israel, for the Germans who are a segment of Christendom, and for Jewry and Germany together who share the fortunes of the whole western world, we have been led into certain general accounts of the origin of the antagonism between Jew and Christian, the rise of feudalism, the attitude of the Church toward the Synagogue, the significance of Protestantism, the career of capitalism, the forces which evolved religious tolerance and political equality, and the history—quite apart from the science —behind our contemporary racial myths.

All of these themes are obviously broader than the story of either Germany or its Jews, but they were not thrown in for good measure. Without some knowledge of them, our tale would be a confusion and an enigma, as the general reader has too often found the fate of what, lacking this knowledge, he calls the "peculiar" people. Yet Jews have no more been the beneficiaries of an incomprehensible good-fortune than have bankers; they have no more been the victims of an incomprehensible hatred than dozens of other minorities.

The Jew has sometimes been called the unofficial critic of our civilization, and rightly so. Viewed through his eyes, the eyes of an ancient people who has contributed to and yet stood apart from the stream of western culture, many of its institutions, movements, and achievements appear in an unconventional light. Renan once remarked that our greatest joy lies in seeing the past as it really was. This is probably a joy no man can experience, but the delight that must come closest to it is to see the past from as many perspectives as we can.

The Jewish perspective, because it is colored by its own interests and philosophies, adds another light and shade and therefore a further understanding to the panorama of the centuries. For a long period the Jews were as distinct an economic class as the artisans or peasants. Besides possessing a special economic perspective, they have been the exponents of a distinctive view of the world, a religion and a philosophy, a manner of life, at once the basis and the antithesis of Christendom. Socially they have been through the ages—and still are— the touchstone of human decency. The distance which separates man from brute, the height which spells civilization, can be measured by the treatment accorded to this eternal minority. All in all, a history of the Jews, whether it be in Germany or any other western land, is therefore bound to reveal new facets in primitive Christianity, the Crusades, the revival of learning during the Renaissance, the character of a Martin Luther or Frederick the Great, the relation of finance to democracy, the birth of nationalism, and the decline of liberalism—to name a few of the diverse elements which shaped the destiny of the Jews and, in doing so, evoked their own appropriate evaluation.

The German Jews are singularly equipped to give us both the gist of typical Jewish experience since the Dispersion and a fresh critique of western culture. Unlike their kin in England, France, and Spain, they were never totally banished from their native land. Unlike the Jews of Italy, who also escaped total expulsion, they usually persisted in comparatively large numbers. And unlike the Jews to the East, they have always been in close contact with every successive phase of European civilization, struggling with every wind of doctrine and every shift in the social structure.

In the later Middle Ages, when the Jews had vanished from England and France and were entering upon their death agony in Spain, it was the German Jews who largely upheld the chain of tradition and became the mentors of the growing and soon to be the dominant Jewish centers of Europe—in Poland, Lithuania, Moravia, and the East. Orthodox Jewry as the western world knows it today is to a great extent the heir, when it is not the creation, of German Jewry.

It was in Germany, too, that a Jewry of size first met the brunt of modern civilization—Revival of Learning, Protes-

tantism, capitalism, science, industry, democracy, and nationalism. And perhaps because of their numbers—or their genius—
the German Jews in meeting modernity have been excep-
tionally articulate. The Jews of France and England early had
to wrestle with the difficulties of adjusting tradition to modernity, but the battles over this adjustment found their most
brilliant reporters in Germany. The best and most telling
words, the classic words, on Orthodoxy and Reform, on Nationalism and Assimilation, on Jewish history, theology, religion, and philosophy were said by German Jews. The very
reluctance of the German to admit the Jew into the modern
world, the very modernity of that world in Germany and her
own distinguished achievements in science, history, and philosophy, gave edge and power to the German Jewish tongue.
Nowhere can the drama of the modern Jew be better seen and
appreciated than in the land where it has now reached a tragic
curtain.

Because the experiences of the modern Jew—the origins of
and the fight for Emancipation and its fruits for good and
evil—have been written so large across the German landscape,
we have devoted progressively greater space to each century,
beginning with the Renaissance, as we approached our own.
Almost every episode, we feel, has its meaning for all men,
Jew or Gentile.

Jew and Gentile may learn that hatred and intolerance
can never be banished, together with all the wanton miseries
they provoke, until we can distinguish between men and their
environment, until we can understand that the real enemies
of humanity are not human beings—not members of sects,
races, or nations—but social systems which breed and perpetuate injustice and exploitation. Jews, Germans, or any

men are guilty only so far as having it in their power to help better society they put no hand to the task.

And pending such betterment, every man owes it to his own honor and dignity, as well as to his ultimate safety, to tolerate even those whom he believes to be his enemies. For they are not enemies but fellow-victims.

MARVIN LOWENTHAL.

BOOK ONE

THE FIRST THOUSAND YEARS

Well it is for us that God loves mankind more than men do.—*Leibnitz*.

1

THE DAYS OF WOTAN AND MARS

THE first civilized people to settle within the present bounds of Germany were the Romans. They came, under Caesar's eagles, at the request of the Gauls who inhabited the left bank of the Rhine and who had invited them to repel an invasion of Germanic tribes. Here as elsewhere, when the Romans came they stayed.

Within a century following the death of Caesar, Roman towns sprang up along the Rhine and its western confluents —Cologne, Trèves, Mayence, Metz, Strasbourg; Roman colonists were planted south of a great wall which arched from the Main to the Danube; and more Roman towns—Ulm, Augsburg, Regensburg, Vienna—guarded the line of the Danube eastward, where Roman territory ran through the Balkans to the Black Sea. The German barbarian, still clad in pelts and roaming the primeval forest, was ringed on two sides by civilization.

Beyond the ring, Roman arts built forums and roads, Roman laws governed their traffic, and Roman arms guaranteed their security. Under their shelter, the commerce of the known world was brought to the wooded trails of Germania. Little hoards of Roman coins, rings, lamps, and necklaces have been found along the Weser in what was once savage jungle, trinkets treasured by the German braves as the Iroquois treasured flintlocks and glass beads. Trade followed the eagle as it now follows the flag.

Chief among the traders of the Roman Empire were Syrians, Greeks, and, to a lesser extent, Jews. As such, all three peoples followed a common Levantine tradition, heirs to the Phoenicians who had ploughed the seas from Britain to India. Indeed the term "Syrian" was a popular synonym for "merchant"—as "Jew" was later to be—and designated more a calling than a race. So much so, that when we meet a "Syrian" in Roman history and literature, it is difficult at this late date to know whether we are dealing with a pagan or a Jew.

When the Rhine and Danube were first thrown open to the colonization of "white men," as we would call the Romans today, the Jews were already trading and settling in a wide dispersion. They were thick along the eastern marches of the Empire, in Egypt, Babylonia, and Byzantium. They had penetrated North Africa and percolated into Spain and Gaul. Numerous communities of them flourished in Italy itself. Strabo, a contemporary of Caesar, notes in his *Geography* that "it is hard to find a spot in the inhabited world where this race does not dwell or traffic." And the destruction of the Jewish state (71 C.E.) sent out fresh waves of slaves, refugees, home-seekers, and fortune-hunters.

Not all, probably far from the majority, of this dispersed people were traders. A whole class were little better than beggars and gypsies. Another class were engaged in the handicrafts, especially smithing, glass-making, weaving, and dyeing. A considerable number became tenant-farmers and landowners. And among the traders themselves, few—except in

2

Alexandria and the East—rose above the level of hucksters. The era of great Jewish commerce was still centuries to come.

We do not know the exact date when Jewish pioneers began to "dwell or traffic" in Germany. It might well have been the first or second century of the Christian era, at approximately the time they first reached China.

The earliest documents that prove their presence on the Rhine are a series of terra-cotta bottle-stoppers dug from the Roman ruins of Trèves. They date from the last quarter of the third century and are of local manufacture. They are topped with sculptured manikins unmistakably caricaturizing Jewish features, even to the point of poking fun at circumcision and intermarriage. Their costumes, postures, and the use to which they were put, show that Jews of Trèves dealt in wine and slaves—the first a traditional and still flourishing industry among the race, born of ritual necessity; the second long a favorite commerce; and both in this case evoking the humorous spite of Gentile competitors.

We know even less of where these Jews came from. First-century tombstones found in Mayence, supposedly of Iturian-Jewish soldiers, suggest that some of them marched to the Rhine in the legions. Fourth-century lamps of Italian manufacture, again found in Trèves, and stamped with the seven-branched candlestick, the immemorial signature of the Jew, point to Italy as the origin of a number of the Rhenish immigrants. Others may have drifted in from Gaul during Roman days, as they afterwards did in the reign of the Franks. A Jewish tombstone, inscribed in Latin and discovered in Lower Pannonia (Hungary), means that immigration cannot be precluded from the East, up the Danube out of Byzantium. Popular legend which settles Palestinian refugees in Worms, Ulm, and Regensburg even before the Christian era is, like much legend, not fiction but inaccurate history.

Written evidence assures us, however, that by the beginning of the fourth century—nearly one hundred and fifty years before the Germans themselves permanently crossed the Rhine —a Jewish community was flourishing in Cologne. In 321 Constantine the Great issued an edict denying the Jews of this city their customary exemption from serving on the *curia* or town-council—"nevertheless, to indemnify them for the loss of their previous immunity, two or three of those nominated for the *curia* shall be absolved from holding office." As the reader suspects, membership in this body was no enviable privilege. "Should anyone propose your nomination," Rabbi Johanan bar Nappaha had long before said, "rather flee to the Wilderness of Judea." The *curia*, in fact, was responsible for the imperial taxes levied in its jurisdiction; and when the taxes did not come in—and because of their magnitude they rarely did—the members of the *curia* had to make good the deficit from their own pockets. And if, wearing togas, they had no pockets, they forfeited their estates. By 321, therefore, the Jewry of Cologne must have been rich enough to furnish attractive candidates for this dubious public honor. The "two or three" nominees still allowed exemption were likely the rabbi and chief officers of the community. Ten years later, another imperial decree freed "the rabbis, heads of the synagogue [*parnasim*], elders, etc." from "all personal obligations" —probably of a fiscal and military nature.

Further written evidence, but of doubtful authenticity, tells us that a converted Jew attained, about 350, the more substantial honor of becoming the seventh bishop of Metz.

By and large these early Rhineland Jews, like their fellows

throughout the Empire, possessed equality under the Roman law. They were eligible to most public offices; they could engage in all trades and professions. They were granted the same opportunity as any other Roman to become a landed proprietor, a tenant-farmer, a *colon*, a freedman, or a slave. Like Paul they could say, *Civis Romanus sum;* and in the social and economic structure of the state, they occupied a position hardly to be distinguished from the majority of the Romans, except for their religion and race. Even in these respects they were not an anomaly, for the races, tongues, and creeds of Rome were innumerable.

Yet two measures showed that the Jew stood on a different footing from his fellow-citizens. After the fall of the Jewish state he was subject to a head-tax which theoretically represented the tithe he formerly paid to the Temple in Jerusalem. The "apostate" emperor Julian finally abolished it (361), but it was to return in a new guise under the German masters of the Holy Roman Empire. The tax was, in a sense, a public, even if an unpalatable, recognition of the religion of its victim, a recognition which took more welcome form in the second discriminatory measure against the Jew, whereby he was relieved from compulsory service in the Roman army. This exemption had its repercussions, too, in medieval history.

But aside from the formality of laws, the cleft between Jew and Gentile, which was finally to become a chasm, already showed itself.

The Jew frankly set himself apart. In doing this, he was moved by the conviction that his national habits were the sole divinely-revealed way of life, and that he alone possessed a positive, if limited, knowledge of God. Other ancient peoples, it is true, felt similarly about their own habits, but never—

the event proved—with the same tenacity. The obstinacy of the Jew, his stiffneckedness, arose in part from his further conviction, which he held with a passion and certainty beyond the reach of all argument, including fire and sword, that faithfulness to his own God-given ways and beliefs would ultimately usher in a reign of peace and justice for the whole of mankind. The pangs of Israel in maintaining the laws of God are the birth-pangs of the Messiah. Finally, the Jew, unlike the wandering Greek, Syrian, Armenian, and other immigrants of Rome, never cut the spiritual bonds which held him to his homeland. In the first centuries after the Roman conquest of Palestine he rose time and again in simple patriotic revolt. And when continued defeat banished the liberation of Palestine from practical politics, the return to Zion became a religious ideal, that is to say, a supernatural event bound to occur at an unpredictable but nevertheless assured date.

This loyalty to his laws, customs, and God, to the Messiah and Zion, to everything implied in his "covenant" with Jehovah, bred in the Jew an exclusiveness unapproached, or at least seldom long maintained, by the pagan creeds of the Empire. It sprang, to be sure, from a natural tribal urge for self-preservation; but it justified itself by a reasoned, coherent view of human salvation, which, embodied in innumerable prescriptions and prohibitions, erected an impregnable wall, not only around the Torah, but around Israel itself. Since this wall, like its Chinese counterpart, was to run up and down the vicissitudes of subsequent centuries in Germany, as wherever the Jew found himself, and because its presence demarcates and in part determines the substance of Jewish history, it deserves more than passing mention.

Jewish law, the bulwark of the wall, was held to be not

merely the teaching—the *Torah*, as "teaching" means in Hebrew—of the everlasting deity, but a direct and solemn charge laid upon the Jewish people. It was a binding covenant and a divine yoke. The ethics of the law, its insistence on justice and loving kindness, and its promise of the universal triumph of peace and righteousness, rested on no philosophizing in porch, colonnaded walk, or grove, but on the word of the one and true God; and its application to the round of daily life became the duty of talmudic masters to expound and of the Jewish people to guard and obey.

Consequently, the exclusiveness arising from submission to the law and from watch and ward over it—an exclusiveness which the pagans were quick to resent—was in the Jewish view an act of defense in behalf of themselves, the future of man, and the glory of God. It did not prevent the Jews from engaging in widespread proselytism. It did not hinder thousands of Gentiles from entering the synagogue gate. It directed itself more toward shutting out pagan influence from within the gate than toward dictating the behavior and beliefs of the outsider. The pagan was considered free to remain unconverted—"let all the peoples walk each one in the name of his god" (Micah 4.5)—but if he did so, he was in the Jewish mind clearly an outsider. The laws concerning food and drink, circumcision, and the Sabbath, which defined the Jew and set the pagan apart, no doubt made the latter feel as much. We catch a hint of this feeling when Seneca, alluding to a wave of conversion to Judaism which swept fashionable Rome, complained that "the vanquished lays down the law to the victor."

Defensive aloofness paved the way for downright aggressive intolerance when Judaism gave birth to Christianity. The

Jew had recognized in the new sect a dangerous offspring; and if we are to follow the Christian account, for contemporary Jewish records say little about it, he turned violently against the new claimants—not as outsiders, but as dissident, internal trouble-makers. Meanwhile the early Christian, usually a Jew by upbringing, learned the lesson of intolerance from the mother-faith, and never was there an apter pupil. The Jew hoped to save mankind by remaining true to himself and so prepare the road for the Messiah. The Christian, convinced that the Messiah had come, took the next step by proposing to save mankind through making it over in the Christian image. And he ended, reasonably enough from the pretensions of having a monopoly on revelation and on saving other people, by concluding that whoever refused to be saved—that is, to become a Christian—was damned; and whoever persisted in remaining damned must obviously be an enemy and an abomination to all right-thinking—that is, Christian—men.

Only one further step remained to be taken—the damnation of the outsider whether he is willing to be converted or not; but for that we must wait until our final chapters.

The rise to power of Christianity—of a group who believed that everyone else must be brought by persuasion or force to share the truth which they alone possessed—has been a familiar spectacle in modern politics. When mostly by persuasion the Christians captured the Empire, they turned to violence as men of absolute convictions are likely to do. What happened has been obscured by our view of it through generations of Christian historians; but as Gibbon and other open minds have attempted to reconstruct it, the story of sacked and ruined temples, of plundered treasuries, of harried and hunted priests, of the forcible closing of schools and universities, of the destruction of literature and free speculation, and of discriminatory measures against masses of unconvinced pagans, reads not unlike our daily headlines from Europe.

In the end the pagan yielded, but not the Jew. This was particularly exasperating, for to the Christian the Jew had become the arch-enemy.

The reasons for this enmity were many. To begin with, no quarrel can be so bitter as a family feud. When the Jew first opposed the Christian, which he did long before the pagans were hardly aware of a difference between them, he employed all the fury of a man fighting his brother; and the Christian, far from turning his cheek, never forgot or forgave this initial onslaught; the memory of it colors both the Gospels and the Acts. The Christians, moreover, had suffered a bitter disappointment. Their way to salvation had been offered "to the Jew first" (Romans 1.16), and he had refused it. Again, Jewish scriptures and their promises furnished the basis of Christian belief; and as long as the Jews, who were the acknowledged guardians of these scriptures and presumably an authority on them, denied that the promises had been fulfilled by Christianity, they proved a painful and potentially fatal embarrassment. Then, too, Christians and Jews were for some centuries missionary rivals over half the globe. Finally, as Christian dogma shaped itself—wherein the persistent and annoying denials of the Jews were explained away through the claim that the Jews by their own prophecies were doomed to reject the Messiah—and as the hope of winning over the Jews waned and as the prospect of capturing the Romans grew more flattering, the Church flung off its troublesome family connections with the Synagogue by enthroning the Jew as its pre-destined hereditary foe. It was clever theology, it was cleverer politics, even if it was questionable history, to assert that the Jews, and not the Romans, killed Jesus.

This simple assertion, based on an obscure and uncertain police incident in a remote provincial capital, was to prove another determining factor in the ensuing centuries of Jewish history. The fence around the Torah became, in the hands of the Gentiles, a ghetto wall. The barrier which the Jews had built for their own preservation and for the salvation of humanity served to exclude them, generations on end, from the enjoyment of the most elementary human rights and decencies —to mark them off as a public enemy and a common object of prey. And the hue and cry to track them down was raised in the name of the very Messiah they had themselves devised as a blessing for mankind.

The first Christian emperor, Constantine, whose edict we met in Cologne, set an enduring example when in other edicts he called the Jews "contemptible" and "perverse"—members of a "shameful" and "bestial" sect. Succeeding emperors one by one stripped this perverse people of their freedom to hold public office, their privileges, and their political rights. "They shall enjoy no honors," decreed Justinian, "but their status shall reflect the baseness which in their souls they have elected and desired." Within their walls, the Jews found themselves without the pale of civilization. Had the Romans, now become Christians, endured in Germany, the history of its Jewry would, as in many other parts of the Empire, have been sealed with an early martyrdom.

But a little after the middle of the fifth century the Franks —pagan and barbarian Germans—swept over the Rhine. And its budding Jewish communities were to enjoy a long respite.

2

TRAFFICS AND DISCOVERIES

FOUR centuries of silence fall upon the Jews of Germany after the vague report of them in the person of Simon, bishop of Metz. But they were fertile, if inaudible, centuries. In them a new world came to birth, the world of Feudalism, which in its first flush brought the Jews prosperity, security and, though probably little noted at the time, the seeds of their subsequent misfortunes. Something of these centuries must therefore be told.

The Franks, in crossing the Rhine and establishing a series of kingdoms which embraced most of France and all of western Germany, were but one of the many Germanic spearheads that penetrated and rent piecemeal the Roman Empire. The barbarians had come not to wreck the Empire, since the Romans had done that pretty much for themselves, but to loot the débris. For previous to their coming, the West had sunk to a near-barbarian level. Currency had depreciated to one twentieth of its nominal value. Stricken by taxation, the small land-owner, the small merchant, and the independent artisan had vanished. The currents of commerce ran slower and slower. Town and country markets dwindled, and in many regions disappeared. Huge landed estates, the *latifundia*, alone able to survive, did so by reverting to a primitive economy, resolving themselves into self-sufficient units which produced from their own resources nearly all that their masters, tenants, and slaves consumed. Cities thereby shrank in population, or were frankly abandoned. And, caught in a vicious circle, the slackened currents of commerce almost ceased. The country-side, too, drew in upon itself and left wide areas uncultivated. Technique in the way of building, road-mending, agronomy, and the manufacture of comforts weakened or passed into disuse. Western Europe became what we are told it will be once again, if we live through many more world wars.

We do, then, the barbarians an injustice if we imagine them destroying a civilization. They merely plundered its last relics and, carting their wives and children on their bullock-trains, occupied as pioneers a wilderness they had found rather than made.

The character of the barbarian has likewise been misunderstood. He was rude, violent, and unlettered; but, perhaps for that very reason, he was incapable of sustained cruelty or rationalized, complacent injustice. He was as quick to repent as to sin—a virtue seldom found among his so-called civilized betters. Judged by the touchstone of decency, tolerance, and good-will, he was superior to his own descendants when in due course the Germanic nations became educated, intellectualized, and Christian. Clovis could cleave a man's skull as readily as a vase, but the refinements of the *Judensau* or of the pyres of the Black Death were beyond his moral horizon. It has often been said that the test of a civilization is its treatment of women and Jews. On either count the German tribesman will stand comparison with, centuries later, the German burgher.

Slowly the Franks and the other Germanic tribes built a new life. Though based on Roman ways, which had no more been destroyed than the Roman population, it differed in many respects from the old order. Some of these differences profoundly affected the Jews.

The rise of petty kingdoms meant a more intensive development of local customs, interests, loyalties, and speech—a development which eventually gave birth to the nationalities of Europe much as we know them today. The Jew of the Rhinelands, as elsewhere in the newly-forming states, had his own social interests and customs which on the one hand bound him to the larger Jewish world, but on the other hand blocked his full participation in the local life. In the cosmopolitan unity of Rome his distinctive blood and breeding were only one among a score of others. But in a state built of Franks or Burgundians he stood apart. Nor—because of religious prohibitions as weighty on the Christian as on the Jewish side— could he break the barrier by intermarriage, as did the Roman-Gallic population.

The development of national differences was further encouraged by the distinguishing mark of Germanic law. It was personal law, whereas Roman law had been, on the whole, territorial. That is to say, Roman law in imperial times had prevailed, theoretically at least, wherever the Eagles spread, regardless of the diversity of races brought beneath their wings—in the reign of Caracalla all Roman subjects became Roman citizens. But a Frank, Burgundian, Frisian, or Swabian governed himself by his ancestral folk-law no matter where he might be; and he saw no objection to other people, whether neighbors or subjects, governing themselves by their own habitual institutions. To this extent Germanic law was not unlike Jewish law, both tribal in origin and juris-diction. But, in the circumstances, it worked to the eventual disadvantage of the Jew.

The Frankish conquerors allowed the Roman-Gallic popu-lation of the Rhinelands the free exercise of Roman law. In the beginning of the conquest, the civil status of the Jew, as fixed by Roman law, no doubt likewise remained unchanged. But when the Franks embraced Catholicism and conqueror and subject merged insensibly into a single Christian-Roman-Frankish people, and as, in the course of time, the older Jewish settlements lost their Roman rights in the battle with the Church, and as Roman law itself fell into disuse, and as newer Jewish settlers arrived without benefit of blood or clergy, the Jew found himself a *Fremder*, a foreigner, a man deprived of the privileges of Roman, Gallic, Frankish, or any other native status.

How gradual the process was, cannot be said. Old usages among a tribal-minded people like the Franks die hard. In Cologne, the Germanic gods were worshiped as late as the sixth century, and a temple of Bacchus remained opened for the Romans until the end of the seventh century. So too, the Roman status of the Jew may have lingered for a long spell. In Frankish Gaul the Jews were demanding from King Guntram (585) reparations due them according to Roman law; and it was not until 614 that Chlotar II promulgated the familiar Christian prohibition against Jews holding public office. But by the time Charlemagne set up his court in Aachen the Jew had become the political outcast he was to remain until the French Revolution.

His position as outsider was still further accentuated by

the nascent feudal order. Old Roman land-owners were reduced to vassalage under the new Frankish masters. Abandoned lands fell to the Frankish crown, to be distributed
among chieftains, warriors, and princes of the Church. New
owners as well as old held their land by an oath of fealty and,
in the case of laymen, by military service. In the course of
events, everyone, in an ascending scale through state and
church, became someone else's "man."

But military service from the Jews, a people long exempt
by Roman law, untrained, and because of their Sabbath and
dietary laws unfit for it, was difficult. And fealty from a
Fremder, a foreigner, and, what is worse, a man whose faith
did not permit him to take an "honest" Christian oath, was
unthinkable. As a result, when the curtain of silence rises,
the Jews are discovered owning, to be sure, scattered vineyards along the Rhine, probably suburban property, on terms
unknown; but they are nobody's "men." Though they were
later to obtain an equivocal "protection" from the emperor,
to become his property rather than his liegemen, they were
otherwise completely dropped from the close-knit hierarchical
texture of society which we call the feudal ages.

Legally, therefore, the Jews were *vogel-frei*—masterless men,
beyond the law. Politically they could be neither *Ritter* nor
Knecht, lord nor vassal, villein nor serf. Economically they
were by and large barred from the land. And in an age when
religion pre-empted more and more of what we should today
regard as secular life; when church, state, and folk were exclusively Christian, the Jews were not merely unbelievers,
but they were classed as *fidei inimici*—enemies of the true
faith.

Altogether, their chances of survival, if confined to these circumstances, looked hopelessly dark.

ii

But there is another side to the story. While Roman commerce sank and fairly ceased in the West, Constantinople and the Eastern Empire flourished as never before. And step by step the East reached out to recivilize the West. The trail of Byzantine tapestry and embroidery, of enamels, jewelry, and carved ivory, of themes and styles in sculpture, painting, and architecture, of mosaic and dome, can be traced in church and museum from Ravenna and St. Gall to Elche in Spain. Awakened to new desires, the barbarian began to buy and sell, and all along the highways of the West have been dropped the bezants of the Golden Horn.

Greeks, Bulgars, Italians, Syrians, and Jews shared in the commerce which brought Eastern goods and ideas to the Germanic courts. In the beginning the Syrians held the lead. But by the seventh century they were yielding place to the Jews. And by the ninth century the words "merchant" and "Jew" became almost synonymous. *Judaei vel ceteri negotiatores, negotiatores sive Judaei, mercatores et Judaei*—"Jews or other traders, traders or Jews, merchants and Jews"—so run the usual phrases in Germanic chronicles, legal codes, and tariff bills.

This was only natural. The Roman Empire had been split into hostile kingdoms of Greeks, Lombards, Ostrogoths, Visigoths, Vandals, Burgundians, Franks, and the like. It had been set at sword's point by the rivalries of Catholics, Arians, Orthodox, and a host of lesser Christian sects. And the rise of Islam in the seventh century shattered for long years the free commerce of Europe with Africa and Asia; the Mediterranean was no longer a Roman lake, but a foreign sea. In this dismembered world the Jews became the obvious channels of intercourse by virtue of their common faith, the common social habits reared upon it, and the assumed community of blood underlying it. The very reasons which prevented Jewry from sharing the inner life of the peoples among whom it dwelt enabled the individual Jew to become an international carrier, to join hands with his fellow in remote lands and across remote seas—to ship, in short, a bale of silk from Constantinople to Cologne.

Jewish ships, in fact, sailed the Mediterranean; and Jewish traders trafficked by raft and cart up and down the valleys of the Rhone, Danube, and Rhine. Venice, Passau, Cologne, and the city-fairs of Champagne became the chief ports-of-entry for Germany. Spices, silks, ivories, and other luxuries of the Orient were sold to Germanic princes, peddled at convent doors, and displayed in episcopal halls. In return, Western furs, weapons, and slaves were carried to Moslem Spain and the East. As early as 472 the bishop of Clermont, Apollinaris Sidonius—while berating Christian usurers—describes these Jewish merchants as "conducting an honest business."

To the Western buyer—duke, count, bishop, or abbess—price was no consideration; he was indifferent as to whether he paid for a coveted tapestry the equivalent of two or twenty peasants' daily labor. Indeed, a Jewish trader (*pace* Sidonius!), "who often visited Palestine," enticed Richulf, bishop of Mayence, into paying twenty pounds silver for "an unheard-of exotic beast" which, to the Homeric delight of Charlemagne, proved to be a much-perfumed mouse. These upper-class Westerners were, moreover, isolated random customers; there lacked the competition of a broad, regular market with its low prices. On the other hand, the slaves and furs much prized in Moslem lands were picked up for little more than nothing in the great Slavic reservoirs of men and beasts. So, naturally, the profits were substantial. The foundations of Jewish wealth, later to be fatally enhanced by money-lending, can undoubtedly be laid to these favorable conditions, in which goods could be bought cheap and sold dear—conditions which bear a marked resemblance to the halcyon days of our modern colonial trade.

iii

The curtain of silence rises in the reign of Charlemagne and his dynasty (768-911). The Roman Empire of the West was reborn, at least in the imagination of the Germans. A revival of art, letters, and commerce, an expansion of territory, and a restoration of order—the Carolingian Renaissance —set Germany on the road to becoming a nation in its own name. And with the dawn, the Jews emerge into clearer light.

Almost anywhere in the new empire something can be heard or seen of Israel. We may stand (in legend) with Charlemagne by the sea; ships are sighted from afar; the king's servants claim they are either Breton or Jewish. We are in the royal palace at Aachen; Charles is despatching Isaac the Jew, together with an embassy, to Harun al-Rashid; four years pass and Isaac, who is probably a seasoned traveler, alone survives the journey, and he has much to-do in getting an elephant—the gift of the Caliph—over the Alps back to Aachen. In the same palace we may talk with the Jew Sedechias, physician to His Majesty, and hear him sigh over Charles' slender faith in cures. Or, a little later, we may listen to David and other Jewish witnesses, apparently less skeptical than Charles, confirm the miraculous cure of a young girl by the holy relics Einhard fetched from Italy.

Later still (ca. 850) we might encounter somewhere along the Danube highway a train of Radanite Jews, incredible continent-girdling merchants. If their caravan is moving eastward, it is bearing slaves, furs, and swords to the Jewish-Khazar kingdom on the Volga, and it will reach its last stop in China. If it is moving westward, it is bringing Oriental spices, silks, and tapestries to "the palace of the king of the Franks."

We could not pass a season at Passau, the German gate to the East, without watching the customs-collectors levy their toll "on Jews and other merchants" at equal rates, according to the tariff-bill of 906. The merchandise, the same bill informs us, includes "slaves and other wares" from Bohemia, Moravia, and remoter Slavic lands. We could follow the slave-trains, as they move in Jewish hands, clean across Germany to Verdun, and thence to Moslem Spain. En route, in Regensburg and again in Worms and Mayence, we could meet Italian Jews or their local Jewish agents displaying Byzantine specialties up from Venice. In Cologne the trade among the Jews is brisk in Frisian cloths and Russian furs. Gloves, veils, snoods, mantles, silken robes, dyes, horses, and hides appear in the early decisions of German rabbinic law. On the western border, we can observe the customs officers in Kiersey, seat of a renowned Champagne fair, collect (in 887) an extra ten percent from the Jewish merchants—augury of the still distant day when Christian competitors will gain the upper hand.

In any one of the few interior cities of Germany we would find Jews and monks striving to corner the market in wine and grain, with oil as a side line; the Synod of Frankfort (794) tries to put a halt to their monopoly. Or in almost any church and cloister, Jews will be purchasing ecclesiastical jewels, plate, and utensils. The clerics think so highly of pleasant spices, warm furs, and stalwart slaves, and care so little for the ritual treasures in their charge that the Jews "boast they can buy whatever they want"; and Charlemagne likewise passes a law against the traffic. Sometimes the clerics pawn the sacred objects—a second early hint of the money-lending business—and there is another law. But we know those laws from of old and how readily they are evaded. They imply, moreover, no hostility of the State toward the Jews. In military camps along the Rhine, Jewish commissaries are active; and Lothar I confirms their concessions, with the "usual tolls" (832). Ludwig the Pious, heir to Charlemagne, gives royal protection to a number of the race, and when he grants a charter of privileges to certain Christian merchants (828), he enjoins them "to serve him loyally as do the Jews." Furthermore, a council in Mayence decrees (906) that anyone who kills a Jew or a heathen "shall be considered a murderer . . . for even foreigners are not to be attacked unless they break the peace."

Enmity toward the Jews was confined to the Church. The ecclesiastics looked with disfavor on any social mingling of the two faiths; the Church was not yet sure enough of its barbarian converts, and the converts were not yet Christian enough to be wary of the Jews. The Synod of Metz (888)

was therefore merely echoing earlier synods in other barbarian lands when it forbade Christians eating or drinking
with Jews, in order, as a ninth-century bishop said, "that no
shadow may fall on the sons of light through social intercourse with the children of darkness."

The Church looked with similar disfavor on Jewish wealth
and the support this wealth gave the State. Fearful of lost
tithes, it had had a share in driving the Jews from the land.
No doubt, too, it had little fondness for its competitors in
wine and grain. Above all, however, it objected to the Jewish
slave-trade. Not that the Church minded the trade itself;
priests, bishops, abbots, and even the popes possessed slaves.
But the Jews (like the Christians) insisted on proselytizing
their bondmen, and the Church resented the consequent loss
of souls. So edicts were passed forbidding Jews to buy or own
Christian slaves, and more edicts denying them the right to
convert their own heathen slaves into Jews—all of which
would have been most inconvenient but for the fact that they
were rarely enforced. It is not, of course, to be assumed that
every cleric was moved by material motives. Bishop Adalbert
of Prague resigned his office and helped win himself sainthood because he spent his fortune redeeming slaves from the
Jews. Here, as often in their checkered relations, Christians
and Jews were rivals in virtue no less than in vice; for the
Jews, too, it was a blessed deed to redeem those—of their own
faith—who were bound.

The motives of Agobard, bishop of Lyons, are not so apparent when he wrote *De Insolentia Judaeorum* ("Concerning the Insolence of the Jews" ca. 822), the first anti-Semitic
pamphlet in modern literature. There is a suspicion of political maneuver against the Jewish favorite of Ludwig's queen,

and possibly against the queen herself. Nor is his famous description of Jewish influence in the Empire beyond suspicion; anti-Semitic observations have been known to be exaggerated. But the charges which have the ring of truth and probably give a fair picture of the Jews in the Carolingian age describe them as building synagogues, flaunting silks, catching the ear of the throne, owning mills and vineyards, arranging that markets should not be held on Saturdays, and preaching sermons that attract Christian audiences. Indeed, a year before Agobard died, they succeeded in winning over an Alleman deacon named Bodo, who "let his beard grow, gave up his military garb, married a Jewess, converted his nephew, and departed for Saragossa." Such is the insolence which even a recent historian characterized as "a menace to Christianity."

iv

Charlemagne's conquest of the heathen Saxons began the *Drang nach Osten*, a drive toward the East which has persisted in German policy to this day. Thousands upon thousands of Saxons were killed, and the survivors, through no coincidence, were converted; for the choice was baptism or death. After the Saxons became proper Christians they took up the drive in turn, and during the tenth and eleventh centuries the Cross was carried against the Wends from the Elbe to the Oder. Meanwhile the South Germans were driving eastward against the Slavs of Bohemia and Carinthia. The conquests brought a flood of Slavic blood into German veins. Bigotry and land-hunger were the compelling forces of the movement, which combined pioneering with religion.

As fast as they had killed and baptized, the Germans

ploughed and built. Frontier-towns girded by palisades and guarded by blockhouses—the *Burgwärde*—rose along the Salle and Werra rivers. Magdeburg, Merseburg, Erfurt, and Halle became outposts against the Wends; and a line of fresh settlements from Passau to Vienna drove a wedge between the North and the South Slavs. Besides protecting the newly-won territory, these Wild East towns—like their Wild West successors in America—served as a jumping-off point for further commerce. The Norsemen had recently opened a road from the Baltic to Kiev and the Black Sea, the invasion of the pagan Magyars had cut off the old Danube route, and Poland and Bohemia now offered the most attractive access to the East.

It is, therefore, no surprise to discover Jews among the first-comers in these pioneer towns. Otto the Great (965) decreed that "the Jews and all other merchants" of Magdeburg were to be governed by the local bishop, and the bishop's powers were in this respect enlarged by Otto II. The latter monarch likewise bestowed upon the bishopric of Merseburg (973) property rights to everything within the city walls, "including the Jews and merchants." Thietmar, the bishop, must have somehow disposed of this property, for Henry II returned to him his merchants and Jews (1004). The same Thietmar has left us a picture from his youth, which was spent in Magdeburg. In that raw frontier post, swarming with burly Saxons, backwoodsmen, and barbarian slaves, he remembers the guards watching in the church over the goods "of the Jewish and Christian merchants." Abraham ibn Jacob was another witness. A Jew in an embassy from the Caliph of Cordova to Germany, he passed through these border lands about the year 970. Near Halle he found Jews owning a salt mine, and in Prague he describes the "Moslems, Jews, and Turks" who bring "Byzantine wares and coins" and who buy "slaves, tin, and lead." The Jewish minister of state to the same Caliph used the services of a German Jew to carry a message through Slavic lands to the Khazar kingdom. More than in the days of Addison, the Jews were "the instruments by which the most distant nations converse with one another."

Before the close of the eleventh century the race had fairly distributed itself in the expanding borders of Germany. It had as well its own *Drang nach Osten*, which took the first German Jews into Poland. A similar urge brought French Jews into the Rhinelands and even eastward to Saxony; throughout the Middle Ages French words lingered on the pens and perhaps on the lips of German rabbis. Every boom town of importance in the Reich, except the northern ports, had its contingent of Jews; and the threads of their trade united the land with far places.

Petahiah of Regensburg may have done something a bit out of the ordinary when he wrote down his travels, or a stroke of luck may have preserved for us what he wrote. But he merely followed old and established routes, well worn by Jewish traders before him, when, setting out from Prague about 1170, he traversed Poland, the Ukraine, Crimea, Tartary, Armenia, Media, Persia and, turning on his tracks, visited Mesopotamia, Syria, Palestine, and Greece.

True, the German Jews enjoyed neither the freedom of the upper classes nor the security of the lower. Their houses, goods, and persons were at the mercy of the king. Yet in the Carolingian and Saxon reigns they managed to stand above, even as they stood apart from, the servile masses. For this they had to thank not the morals or the "rights" of the age.

Their claims were more substantial. They served a necessary purpose, they performed an indispensable function, in feudal economy. The importation of comforts and luxuries, the exportation of surplus labor and products, the maintenance of home markets, and the provision through it all of revenue to the state, guaranteed the Jews place and survival in the Germanic scheme. Ludwig the Pious gave utterance to more than piety when he said, "We must not harm the life, limb, or property of the Jews who live among us."

3

THE DISCIPLINE OF LIFE

THE Jews of Germany did not cling to Judaism in order to become merchants, although that was often the consequence. On the contrary, they became merchants in order to remain Jews. Trade was one of their few available means of livelihood; but, more than that, its profits were their chief bulwark against oppression. "Christians," said Gershom ben Judah, the great tenth-century rabbi of Mayence, "cannot be appeased with pleasant words; only money will satisfy them, and whoever falls into their hands will not go free without payment." Trade, then, was the price of survival. But the Jews, it must be understood, insisted on surviving largely because of their loyalty to an inward light.

Merchants, as such, have neither the reason nor the urge to become martyrs. They will not be found among "those nameless knights of the Holy Spirit," as Heine characterized his medieval forefathers, "who fell on all the battle-fields of human thought." Nor is the tribal instinct for self-preservation enough to make a people rise unbeaten from endless defeat; the instinct sadly failed the Saxons and the Wends. But a Jewish merchant, even the meanest huckster, found himself, upon the test, the slave and champion of an idea.

26

Though he died in helpless combat, though generations of him suffered, fought and died, the idea ran like ichor in his blood and wrought a perpetual resurrection.

It is, however, unnecessary to suppose that the marketmen of Mayence or Worms thought of themselves as incipient knights or martyrs. Or that they looked upon the *Judengasse* —the Jewish quarter—and its synagogue as a training camp for the coming centuries of warfare. They were concerned with more immediate wants.

The *Judengasse* lived by its own law—by the Bible and Talmud. Oriental in spirit and derived from remote conditions in Palestine and Babylonia, it had, perforce, to be made Western and brought up to date. The inhabitants of the *Judengasse*, moreover, stood in need of authority and discipline: authority to regulate the conflicts and limits of individual and communal interests, and discipline to steel their ranks against an alien and often hostile world. In these communities where the sword and the sanction of brute force were banished, authority and discipline could be attained only by a voluntary surrender to the power of tradition and its recognized exponents. This meant a continual re-dedication to the Torah, to the biblical word, a continual instruction in it and interpretation of it. It meant the rule of the teacher. The teacher was the master—in Hebrew, the *rabbi*.

Since nearly every concern of life was directed by the Torah and the Talmud, the medieval rabbi was religious leader, scholar, schoolmaster, moralist, poet, legislator, administrator, and judge. At the same time he was often a man of affairs, a merchant like Eliezer ben Nathan, or a grapegrower like Rashi. He governed, not by power of wealth, lineage, or office—though all three counted for something;

but by virtue of his learning and character. He was a *Leader*, as the present-day German likes to say; but his was primarily a moral leadership; and under its guidance the community was unified—*gleichgeschaltet*—to a degree approached perhaps by Islam, but unequaled by the most intransigent of our modern nationalisms. From the tenth century onward, first in the Rhinelands and France and then in the widening centers of Germany, an august procession of these rabbis bore "the chain of tradition" which linked the ancient East to the new West, created out of it a morale which preserved the Jewries of Central and Eastern Europe until the dawn of today, and thereby shaped the spirit of traditional Judaism, the Jewish soul, as it now survives.

The procession begins with Gershom ben Judah of Mayence (960-1040). He was preëminently a legislator. He established fundamentals in government which provided majority rule in communal affairs, secured the jurisdiction of the rabbinic courts not only over the residents but the passersby in a community, employed the ancient rite of excommunication as a sanction for enforcing law and order, and assured the right of an aggrieved party to get his case judged by means of interrupting the synagogal service. On the last point, it is interesting to compare Christian and Jewish procedure: the medieval Christian who was denied justice could cry "Haroo, my prince, I am wronged!" provided he found his prince; the Jew simply rose from his pew and put a stop to prayers.

Gershom likewise lessened the anarchy inherent in the dispersed communities. He created a loose federation of Rhine Jewries, centered in a synod. And later synods, modeled on his device, furnished a measure of unity in Israel.

Three of the many ordinances credited to his name rendered perhaps even greater service in their day. One of them forbade a Jew to rent the house of a Gentile who had unjustly expelled a former Jewish tenant, a safeguard against chicanery in the cramped limits of a *Judengasse*. Another assured the privacy of personal correspondence, no light matter for a commercial people in an age without government mail facilities. The third prohibited anyone from insulting a converted Jew after his return to Judaism. Here, perhaps, is a touch of personal drama, for Gershom's own son became a convert upon the expulsion of the Jews from Mayence in 1012; if so, the father's delicacy was in vain, for the son never came back to the fold. It is said that he died soon after the expulsion and before he had the opportunity to return.

Gershom, however, is most remembered for his influence on family life. He abolished polygamy and ordained, in terms appropriate to Occidental custom, the rules governing bigamy and divorce. His, too, was the lion's share in inaugurating the study of the Talmud in northern Europe, a study which meant the cultivation of Jewish letters, the birth in Germany of a Jewish culture, and the entry of its Jews into their spiritual homeland.

All in all, later generations indulged in no Oriental hyperbole when they called Gershom "the Light of the Exile."

The coming of the Talmud is likewise closely bound up with the fortunes of the Kalonymus family, Italian Jews of long and distinguished lineage. After the defeat near Cotrone (982)—as Bishop Thietmar tells the story—the German emperor, Otto II, was rescued by "Kalonymus a Jew," who got "his beloved lord" safely on a passing ship. A short while later, a Kalonymus appears in Mayence; and for generations the family supplied Mayence and Spires with protectors, leaders, and rabbis. More than that, it appears that they helped bring the study of the Law from Italy, where it had been transported from the fading schools of Palestine. "Out of Bari shall go forth the Law, and the word of the Lord from Otranto" was the old saying. It was no less true of Gentile than of Jewish learning. Peter of Pisa, Paulinus of Aquileia, Paulus Diaconus, and John of Gorze, they too brought the light of antiquity across the Alps to Germanic Europe.

And now the Law went forth from the new Rhine schools. Rashi studied in Worms—perhaps in the synagogue built in 1034 and still standing—at the feet of the scholar who studied under Gershom. And with Rashi began the line of commentators and jurists, in Germany and France, who made the Law a living thing down succeeding generations. His clear patient explanations adorn to this day the margin of Bibles and Talmuds; and the notes of his followers, the Tosafists, rank close in honor with the text itself.

It was, to be sure, a meticulous, straitened Law, hard and precise as the columns in which it was written. There were but few glints of philosophy, science, or secular delights. There was no flowering of poetry and the arts as in the Jewries of Spain. But in a land like medieval Germany which itself had little enough philosophy or science, it served its high purpose. The cult of the Talmud was not a conquest of nature or a liberation of humanism; but neither was it, at this early date, a flight from reality. For an outlawed harassed people it meant coming to grips with the necessities of daily life.

Material necessities, first of all. Reading the decisions of the Rhine masters, men like Gershom or like Eliezer ben Nathan of Mayence (11th-12th cent.), sweeps one into the tide of the practical world. Problems of partnership, loans, credit, and collateral, and the difficulties and conflicts of doing business in an age when the currency varied at a monarch's wink; when each Jewish community claimed the right to make its own commercial law and usages; when travelers were exposed to frequent shipwreck and robbery; when confiscation, extortion, or imprisonment was likely to put an end to a customer, a partner, a debtor, a bill-of-goods, or oneself; when Christian authorities—count, bishop, or judge—were generally open to collusion or bribery; when the exclusive "right" to a customer—a wealthy abbot or a needy knight—was a matter of constant and vital dispute; when the purchase of war-booty—and there was always a war—made the victor a friend but the vanquished an enemy; when "permitted" and "forbidden" held for the goods one sold as well as the food one ate—when the Church forbade Christians to buy *kosher* wine or *trefa* meat, and the Synagogue allowed Jews to sell wax, cups, altar-mantles, and embroideries to a church, but not crucifixes, statues, incense-burners, or incense; when it was doubtful whether a Jew might be permitted to trade with a Christian pilgrim en route to the Holy Land or saintly shrine or whether he must wait until the pilgrim was on his way home; when it was a question whether community taxes could be levied on the goods one held in pawn, and what a man's share might be in a fine or frank extortion laid upon the whole of a Jewry; when interest could be taken from Christians, but not from Jews, and the Jews stood nevertheless in equal need of borrowing and lending—all these complexities were grappled with and ruled upon by the talmudic schoolmen. Two centuries before the Hanseatic League, these Jews had developed a rounded body of commercial law.

"Reuben and Simon," relates a case brought before Eliezer ben Nathan, "lived in a Christian community, each on a different street and each engaged in the same business. Simon moved from his street and rented a house next to Reuben's, so no one could enter Reuben's shop without passing Simon's door. Reuben complained, 'You are taking the bread from my mouth.' But Simon answered, 'Everywhere that Jews have their own quarter, they live next to one another and gain their livelihood from the same source—from trade or money-lending. In what way, then, are we different?' Whereat Reuben explained, 'In all Jewish quarters the street is open at both ends, and customers come from both directions—now they pass by one man's door, and again another's. But ours is a blind-alley; and before a customer can reach my shop he is bound to pass yours.'" A light dispute to set before a prince of the Law, but a typical detail of the times; and the genius of the Law, like other genius, lay in its mastery of detail.

Behind the material problems, and coloring their resolution, pressed the necessities of the spirit. These same Talmudists who reckoned the shifting quotations of wheat built the foundations of a school system in which education was practically compulsory and universal. They added in joy and without stint to the arsenal of prayer. They made children lisp in morals and elders think in homily. And in common with the Christian clerics, they pushed against the clay walls of the world and broke into the great intoxicating spaces of mysticism. They made God the conscience and the partner of man.

The "Testament" usually attributed to Eliezer ben Isaac of Worms (mid-11th cent.) puts this multiple endeavor in a small compass. "Come," says Rabbi Eliezer, borrowing freely from Bible and Talmud as well as from contemporary wisdom, "I will teach you the paths of life." They are very human paths, now picking their way among the humblest daily routine, and now mounting to heady spiritual peaks. But the petty and sublime are forever rubbing elbows in Jewish literature—from Proverbs to the *Memoirs of Glückel* —a token, no doubt, that such distinctions were felt to be an illusion. It is this sense of an equal weight in worshiping God and in washing the hands—which latter, says Rabbi Eliezer, "is one of the sublime things of the world, for when you wash your hands you are bound to lift them in adoration to your Maker"—that imbues the crassest legalism of the Jew with a mystic and saving significance. "Do not say, 'This is trivial' and 'That is important,'" explains Rabbi Eliezer, "for you do not know the reward thereof—let all deeds be done in the Name of Heaven."

"Give glory to God," he begins, as step by step he guides us through the day's work and the night's rest, "for you have need of Him, and He has none of you." When you rise in the morning, "do not begin to dress without washing the hands, for the spirit of uncleanness rests upon them"; and do not touch your eyes with your unwashed hands if you plan thereby to work a little medieval magic against your enemy, "lest your plot fail and your gaze proves harmful to your friends." Once dressed—with the proper benediction—do not hurry to visit a neighbor before you have greeted God; but

"be among the first ten at the synagogue, that you may enjoy the reward of all the ten, and since each of the other
nine are reaping the same advantage, your reward will be
increased a hundred-fold"—a happy calculation! Once before
your Maker, "exert all your powers to achieve holiness, to
subdue your will to God." Next, when you pass to the house
of study, "consider nothing negligible, and despise no one,
for many pearls are found in a poor man's tunic." Visit the
sick, and, if the sick man be poor, never come without a gift,
"but don't tire out the patient by staying too long, for his
malady is heavy enough as it is." Help bury the dead, for "to
one who does a kindness that the receiver cannot return, God
renders unmerited favors." Join the wedding throng, for
"bringing the bride to the canopy" is to the wedding-guest
"as though he attended the giving of the Law at Sinai."
Honor the poor "and draw out your soul to him," but "make
your gift in secret—give him food and drink in your house,
but do not watch him while he eats." If you are poor yourself, "eat herbs rather than beg"; but if beg you must, "ask
for no more than you absolutely need." Prepare for the Sabbath joy by providing three meals "even beyond your means."
Do not enter your house suddenly, "and still less the house of
a neighbor." When you sit down to eat, "remember you are
in the presence of the King, and be not a snatcher or a glut-
ton." Salute all men, speak the truth, and "do not betray
another's confidence, even if you are at strife with him."
Beget children and rear them for the study of the Law, because "for their sake you will merit eternal life." Avoid all
grossness "and do not pass behind a woman on the street, or
between two women."

And so, with similar admonitions regarding the choice of

a wife, the rearing of children, the management of the household, the preparation of food, the duty towards a neighbor, the day is brought to a close. When you have gone to bed, "recite the prayers of Unity and Love, and when you have in this way adored the Lord and sanctified yourself, speak no idle words and do no carnal act, for you are hallowed with the holiness of your Maker, your soul mounts and you do not know if it deserves to appear before Him—sweet and goodly it is, to be always prepared to join the righteous who enter with God, thus drawing upon you the thread of His love."

Like a rising tide, beginning with the tenth century, schools, synagogues, laws, preachments, and manners joined in a common discipline. Together they instilled Jewry with the conviction that its view of the world, in which Israel was a divine witness, in which the behavior of every Jew meant, from day to day, either the sanctification or the desecration of the Holy Name, was something to live for, even if in ignominy and pain, and, when needs must, something to die for with a cry of gladness.

4

"GOD WILLS IT"

THE occasion for dying came soon enough. With almost mechanical precision, the forces which rendered the Jew an outsider ended by making him a martyr.

The early steps in the process warrant retelling. His religion, to begin with, set the Jew apart spiritually and socially. Then, Christianity, the issue of his loins, by appropriating and further extending the Jewish claim to a divine patent, did all it could to keep him apart. Since he could not become a Bavarian in Regensburg or a Frank in Cologne, he drew closer to his own people whether in Constantinople or Cordova. Because he enjoyed these wide contacts abroad and could do little else at home, he therefore turned largely to trade. Thus, in a dismembered feudal Europe, his demarcation from other peoples made him a successful merchant. But now fresh merchant classes were to dispute his place, and a needy populace to reach for his wealth. And, in doing so, they naturally took advantage of the fact that he was a marked man. Old stigmas were used to settle new scores.

The omens of change and attack were many. As early as the tenth century, the star of fortune rose over Venice, Bari, and Amalfi; and Italian merchants began to dominate the commerce with the East. Petrus, doge of Venice (932-36), wrote to the archbishop of Mayence urging out of purely religious fervor that Jews be forbidden to deal in coins, textiles, or other objects marked with the sign of the Cross, which, had the suggestion prevailed, would have left a great share of Byzantine trade in pious Italian hands. In 945 the project was further advanced, when Doge Arso forbade Venetian ships from carrying Jewish merchants. Fifty years later, not only Jewish merchants but Jewish goods were banned from the sea-queen's galleys. So one Jewish thread between Germany and the Orient was broken. Then, the Magyars accepted the Cross (1000), and Christians were as free as Jews to use the Danube route to Constantinople; and another thread was weakened.

The next century saw a great growth of cities in Western Europe. When the Saxon dynasty first came to the throne in 919, Germany could count thirty towns. By 1125 the number had risen to one hundred and fifty. Towns meant commerce and merchants, and for the Jews new business. Rüdiger, bishop of Spires, ambitious for his episcopal seat, endowed the Jews with lavish privileges and provided them a special quarter inside the walls (1084). "Wishing to make of Spires a city," he wrote, "I thought to increase its honor a thousand-fold by bringing in the Jews." Doubtless Rüdiger was not alone in the idea; and probably similar motives, along with cash inducements, impelled Henry IV to grant, in 1090, privileges and protection to the Jews of Worms as well as Spires. Tangible monuments of their prosperity may still be seen in the old synagogue of Worms and the great twelfth-century ritual baths in both cities.

But the new business brought new competitors. With the

rise of the cities, Christian merchants rapidly outnumbered the Jews; and though both stood at first on the sufferance of special privileges, the Christian merchant, as a full-blown subject and citizen, as kin in faith and blood to his protectors and customers, soon gained the inside track. Like merchants the world over, he used his commercial resources to increase his political power and made, in turn, his political power serve his commercial growth. In Germany of the eleventh and twelfth centuries, this growth was bought at the expense of the Jews. "Native business," says a German historian of capitalism, "was built on the ruin of the alien. The leadership of the latter, sustained through the centuries, ceased to be a necessity; and the alien had to make way for the native trader and manufacturer."

Nor was the new business purely mercantile. Monasteries had hitherto engaged in rudimentary banking; and its profits, as well as the huge receipts from gifts and bequests, had been invested in land. But the rise of the cities had knocked the bottom out of the land market and plunged innumerable monasteries into bankruptcy. As a result, the impoverished monks and their former clients together turned to the Jews as a source of further capital. Lured into the new field by its high profits and in part driven from their old position in commerce by the competition of their politically-stronger Christian rivals, the Jews insensibly slipped into money-lending. The upshot was, they multiplied their enemies. The Christian merchants, on the make, were hardly friends. And now they were joined by the clerics who, quite apart from religious animosity, had lost a paying business, as well as by the rank and file of borrowers, whether churchmen, nobility, or commoners. The enmity, to be sure, was slow in bearing fruit. For the present it is enough to know that the eleventh century ushered the Jews into this fertile field of friction and disaster.

The transition from commerce to usury began, moreover, at a ticklish juncture. To the ruin of the monasteries, which owned an unconscionable share of Germany, was added the turmoil of the War of Investitures, a struggle between church and state which disrupted political authority and all but swept the country bare. Hard times ruled in France as well; and Western Europe was beset by what we are accustomed to call "general unrest," meaning that the poor became poorer, and the rich, for lack of their normal victims, began to prey upon one another. In 1095 Pope Urban II summed up conditions at a famous council in Clermont by saying, "You have seen the world disordered for a long time, and to such a degree . . . one scarcely dares travel for fear of being kidnaped by force or craft, at home or out of doors." The stage was set either for a relapse into Merovingian anarchy or for the blazoning of a new ideal capable of uniting and reviving society.

Pope Urban, at this same Council, provided the ideal. In trumpet tones Christendom was summoned to "imitate" its Master—"if any man will come after me, let him take up his cross and follow me" (Luke 9.23)—which to the mind of Urban meant that the faithful should "hasten to exterminate the vile race" of Moslems who possessed the tomb of Jesus— to the modern mind a rather strange Imitation of Christ. As a reward, the faithful were to win salvation for their souls; "and if those who set out," promised Urban, "should lose their lives, their sins shall be remitted."

The Crusades as religious warfare were not the invention

39

of Urban. They lay implicit in the theology of the Church. Charlemagne had carried the Cross against the Saracens and heathen Saxons, and the early campaigns against the Wends and Magyars saw "religion painted upon banners." Nor were mass movements to the Holy Land a novelty. Ever since the fourth century pilgrimage to Jerusalem was fashionable. A generation before the First Crusade, some seven thousand pilgrims had joined in a common cavalcade through Hungary to Palestine, and had set a precedent by leaving two-thirds of their number dead by the way.

The originality and import of the Crusades lay in the backing they received, from popes and kings to the meanest monks and knights. And it may be observed that when the ruling classes go out to "save" something, whipping their underlings into an idealist frenzy, it is generally to save themselves. In the case of the Crusades, the Church, despite Canossa, was saving itself from lay revolt, the kings were saving themselves from a recalcitrant feudalism, the knights from boredom and debts, and the masses from starvation. "The French could easily be induced to leave their lands," reports Ekkehard, an eye-witness of the First Crusade, "since for several years Gaul had suffered from civil war, famine, excessive mortality, and plague." As for the debts, Ekkehard explains that many Crusaders "confessed they had been forced to take the vow by embarrassed circumstances." If further evidence is necessary, it may be noted that the only social class which showed a reluctance to save their souls by fighting in distant lands were the merchants. When knights were selling acres and castles for a song, when everyone who sewed a cross on his shirt front was ready to give all he owned for a little travel money, the merchants found it altogether more attractive to remain at home.

But these ulterior motives did not invalidate the moral earnestness of the cause. It was a genuine and magnificent enthusiasm which moved thousands of throats to respond to the plea of Urban with a single cry, "God wills it!" The proof lies in the sacrifice those who raised the cry offered to their Lord. As a token of their devotion, almost the first thing they did was to kill the Jews. Again to quote Ekkehard, who is now speaking of the forces which passed through Germany, "they either utterly destroyed the execrable race of Jews wherever they found them (being even in this matter zealously devoted to the Christian religion), or forced them into the bosom of the Church."

The first irregular bands of cross-bearers set out eastward from France; and the French Jews, who knew their mettle, despatched a warning to the communities along the Rhine. With a sense of loyalty which has so often marked the German Jews—*Deutsche Treue* the Germans call it, and no one has relied more firmly on it than its habitual victims—the Rhine Jewries disregarded the French storm-signals. The Mayence community, in fact, replied that while they were much concerned for the possible fate of their French brethren, neither now nor in former times had the lives of the Jews in Germany been endangered.

They were lulled, it must be said, partly by a prevalent hope in the coming of the Messiah. His advent had been calculated for the end of the 250th cycle of the moon, between the years 1096 and 1104; and their faith in the living Redeemer was stronger than their fear of—as they would have said—a dead Pretender. Yet they might have known better. They could have recalled a series of portents: reports, over a century before, of assaults upon Palestinian Jews by ardent pilgrims; the expulsion of the Mayence Jews in 1012; expulsions and confiscations, forty years later, in Bohemia, upon a charge of burning churches; and in 1066 an attack upon the Jews of Trèves for dabbling in black magic.

Anxiety arose, however, when Peter the Hermit and his swarm descended upon Trèves (April, 1096) with a letter from the French Jews ordering "that wherever he comes, the Jews shall furnish him with supplies; and he will bespeak good for Israel, for he is a monk and his words will be obeyed." But Peter abided by the canonical code. He allowed no violence, and merely contented himself with "gifts," no doubt blinking at the spirit in which they were given.

The laity were bound by no such code. According to contemporary Jewish records, the cross-bearers "as they approached a city where Jews dwelt, said to one another, We are going on a far journey to seek the Holy Sepulcher and wreak vengeance on the infidels who possess it; and, behold! right among us live the Jews, whose fathers crucified our Lord; let us, therefore, revenge ourselves on them first of all, let us wipe them out from among the peoples—or let them become like us and recognize the true faith." A certain Count Ditmar was credited with the vow that he would not leave Germany "until he had killed at least one Jew." And Godfrey of Bouillon—"may his bones," the chronicler piously adds, "be crushed!"—took an oath that "wheresoever he found himself, he would avenge the blood of God upon the blood of Israel."

At these threats and rumors, anxiety turned to panic.

Kalonymus ben Meshullam, head of the Mayence community, sped a report of the impending danger to Henry IV, who was then in Italy; and with the report went 500 silver marks from the Mayence Jews and another 500 marks from Cologne. Fasting and prayer were instituted throughout the Rhine Jewries. Henry responded nobly by sending letters to "all princes, bishops, and counts" of the Empire, and to Godfrey as well, commanding them to maintain peace; but a greater King, says the chronicler, "turned His eyes from His people and gave them over to the sword."

The sword fell, lightly to begin with, in Metz and Spires. Metz counted twenty-two dead. In Spires an unofficial crusading riff-raff—French, English, Flemings, and Lorrainers— joined with the local burghers and besieged the newly-built Jewry (May 3, 1096). But the bishop, Johannes, managed to bring its inhabitants to safety, the rioters were quelled, and only eleven victims "sanctified the Holy Name."

Worms was next. Part of its terrified Jews clung to their homes, depending on the aid of Christian neighbors, "who promised them protection." But the promises proved to be "broken reeds," largely because the Jews were so indiscreet as to leave their wealth, for safe-keeping, in these same neighborly hands. On May 18, the crusading horde, under the leadership of another flower of knighthood, Count Emicho, and joined by the burghers and peasantry, descended like "wolves of the desert" and put the trusting stay-at-homes to sack and slaughter.

Meanwhile the remainder of the Worms community had taken refuge in the bishop's palace. The bishop, Adalbert, was either helpless or else, as an opponent of Henry, indifferent to imperial orders. A week later (May 25) the palace was successfully stormed; and the refugees "passed," as the chronicler says, "into the great light of Paradise." In their extremity, many of them imitated their ancestors trapped in Masada, and heroically killed their dear ones rather than let them be contaminated by Christian swords. "They slaughtered, this one his brother, that one his wife and children, bridegrooms their brides, tender women their young babes . . . one and all they accepted the Divine Judgment with a devout heart, and, recommending their souls to the Creator, they cried, 'Hear, O Israel, the Lord our God is One!'" A very few saved themselves at the baptismal font. One youth, Simhah Cohen, whose father and seven brothers had gone down in the massacre, made a show of accepting baptism. Within the church door, at the moment of receiving the sacrament, he unloosed a dagger and—no doubt missing the prelate himself—killed the bishop's nephew. Naturally, his name was added at once to the eight hundred which made up the toll of the two days' work.

From Worms the warriors of the Cross moved upon Mayence and spread their tents before its walls. Hurriedly the Jews took counsel with the archbishop—Ruthard—and with the local count. They sweetened the counsel with a gift of 500 silver marks. The result was, they placed their wealth in the town treasury (where it eventually paid for their burial), they were given refuge in the episcopal palace and city castle, and both bishop and count swore "Either we shall save you or die with you." As an additional precaution, seven pounds in gold were sent to Emicho outside the walls and the promise of a letter-of-recommendation if he departed in peace. But the older and saintlier men shook their heads; they had seen

visions, they had heard wailing by night in the synagogue—
"The Heavenly decree hangs over us and cannot be averted."

After two days' parley with the reluctant but not obdurate
bishop—it was May 27, the day of the giving of the Law on
Sinai—the city gates were opened. Crusaders and burghers
marched "with waving banners" upon the palace. The Jews
"quickly put on their coats-of-mail and girded themselves
with swords," Kalonymus placed himself at their head, a
grey-beard bade them behave like the sons of Jacob; and
from the outer to the inner gate of the palace they fought a
losing fight. When the last barrier yielded, the episcopal
guards, who had sworn protection, "were the first to flee";
and the bishop, threatened with his life, fled after them.

The scenes that followed, through room after room of the
palace and castle, were a repetition of Worms—the Jews
vying with the mob as to who should kill the women and
children first. In the beginnings there had been an effort at
resistance. Defy and insult were hurled at the invaders—
"Spawn of abomination! believers in a dead savior! worshipers of a hanged corpse!"—and loyal acclaim to God. The
very women fought with stones torn from the chamber walls.
Then a delirium of self-destruction drove the doomed victims
to drink death like strong wine. Women threw their trinkets
to the mob to gain time "in order to fulfill the will of the
Creator and"—rather than allow them to suffer baptism—
"kill their beloved children." "Men and women slaughtered
one another . . . and girls and brides cried from the windows, 'See O Lord our God, what we are doing to keep holy
Thy great Name!'"

At Masada in Roman days, at York, Barcelona, and in the
Ukraine of later centuries, as now along the Rhine, this has

been the supreme gesture of the Jew. There was in it the breaking of desperate nerves and something, too, of the ancient stiffneckedness which refused a foe the satisfaction of the last blow. But more than that was the humane man's horror of bestiality, the fine resolve to keep a fellow-creature from the degradation of murder, by taking the crime and the blood upon one's own hands. And above all was the lure of a divine *Liebestod*, wherein death brought the lover to a perfect union with God. Two young girls, Bella and Madrona, sharpened the knives for their own execution. "Then they bared their necks . . . as a sacrifice to the Eternal, who has commanded us to *give ourselves utterly to Him*."

Before the sun had sunk twice, the palace and castle yielded the last soul, the ghetto was mopped up for stray victims, the synagogue burned by Jewish hands lest it, too, be "converted," and Kalonymus, together with a band of fugitives, hunted to death in a neighboring wood. Mayence reckoned its dead at eleven hundred. As a measure of public economy—for the wealth deposited in the town treasury never returned to Jewish hands—the bodies were buried in a single trench.

In Cologne, where the Jews had been acquiring status and repute for some eight centuries, the archbishop made a serious effort at protection. He evacuated them from the city and distributed them among a number of episcopal strongholds in outlying villages. However, May 30, the Jewry, almost empty of inhabitants, was pillaged; and, shortly after, the refugees were routed out of their strongholds and, despite the centuries and the archbishop, put to the sword. The turn of Trèves came early in June.

Moving eastward, the Crusaders won a victory at Regensburg by driving its entire Jewry into the Danube and baptizing them at one wave of the hand. Prague and other Bohemian towns completed the tale of forced conversion and slaughter.

And then, to the satisfaction of both Jews and honest Christians, Emicho and his cohorts were destroyed by the Hungarians, who stood for no nonsense from foreign marauders merely because they wore a cross. Albert of Aix, the one Christian chronicler who gives the story in detail, puts his satisfaction on curious, though perhaps typical, grounds. The disaster inflicted on Emicho's crusaders was a divine punishment, he says, "for their slaughtering the Jews through greed of money *rather than for the sake of God's justice*"— and a little, too, for "their excessive fornication" and for using, as oracular guides on their journey, a goose and a she-goat.

Altogether, the First Crusade cost the Jews of Germany close to 12,000 lives. A contemporary writer grimly consoles himself with the thought that "God had chosen the entire generation to be His portion, in order that the generations to come might reap the reward of its merits."

But lives were the least of Jewry's losses. Compared, in fact, with the casualties suffered by Saxon and Wend at Christian hands, or by fellow-Christians in Greece and Syria when the Crusaders neared their goal, the Jews could count themselves lucky. Among the wounds which really pierced the marrow, wounds not healed to the present day, the crusade of 1096 set an undying precedent. Succeeding crusades brought, with macabre variations, the same round of terror, pillage, and death. Once aroused and fed by a rich booty, religious hatred proved ingenious in providing new charges.

To the crucifixion of Jesus was added the ritual murder of children, desecration of the Host, conspiracy with the enemy, complots to destroy Christendom, and congenital greed and treachery—each leading to further humiliation and plunder. *Hep, Hep!*—"Give, give!"—an insult and a demand—the cry of the pack when the prey was winded—became the familiar Christian salutation. Jew-baiting acquired a technique and served, from age to age, as a sovereign remedy for the ills of the land.

The Jewish soul was seared. Medieval chroniclers and poets show the scar of it in their narratives and plaints, which move in a world of incredible hope, horrid despair, and impotent visions of revenge. Much of these writings is magnificent. The liturgy overflowed with *selihot*, penitential prayers which are masterpieces of agony, pleading, and self-reproach. The narratives, a compound of homely reporting and sweeping eloquence, would well repay English translation. But all are touched with abnormality. Even his faith in God which, if not wholly responsible for the survival of the Jew, did most to keep him sane, seems in the face of his trials to strain perfection. A Benjamin ben Zerah is rare. Living in the eleventh century, at the outset of the storm, he is still human enough to protest, "Am I made of iron? Is my flesh steel, to bear this burden? I am weary of exile and servitude, tired of letting the nations tread me down on all sides. When they cry at me, 'Where now is the Rock of your salvation? Why does He not stretch out His arm to uphold you?' I want to hide my face in the earth." And rare the bitter Hebrew pun which altered the boast of Moses (Ex. 15.11), "Who is like unto Thee, O Lord, among the *mighty?*" to read, "Who is like unto Thee, O Lord, among the *dumb?*"

For the most part, in the five centuries of degradation which followed the First Crusade, the Jew repeated the perversity of the Christian. "Gods wills it," said the "imitator" of Jesus as he raised his sword; and the Jew, upon receiving the stroke, echoed after him, "Gods wills it." An old *selihah* of German origin, still preserved in the standard prayer-book, puts it at greater length, "They were swifter than eagles to do the will of their Master, and the desire of their Rock." There lurks, however, another difference—the perversity of the Jew was heroic.

BOOK TWO

DEGRADATION

If sincerity and honesty are to prevail between two peoples, each must make a large and generous effort to this end; if, however, one of these peoples believes it a religious duty and a profitable business to persecute the other—what then?—*Lessing*.

5

THE GOLD TRADE

As far as the Jews were concerned, the First Crusade was quickly liquidated. Henry IV permitted the forcibly baptized victims to return to their old faith—a matter of principle and prerogative hotly contested by the papal claimant Clement III. An imperial investigation honored the pillage of the Mayence Jewry; Archbishop Ruthard, suspected of connivance, was laid under the ban; and Henry pocketed what remained of the spoils. The *Landfriede*, or general immunity, proclaimed by Henry in 1103 and valid for four years, added the Jews to the usual list of unarmed beneficiaries: "clerics, women, nuns, peasants, merchants, travelers, fishermen, hunters, and Jews." Actually, the Jews enjoyed peace for more than a full generation.

It was the generation which, without abandoning commerce, plunged largely into money-lending. A start in this direction had, we saw, been made in the previous century. Meanwhile, the need for cash in the Crusades and the continued growth of the cities, with their expanding trade and manufacture, enormously increased the demand for loans. In many crafts, the guilds united manufacture with sales, thereby eliminating the independent and particularly the "alien" merchant, but widening, instead, the market for finance. Trade and manufacture themselves waxed on the flowering of knighthood with its attendant luxuries and on the vast boom in church building—both encouraged by the spirit of the Crusades. Plumed knights and stained glass demanded more loans. Princes and kings became expensively engaged in enlarging their power; the rising bourgeoisie joined the knights in cultivating a taste for the amenities of life; and crowns and comfort demanded still more loans. Serfdom likewise bettered its condition through the influence of the Crusades. The peasants entered upon a tedious emancipation. Instead of working directly for the masters, they began to pay for their existence by deliveries in kind and, to some degree, money. Here, too, advance loans on crops and rentals grew in demand.

Behind these many demands lay a slow economic revolution. In a gestation covering centuries, feudalism was painfully giving birth to capitalism. And by inescapable circumstance, from that day to this, for good and for evil, German Jewry found its fortune tied to the wheel of capital.

The story of Jewish money-lending differs little from that of Jewish commerce. The Jews were not alone engaged in the traffic. But when they had outstripped their rivals, and the benefits to society and themselves grew worthy of plunder, they were pushed aside by terror, by bloodshed, and by the force of superior political, social, and religious power on the part of their competitors. In both cases they were enabled to break ground in a new economic endeavor because, as outsiders, they could not share on equal terms in the old. And in both cases the harvest was snatched from their hands likewise because they were aliens.

From the outset, Christians plied the trade as well as Jews.

Clergy, nobility, and burghers were berated for it as heartily as any son of Judah. From the twelfth to the sixteenth century —until, that is, the growing influence of business *mores* upon society led to the discovery that usury* under the name of banking was a public service—preachers, moralists, and poets incessantly attacked Christian money-lenders. Bernard of Clairvaux led the assault, in 1146, by claiming that Christian usurers were worse than Jews. A century later, the minnesingers played variants on Freidank's theme: *"Swaz verstât in Römer hant, lither loest man juden pfant—*it is easier to redeem a pledge from the Jews than from the Church." And by the sixteenth century, when Israel was out of the running, Johann Purgolt, the scribe of Eisenach, can even find apology for the Jews. Because, he says, they were excluded from trade and crafts, "they were compelled to take up usury." "But," he continues, "the Christians have no excuse save greed and wickedness." Indeed, it was not uncommon to find Jews borrowing from Christians, or to find Christians turning to Jews as a relief from the usurers of their own faith.

The latter point hints at the circumstances which in the first heyday of the trade gave advantage to the Jews. The Church stood in principle against taking interest on money, a principle grounded in Scripture (Luke 6.35) and deepened by concern for the welfare of society. But the Church had to live and prosper; and legal casuistry—whereby interest was considered to be a payment for possible loss, damage, labor, or delay— devised ways to maintain papal bankers in Italy and ecclesiastical pawnbrokers everywhere else. As a medieval cynic observed in expounding canon law on usury: "He who takes it

---

* Usury, in medieval times, meant lending money at interest, irrespective of the rate.

goes to hell, and he who does not goes to the poor-house." The Church, nevertheless, was ill at ease in the business. It roundly prohibited competition by the laity—always excepting its protégés, the Lombards. It was stringent and pitiless in its own transactions. And fanatics were forever rising in its ranks to denounce the whole traffic.

As a result, money-lending suffered in Christendom somewhat the same taint as liquor-dealing in America. It bristled with vexations and restrictions, it might be necessary but the devil was in it, and the cost of its services mounted accordingly. The payment of interest was often disguised—bootlegged—under clever masks: property was "sold" below its market value with the right, after a set time, to rebuy it above its worth; or rents, taxes, and tithes were "sold" for less than they yielded. However, with respect to money, one class of people lived in the Christian world over whom the Church claimed no authority—the Jews. Taint or no taint, they were legally free to lend when, where, and whom they pleased.

More than free, they were invited—nay, urged. Christian borrowers flocked to lenders who were licit and accommodating, yet who in a pinch could loose no thunders of church and state to compel repayment of the last pfennig.

The secular authorities encouraged the Jews; first, because in the beginning the Lombards and other ecclesiastical bankers held aloof from the laity as risky clients over whom the Church had no effective power when the time came to pay, and better yet, because the richer grew the Jews the bigger the immediate taxes and ultimate spoils of the state. Augsburg and Regensburg were not exceptional in basing their protection of the Jews on the ground that they were "useful citizens and indispensable to the common man." So useful that local governments—Cologne 1266, Austria 1316, Winterthur 1340, among many others—granted them a monopoly on usury. And so indispensable that prince and city often forced them into lending money. Conrad IV (1242, 1243), Cologne (1250), Passau (1260), Regensburg (1328, 1333) do not begin to give the tale of these compulsory loans. By a neater device Henry IV of Silesia (1270) attained the same end through forbidding the Jews any other occupation.

Then, too, the Jews found themselves advantageously equipped by the possession of large stocks of cash—in part the accumulation of commerce, in part the proceeds of its liquidation under pressure of Christian competition, and in no slight degree the result of their precarious existence, in which mobile wealth was cherished as a means of protection or flight.

Finally, they were driven into money-lending for the same reason they had once embraced commerce. There were no alternatives. The land had long been closed to them—"we have neither fields nor vineyards," pleads a twelfth-century apologist. And now Christian merchant- and artisan-guilds made commerce increasingly difficult and handicrafts almost impossible.

To be sure, the Jews likewise had their principles and sacred texts (cf. Talmud, B.M. 71a); but when needs must, the casuist thrives. They had their prohibitionists as well. "He who lends money at interest," warns Judah the Pious of Regensburg (12th-13th cent.), "will be ruined—he, his children, and all his associates will pay the penalty."

In countries where other vocations remained open—Spain, Portugal, Provence, Poland, and the Moslem states—the medieval Jew never became synonymous with the usurer. In Italy, where the Christian usurers practically monopolized the favor of the Church, money-lending never monopolized the Jews. Usury as a dominant Jewish calling was confined to lands where conditions made it inevitable: Northern France, England, and Germany.

It was not only pardonable casuistry but grim good-sense when Isaac of Vienna (ca. 1250), repeating common rabbinic opinion, wrote, "In ancient talmudic times when the Jews lived among themselves and did all their business with one another, it was forbidden to take interest from non-Jews. But now that we dwell among them and cannot withhold dealing with them, it is permitted to take interest from them; since everything we lend is necessary for our livelihood and we cannot know what taxes the king will exact of us . . . threatened, as we are, by bitter demands and needing, as we do, huge sums for bribery, money-lending is the price of our existence."

ii

Swifter than commerce, the stream of gold carried the Jews like mobile cells into the body, limbs, and heart of German economy. A creditor has access and power that a salesman cannot dream of. For three centuries money-lending opened to the Jews intimate and potent contact with a world which, by a paradox, was thrusting them socially further and further aside.

Even the Church—which sanctioned loans only in case of "direst need," which hedged the pawning of its ritual treasures with elaborate precautions, and which particularly disapproved of the influence accruing to "unbelieving" creditors—was a long and steady customer. "Direst need" for the Church included, on occasion, the financing of military expeditions (Würzburg 1161 and 1173), the ransoming of dukes (Prague 1107), the maintenance of abbatial pomp (Ebersheim 1228) and, we are led to suspect in an age of simony, the purchase of episcopal chairs and cardinal's hats. The very priests of the village pawned their weekly tithes. Monasteries and bishoprics went into silent partnership with the Jews. Clerics likewise furnished collateral—sacred jewels and plate—for hard-pressed barons when, by doing so, they could shrewdly relieve the Church of rentals due these same noblemen, or, if the repayment of the loan could not be met, the Church could take over the unlucky debtor's temporal possessions (Herrenhalb; Merseburg 1234). From partners, the Jews were turned into cats-paws. "Whoever does business with a priest," said Judah the Pious, "loses his money." In the end, this immersion of the Church in the business, together with the burden of its debts, sharpened the edge of its reaction to Jewish usury. The preaching orders, founded in the thirteenth century, could play upon an uneasy conscience as well as on more practical considerations when they stirred the masses against the Jews.

The nobility furnished probably the most important class of customers. Imperial loans were infrequent until the fourteenth century—the emperors had, we shall see, other means of coming by Jewish money; but princes, dukes, barons, and counts are to be reckoned by the dozens. Loans to landed gentry were especially attractive, because if the borrower pledged his land as security, the lender enjoyed both the interest on the debt and, for at least a year, the revenue of the acres. And not only acres. Whole villages, towns, and dominions fell into the fiscal possession of the Jews.

Closely related in importance and effect to the aristocratic clientèle were the state and city governments which, it might be recalled, were as likely to be ecclesiastic as secular. The accommodation of public treasuries sometimes led to the appointment of money-lenders, as men demonstrably wise in the ways of gold, to the offices of mint-master, tax-collector, and director of finance. Jewish mint-masters are found scattered over Germany (Austria 1177-1194, Saxony 1180-1212, Würzburg 1207-1223)—at the same period when Jews in Poland were coining specie with Hebrew inscriptions. Jewish tax-collectors appear in numerous localities (Sayn 1160, Mecklenburg [?] 1266, Gersenheim 1296 and 1342, Bacharach 1317, Miltenberg 1341, Lahnstein 1336, Ehrenfels 1337, Coblenz 1345, Bingen and Kreuznach). Ministers of finance, in fact if not in name, were mostly prevalent in eastern Germany— Austria, Bohemia, and Silesia; though in the west Trèves set an example with a treasury directed and enriched by generations of Jews (1260-ca. 1350).

Men of this type—*Hof-Juden* or Court Jews—deeply influenced Jewish destiny in Spain, Provence, and the Germany of a later age, by serving as a link between the Jewish and Gentile cultures of their time. They were patrons and servants of the mind. It is perhaps, therefore, a commentary on conditions in medieval Germany (and for that matter, England, France, or Poland) that although this link existed there was nothing for it to join. Both of them untouched by anything resembling the liberal breath of Moslem science and literature, the northern Jew was still predominantly talmudic and self-absorbed, and the northern prince still an intellectually unawakened boor. The rare German ruler who felt a twinge in his brain-cells—an Emperor Frederick II—managed to pass the best of his days in southern Italy and Sicily, where Arabs and Jews had a place in the sun. Indeed, it is no less a commentary on the *Hof-Juden* of medieval Germany to discover that contemporary Jewish references to them chiefly betray their willingness to use their station for reducing their personal taxes or—an occasional failing in Jewish bankers—to finance the avowed enemies of Israel.

Burghers made up the remaining bulk of customers. The little man and the peasant seldom appeared in the early pages of Jewish ledgers. They grew into prominence—beginning with the late thirteenth century—only as the larger customer shifted his business to the Lombards or had exhausted, by means readily surmised, the resources of the big Jewish lenders.

At the peak of the money-lending trade and before commerce had dwindled to peddling, the wealth of the Jews was huge. However, it is significant that research mainly learns of it through the taxes, extortions and forced loans inflicted on its owners. It may have been "easy come"; but what with threats, imprisonment, and thumbscrews, it was hardly "easy go." A fine imposed on the Jews of Cologne in 1179 netted the archbishop 4200 silver marks. The archbishop of Magdeburg did better, in 1261, by extorting from its rich Jews 100,000 marks ransom. Duke Vladislav I of Bohemia, about 1124, did better yet when he extracted 3000 pounds silver and 100 pounds gold for the release of a single Jew.

What purchasing power did these fortunes represent? It is hard to say. Let us take some items close to the dates mentioned. In Cologne of 1140 the yearly rental of a medium dwelling was ½ to 1 mark; a coat cost 1 mark; a horse rented weekly for 6 pfennigs. Around 1270 the daily outlay of a Jew who traveled at community expense—presumably before the invention of the swindle-sheet—was reckoned, exclusive of shelter, at 18 pfennigs. Gold, in the period, had about twelve times the value of silver. According to modern standards, these disparities are confusing. But a comparative estimate may be gleaned from the taxes. In 1241 the Jews of Germany paid 12% of the total imperial levies, although the population of the Jews—this may interest the devotees of the numerus clausus—was proportionately about where it stands today, that is, 1% of the whole. Even this 12% fails to include Nuremberg and Würzburg, and in addition omits such important cities as Mayence, Erfurt and probably Cologne and Trèves, none of whose Jews were at that date subject to the imperial fisc. In fourteenth-century Nuremberg the Jews paid 4000 thalers taxes, while the entire city paid but six or seven thousand. Yet then no more than now were the majority of Jews wealthy. In Breslau (1330-1360), out of 170 self-supporting members of the Jewry, only sixteen were taxpayers and eleven outstandingly rich.

At first blush the interest rates—which accounted for much of this wealth—seem incredible. The average loan brought in from 43% to 50% a year. The usual range was from about 21% to 108%.

Astonishment vanishes, however, upon a glance at the circumstances, risks, and needs of the case. Cash was exceedingly scarce—not, in fact, until the discovery of America did Europe have anything like an adequate supply of bullion; and the use of credit was in its infancy. What specie there was had a disconcerting trick—developed by the governments issuing it—of shrinking overnight in its gold or silver content. The majority of loans ran for short terms, which made the effect of the high rates less monstrous in fact than on paper. Again, most loans were of a consumptive rather than productive nature; the borrowed money was spent rather than invested; and repayment, even when the debtor was in good faith, depended less on the returns of a going enterprise than on a stroke of luck in war, politics, weather, or marriage.

Too often the debtor was not in good faith. "So-and-so, the debtor, is a man of violence and refuses to pay interest or capital," became a stock formula in the cases brought before rabbinic judges. Consequently the common hazards, which the money-lender accepted as part of the day's work, included the "violent" man's denial of the bond; the difficulties encountered in taking possession of a pledge if it belonged to a vassal whose title to it was neither free nor clear; the appeal, backed by appropriate bribes, to the recalcitrant debtor's overlord; the evasion of the vengeful debtor's strong arm, and, when unsuccessful, the cooling of one's heels in his donjon keep. Outlays for bribery and ransom were part of the regular overhead in the business. And if the creditor, in prudent fear, took flight without first securing permission, at due price, from the authorities—the prince, count, or bishop to whom the Jew "belonged"—he forfeited his loan; and, what is more, the local Jewry had to indemnify the said authorities for whatever fiscal loss the flight entailed. The death of a debtor often meant the loss of the debt; and the death of the creditor, likely as not, ended in the frank appropriation of the claim by the authorities. Finally there were, as we have seen, the taxes. They seldom came to less than a fifth of the total wealth of the Jewish communities, and often took a quarter or a third.

But these were merely habitual risks. For four centuries,

beginning with the twelfth, there was not a generation of Jews in Germany which did not at least once in its lifetime face the threat or reality of mass persecution and death. Aside from plunder by the mob, these persecutions struck directly at the Jewish purse through wholesale remission of interest, cancellation of debts, and confiscation of fortunes.

Monumental interest rates and dangerous living were not, however, the sole rewards of the trade. We have already hinted at the process whereby the swift circulation of gold fertilized the land. In spending what they borrowed, baron and bishop stimulated arts, commerce, and crafts. Merchant- and manufacturing-guilds benefited by the growing knowledge and use of credit. Kings and dukes found in gold a weapon sharper than the sword for destroying feudalism and fortifying the power and security of the land. And when in the late twelfth century Jews filtered into small towns and villages, and when a hundred years later the competition of the Lombards forced their gradual withdrawal to petty loans, the little craftsman, shopkeeper and husbandman began to share in the services familiar to the more affluent classes.

Jewry itself reaped advantages quite apart from the evanescent profits. Money-lending, to a larger extent than commerce, threw an enormous responsibility on the local community. It became, more than ever, the favorite quarry for extracting public revenue, a mine from which princes of the church and state could dig their fill. Upon it, too, fell the dangers and disasters of its money-lending members. As a result, it strengthened its control over the individual, often dictating to whom and under what conditions money could be lent. By tightening the common discipline, it steeled

Israel for the shocks to come and, by the same measures, deepened the loyalty to Judaism as a way of life.

But the cost of these gains was too great, both for Germany and the Jews. When joined to the average lender's zeal for gain—a zeal surpassed only by the average borrower —the hazards of money-lending terminated in a vicious circle. The risks enlarged the rates and narrowed the terms, in this way increasing the burden upon the debtor, and ultimately upon the entire German people. And the weight of the burden, expressed in hate, chicanery, and violence, heightened the risks. The cleft between Jew and Gentile became in the economic sphere as tragic as in the religious. Literally tragic, for the antagonists, each in his own light, were justified and driven by forces beyond their control.

An immediate consequence was the progressive declassment of the Jew. In earlier centuries when Jew was synonymous with merchant, he was looked upon as an alien, yet not intolerable and certainly harmless. But now that he was synonymous with usurer—St. Bernard of Clairvaux used and perhaps invented the verb "to Jew" (*judaizare*) with the meaning "to lend money at interest"—he became despicable and vile. He sank from alien to pariah. The close intercourse between borrowers and lenders, the frequent demonstrations of loyalty on the part of the Jews—mourning at bishops' funerals and fighting shoulder to shoulder with the burghers —the neighborly give and take bound to arise between any two peoples living together, could not prevail against the tide of contempt.

Almost invariably the medieval German writer on manners and morals, when he mentioned the Jew, spared nothing of loathing and vituperation. "Blind—false—stumbling-blocks

—stinking unbelievers!" were the common apostrophes. "I hate the Jews without stint," avows Regenbogen (13th century). "Accursed people, the unslaughtered Jews!" exclaims David of Augsburg (in the same century). "The devil would long ago have broken your necks, without our angels to protect you," adds his pupil, Berthold of Regensburg. When Berthold storms against feminine vanities and prinking, he says they are indulged in only by "prostitutes, church concubines, and Jewesses." About the worst thing he can call a man—and he seldom loses a chance—is "a Christian in name and a Jew in deeds." "If I were king," sighs Helbing, an Austrian contemporary, "I'd burn you Jews, one and all, wherever I found you." This garland of friendship could be woven, indefinitely, through the succeeding generations. "Jewish sow" and "Jew dog" remain popular epithets to the present day.

When the tension of the vicious circle became too acute, the debtors generally resorted to two wholesale remedies. One was to kill the Jews. But this had its drawback; if the promissory notes or other documentary evidence of the debt survived, the king or provincial lord was ready to step into the shoes of the dead creditors. The other and surer remedy was to "kill" the documents. This was accomplished by decree of the ruler, who reduced or abolished the debt "for the salvation of his soul or in honored memory of his forefathers." As for the masses, who indirectly bore the brunt of the whole traffic, they simply rose in blind wrath and, on whatever the passing pretext might be, gave themselves over to pillage and slaughter. Too often what the Jewish historian has seen as persecution was, at the bottom, social revolt.

"What we now call the hatred of the proletarian against the rich," said Heine, "was formerly called Jew-hatred."

iii

The Second Crusade (1146-47) was a case in point. Peter the Venerable inveighed against the wealth of the "enemies of Christ in our midst." While denouncing any bodily violence—for which service, observes a contemporary Jewish chronicler, he received neither bribe nor gift—St. Bernard of Clairvaux fastened on usury as the source of this wealth. Pope Eugenius III remitted interest payments—along with sins—for all who took up the Cross. And a pious monk, Rudolph, marched through the Rhinelands preaching death to the wealth-owning Jews.

But, aside from the plunder and the saving of interest payments, the harvest was slim. A Jewess in Spires lost her ears and thumbs; another in Aschaffenburg was drowned. A few Jewish travelers, among them distinguished scholars, were slain on the highways. Twenty-two victims fell in Würzburg. For the most part the Jews owed their skins to the eloquence of Bernard and the power of their purse. "We gave our wealth as the price of our lives; whatever was asked of us, silver or gold, we did not refuse."

The Third Crusade (1189-92) occasioned a similar technique in England and France: annulment of debts, confiscations, expulsions, and massacres. The fall of Jerusalem into Saracen hands brought German Jewry nothing worse than a reign of terror, graphically described by Eleazar ben Judah of Worms (author of the *Rokeah*), who was later to taste its fruits.

As a preparation for the Fourth Crusade, Innocent III,

who had just followed Alexander III in confirming the inviolability of Jewish property, balanced the score by following Eugenius III and again decreed a moratorium on interest due to Christian creditors (1199). If the Jews demurred, they were to be coerced by a general boycott.

Meanwhile the Rhinelands were visited by excesses which, in their irrelevant origins, showed how deeply ran the religious and economic roots of Jew-hatred.

A woman is found murdered in Boppard (1179): Jews on a passing ship are suspected of the crime, vainly proffered baptism, and promptly drowned; and the affair does not end until the Jewries of the diocese pay Emperor Barbarossa and Archbishop Philip of Cologne 4700 silver marks. In Neuss (1187?) a Jewish madman kills a Christian girl: not merely the assailant, but his entire family—the mother is buried alive—and six leaders of the community are horribly executed, and their bodies exposed to public view; 150 marks are paid the local archbishop and a number of wealthy Jews tapped for compulsory loans before permission is granted for the removal of the remains, and even so the permission is postponed five weeks. Spires 1196: a Christian is again found murdered by unknown hands; in consequence, the leading rabbi and eight other Jews lose their lives, the community buildings are fired, the Jewry is pillaged, the body of the rabbi's daughter dug from her grave, hung naked on the street, with a dead mouse tied to her hair. Boppard, one week later: a mob kills eight Jews. (In both these cases the authorities forced the Christians to pay an indemnity.) Worms, the end of the same year: crusaders burst into the home of Eleazar ben Judah, slaughter his wife and two daughters before his eyes, and leave himself, his son, and his pupils for dead.

The gruesome cruelty and explosive violence of these acts —which were paralleled in France and England and repeated through the next centuries—can no longer be regarded as "medieval." To its sorrow the modern world has learned that they are perennial means of relief for morally undisciplined peoples when their pockets are robbed, their stomachs emptied, and their heads filled with national or religious ecstasy.

Although it meant a desperate and barren existence, the Jews of Germany must have likewise felt relieved when the paroxysms of the Black Death and the final triumph of the Lombards (14th-15th cent.) drove them from the cream of the gold trade. In the Polish exile, in the isolated Bavarian villages, and in the gloomy ghettos of the few larger cities, to which they were reduced, they had leisure to ruminate the words of Judah the Pious, "He who lends money at interest will be ruined—he, his children, and all his associates."

6

SERVANTS OF OUR CHAMBER

IF WE are to believe the medieval Germans, the Jews of the Reich owed their political status to Titus. As the *Sachsenspiegel* (1224-32) and more particularly the *Schwabenspiegel* (1275) tell it, Titus, after the fall of Jerusalem, took personal possession of conquered Israel, passed his title on to his imperial successors, and bound them to protect their "property"; and in due course the German emperors, having fallen heir to Rome, fell heir to the Jews as well. At the outset we may note an important difference in these heritages. The Holy Roman Empire of the German Nation seldom amounted to more than a flattering myth, whereas the ownership of the Jews by the German crown came to be an altogether solid fact.

Its title to Jewry, however, was not so simple and ancient as the writers of these *Spiegel* would have it. In the ninth century Ludwig the Pious, far from assuming that he already possessed the Jews or owed them security, bestowed his protection on several individuals of the race as a special favor. It is true, *Judenmeister,* royal officials having authority over the Jews, appear in his reign; but the character and basis of this authority is unknown—presumably it was fiscal and derived from Jewish commerce.

A century later, what historians call the "particularism" of Germany began to complicate matters. The Empire was, as we said, largely the shadow of an ideal. Old tribal differences, fed by party strife and material interests, persisted in the form of quasi-sovereign states and provinces—Saxony, Franconia, Swabia, Bavaria, Hessia, Thuringia, and the like—which made a formal bow of fealty to the emperor and otherwise did as they pleased. Dropped in the middle of these provinces were ecclesiastical and secular city-states which also exercised a great measure of autonomy and often possessed outlying territory, towns, and villages.

When the emperors were men of strength—the Saxons or the Hohenstaufens—something like unity blanketed the land. When the popes or princes were men of greater strength, or the emperors weaklings, the map of Germany returned to its customary look of a crazy-quilt. To add to the confusion, much of the energy of the emperors, not content with failing to rule Germany, spent itself in failing to rule Italy as well. And, together with other sources of revenue, such as acres, mines, and serfs, the Jews were shuttled to and fro in the interminable four-cornered fight for power on the part of emperors, princes, bishops, and burghers.

The Jews of the early days lived chiefly in the city-states, and at first the cities had it all their own way. The Saxon emperors, Otto I and Otto II, it will be recalled, gave "the Jews and other merchants" of Magdeburg and Merseburg to their respective bishops. In Mayence, Cologne, Trèves, Metz, Spires, and Worms—which latter, by a refinement of crazy-quilting, was until the reign of Otto II one-third secular and two-thirds ecclesiastical—the bishops ruled and taxed their Jews, with or without royal consent. Friction between emperor and bishops was, moreover, in the nature of things reduced to a minimum, for the good reason that the Saxon monarchs—who gave Germany a unity no other European nation achieved for centuries and Germany itself never recaptured till the days of Bismarck—appointed their own bishops, investing them not merely with their temporal possessions but with their sacred ring and staff.

In the eleventh century, ring and staff became the stakes in a war between state and church, emperor and pope, which sent Henry IV to the snows of Canossa, Hildebrand to an exile's death, and Germany to a long ruin. The War of Investitures, it was called. But it is a chronic war which has since worn many masks: the sixteenth century knew it as the Reformation, the seventeenth as the Thirty Years War, the nineteenth as the *Kulturkampf*, and what name Chancellor Hitler and Cardinal Faulhaber will give its current guise remains to be invented.

It was hardly a coincidence that in the course of Henry IV's struggle, the imperial claim upon Jewry reappears in his grant to the citizens of Worms, as a reward for good behavior, of the taxes due him from the Jews of that and other cities (1074). Or that in the consolidation of his power, when Hildebrand was broken, he gave Jews in Spires and Worms generous privileges and letters of protection (1090); the recipients, it may be assumed, were no less generous in paying for the gift. Or, finally, that after the First Crusade, in the year Henry proclaimed his *Landfriede* (1103), the Jews of Mayence are given the title *Kammerknechte*—"servants of the imperial chamber."

What was a *Kammerknecht*? It hardly serves to consult the dictionary. *Kammer* means "treasury" as well as "cham-

ber"; *Knecht* means "thrall" and "vassal" as well as "servant."
Nor will historical analogies help. *Adelknechte* were noblemen, and *Landsknechte* were freebooters.

The meaning of the term begins to emerge in the reign of
Frederick Barbarossa (1152-90). The same change in society
which developed usury was now making money itself a
power, quite as much as wealth in land, goods, or men. Accordingly, in his royal schemes Barbarossa—who, with
Charlemagne, won his greatest empire in the poet's heart—
devoted a great deal of attention to his purse. He just failed
of appropriating the Lombards as that fine source of income
they were later to become. Turning to the Jews, he decreed
the whole community of Worms and perhaps of the Rhinelands a direct possession of the Reich (1157). In the *Landfriede* proclaimed in Würzburg and valid for Franconia, he
included the Jews because, so he declared, "they belonged to
the imperial fisc" (1179).

With the approach of the Third Crusade, the anxious Jews
welcomed this proprietorship, despite its probable cost—of
which they could gather a hint in the 500 marks which Barbarossa took as his share in the Boppard affair. A Jewish observer at the Mayence diet (1188), which completed the
plans for the Crusade, notes with satisfaction that the princes
who were present "realized how beloved we are by the
emperor" and he reports, "it was written and sealed as well as
proclaimed by word of mouth that they must watch over the
Jews, even as the apple of their eye." Not only did Barbarossa
enforce this promised protection, but, in comparison with the
way things went in contemporary France and England, he
treated his fiscal wards with admirable restraint; "he de-

manded," says a Jewish chronicler, "merely a small share of our possessions."

The same year, 1188, Barbarossa took occasion, upon granting privileges to the Jewry of Regensburg, to lay down principles of tolerance and protection which, if they could have entered into the mind and heart of the age, might have banished the Jewish problem.

"It is the duty of our imperial office," he declared, "demanded alike by justice and by reason, that we safeguard the property, persons, peace, and ancestral customs of all our subjects, not only those of our own faith, but those who live after the tradition of their fathers. We therefore make known that we shall assiduously protect the Jews of our empire, who enjoy a special claim upon our regard in that they belong to the imperial treasury." Fairer words were never spoken from the pagan interlude of Julian the Apostate to the no less pagan Age of Reason which ushered in the French Revolution.

But the principles of monarchs or philosophers seldom determine history. The religious set-up of the times, the whole economic and political bent of things, deafened Germany to Barbarossa's words. Even the principle was at once contested. The bishops set up a howl, and Otto IV conceded, in 1209, that the crown held no claims on Jews inhabiting ecclesiastical cities. Not long after, the principle was perverted, in typical medieval fashion, when Henry VII presented his fiscal rights in the Jewry of Jülich to its local overlord (1227) and of Regensburg to its bishop (1233), and when he declared his wrath appeased against the count of Freiburg for the imprisonment of "our Jews" (1230).

Frederick II, grandson of Barbarossa and the best intellect

to grace a German throne down to his namesake, the king of Prussia, established the *Kammerknechtschaft* of the Jews in its classic form. The old war between church and state had broken out with renewed vigor; and an emperor who despite his oath refused for years to go crusading, who chased the papal troops across the heel of Italy, who got himself excommunicated twice, who hobnobbed with Jews and Arabs in his Sicilian palace, who wore if he did not earn the name of heretic and atheist, who read books and was even accused of writing them, such an emperor was not likely to stickle at a bishop's protest when it came to asserting imperial claims.

On the Jewish side, the need for shelter was graver than ever. The civil strife which had raged during Frederick's long minority—he was only three when his father, Henry VI, died—went hard on the Jews. How hard may be gauged from the fact that Rabbi Eleazar Rokeah, the rabbi of Worms, when this city was besieged by a royal claimant, allowed its Jews to bear arms on a Sabbath (1201). In the general upset of the *schreckliche kaiserlose Zeit*—"the terrible kaiserless days"—and the years immediately following, the Jewry of Halle was put to fire, sword, and sack (1206), the bishop of Cologne squeezed enough from the servants of *his* treasury to build the castle of Godesburg (1210), one Uri ben Joel Halevi, son and brother of famous rabbis, was burned in Cologne (1216), Frisian merchant-pilgrims instigated the murder of twenty-six—or ninety-six?—of their Jewish competitors in Erfurt (1221), and the Jews were banished from Breslau (1226) until they agreed to pay their way back.

The plight of the race was further aggravated by the newly sharpened attack of the Church, in the stringent decrees of the Fourth Lateran Council (1215) and the synod of Trèves

(1227), and in the complaints of Gregory IX (1233)—of which more in our next chapter. And it was hardly improved by Frederick's decision, at long last, to take up the Cross (1227).

Finally, the whole situation was rendered acute by a wave of blood-accusations. They came in a rush. In one year, 1235, destruction, torture, and massacre overwhelmed the Jews of Lauda and Tauberbischofsheim for the imputed murder of a Christian child; sixteen fell in Wolfshagen and eighteen in Wolfsheim on a similar score; and the citizenry of Fulda, aided by Crusaders who happened by, killed thirty-two Jews and Jewesses because five children were found dead in a burned mill. The bodies of the children were brought by the incensed populace to Frederick. "If they are dead," he said, "go and bury them, for they are good for nothing else." The populace thought otherwise; felt, in fact, they were indubitable proof of ritual crime.

With that modernity which colored Frederick's life, he appointed a commission to investigate the entire question of ritual murder. The commission, like many another, came to no agreement. Then, with common sense rare in any age, Frederick took, as he said, "the simplest way" and turned to experts. He summoned from various lands of Western Europe a conference of Jewish converts to Christianity, men who knew Jewish laws and ways, but who, "as opponents, would conceal nothing that might be said in this connection against the Jews or their sacred writings."

In 1236 Frederick published their findings which, as he had anticipated, completely exonerated Jewry. This exoneration was later confirmed by Innocent IV who, in his bull of 1247, declared the charge of ritual murder false in fact, unwarranted by Jewish scriptures, and, more than that, "a mere pretext for persecuting the Jews in the cruellest manner." It was probably the only point on which Frederick and the Papacy ever agreed.

Frederick took a further and what he doubtless felt was a conclusive step in settling the Jewish problem. "In order," as he wrote, "to assure the Jews of Germany peace and security," he prefaced the finding of 1236 with a decree—solicited, he notes, by the Jews themselves—which was to give effect to the principles of Barbarossa. It proclaimed all the Jews of the Empire to be *servi camerae nostrae*—"servants of our treasury." Frederick justified his action to Gregory IX— for the Church had its own claims to protecting the Jews— by explaining that it sprang from his "common right" over them. Writing to Vienna with regard to privileges he had extended Austria, he justified a paragraph which excluded Jews from public office, on the grounds that "for their crime against God they are condemned to eternal servitude." Thus, so far as Germany was concerned, populace, popes, and Jews were put in their place; and Frederick could go back well-pleased to his civilized Palermo—where he saw to it that Arabs and Jews enjoyed the same rights as Christians.

Far from settling the problem, the privilege of being "servants of the treasury" gave it new form and direction. Theoretically, the Jews got protection and the treasury got the Jews. No longer public prey, imperial game-laws preserved them for the exclusive provision of the imperial larder. The theory worked fairly well in France and better in centralized England, until, that is, the royal appetite overreached itself, and the people—who fattened the game which fed the king—rebelled, and the Jews were ejected in a body.

But in Germany the scheme broke down from the start. The inherent weakness of the Empire prevented it from protecting—or mulcting—even the Jews on an imperial scale.

Contrary to the intentions, or at least the decree, of Frederick, not all the Jews became "servants of the treasury." Magdeburg, Mecklenburg, and the principalities east of the Elbe, as well as many western states and cities, continued to exercise their own traditional control. Moreover, the right to belong to the treasury had to be sought—and paid for— before it was granted. Since the bestowal of the right lay in the hands of the emperor, and not in the Empire itself, it lapsed on his death and had to be renewed—and again paid for—at each coronation. Often, too, it ran for a limited term within any one reign, which meant another payment for its extension. Ultimately the annual taxes, renewal fees, and not infrequent arbitrary levies which the right poured into the imperial coffers wrought its undoing. Not that the Jews refused or failed to pay. But the revenue which the Jews represented proved an irresistible temptation to the emperors when it came to rewarding liegemen, bribing foes, or climbing out of a financial hole.

As a Jewish contemporary saw it, the fiscal procedure was simple. "The authorities make a practice of demanding ten times what a man possesses, in order to worry or frighten him into buying his way free." Under such procedure, the obligation to protect the "servants" was rapidly forgotten, and it was only remembered that they "belonged" to the treasury. *Ipsi Judaei et omnia sua regis sunt*—"the Jews and all they own are the king's"—became the ruling formula. So much so that one of the few advantages of the Jew in the medieval world, his freedom of movement—"The Jews may go wherever they wish, just like the knights," boasted a twelfth-century talmudist—was taken from them. Hereafter they were chained to their ghetto counting-tables as the serf to his acres. As for protection, it was Charles IV, in 1347, who boasted, "We can do with them as we choose."

Usually the emperors chose to treat their Jews as they did their other chattels and regalia—pawn, barter, or give them away. This ensued naturally from the rag-bag character of the Reich, in which kings, princes, and bishops did the picking while the emperor held the bag. Entire populations of cities, counties, and states fared no better than the Jews.

The disposal of the Jews as prize-packages antedated, we have seen, the decree of Frederick. Its tempo was hastened by the anarchy of the Great Interregnum (1250-73) which followed Frederick's death—a generation of turmoil, in which rivals vainly fought for the imperial throne while dukes and electors garnered the spoils.

Conrad IV, who ruled Germany in Frederick's absence and for some years after his death, set an example in retail and in wholesale. He pawned three Jews to Heinrich of Pfalzel against a loan of 500 pounds, with the understanding that if Heinrich failed to recoup interest and principle from the three pawns, he would make good the deficit (1242). To pay off 3,000 marks military expenses he pledged the whole city of Rothenburg *and* its Jews to Gottfried of Hohenlohe (1251). His rival for the throne, Henry Raspe, was no less enterprising: he ceded the Jews of Würzburg (1247) to its bishop for 2300 silver marks, which was not to be repaid as long as the bishop lived—obviously nothing but an untimely taking-off would prevent the prelate from gaining by the bargain. Altogether, in the century which elapsed between the reign of Barbarossa and the end of the Interregnum, the records, which are of course incomplete, preserve over fifty similar deals.

Rudolph of Hapsburg initiated the new dynasty into the old ways. He too stooped to small change when he pawned five Jews in Leimburg (1276) for 300 marks, and the Jewry of Limburg (1287) for a like sum. His successor, Albert I, bought his election to the throne by ceding to the Archbishop of Mayence a tenth of the annual revenue from his Jewry (1298), and neither did he scorn a paltry 150 marks on the pledge of three Jews to the Count of Daun. Meanwhile, Adolph of Nassau, claimant to the crown, liquidated a debt of 3500 marks by surrendering to his creditor the Jews of Oppenheim (1298).

In the next century the business thrived more lustily than ever. Ludwig the Bavarian (1314-1347) showed himself the master at it he needed to be, in view of his costly quarrels with pope, anti-pope, French king, and German underlings. Despite the fragmentary records, a statistician could produce a handsome graph showing our own price-loving age the market fluctuations on Jews through nearly every year of his reign. The variety of the trade testified to Ludwig's ingenious head. Perhaps his most original stroke was giving the Jews of Heilbronn to this city for a term of six years, on the understanding that the city was to use the gift to reduce the municipal debt by 4,000 pounds; the race to collect may readily be imagined. His lenders and beneficiaries ran from simple knights unable to advance more than a few pounds on mere village-Jews, up to mighty princes (like Frederick the Earnest) who received the entire Jewries of Austria, Regensburg, Augsburg, Strasbourg, Spires, and Worms. And when he had fairly exhausted these means, he was still able to make the Jews, even those he no longer possessed, a source of royal revenue. With shrewd romanticism he revived the old tax which Titus laid on Israel in place of the tithe paid to the vanished Temple. In 1342 he introduced the *Gülden Opfer-pfennig*—the "golden penny offering"—an annual poll-tax of one gulden payable by every Jew and Jewess, above the age of twelve, whose property was worth twenty gulden or over.

Charles IV, who succeeded Ludwig, managed if anything to surpass him. He was probably encouraged to give away his Jews on the best possible terms since the property was sadly depreciated by the Armleder uprising (1336-1338) in the previous reign and the Black Death massacres (1348-1349) in his own. The Golden Bull (1356) brought his efforts to a climax. This decree—which one historian calls "written testimony to the fact that the Empire ceased to exist except in name"—bestowed upon the principalities of the Reich the imperial rights, lumped together, in mines, salt, tolls, and Jews. The "servants of the treasury" became, like the Empire, a nominal title.

The results of the *Knechtschaft*, while it flourished and after, were not, however, nominal. The ghost of imperial servitude returned in the shape of *Schutz-briefe*, letters of protection issued by emperor, king, or princelet to favored and paying *Schutz-Juden*, protected Jews, who stalk through German history till well into the nineteenth century. The *Gülden Opferpfennig* strengthened the use of the head-tax—trace of which goes back to 1226—and the equally odious body-tax, a toll placed alike on cattle and Jews and lingering in some parts of Germany, Saxony for example, until long after both cattle and Jews are riding on railroad trains. The authority granted the local powers "to have and to hold" their Jews likewise played a part in the development of the compulsory ghetto as a means of enforcing this authority.

The encouragement which the whole system gave to looking upon the Jew as a mere commodity aided the Church in her program of demeaning the race and helped instill an abiding contempt for it among the people. However, in this respect, it must be remembered that most German subjects were similarly treated—Americans will not forget that Hessians were once sold like beasts to an English king. The flavor of the word *Untertan*—"subject"—has carried over to modern times a sense of abasement and self-hate peculiar to the German people. And no one is readier to despise another than the man who secretly despises himself.

Graver still, the Jews, in the course of pawn, cession, and sale, fell from one frying-pan into a hundred fires. They were placed at the mercy of the whims and vacillating policies of innumerable petty and conflicting masters. But, on the other hand, the number and disunity of these masters spared them the mass-expulsions which overtook the Jews of England (1291), France (1394), and Spain (1492). Whenever, in the tide of German fortune, they were driven from any single barony, free city, or mark, they usually found refuge in another. Or, whenever they left a state because of intolerable conditions, they were usually invited back. During the wildest times of the Interregnum, the federation of Rhine cities, for example, took energetic steps to safeguard its Jews. When Nuremberg expelled the race, Fürth, five miles away, opened its gates.

Taking it all in all, Germany could live neither with its Jews nor without them.

7

THE LIVING WITNESSES

THE course of medieval business and the tactics of the
state were not alone in shaping Jewish fortune. There
remained the Church. And much like commerce and state-
craft, its policies culminated in the thirteenth century.

But in writing of the Church we must, as the scholastics
would say, "distinguish." Throughout its career there have
been three churches. First the temporal Church, the work of
human frailty and busied with the fleeting goods of the
world. Every medieval cathedral, faithful mirror of the Christian mind, reveals this church in its ranks of sculptured kings,
or better yet in the homely thrusts at priests and monks
carved beneath the *misericordia*. Then there is the dogmatic
Church, reared on no less human doctrine concerning the
purposes of God and the well-being of society. For the Jew—
who is our concern—this Church has provided a niche by the
cathedral door, where the Synagogue Defeated stands as a
stone symbol and rebuke. Finally there is the Church Invisible, true edifice of Christ, its plan unknown save to the
divine Architect, its builders unrecognized of one another,
its site the New Jerusalem, its spires glimpsed by the eye of
the mystic on rare occasion and from afar—the spires which

point the goal and home of humanity. Glowing from the heights of nave and choir, the windows of its earthly counterpart shadow but a poor ray of its glory; perhaps because of the very crimson, purple, and gold, it is seen through stained glass darkly.

The church that history knows best, the church of power and doctrine, was, with respect to the Jews, in a quandary. Heathen and upstarts like the Moslems made no problem. They were to be converted or, if dangerous, killed. Heretics were to recant, or likewise feel the edge of the secular sword. But the Jews were neither heathen nor heretics; and, most perplexing of all, they were not upstarts.

They had, by divine authority, an abiding part in the Christian scheme. It was a fortunate day for Israel when Isaiah was inspired to write, "You are My witnesses, saith the Lord, that I am He, that before Me there was no God, neither shall any be after Me . . . the things that are coming to pass, have I not announced to you of old, and declared it? Therefore you are My witnesses" (Isa. 43.10; 44.7-8). For the Church, the things declared and come to pass were naturally the mission of Jesus, his passion, the Jewish guilt in it, and the triumph of Christianity. Of all this the Jews were the eternal testimony. "They are living symbols for us, representing the Lord's Passion," said St. Bernard; "for this they are dispersed in every land, so that, while they pay the just penalty of their great crime, they may be witnesses for our redemption."

There were other cogent reasons for preserving them. Paul bore record to their zeal, mistaken though it was, for God (Rom. 11.2). They were the guardians of the Scriptures, and to them pertain the covenants, the giving of the Law, the service of God, and the promises (Rom. 3.2; 9.4). A remnant of "all Israel" was ultimately to be saved (Rom. 9.6, 27; 11.1-5, 26). And with a fine sense of historical justice—a veritable gleam from the Church Invisible—Paul understood and declared the tragedy of the Jews. "As concerning the Gospel, they are enemies *for your sakes* . . . through their fall salvation is come to the Gentiles." But as "touching the election" to that unseen Church itself, "they are beloved for the fathers' sakes" (Rom. 4.28; 11.11). However, Innocent III reiterated the salient point when, in a bull (1199) confirming the traditional attitude of the Holy Chair toward the Jews, he wrote, "They are the living witnesses of the true faith."

Yet what witnesses! It was not enough that they disputed the efficacy of the sacraments, such as baptism, or the validity of the mysteries, such as the Trinity; but what they were above all supposed to confirm—that Jesus was the Messiah—they ceaselessly denied. By their example if not by their efforts, they were a standing encouragement to backsliding and heresy. "As long as there remained a member of the Old Faith who denied the New," writes Darmesteter in an unforgettable passage, "the Church felt ill at ease in its heritage. More than one Christian, entering a sordid ghetto house to raise a loan or have his horoscope read, left for home a troubled soul and fit for burning. The Jew was skilled at laying bare the weak spots of the Church. For this purpose he had not only a profound knowledge of the Scriptures, but a wit sharpened by oppression. He was the master of incredulity, the mentor of rebellion. He was to be found at work in the blasphemy plants of an Emperor Frederick or the princes of Swabia and Aragon. It was he who forged the weapons of reason and irony which the skeptics of the Renaissance and the Free-thinkers of the seventeenth century were to wield with deadly effect. A sarcasm of Voltaire is nothing but the last echo of a quip whispered six centuries before in the dark alleys of the ghetto."

Accordingly, the "living witnesses" were in the same breath the "enemies of the faith." Paul had once described Christ crucified as a "scandal" to the Jews (I Cor. 1.23). Now the word came home to roost, and it was the Jews who had become a scandal to the Church.

The obvious remedy was to convert the Jews, even if it meant the disappearance of the historic witnesses. Moreover, there would be other recompenses. Souls would be saved, for as matters stood the Jews were damned by misunderstanding their own Scriptures. Then, too, by a neat *a fortiori* argument, it was evident that if the downfall of the Jews had brought salvation to the Gentiles, their return to grace would bring still greater benefits. "Now if the fall of them be the riches of the world, and the diminishing of them the riches of the Gentiles, how much more their fulness? . . . if the casting away of them be the reconciling of the world, what shall the receiving of them be, but life from the dead?" (Rom. 11.12, 15). And lastly, every Jew led to the font hastened the day when their total conversion would signal the second coming of Jesus and the redemption of humanity.

But just as the testimony of the Jews was vitiated by their contrariness, so their conversion was balked by an hereditary stiff-neck. Luther summed up the centuries of proselyting endeavor, including his own, with the verdict, "It is as easy to convert the Jews as the devil himself."

The very process gaped with pitfalls. There always lurked the chance that the Christian who tried to win the soul of a Jew might lose his own. Berthold of Regensburg was only repeating the tenor of papal instructions when he told the German laity, "You are as ignorant with respect to the Bible as the Jews are learned, and they can always throw up to you that your own faith is weaker than theirs," and when, in conclusion, he warned against "the treacherous babble of the stinking Jews."

On the practical side, the contradictions were painful. The Church lost heavily from the tithes which were neither due nor paid by Jewish money-lenders who held Christian collateral; and it was not backward in complaint. Princes, wrote Innocent III, "allow the Jews to take Christian castles and villages in pawn, and the worst of it is that the Church loses the tithes . . . while Christians are banned for favoring the Jews, the latter are laughing up their sleeves because, on their account, the harps of the Church are hung on willows and the priests deprived of their revenues." Yet little was to be gained by converting the money-lenders, because the Jew who entered the Christian fold left his property behind him— the Jewish community and the Christian debtors and princes saw to that. And the Church not only failed to recover its revenues, but it was put to the expense of supporting the converts. The thirteenth-century popes were willing to overlook the expense, but not so the bishops on whom it fell.

When a conversion was finally effected, it still remained to be seen how long it would last. The medieval German writers who dwelt on the subject seemed pessimistic. They agreed with Conrad of Megenburg, who in the blunt speech of his day remarked that the faith of a converted Jew is like the droppings of a sparrow—hot when it falls, but cold by the time it hits the ground. Everhard, a convert himself in thirteenth-century Cologne, likewise agreed. After spending most of his life as a canon, he refused to take the sacraments on his death-bed. Instead, he ordered brought to him a cat, mouse, dog, and hare. "Look," he said, "at these four animals which have never seen one another before—the cat chases the mouse and the dog chases the hare—as well expect them not to follow their instincts as expect a Jew to turn Christian."

Altogether, the Church pursued conversion as obstinately and unremittingly as the Jew refused it. Consequently we can learn what happens when an irresistible force meets an immovable object. Nothing happens.

Other measures were therefore in order. They one and all sprang from, or rather see-sawed between, the two horns of the Christian dilemma. Because the Jews were God-ordained witnesses, they must be protected. But because they were enemies of the faith and condemned by the Judgment of God to "eternal servitude," they must be segregated and degraded.

By way of protection, the Church recognized the right of the Jews to keep to the Old Faith. Gregory I (560-604) established this right when he ruled that "just as Jews should be forbidden to do anything in their synagogues contrary to law, so no injury should befall them for doing what the law permits." Gregory IX took the Fifth Crusade—just four crusades too late—as an occasion for condemning the exuberant zeal of the warriors of the Cross (1236). "Their excesses," he wrote Louis IX of France, "are horrible and outrageous, an offence against God and a dishonor to the Holy Chair, through whose privileges the Jews are protected." At the outset of the Interregnum, Innocent IV enjoined the German bishops to tolerate no persecution of the Jews (1247). The papal claim to protect the Jews rested on impressive authority. Backed by the Scriptures—"the elder shall serve the younger," said Paul

(Rom. 9.12)—and fortified by the scholastic doctors, especially Thomas of Aquino, the Church asserted, in the teeth of the Reich, that Jewry was *its* servant. And both on this general principle and through the accidents of politics, German bishops frequently exercised, as we have seen, government over the Jews in episcopal city-states. Cologne was an old and striking case, where for generations Jews enjoyed the shelter of the Church.

That despite papal edicts and episcopal assurances the Jews seldom escaped the violence of the masses need provoke no wonder. The Church was caught in its own contradictions. What it proffered with one hand it was compelled to take back with the other. Fair words of tolerance and security were, in the nature of its dilemma, matched by foul pleas for ostracizing and abasing Israel. The ordinary Christian was asked to protect a people whom at the same time he was taught to subject and despise.

The same Innocent III who cherished the Jews as living witnesses proclaimed their eternal slavery. "It is pleasing to God," he wrote, "that they should be oppressed by the servitude they earned when they raised sacrilegious hands against Him who had come to confer true liberty upon them." He was unsparing in accusations calculated to arouse hatred against the race:— they mocked the faithful for believing in a crucified peasant, they provocatively dressed in finery and paraded the streets during Holy Week, they were given to the secret murder of Christians, they abetted thieves, robbed, and kidnaped, and they built their synagogues higher than churches.

The same Gregory IX who reproved the bloody methods of the crusaders drew up a bill-of-complaint against the Jews of Germany (1233) which was not likely to keep crusading swords in their sheaths. The Jews, he charged, arrogated to themselves public office contrary to law, seduced the faithful from the Church, circumcised Christian slaves, employed Christian servants and nurses, and forced the latter to spill their milk in the latrines for the three days following Good Friday.

In this spirit the ecclesiastical councils went to work. Their venom was understandable, for the nerves of the Church were jangled by the Waldensian and Albigensian heresies, by the continued victories of the Saracens, and by the endless quarrels with the German throne. In its most triumphant century the Church was fighting for its unity and its life. The degradation of the Jews, like the suppression of heresy and the war against the Moslems, was part of a common campaign of self-defense. When it talked of protection the Church, with sound judgment, meant protection for itself.

The Fourth Lateran Council (1215)—of which Innocent was the guiding light—sanctioned the crusade against the Albigenses, launched the Franciscans and Dominicans on their mission of preaching and burning, and confirmed the old strictures against the Jews. It even added new ones. Christian property when it passed into Jewish ownership was subjected to the tithe. Exorbitant interest rates, whatever that meant, were forbidden. Ground was broken for the Inquisition by proposing "salutary compulsion" to discourage converts from relapsing into Judaism. And Judaism itself was made as despicable as papal ingenuity could contrive by compelling the members of the Old Faith to brand themselves with the Badge of Shame.

Succeeding synods—particularly Trèves (1227) and Mayence (1233 and 1259)—put the finishing touches to the work of the Lateran Council. Significantly, many of their measures harked back to the sixth and seventh centuries when the Church was fighting to make Europe Catholic, as now it was fighting to keep it so. Little remained to be done, as far as the Jews were concerned, after the Synod of Breslau (1267) ordained the compulsory ghetto.

In the field of religion, a *cordon sanitaire* was thrown around Jewry to prevent any infection of Christian souls. The common man was forbidden, under pain of excommunication, to discuss matters of faith with a Jew. If he took the risk and yielded to the persuasion of his opponent, he was branded a heretic—though Judaism itself was obviously no heresy—and found himself in line for the dungeon, rack, and fagot. On their side Jews were forbidden to indulge in blasphemy—a blanket curb, under which it was possible to prosecute as one pleased, for a Jew by his mere existence implied a blasphemous interpretation of the divinity of Jesus. In keeping with this ban, Jewish books, above all the Talmud, fell to the censorship and bon-fires of the Dominicans. A Jew, moreover, was forbidden to show his face at door or window during Holy Week. And, unless unavoidable, he was not to cross the threshold of a church. Only with great difficulty could he secure permission to build a synagogue. Permission granted, it had to be a small, unattractive structure. And once built, it was highly liable to confiscation. In Germany alone, there survive some dozen medieval churches and chapels which were originally synagogues, or were erected on their site.

The daily existence of the Jew, as the Church regulated it, proved the contention that he had been rejected by God. His livelihood was undermined by the repeated remission of interest, which destroyed any sense of economic obligation to him. Before the bar of justice he was made to feel his inferiority as a witness and a man of honor, by being compelled to take a blood-curdling oath while standing barefoot on the hide of a swine—a procedure which lingered in the statutes of Germany until 1877. The door to political office, which began to open for court-Jews, was slammed tight.

Social relations between the sects were reduced to an incredible minimum. Christians were forbidden to buy food or drink from Jews—especially meat and wine, which had, of course, been prepared in accordance with Jewish ritual, and milk, which was presumably poisoned. They were forbidden, for the same reason, to use Jewish physicians or medicines. They must not eat or drink with Jews, attend Jewish weddings, dances, or other festivities, and naturally they dare not set foot in a synagogue. On the other hand, Jews were forbidden to use Christian inns or baths, and hire Christian servants or nurses. They were ordered to behave in public and private with the humility and shamefacedness proper to a servile, guilty, and God-stricken people. Illicit sexual intercourse between Jew and Gentile incurred penalties running from fines to whipping, burial alive, or death by fire. Licit unions, by ordinance common to both sects, did not exist. Fortunately for the good name of mankind, few of these decrees went further than the paper they were written on. But their moral effect—the eeriness which everything Jewish assumed in the Christian mind—ladened the air of Germany.

Two decrees, and the most blighting, did not however fail of application. The sign which the Lateran Council prescribed to distinguish the Jews as moral lepers suffering from noxious and contagious beliefs received general enforcement by the fourteenth century in Germany, where it usually took the form of a yellow-fabric ring stitched on the sleeve or breast. In addition, a high-peaked hat, the *Judenhut*, probably first adopted by the Jews out of choice, was made obligatory, in case, no doubt, the ring escaped notice. Still unsatisfied, the authorities often ordered the use of a long cloak, sometimes specifying the color and the inches. Yet despite these precautions, the Jews apparently looked too much like Germans to suit the popular taste. So, in a number of cities, the cloaks were not only ordered lengthened, but the beards shortened. For the women there were blue stripes on the veil or headgear, bells on the skirts, and, on occasion, their finger-rings numbered and weighed. Medieval life, to be sure, ran riot with distinctive and obligatory costumes; but for the Christians they meant badges of honor—uniforms of rank, calling, or craft. For the Jew, these bizarre regulations shut every man and woman in, as it were, a personal walking ghetto. Clothes made the man, and of the Jew, a marked man, ringed or striped like a convict.

The communal ghetto completed his humiliation. A wealth of apology has been wasted on this institution by modern romantics. It is true, the ancient and early-medieval Jew elected to live, like other distinct racial and economic classes, in a quarter of his own. The *souks* of the Orient, the collegia of the Roman world, and the medieval guild system made such congregation natural and profitable. And the social requirement of Judaism—the daily use of the synagogue, the need for a special bakery, slaughter-house, bath, court of justice, and cemetery—rendered it almost inevitable. From the earliest period the Jews of Germany appear to have lived together, either near the town-hall (Cologne), the cathedral (Frank-fort), or one of the main city-gates (Worms). It is likewise true that the segregated Jewry with its gates and police and massed population served as a protective device, a defense against the outer enemy and a preservative of the inner life.

But neither romance nor utility can obliterate the differ-ence between a Jewry and a ghetto—a home and a prison. Not gates nor overcrowding defined the ghetto; the Jews could be thankful for the one, and all medievals seemed to enjoy the other. It was the compulsion which stung, and which turned the Jewry lane into what the Church meant it to be, a habitation of cruelty, whose doors closed on houses of darkness.

The first compulsory ghetto was decreed, as we have said, by the Synod of Breslau, "to prevent the Christians from fall-ing under the influence of Judaism" and because Silesia was "a new Christian land." In the fourteenth century the move-ment to coop up the Jews spread throughout the Reich. Where the race dwelt in a desirable section of a city—as their early settlement and commercial needs made it likely—they were often driven to remote or unclean quarters, as in Breslau, Leipzig, Nuremberg, and Frankfort. Pius II expressed his astonishment that the Jews of the latter city were allowed to keep their ghetto "close to the chief church" where "they can even hear the chanting of the Holy Mass"; and he warmly praised the burghers for moving them beyond the town-walls (1462). Frequently the burghers, it must be noted, joined to these pious motives a prudent desire to place the Jews where in case of siege they would receive the brunt of the attack, and a less pardonable desire to wall in the peaked-hatted, long-cloaked, yellow-ringed people so that when the time came for a little local pillage and cancellation of debts, the victims could not flee.

The fruit of its labors was probably bitterer than the Church anticipated. What the higher clergy and the learned theologians proposed as wise prophylactic and pious obedience to the manifest intentions of the Almighty became, in the hands of the ordinary cleric and layman, a ready implement of superstition and greed.

If Innocent III could accuse the Jews of secretly killing Christians, it was only a step in advance for the masses to convince themselves that the crime served the dark purposes of Jewish ritual, and that any local murder-mystery might be reasonably solved by tracing it to the "enemies" of Jesus. Christian preoccupation with the blood of the Savior, which in the fervor of medieval faith rose to an obsession, likewise played a sinister part. Belief that the Jews drank of Christian veins was a distorted image of the most sacred rite of the Church—a distortion akin to the perverse imaginings of the Black Mass.

In any case, once the Lateran Council set in motion its Europe-wide campaign against the Jews, blood-accusations became epidemic. However, in due justice to human nature it must be added that more than fanaticism was at work. Innocent IV put his finger on the spot when, in his solemn denial of the charge, he observed that it was brought against the Jews of Germany "in order to plunder their wealth."

The same overheated imagination was responsible for another devastating accusation—that the Jews made a practice of stealing a wafer of the Host, which they thereupon pierced, burned, or otherwise defiled. The charge first appeared after Innocent III recognized the doctrine of transubstantiation and so encouraged the public and general worship of the Host. As in the case of ritual murder, it was based on the supposition that Jews, like Christians, identified the wine and bread of communion with the presence of God—the wine His blood and the bread His body. Hence, by inversion, the Jew would use Christian blood for wine and Christ's bread for mockery.

Although known to France and Spain, the charge grew to be a German specialty. Over thirty cases have remained in the records covering the thirteenth-fifteenth centuries, with the usual massacres and burnings as the penalty. The victims sometimes numbered in the hundreds, and even thousands. Nor was the zeal for profit absent. Reacting against its mistreatment by the Jews, the sacred wafer usually managed to bleed—again the obsession with blood—miraculously. After being cleansed of the culprits by fire and sword, the scene of the miracle—in general a synagogue—was promptly dedicated as a chapel, where cures and pilgrimages, enlivened by mystery-plays rehearsing the crime, brought in sizable revenues. The Salvator church in Passau, to take a well-known example, is built on the site of a synagogue and commemorates the desecration of a Host in 1477; it was long a profitable shrine, and across the river the Ilzstadt church preserves for the modern sightseer a series of stained-glass windows depicting the event and the execution of the ten recreants. In Deggendorf, farther up the Danube, one may still visit the Church of the Holy Sepulcher, erected in gratitude for a miraculous deliverance of the Host (1337). The citizens could well be grateful, for Duke Heinrich of Landshut, their overlord, not only praised them for "burning and exterminating our Jews of Deggendorf," but canceled the bonds and debts and released the pawns in the possession of the burned creditors.

Compared with these enormities, the other charges habitually laid against the Jews sink into misdemeanors. Yet the presumed stoning and mocking of the crucifix, disturbance of holy-day processions, practice of black magic, and the imputed blasphemies and sarcasms of the Talmud—charges directly or indirectly traceable to the papal assurance that the Jews were the sworn foes of Christendom and to the obloquy heaped on their heads—cost them torture, death, and an ever-mounting hatred. The proficiency of the Jews in magic and their kinship with Satan would reveal, if we had the stomach to pursue the subject, the ultimate spring of medieval Jew-hatred. It may suggest enough to say that Satan, whether clothed in theological finery as the Spirit of Evil or stripped to his horns and hoofs as the Devil himself, fairly carried the day against God; and in popular German speech *Judenblick* meant the Evil Eye; *Judenpech,* bitumen or the fuel of hell-fire; and *Jüdel*, the name of a familiar demon; while the Jew in person served for any devilish purpose, from instigating heresy to putting children into a wholesome fright.

The sign and symbol of the whole sorry tale we have seen in the image of the Synagogue Defeated, her brow sunk in dejection before the cathedral door. But the genius of Germany invented a further symbol. In Wittenberg, in Magdeburg, Regensburg, Kehlheim, Friesing, Heilbronn, Wimpfen, Heiligenstadt, Basel, and other Germanic towns is carved on choir-stall, pillar, or eaves—and may there be found to this day—a sow giving suck to piglets and Jews. This is the *Judensau,* the Jew-Pig, repeated in block-prints, broadsides, and leaflets recounting ritual-murders and other edifying religious themes. In Wittenberg, a rabbi stands behind the sow, holds up its tail, and, as Luther describes him, "looks into— the Talmud." To this shame, exposed in Christian houses of worship, had come the living witnesses of the Lord.

Meanwhile, one may ask, where was to be found, not the churches of *Judensauen* and stained-glass calumnies, but the true temple of Jesus? Apparently it stayed as it was named, the church invisible.

8

BEHIND THE GATES

THE survival of the Jew is often considered a riddle, if not a miracle. Yet it is likely neither one nor the other. Whenever the forces of society—church, state, and business—have wholeheartedly combined to exterminate an unpopular people, they have generally succeeded. Such was the fate of the Albigenses, Pastoureaux, Jacques, Lollards, Templars, and Moriscos. Such, of Jewish lineage, was the fate of the Marranos.

But the Jews, as we have noted, never suffered this combined whole-hearted attack. Their antagonists always balked at taking the last fatal measure of destruction: the church on theological grounds, the state out of concern for taxes, and the bread-and-butter world because it needed Jewish butter for its bread. Moreover, when matters reached a critical point and destruction seemed inevitable, the forces arrayed against the Jews showed no hesitation in balking one another. With respect to Israel as a whole, and not the fate of the individual, the worst to befall them was mass-expulsion—which German Jewry even managed to escape.

A curious spectacle results. The Church is seen burning Christians for secretly embracing the mere shadow of disbeliefs which the Jew preached openly and unmolested in his synagogue. The state raises armies to crush unbelievers at home and abroad, while it shields the Christ-denying servants of its treasury. And in the midst of its storm against usury, society assiduously patronizes the money-lenders of the ghetto.

However, there is more to Jewish survival than the reluctance or cross-purposes of the enemy. The medieval Jew had a home in the universe. His faith was not merely an interpretation but, as he saw it, a part and parcel of reality. He shared in, as well as understood, the divine scheme. However battered by tempests he had no doubt that his place in it was secure.

The fence he had staked about his home—the Talmud—was not meant, like monastery walls, to be a rampart against life. Indeed, it had been raised to ward off the enemies of life. Historically the talmudic discipline had been a defense against Rome—we need only remember Johanan ben Zak-kai and the school of Jabneh. And now it rendered a similar service against the heirs of Rome: the Holy Roman Empire and the Roman Catholic Church. Within the shade of the thorny hedge planted at Jabneh and re-planted along the Rhine, the Jew cultivated his garden.

But his security had a broader base. He not only had a home in the universe, but he lived in the same universe as his medieval neighbors, whether friends or foes. Their houses all stood up the same street. Church, mosque, and synagogue prayed to ostensibly the same God, preached more or less the same morals, feared the same evils, and hoped for the same heaven. Paradise, the Garden of Allah, and *Gan 'Eden* were geographically one. Conversion, repentance, *teshubah,* the road to the garden, traveled the same route. The very things

the medievals fought about—the nature of God and the way
to salvation—they largely held in common. The bitterness
of the battle testified that though their language differed,
they agreed in their knowledge, or presumed knowledge, of
what they were fighting about—a world and goal as real and
familiar to one combatant as another. No one on that street
ever spoiled its violent blood-stained harmony by asserting
there was no God, there was no salvation, by suggesting they
were pursuing figments, and cracking skulls for the sake of
shadows. So firm were their common religious convictions
that no one—except in Heine's imagination—dreamed of dis-
arming priest and rabbi, or rabbi and imam, with the summary judgment: *sie alle beide stinken.*

And, finally, in that medieval street—with God at one end
and the Devil at the other—the Jew, by an unwelcome but
general consent, was recognized to be the oldest inhabitant.
The synagogue might be a drab cell compared to the cathedral of Cologne, the Jew might be insignificant in numbers
and his house sequestered and spat upon, but he enjoyed all
the pride, the inner dignity and strength, of a first settler.

The stiff-neck of the Jew—a stumbling-block to the German moralists and missionaries—was partly the stubbornness
of an oak aware of its gnarled centuries. The refusal of the
Jew to commit an act which, though innocent in itself, might
injure the good repute of Israel and thereby cast a reflection
on God—"profane," as he said, "the Holy Name"—a naive
and sublime impudence—was the last word in *noblesse oblige.*
"Jews," reads the *Book of the Pious,* "shall not indulge in
pleasures from which Christians hold aloof—if a Jew sees a
Christian about to do wrong, he shall make every effort to dis-
suade him—else the Name of God be profaned." These are

the maxims of aristocrats. When we remember that the men who preached them had every incentive to lose themselves in hatred and malice—to rejoice in pleasures denied their enemies or triumph in a Christian's fall from grace—we may well call them the aristocrats of God. Their refusal, to be sure, had a practical bearing. When the incautious act of an individual Jew might literally plunge his family and the community in blood, the "profanation of the Name" was more than a theological delicacy. But for all that, the sense of communal responsibility—certainly the strength and tone of it—issued in part from a well of ancestral pride, from the consciousness of a tradition which, as the Jews believed, harked back to the dawn of the world. A first family keeps more than wine in its cellar to fortify its long thin line.

The medieval Jew, it is true, constantly bewailed his "exile" —but so did the Christian, who liked to repeat he "was not of this world." The point, in fact, is worth pressing. Theoretically—or spiritually—a good Christian was bound to feel in perpetual exile from heaven. Actually he possessed and enjoyed the earth. For the Jew it was the other way round. Actually and physically he possessed only his ghetto lane, and that on a precarious lease. Practically he was stripped of almost every vestige of temporal independence and power. He was literally in exile from a land he could call his own. But the exile weighed so little on him that throughout the Middle Ages when populations shifted enormously—and never more so than in Germany with its *Drang nach Osten,* its Frisian and Flemish migrations—and later when discovery opened the continents of Africa and America, the Jew made no concerted effort to stake out a claim for himself. The reasons, of course, are many. But not least among them was the fact that spiritually the Jew was reconciled to the world, and, more than that, congenial to his medieval environment. The modern Jew who is impatient with the submission and apparent torpor of the ghetto is reading his own homelessness—a totally different thing—into the past.

This fundamental harmony between the medieval Jew and his world reveals itself at almost every turn. In Spain the Moslems cultivated science, medicine, philosophy, and poetry; and the Spanish Jews became mathematicians, doctors, Aristotelians, and poets—not in Gentile terms, but in their own. When the Spanish Christians followed the tracks of the Moors—except in philosophy—the Jews accompanied and indeed often led them. And when the Spaniards substituted mysticism for philosophy, so did the Jews. Ramon Lulle and Juan de la Cruz had by their side Abraham Abulafia, Moses de Leon—and the *Zohar*.

A similar correspondence reigned in Germany. The medieval Germans, at least until the fourteenth century, were weak in philosophy—the Jews altogether untouched by it. In Spain it was a Jewish refugee from Germany, Asher ben Yehiel, who shared in the fight against Maimonides and Aristotle. In Germany itself, the Jews were not even concerned enough to create a philosophic school which they could fight. Judah, the son of Asher, who fled to Spain with his father, reflects the attitude of German Jewry when he wrote, "As to secular sciences, blessed be the Merciful who saved me from them." The attitude persisted as late as the seventeenth century when Isaiah Halevi Hurwitz warns us, "Philosophy has long been banned by our teachers, old and new, and we should keep aloof from it, as well as from the secular sciences." Asher himself probably absorbed this repugnance from his master, Meir of Rothenburg, who entertained the notion that birds grew from trees—a bit of natural science which can be matched by many thinkers of northern Europe, even the redoubtable Albertus Magnus. As a matter of more than coincidence, both the Christians and Jews of Germany lagged far behind Spain and Italy in the most practical and urgent of the sciences—medicine.

When the foundations of German science were laid in the fourteenth century, German Jewry was pulverized and impoverished by the massacres and expulsions attendant on the Black Death. For the German Jews the first break from their traditional scorn of secular learning came precisely where it might be expected: at prosperous Prague in the reign of Rudolph II, a mad monarch not the least of whose madness—considering the record of German royalty—was a love for science. Rabbi Judah Löw (d. 1609), who frequented the court of Rudolph and who is usually remembered for the childish legend of the *Golem*, dared evoke the name of Maimonides and declare that secular science "is the wisdom of all men." "It too," he makes bold to add, "springs from God and differs from the Torah only in its subject matter." At Löw's side, in the court of Rudolph, was Tycho Brahe; and Löw exhorts the Jewish world "to study, above all, astronomy, for through it we can learn the greatness and power of the Lord." David Gans—Löw's friend—not only studied and published works on astronomy; he wrote a compendium of Jewish history and, bolder yet, added to it a compendium of world history. The *Book of the Pious* was confirming events when it said, "As the Christians behave, so do the Jews."

Offsetting their indifference to philosophy, the medieval Germans produced a distinguished and prolix crop of moralists. And nothing they wrote was more distinguished, exhaustive, and exhausting than the books of manners and morals—*Moralbücher*—penned by their fellows in the ghetto. Chapter and verse the parallel has been drawn between Eliezer ben Isaac of Worms—whom we met in a previous chapter—and his fellow-Rhinelander, Winsbeke. At times there is only the difference of a name between Judah and Berthold of Regensburg. The life of Judah (d. 1216) is clouded with legend; and his great work, the *Book of the Pious*, which helped, together with legend, to win him the title of Saint (*Hasid*), is more than the product of his own pen. Not merely that his father and other scholars had a hand in it, but it enjoyed the collaboration of an age. Its contents were drawn from the folk-mind and moral aspirations of generations of Jews; and it set a literary fashion which prevailed in the Jewish centers of Germany and Eastern Europe until the last century. The *Little Book of the Pious* by Moses Cohen ben Eleazar (1473), the anonymous *Sittenbuch* (1542), and Isaiah Hurwitz' *Two Tables of the Covenant* (ca. 1625), together with a host of their kind, added in each generation to the popular stock—much as the early stream of German moralism was replenished by a Sebastian Brant, Thomas Murner, and others as forgotten as their Jewish fellows and whose similarities to their roundly-despised rabbinical contemporaries the modern reader will gladly take on trust.

The German moralists, in their aversion to formal thinking, drew their sustenance from mysticism. In the *Gottesminne*, the troubadours of God mounted the medieval empyrean; and the mystics of the ghetto kept wing with the flight of a Winsbeke or Master Eckhart. Judah the Saint, Eleazar ben Judah of Worms, and his pupils Menahem (author of *Crown of the Name*) and Abraham of Cologne (who carried the Jewish *Gottesminne* to Alfonso X of Spain) founded a discipline which gave German Jewry a predominant reputation for mysticism as well as piety. To them, as to their Christian contemporaries, piety and mysticism were one. Subordinating theory to practice, they emphasized the moral rather than the philosophical aspects of saintliness and divine communion. Despite their angelology and visions, right praying and right doing meant more to them than the attributes of the *Sefirot* or the mechanics of the invisible world. Perhaps the profoundest word in the conduct of life came from the mysticism of the German ghetto. "Who is a saint? He who acts kindly with his Maker."

A cold reception seems mainly responsible for keeping the Jews from the lists of the Minnesingers, who represented another great current in German cultural life. Süsskind of Trimberg made a trial flight in the thirteenth century, and turned back, as he said, "to the old Jewish ways" after discovering "I have gone on a fool's journey with my art, for the great lords spurn my song." In the next century, one Samson Pine, a Jew, aided Claus Wysse and Philip Kolin translate a French version of Parsifal. But the social cleft between the races was too great to be bridged by poets. Jews with an itch for writing secular literature—not a few in number and with tastes altogether akin to the Germans—either chose baptism, like Johannes Pauli (fl. 1500), or imported, as we shall see, a freight of medieval romance into their own vernacular.

But the parallels go further than book making or the rarities of saintliness. The Christians had their *Ordo Vagorum*, wandering scholars, hundreds of them, who tramped (and studied) from school to school. So did the Jews. For every

Bachante sleeping on straw and copying the words of a *Meister* in the cold of the morning, there was a *Bahur* at the feet of his *Rab*; and often enough rabbi and disciple were compelled to flee along the roads in search of a new asylum of learning. Coming closer to the life of the masses—the flirting with magic and devils, the homely wisdom of housewife and husbandman as well as in the fancies of the learned —we find the superstition of the Jew going hand in hand with the German. Fables, folk-medicine, amulets and incantations, symbols and omens had no respect for church bans or ghetto regulations. There, at the lowest rung, in the things people lived by, not under the cloak of eternity, but from hour to hour, the Jew was at one with his world.

There is no need to talk of influence, borrowing, or plagiary. Jewish *Geist* moved with the *Zeitgeist*. Common views and common visions were plucked from the common air. The ghetto walls were porous. On double-hinges its gates swung both ways.

In fact, the Jew was so much at home he was able to remain himself. He maintained and even deepened the differences which marked him off from his neighbors. His own compelling will to be himself as well as the chains and walls which prevented him from becoming anything else had their share in the preservation of his peculiar life. But he was aided— as the modern world could never aid him—by the character of the Middle Ages which, apart from such realms as God and Heaven, singularly favored diversity. This is not to be credited to a love of tolerance and freedom: the dominant Christian mind understood little of either. It was, rather, the product of physical isolation and a system of rigid privileges.

The world was much vaster than it is now. Cities lay days

apart, and the next parish was likely a foreign land. Men lived unchanging parochial lives, fixed and guarded by immemorial privileges. However hard they were to win and, certainly for the Jew, however few in number, they were profoundly respected by public opinion. Every group in a population not only dared be, but was supposed to be, itself. When the traveler of today stumbles on a group of this stubborn metal surviving in the hinterland of Germany or Italy, with their age-old houses, dress, customs, and dialect, he calls them quaint. But in the Middle Ages all the world was quaint.

In the welter of local manners and privileges the Jew could keep his diet, habits, costume, learning, speech, and even his soul, without running contrary to the trend of the times. Every other people, each in its own fashion, was doing as much. For the Jew it meant unquestionably an unrelenting battle; but he was not alone in the fight. To cling to his privileges, to fight for his tradition—whether it was the cut of his ear-locks or the number of persons in his God—did not, at least, stamp him as an eccentric.

Nowhere was the world more diverse than in Germany. Like every other medieval land, it had its innumerable and sharply divided social, economic, political, and religious strata. In addition, as we have noted in another connection, it was split up and down into literally scores of petty states; their government was complicated by the rivalries of church and secular power; and the whole lacked the cement of any effective central authority. Not till 1870 did Germany have so much as a central capital; and even today the German world does not altogether revolve about Berlin.

It is therefore not surprising that traditional Judaism flourished so hardily in the German ghettos, undistracted by science, arts, and secular opportunity; that its piety grew to be a by-word, and that its discipline, when carried to Slavic lands, became the backbone of European Jewry. Though it drew its food from a common German soil, the seeds were of another and older clime; and the plant bred true to its seed.

Inside the ghetto gates the Jew surrounded himself with the institutions his fathers had created time out of mind— institutions which both expressed and reinforced the pervasive discipline, which slowly changed in response to his needs, regardless of the world's calendar, and which gave to Israel its hall-mark among the nations.

The synagogue stood in the center of the stage, as it had ever since the Temple disappeared; but it did not stand still. Hardly a generation passed without swelling its store of canticles, laments, and prayers, many of them chanting the death or deliverance which alternately befell the community. There grew up, as well, a cult of the prayer book, which fondled its every phrase, counted every word, played cabalistic games with the letters, and left a library of some seventy-three volumes of commentaries. The rabbinate, too, as we shall learn, underwent profound changes after the demoralization following the Black Death.

Associated with the synagogue were the schools: primary class-rooms, colleges, and for the adults a reading- and study-hall. In touching on Gershom of Mayence we have already seen that schooling was the distinctive and controlling feature of Jewish life. We saw how the net of education caught the humblest ghetto-dweller in its toils. Every community of ten men or more had a synagogue, every synagogue its school, and with few exceptions every child sat in its benches. Moreover, schooling seldom ceased with childhood. Throughout his life a man spent on his books every hour he could snatch from work or sleep. We saw, too, how the purpose of this learning, the endless question and debate, was not, like scholasticism, the discovery of abstract truth. The letters the Jew pored over he lived by.

The masters of this learning, beginning with Gershom, ran in an unbroken line to Meir of Rothenburg (d. 1293), the light of the thirteenth century. After the interlude of the Black Death, it resumed its course with Jacob Mölln (Maharil, d. 1427); and when thousands of German Jews took the road of exile, it radiated eastward into Bohemia, Moravia, and Poland, and south into Styria and Italy. If we seek to classify these masters we can say that they stood feet on the ground, the solid ground of talmudic tradition, somewhere between the soaring mysticism of a Judah Hasid and the philosophy of a Maimonides. The classification, however, is misleading; for Judah and Maimonides were no less grounded in the Talmud, and Meir and Mölln paid their proper respects to the *altitudo* of the mystics.

As to the mass of German Jewry, who had no gift for sainthood or science and whose loyalty gave to a Meir or Maharil their real significance, they strove as hard as ever men could for an understanding and control of life in the only terms they knew or could conceive, the terms tradition had provided them. It was neither idiosyncrasy nor unusual talent, but a sturdy effort to face existence that gave almost any German village—where the priest perhaps could not so much as read the missal—a dozen hucksters at home in ten folios of the Talmud.

By the time of Meir an inevitable change, it is true, cast its shadow over this learning. Men began to yield to the insidi-

ous delight of considering it an end in itself. When nothing
remains to be said, sophists and quibblers will have their say.
Judah the Saint could well complain that his contemporaries
"putter too much over the Talmud." The puttering grew to
be an obsession. The hours devoted to it lengthened until they
consumed a man's whole life, leaving the wives and daughters
to earn the daily bread. Nay, the Jewess spurred her son and
husband on to study much as the Christian woman spurred
her men to fight. By the fifteenth century the learning of a
great part of German Jewry had sunk to logic-chopping and
formalism.

It is a commonplace to say that the Jew lost himself in letters as a relief from oppression, an escape from reality, and a
substitute for all that the world refused him. But there is more
to the matter than this. Scholasticism, without oppression,
likewise lost itself. History is filled with movements in art and
letters which, with no compulsion of ghetto walls, ended in
the sands of sterility. Decadence and death—as we can learn
from the psalmist or the nearest tree—are a process of life.
The plight of the German Jew differed from the German
monk who saw his learning turn to ashes—or the German
minnesinger who saw his song sink into the pedantries of a
Meisterlied—only because Jewry had staked its whole strength
and soul on a single art. In itself this consecration was not a
retreat, but an affirmation. The Talmud was the homeland of
the Jew, the prayer shawl, his flag; and his single-hearted devotion to them gave him, to say the least, the same sense of
honor, expression, and service that other citizens find in other
patriotisms. Talmudism, as the Jew felt it, even in his utmost
subservience to it, meant a preoccupation with reality, not a
denial of it. It may be the depths of slavery for a man not to

recognize his chains; but in failing to do just this, the Jew felt himself arbiter of all he held most dear. And what other freedom is there, under any discipline, or in any society?

Besides synagogue and schools, the Jew maintained, as evidence of his victory in the fight to be himself, his own courts and administrative offices. Sometimes—a famous example survives in Prague—they even achieved the dignity of a town hall. Baths, wedding-hall, bakery, slaughter-house, inn, cemetery, laundry, and prison were likewise administered by his own elected authorities. The government of the community was vested in a body of self-perpetuating *parnasim* (leaders), usually numbering twelve in the larger centers. One of them, or else the most prominent rabbi, was recognized by the secular authorities as the responsible head of the Jewry—the *Hochmeister* or, as he was often called, the *Judenbischof* (Jews' Bishop). It was no irony, but simple pride and affection which led an old inhabitant of a typical ghetto to exclaim: *Was diese kleine Gasse doch für ein Reich an sich war*—"Our little lane, what a kingdom it was!"

Walking its streets the Jew came to regard his habitual dress—"the long cloak covering me from hood to shoes" as Süsskind of Trimberg described it—a privilege of his race. Eleazar of Mayence (d. 1357) bade his sons "on no account adopt Gentile fashions . . . dress after the manner of your fathers and let your cloak be broad and without buckles." Although he eventually submitted to the march of fashion, the Jew lagged at his own pace. In the Renaissance he dressed as a medieval, in the eighteen-hundreds as a man of the Renaissance—what did a century or two behind the styles mean to an Eternal People?

Quite apart from the spirit of parochial independence, the

dictates of religion saw to it that his courts, baths, wedding-hall, slaughter-house, and cemetery kept a *cachet* of their own. Even the inn had its peculiarity; a local fund provided the needy traveler with three days' free board and room. As for the bakery—home kitchens were the luxury of the rich—the ghetto housewife stuffed the necks of geese and cooked *Schalet, Simetkuchen,* and sweet-and-sour fish with equal individuality and perhaps greater obstinacy. From the Black Death to the Brown Shirts it may be assumed that as long as she had a goose, she felt free to stuff its neck *more Judaico.*

Indifferent to the world outside the gates the Jew cherished the language he took with him when they first closed on his heels. His Judeo-German or Yiddish was a prevalent South German vernacular of the thirteenth century. He spiced it, and thereby helped preserve it, with a few holy grains of Hebrew. He dignified and endeared it, especially to the women-folk, by translations from Scriptures, prayer book, and moral writings. He opened it to popular medieval romances —King Arthur and his knights, Bevis of Hampton, and other heroes destroyed by Cervantes—as well as to fables from antiquity and the Orient. He recreated in it a wealth of folk-tales and anecdotes, best represented by the *Maase-Buch* (Story Book), now available in English. In the course of trade, emigration, and exile he carried it to Eastern Europe where it supplanted the Slavic speech of Bohemian, Polish, and Russian Jews. It spread through Hungary and Rumania, and was only halted by the equally stubborn Spanish dialect of the Balkan Jews. Today, perhaps one-half of Israel speaks this Germanic tongue. In Germany itself, the Jews persisted in using it until down to the last century; and even now, in remoter German towns and villages, the twang of it survives the mockery of Christian neighbors and the repugnance of "educated" Jews.

On a higher plane the medieval Jew asserted his freedom by transforming the character of his race. The world had deprived him of temporal power and with it the opportunity to indulge the all-too-human love of militancy, force, and brute exploitation. He made of this loss not merely a virtue, but an almost indelible trait. The Jew was by no means a born lover of peace. His history, well into the Christian era, was bloody with conquest or revolt. As late as the thirteenth century—when western Jewry, except in the extremity of self-defense, had banished the sword from their hearts—Jewish or Judaized troops marched in the armies of Genghis Khan. More than the pressure of outer circumstance, it was an inner revolution—begun by the makers of the Talmud—which made the spirit of European Jewry synonymous with a renunciation of physical power and brutality. The entire weight of Jewish learning, mysticism, and morality was thrown into this surrender. "Israel shall trust in the Lord," says the *Little Book of the Pious*, "and whoever, therefore, carries a sword shows nothing but his pride." At this point it can be said: As the Christians behave, so do the Jews—not.

Out of their renunciation, compulsory though its origin may have been, welled a humanity which again owed nothing to the example of their neighbors. Meir of Rothenburg quietly observes, "Unlike other peoples, we are not accustomed to beat our wives." There are volumes of social history in this casual word.

True, the Jews may have learned to abstain from violence in the school of necessity—no people have sat longer on its hard benches. But they learned. And so well that they practiced their lessons not only on creatures stronger, but weaker than themselves. "You shall kill no animal unless you need it for food or clothing," says the *Book of the Pious*, "and God will require a reckoning of the man who spurs his horse." "If you possess cattle or fowls," continues the *Little Book of the Pious*, echoing the Bible and Talmud, "feed them before you give yourselves to eat. Neither maim nor torment animals, fowl, or reptiles. Kill neither flies, wasps, gnats, nor ants. Be compassionate toward all living things which God has made; feed them and learn from Him who feeds and loves all His creatures."

A harder lesson than compassion toward the weak, the Jew learned humanity toward the strong. In the face of humiliation and oppression, he remembered that his enemies, who treated him as he was forbidden to treat his dog, were his fellow-men. "If a man does a good deed, whether he be Christian or Jew, one may say, 'May it bring him his reward'" (*Book of the Pious*). "In no way deceive a Christian, for it is a worse sin than eating swineflesh. If a Gentile does you a favor, hasten to repay him in kind; if you do him a favor, do not expect of him to reciprocate" (*Little Book of the Pious*). These may sound like commonplace rules of conduct today; but they were so little commonplace in the Middle Ages that you may vainly search their Christian writings for a similar attitude toward the Jew. It is singular—and saddening—that the only indisputable "contribution" of a cultural nature which the German Christian accepted from the ghetto was a rich vocabulary of thieves-slang and beggars-cant based on Yiddish words and phrases.

Finally the Jew—a bigot to the general eye—learned the real meaning of freedom. He learned tolerance. His soul truly at home, out of the very strength of his convictions and the serenity of an undivided mind and clean conscience he bade other men seek salvation in their own way. The schooling—a process of tens of centuries with many relapses—began with the Bible. Micah, we remember, dreamed of a day when all peoples shall walk, "each one in the name of his god." And the God of Isaiah said, "Blessed be Egypt My people, and Assyria the work of My hands" (Isa. 19.25). Despite their jealous preoccupation with Israel and terrible flashes of fanaticism and wrath, the rabbis of the Talmud played generous variations on the theme of Joshua ben Hananiah: "The pious of all nations have a share in paradise" (Tos. San. 13.2). Bound by their rigid principles of conversion and redemption, the Church Fathers could hardly imagine, as did the talmudic rabbis, that "The Holy Spirit may rest upon the righteous heathen even as upon the Jews" (*Seder Eliyyahu Rabba,* 10, ed. Friedmann, ch. 9, p. 48).

The medieval masters were as broadminded as Joshua ben Hananiah and as precise as Isaiah in extending their blessing, not to vague remote "nations," but to their enemies next door. Maimonides believed that "every human being, no matter of what people, who devotes himself to God and walks upright before Him will share in His eternal inheritance, and God will provide for him as He did for the priest and Levite of old." Both Maimonides, the rationalist, and Judah Halevi, the strict religionist, agreed that Christianity and Islam—the words are Maimonides'—"help bring all mankind to perfection." The leaders of the Franco-German schools—Gershom, Rashi, the Tosafists—and down to Isserles of Poland in the sixteenth century, united in declaring that non-Jews were not obliged to believe, as a matter of dogma, in the Unity of God, and that Christians, despite their images, were not idolaters.

Such were the views of the teachers; and before dismissing them as probably irrelevant to the behavior of the masses, one might try to find their like in Thomas Aquinas, Luther, or Calvin. Although he gives them pleasant quarters, even Dante put the virtuous pagans in Hell. There was only Abelard, whose *Dialogue* made a discreet plea for the tolerance of Moslem and Jew—and a century later Abelard, always under a cloud, would have ended literally in smoke.

But we may, if you will, disregard the words of the masters, admittedly men of exceptional mind. There is likewise no denying that lesser men, inflamed by the agonies of persecution, gave vent to malice and vituperation in language not surpassed by the worst Christian models. "Hath not a Jew eyes? hath not a Jew hands?" He had a liver as well, and for long dark years its bile flowed copiously. Nevertheless, the codes which ruled the ordinary man, the precepts which made up the stock of his intellectual life, ran counter to the natural tide of hatred and revenge. The stream of humanity and tolerance, fed by the masters, was distilled in the *Shulhan 'Aruk* and similar compendiums which were to be found at the elbow of every student in a Jewish school and every judge in a Jewish court.

And when the Middle Ages drew to a close and the Christian world rediscovered the free men of antiquity; and when the Germans, too, went to school in the Protestant battlefields, and heard the precepts of French Revolutionary guns, they found in granting something like equality to the Jew that, while he might be long on beards and short on social graces, he had nothing to discard or acquire in order to embrace what to him was the old-new lesson of the brotherhood of man.

9

THE REIGN OF DEATH

B Y THE middle of the thirteenth century the Jewish problem
had become a fixture in Germany. If the medieval world
had been stable—if it too could have become a fixture—the
clash between the Jew and the Christian might have settled,
like the thrust and counter-thrust of an arch, into some sort of
equilibrium.

But history stood still for neither one nor the other. Medieval economy, particularly where it touched merchants and
money-lenders, continued its painful evolution toward capitalism. Politically, the Reich never halted its slide toward dissolution. Socially, a new class, the burghers—guildsmen and
merchants—were pushing up toward power. As to religion,
heresy was in the air, and keen ears could have detected the
distant accents of John Huss and Martin Luther. And the
strain of these changes, as well as the fears they evoked, took
their toll from the weakest link in society—the Jews.

Against this background the events of the succeeding centuries could be made to appear as inevitable as an operation
in arithmetic. Each decade brought an addition to the list of
victims and a subtraction from the sum of human decency.
England, France, and ultimately Spain solved their incom-

mensurable Jewish equation by wiping the Jews off the slate in a series of mass-expulsions. Germany failed to imitate them because, for the purpose of united action, there was no Germany. Instead, four centuries of wrestling with the problem —of hating, burning, and killing—distorted the soul of both German and Jew. And this distortion lingered, as a medieval heritage, throughout modern times.

Yet in perhaps a truer light there was no logic in the long tragedy, no fatal unwinding of cause and effect. At any moment the Jew might have halted the agony by the surrender of his faith. The Marranos of Spain had not yet demonstrated the pitfalls in this course, and on the Christian side no one dreamed of closing the door to conversion and assimilation. But Heine was more than witty when he called Israel "the Swiss Guard of Deism"; the Lion on Lake Lucerne is of the same breed as the Lion of Judah. That the Jews died rather than surrender makes their history not a syllogism but a battle. In the Nuremberg *Memor-Buch* and similar martyrologies treasured by the synagogues and libraries of Germany are to be found neither mathematics nor logic, but the death-rolls of men and women who fell on the field of honor.

The events of 1241 offer a pattern which reappeared in every generation. That year the Mongolian armies of Ogdai Khan, in their triumphant sweep against the West, broke into Silesia and put Breslau to sack. Their invasion was an inverted Crusade which struck Christendom with terror. The Germans not unnaturally transferred their fear of the Mongols into suspicion against the Jews. It is always easier—and safer—to manufacture an enemy at home than fight one abroad.

Caucasian and Khazar Jews were said to be marching in the Mongolian ranks, and they probably were. From this it was a simple step to believe, as Christians did, that the Western Jews had decided in secret conclave to unite with the Mongols in an effort to overthrow Christian society, and that barrels of arms had been smuggled over the Silesian border. So old is the "world conspiracy" of Israel against the nations.

The Jews showed a similar naivety. Transferring their fear of the Christians into a hope for salvation, they read in the Mongol advance a sure sign of the long-prayed-for appearance of the Messiah. "The Jews," records the Chronicle of Trèves, "are transported with joy, for they expect the coming of their Redeemer."

But when the year drew to an end history could only record that the Mongols had abandoned Germany for a campaign against Hungary, and that the Germans—either as evidence of their fright or on the pretext of avenging a ritual-murder —killed 180 Jews in Frankfort.

Five years later Conrad IV pardoned the citizens of Frankfort for the damage done his treasury by the murder of its "servants," which he recognized was due mostly to "carelessness and accident." Meanwhile (1243-44) the same lack of care led to the torture and execution of several Jews and Jewesses in Kitzingen on the charge of ritual murder; a bonfire of Jews in Belitz, accused of desecrating the Host; a massacre in Ortenburg and Meiningen, charges unknown; and a similar tragedy in Pforzheim, where many victims spared the Christians from their own carelessness by committing suicide.

Next, the Interregnum (1254-73)—when there was no king in the land—encouraged the lawlessness which drenched the last half of the century in blood. The burghers used the absence of royal authority to further their drive against the nobility who barred the road to political power and against the money-lenders who stood in the way of profits. The peasants stirred with a discontent soon to be epidemic in Western Europe. For the Jews it meant bowing to a crescendo of violence.

It would be painful and useless to pursue these outbursts in detail. Like storms relieving an invisible pressure they broke at scattered points, each cycle of increasing magnitude. In 1264-70 the lightnings of hate struck Augsburg in the south, Arnstadt in central Germany, Weissenberg in Alsace, and Coblenz, Sinzig (where 72 victims were burned in a synagogue) and other Rhineland cities. A *Landfriede* which was proclaimed in a number of Hessian towns said that "irresponsible city-folk had provoked and committed excesses and cruel murder upon the servants of the Reich—though it was against the will of God, in whose memory the Jews were maintained by the Church."

When Rudolph of Habsburg captured the imperial throne, it brought the Interregnum to an end and substituted an era of high taxes. Old debts, new bribes, and the damage of twenty years' internecine strife had to be paid. Germany groaned under the burden and the Jews groaned under Germany. Taxes, debts, and religious passions—inextricably tangled together—led to renewed martyrdom in Franconia, Brandenburg, Bavaria, and again the Rhinelands (1283-1290). Ninety Jews fell in Munich alone.

In misery and terror the "servants" began to desert the Reich. Among the refugees was Meir of Rothenburg, the most eminent rabbi of the century and the spiritual leader of German Jewry—one of the rare men to share with Gershom the title "Light of the Exile." His fate epitomizes the epoch. In 1286 he fled across the Alps to escape the exactions of Rudolph and probably with a view to settling in Palestine. A converted Jew betrayed him to the imperial authorities while he was passing through Lombardy. At the command of Rudolph he was imprisoned in the castle of Ensisheim (Alsace), where he was held for a vast ransom. Rudolph's purpose was not merely to turn Meir into cash, but, like another Pharaoh, to discourage a general exodus.

But the stubbornness of the Jew was a match for the greed of the Emperor. Meir forbade the Jewish communities to raise the sum demanded for his release, and he spent the last seven years of his life a prisoner—studying, teaching, and governing to the end.

Death, however, did not free his body, which the government judged was as valuable as ever. Some years later, when the dead rabbi could no longer enforce his ban, Alexander ben Solomon, a Jew of Frankfort, managed to collect the ransom; and Meir came to his last rest in the graveyard of Worms. Alexander asked but one reward—to be buried next to the master he had redeemed. To this day their tombstones stand side by side, one of the many Jewish memorials in Germany which have not lost their eloquence or point.

The death of Rudolph occasioned seven years more of civil war (1291-98). German nerves reached a breaking point; and a report that Jews in the Franconian town of Röttingen had desecrated a wafer of the Host provided a much-needed diversion. Under the leadership of a local knight—or perhaps a humble butcher—named Rindfleisch, a mob burned alive the Röttingen Jews. Then, swelling their numbers and widening their range, the horde destroyed the Jewries of Würzburg and Nuremberg, ran riot throughout Franconia, Bavaria, and Austria, and within six months made an end to some hundred and forty communities. Rothenburg, its Jewry thrice put to sack and slaughter, earned in Jewish elegies the unsavory title of "Red Burg"—a city red with blood. Altogether the number of lives extinguished have been estimated in the tens of thousands.

Yet these closing years of the thirteenth century served only as a *Vorspeise*, a foretaste and a prelude, to the tragedies of the fourteenth. "Never was there a harder century for the children of Israel," says Johann Schudt, a quaint old Christian writer on Jewish curiosities, "and it is a marvel that a single Jew in Germany managed to survive." It is probably no less a marvel that the Germans themselves survived. Schmoller, an historian of guild-life, which came into its own in this century, calls it "a savage era of ferment, full of raw impulses and strong passions. Even as a handful of German princes killed the Emperor on the open highway, so they hung and beheaded patricians and guild-masters by the dozens in the cities, and to be relieved of their indebtedness to them burned the Jews by the thousands. Wholesale confiscations became the rule among kings, princes, cities, and guilds."

From top to bottom the mills of society ground the Jews exceedingly fine—and not over-slowly. While Ludwig the Bavarian set the upper classes an example with his mastery at exploitation, culminating in the Golden Penny tax of 1342 (see p. 81), at the bottom the mob—led by a Franconian nobleman—repeated the work of Rindfleisch. Their heads were filled with tales of desecrated Hosts—Jews, it was said, had outraged the sacred wafer in Gustrow, Überlingen (1330-31), and Deggendorf (1337). Their pockets had been emptied, directly or indirectly, by the efforts of the Jews to meet the insatiable demands of king and nobility. And, in consequence, their hands were armed with pitchforks, flails, and axes. *Judenschläger,* Jew-beaters, they called themselves and proved their title from the Rhine to Moravia (1336-38).

Meanwhile, perhaps in imitation of the Shepherds Crusade, the slaughter of lepers, and the campaigns against heretics which swept France in the twenties and thirties, the Alsatians staged a "home crusade" against the Jews. Inspired by an inn-keeper, who tied a strip of leather about his arm as a badge and ordered his followers to do the same, the *Armleder*—Arm-leather—hosts devastated Alsatian Jewries for two years (1337-38) with little hindrance from the authorities.

In all some 120 communities were plundered or laid waste, and everyone, except the Jews and possibly the king, felt the gainer: the mob with its booty, the debtors with their bonds and notes destroyed, and the religious-minded with God's honor revenged.

ii

Ten years later came in grim climax the Black Death (1348-50), the plague which destroyed at least a quarter of the population of Europe. Nothing, dramatists have long observed, reveals men and society in their true light as do the fear and presence of death. Then, as Lucretius says, the masks fall and reality alone remains.

The very emergence of the plague, as of all medieval epidemics, meant a society ill-fed, wretchedly housed, and oblivious to drains, soap, and water. And the physical poverty it disclosed proved to be no filthier than the spiritual poverty and inhumanity which the fear of death stripped for even their beneficiaries to see and acknowledge. *Caritas mortua, spes prostrata*—"Kindness dead and hope fallen"—was the pathetic motto of the times.

Probably imported from India, the plague made its first appearance in Provence early in 1348. Fear galloped through Germany many months before the pale horse itself had crossed the Alps. And with the fear came a fearful and panic-born remedy.

In their terror the French had revived absurd stories of poisoned wells as the origin of the pest. At first the rich blamed the poor and the poor blamed the rich, then both blamed the lepers, but in the end, no doubt to the intense relief of the lepers, they all agreed upon blaming the Jews. The admissions wrung by torture from a few Jews in Savoy and again in Switzerland were enough to demonstrate the guilt of the race and dispense with even a cursory test of the well-water. This procedure, it should be observed, was no parody of justice, medieval or otherwise; Death had merely begun his work of plucking away the masks.

Goaded by fright the Germans did not wait for the onslaught of the plague in order to take prophylactic measures. Henricus of Erfurt has left us a rhymed description of what happened:

> The Pestilence like fury broke
> And took its thousands of our folk;
> The Earth against us fiercely turned
> And many Jews were therefore burned.

Early in the summer of 1348 the Swiss were burning the Jews as actual or potential well-poisoners. By autumn the burnings spread to South Germany and the Rhinelands, and by winter into central Germany and eastward. In many cases the plague did not arrive until a year after the pyres had grown cold. Unlike earlier persecutions, the burnings and massacres were carried out, as sanitary and financial measures, under the auspices of the local authorities.

Other measures, of a more spiritual order, were born of the terror and likewise embraced the hapless Jews. Christian consciences became convinced that Christian sins had provoked the wrath of God. Bands of flagellants marched from town to town flogging themselves in the hope of averting divine punishment with their own blood. And together with practicing penance and preaching repentance, it was natural that they frequently spurred the populace to the extermination of Israel as an act of piety. Papal authority decried the claims and behavior of these fanatics, even as both papal and imperial authority denounced the accusation that Jews had poisoned the wells—but in vain. For not only panic, deaf to reason and authority, was at work; but social forces too had dropped their masks and bared the brutal realities of the medieval economy.

The Flagellants themselves represented more than a religious movement. Behind their piety burned a rancor against the wealth and power of the ruling classes within and without the Church—a spirit that was to flame again, and higher, in the Reformation.

The guilds were eager to come to blows with every class that threatened the socialism of their closed corporations: patricians, merchants, and Jews. The latter—while still without gaining the right to hold office or losing their peculiar disabilities and obligations—were beginning, as individuals, to be admitted to citizenship in many of the larger cities. This advance, especially marked in the first third of the century, was probably a response to the need of the growing cities for Jewish brains and money and to the closer partnership between patricians and "capitalists" against the coöperative economy of the guilds. By striking down the Jews, the guilds not only destroyed a hated money-power, but hoped to weaken the patricians and nobility who depended upon that power. The lower masses rose against the Jews with the vague instinct—assiduously nurtured by the other classes—that Jewish wealth was responsible for their own poverty, and with the clear and quite correct belief that this wealth—even if it were but a candlestick stripped from the poorest ghetto den—was worth looting. For their part the patricians and nobility saw in the attack on the Jews a welcome diversion of popular wrath from their own heads; and they were not loath to see their notes and mortgages tossed into the same bonfire with the bodies of their creditors.

Charles IV who began by forbidding the people to touch so much as a hair of his Jews ended by contracting with the city councils to share in the spoils. The attitude of most of these councils may be read in a letter the city-fathers of Lübeck addressed to their overlord, the Duke of Luneborch. "It is to be feared," they wrote, "that neither the plague nor the misery of humanity—through which the Christian populace are exploited by the Jews—will cease as long as the Jews are permitted to remain under the protection of lord or prince and can bribe these lords in order to continue their nefarious work."

The lords and princes showed themselves ready enough to substitute immediate booty for prospective bribes. Archbishop Wilhelm of Cologne pardoned the sack and slaughter in Bonn on condition that all debts accruing to the dead became payable to himself. Archbishop Gerlach of Erfurt refused to pardon the massacre in his episcopal seat until the city obligated itself to indemnify him to the amount of 100 marks a year—a tribute which was long known (and paid) as the *Judenzins*—the Jews-interest. But probably no titled holder of power quite surpassed Friedrich, the Margrave of Meissen. "Rathmeister and Members of the City Council of Nordhausen!" he wrote to, as it proved, his obedient subjects, "You are aware that we have everywhere allowed our Jews access to our wells, with the result that out of their hatred for Christians and Christendom they have poisoned all our water. Since we have in our hands assured proof of this, we herewith counsel you to allow the Jews to be put to death [*das ein uber joden lasset toten*] for the glory of God."

The masks fallen, contemporaries were as aware of the true forces at work as any later historian. The Strasbourg chronicler knew that, although they were accused of poisoning wells, "money was likewise the poison which killed the Jews . . . if they had been poor and if the nobility had not been in their debt, they would not have been burned." The chronicler of the Peter's Kloster is even more explicit. Regarding the wells he writes, "I do not know if what they say is true," and then continues, "but I rather believe that the real grounds [for the *Judenbrände*—Jew-burnings] was the huge, indeed immeasurable, amount of money which barons and soldiers, townsmen and country-folk, were obligated to pay the Jews." Archbishop Gerlach, secure in his 100 marks annual tribute, was not fooled by the tale of poisoned wells, which he expressly declared to be unproved. "The Jews had a multitude of debtors," he was free to say, "and in order to avoid paying them, the debtors put them out of the way—for a dead dog no longer howls."

Nuremberg tells the typical story. In June of 1348 the guilds rose in revolt against the patricians. Less than a year later the Flagellants whipped themselves and the mob into renewed fever. The situation became so precarious that in April 1349 Emperor Charles—for a consideration—bestowed on a nobleman future title to most of the ghetto houses, that is, in case they should be emptied of their inhabitants. In June he arranged, at a price, with the Count of Nuremberg that if the eventual disappearance of Jewish tax-payers should embarrass the civic finances, the loss would be made good through the seizure of whatever property was left behind. In October he presented the city council with a letter exonerating it in advance from any responsibility for whatever harm might befall the "servants" of the imperial treasury. Charles' foresight was justified; for when the plague at length appeared, late in 1349, the Jews were driven to a square, thereafter known as the Judenbühl, and burned or slaughtered to a man.

In Strasbourg the city council tried to stem the tide. Whereat the populace, under pressure from the guilds, installed a new council who quickly satisfied the popular demand. "On Friday all the Jews of the city were imprisoned," records the Strasbourg chronicler, "and on Saturday, St. Valentine's Day [1349], the prisoners, numbering two thousand, were burned alive in the Jewish cemetery. Those few who consented to be baptized were spared. The money belonging to the victims was seized by the council and divided per capita among the artizans of the city." Before the year was out Charles sent the inhabitants his forgiveness "for any judgment or act" they took against "our servants" the Jews, and declared the citizens "free and quit of any present or future claims against Jewish property, no matter how it came into their hands."

Social revolt, death-driven terror, religious penitence, misery, greed, lies born of them all, and at their heels the plague itself together fed the blistering pyres. German Jewry was almost literally consumed in the flames. In many towns—Worms, Mayence, Spires, Erfurt, and elsewhere—the victims desperately set the torch to their own homes and locked themselves to a fiery death. A few communities made show of resistance, notably Mayence and Worms; and an occasional city council, as in Cologne and Erfurt, tried to forestall the massacres—but the efforts of both the Jews and their defenders were hopeless. Still rarer, as in Hanover, a merciful expulsion was substituted for fire and sword. Only one city of any size succeeded in protecting its Jewry—Regensburg.

Within two years nearly 350 communities were exterminated—"felled, drowned, burned, hanged," to quote the Nuremberg memorial lists, "broken on the wheel, throttled, buried alive, and tortured with every means of death for the sanctification of God's Holy Name."

Naturally, untold property, real or personal, fell into the hands of the mob, the local authorities, or the overlords. The scramble for the loot was keen: in Spires the city council, with an eye to its own pockets, barred the smoking ghetto from the populace; in Cologne Jewish land and houses were sold to the right people for a song.

In almost every instance the survivors were banished and the gates closed against the Jews for terms running from one hundred years, as in Strasbourg, on to perpetuity. Unlike the Spanish Jews in similar circumstances, very few consented to save themselves through baptism—although the chance was

frequently given. Instead, refugees and exiles streamed to Bohemia and Austria, and especially to Poland where, under the
friendly rule of Casimir the Great and the simpler economic
structure of an undeveloped land, there was only the plague to
fear. As nearly as ever in her history Germany was *Judenrein*
—clean of Jews.

iii

The results of the plague were as varied as they were doubtless unexpected. Enriched with offerings, bequests, and inheri-
tances the Church entered on a career of luxury, venality, and
oppression which in the end brought it face to face with
ninety-five theses nailed to a door in Wittenberg. The sudden
drop of population, in a world which lived on hand labor,
boosted wages and prices. Rising values, together with a post-
war spirit of high and expensive living, launched a wave of
prosperity and commercial expansion which carried Germany
to the front rank in material civilization. With the exception
of Prague, founded the year of the plague, the first universities
of German lands came into being during the next century.

The very motives which drove the Jews to the pyre and exile
brought about their return within a decade or two—and sometimes within a year or two—after they were banished "forever." Christian money-lending was still banned by the
Church, and the Jews were needed for their financial resources and abilities. And, it must be noted, they accepted the
invitation to come back partly from the same motive which
proffered it—and partly, of course, from a love for their home
and country in truth pathetic. Moreover, their return supposes,
as the discerning reader suspects, that not every rich Jew was

burned and not all Jewish wealth confiscated. Wealthy men, and wealth too, had means of concealment and flight in the 14th century no less than in any other.

But, rich or poor, the Jews returned to a harder world. Bought at the usual heavy price, the right to live in a town that had been their home for generations was now in general limited to a brief and expensively renewable term. More than ever the opportunities for earning this right and an incidental living were restricted to money-lending and petty trade. The vilest section of a city was leased to them, and only seldom were they permitted to own the roof over their heads or the ground beneath their feet. Enforcement of ghetto confinement, distinctive dress, and other devices of exclusion and degradation became more stringent. Letters of protection and the body-tax grew into wider use, emphasizing the hazards and ignominy of their existence. From a people with a fixed and generally recognized status, they sank into "tolerated" puppets allowed to play their part so long as it served and then to be cast aside.

The virtual dissolution of the Empire, marked by the Golden Bull (1356), placed the Jewries at the mercy of its innumerable states and cities. *Kammerknecht,* "servant of the imperial treasury," became little but a name. Yet the Emperor made the name pay royally before it too vanished from practical life. Topping a series of similar acts, Wenceslaus, the successor of Charles IV, decreed in 1390 that in wide areas of Germany all debts owing to the Jews were, so far as these luckless creditors were concerned, null and void. Instead, they were made payable to the states and cities upon condition that one-quarter of the proceeds went into his own pocket. Under Wenceslaus and the next Emperor, Rupert III, the Golden

Penny tax was made a precedent for huge impositions on the imperial servants, despite the fact that they were for the most part already bound and delivered to lesser masters. Sigismund, who followed Rupert, proved a genius at inventing excuses for these levies: his coronation, his traveling expenses to the Council of Constance (1414), an intercession with the Pope, the grant of rosy but empty privileges, all served to mulct the Jews.

The cities and states—a hundred volatile masters instead of one—alternately cajoled and oppressed their Jewries. All of the ruling or aspiring classes—rural lords, town councils, guilds, and church princes—fished zealously in the troubled waters of the dissolving Reich; and their favorite bait were the Jews, to be fattened, hooked, and abandoned depending on their fisherman's luck. And when the Lombards overran the banking field in the fifteenth century, even the value of the bait waned.

Jewish emigration to Poland and Italy increased its flow. Polish Jewry was largely built on these and similar flights. In Venice, Padua, and other towns of the Venetian Republic rose synagogues dedicated to the German ritual, and the grave-yards of these towns still keep the stones of a Katzenellen-bogen, Eilpron, Jacopo di Norimbergo, Lupo di Battenberg, and fellow-wanderers from north of the Alps. When the Turks captured Salonica in 1430, another haven was opened. Isaac Zarfati, settled in this paradise where Jews were treated no worse than Christians, addressed a circular letter to his unhappy brethren in Germany. "Turkey is a land," he wrote, "that lacks nothing. Here you may dress as you please, whereas in Christendom you dare not clothe your children in colors without the risk of their being flayed red and beaten blue."

So many refugees answered the call that a rabbi from Nuremberg deemed it necessary to compose a special ritual for their use.

The flight of the Jews was hastened by the recurrence of the usual religious outbursts—themselves a token of where the ultimate burden of oppression lay. It cannot be recalled too often that the Jews, any more than other financiers or bankers, did not create money. The vast sums—or the goods and services they represented—which were decade after decade pumped or seized from the money-lenders came from someone else. When, as at this period, every class in society save the largest was organized and on the make, this someone else was in the last analysis the peasant and the unskilled worker. The prosperity which followed the Black Death was enjoyed by the nobleman, city patrician, merchant, and guildsman, at the expense of the backward and defenseless masses. Peasant uprisings and city rebellions—heralded a century before—became continental in scope. John Ball "the mad priest" and Wat Tyler in England, Jacques Bonhomme in France, the communists at the heels of John Huss in Bohemia, and a little later John of Leyden and his Anabaptists in Germany were one man: the forgotten man reminding the world that he was forgotten.

Parallel with these unsuccessful revolutions and fed by the same grievances were the reillumined pyres and massacres of the Jews. As the wealth of the nation passed into the pockets of the powerful and built itself into castles, city mansions, guild-halls, *Rathäuser,* churches, cloisters, and universities, enough of it lingered for one bright moment in the hands of the Jews for all the world to see. And much as the revolt of the masses, from priest Ball to anabaptist John, took its flame and watchwords from the humanity which dwells in the Jewish-Christian faith, so the attack on the Jews when it was the work of the mob sprang from a religious groping for social justice—and when it was the work of the dominant classes, from a defense of injustice likewise in the name of religion.

Outbreaks, inspired by the men on the top or the bottom, occurred with pitiful regularity. In 1384 it was the guilds who revolted against the patricians, and Jewish blood flowed in Nördlingen and other towns. Five years later Prague, the imperial capital, saw the mob put thousands to death—rather in vain, for the emperor bagged most of the spoils. After a series of "incidents"—Posen, 1399, fourteen Jews burned; Prague, 1400, seventy-seven killed and three burned; Glogau, 1402, death through the imputed desecration of a Host—violence again culminated in the Catholic reaction to the Hussite Wars of 1419-36. Vienna was purged of its "Jewish dogs"— so runs the inscription, dated 1421, still to be seen in the Judenplatz—who were carted to the Prater in eighty-six tumbrils and burned alive; while fire and expulsion did for the rest of Austrian Jewry, and terror was spread by the anti-Hussite forces to the ghettos of South Germany and the Rhine.

The next peak came in 1452-53 when St. John of Capistrano crusaded against the Hussites of Silesia and won the title "Scourge of the Jews"—well-earned as the burned and banished of Breslau and its province could testify. The final blow of the century was a moral one and therefore more deadly— the work of another monk, Bernardino of Feltre. His was the moving spirit in the ritual-murder trial at Trent (1475-78)— he had already campaigned against the money-lenders of Italy—and, thanks to the newly invented printing-press, the trial became a notorious case throughout Germany and much of Western Europe. The guilt of the Jews was widely believed, expulsions became epidemic; and even today, whether one has heard of Trent or not, the work of Bernardino marches on.

Expulsions, indeed, were the mark of the fifteenth century as burnings had been of the fourteenth. It would be futile to list the towns from which the Jews were banished temporarily —for a month, a year, a decade. If ever the Wandering Jew was personified, it was along the hard roads of Germany.

Cities and provinces gradually rid themselves of the race for good—that is, until the French Revolutionary armies made the city fathers change their minds. Cologne saw the last of its Jews in 1426, Augsburg in 1439, Erfurt in 1448, Nuremberg and Ulm in 1499. Regensburg held out till 1519, Rothenburg till 1520, and Würzburg till 1565. Bavaria, Mecklenburg, Brandenburg, and Alsace were practically emptied by the dawn of the sixteenth century.

Unlike, however, the expulsions in England, France, and Spain—as we have already remarked—the Jews generally found refuge in a neighboring town or province. The Jewry of Cologne, for example, moved across the river to Deutz, the Jewry of Nuremberg down the river to Fürth, the Jewry of Würzburg a few miles away to Heidingsfeld and other towns of the vicinity. Tiny communities received shelter in the rural centers back from the Rhine, in the hills of Württemberg, and along the Polish and Bohemian border. The village Jew became a familiar figure. He served as intermediary in the commerce with the larger towns where he traded at the fairs and markets, made loans on the side, and paid a stiff tax for every day spent within the city walls. Strings of village ghettos, each with a synagogue and inn, ran like caravanserais along the trade routes joining Breslau to Poland, Fürth to Bohemia, Passau and Vienna to Italy. The Hanseatic League still closed the ports and routes of the North. By the middle of the sixteenth century only a few Imperial cities, such as Frankfort, Worms, Prague, and Vienna, possessed Jewries of considerable size.

iv

Spiritual life dwindled together with material existence. Talmudic knowledge grew thin among the laity, and the vital importance of money as a means of paying for the individual and communal right to live gave the reins of leadership to such wealthy Jews as a community could command. As a result the rabbinate became a paid office and thereby ceded to the rich laity a good measure of its influence—a change which has affected the tone of communal life to the present day.

The introduction of systematic ordination for the rabbis—effected by Meir ben Baruk Halevi, chief rabbi of Vienna (1393-1408)—set a fairly high and uniform level of moral and intellectual requirements. The predominant influence of lay leaders—financiers and eventually court Jews—encouraged in later centuries the spread of secular knowledge and attainments among the Jewries and prepared them for modern life. All this was pure gain. On the other hand, the rabbis too fell under the spell of money in order to further their place and rank. Bans and fines and even marriage-broking served their ambitions. Their quarrels—to quote Zunz—"recall the bickerings of popes and anti-popes." And when the rabbis and learning itself lost their amateur standing, the soul of Jewry suffered a loss from which it has never recovered. Although reasons were provided in plenty and are still provided, the *reason* of a Jewish life became something to be heard or read, not lived. Much of the tragedy, the inner shame and outward strain, of the modern maladjustment may be plausibly traced to this loss.

Demoralization showed itself in the divergence among the local rituals and in the meticulous zeal of the rabbis to register and perpetuate these differences. Such preoccupation, as well as the assiduous compiling of rabbinical letters and opinions, although invaluable to modern research, meant that intellectual traffic, like traffic in the market place, had shrunk to *Kleinhandel*.

Yet even this disintegration and jealous separatism responded to a conscious will-to-live. The emperors Rupert and Sigismund made enticing efforts to unify German Jewry through the appointment of an imperial chief-rabbi; and the efforts failed because the Jews understood it would merely facilitate their exploitation and destruction. Like seeds cast to the wind they realized that in disunity lay strength.

Not that unity or leadership altogether vanished. Synods met to grapple with financial burdens, blood accusations, and perplexing social needs. And great figures can be discerned through the veil which ignorance and indifference have drawn between the modern and the medieval Jew. Jacob ben Moses Mölln of Mayence (Maharil—see p. 110), whose work on local customs in the ritual brought him wide authority, steadied the fears of his people when the anti-Hussite army threatened the Rhine Jewries. Israel Isserlein of Neustadt (d. 1460) brought hundreds of students to sit at his feet, and on one ominous occasion helped thwart the schemes to bring about a rightly-feared unity. His writings deeply strengthened the waning life in Germany and the fresh life in Poland. The chain of tradition sagged and coiled, but it did not break.

While the Jews held on and, if they searched the heavens at all, searched in vain for a sign, new forces released by the Black Death were subtly and invisibly working in their behalf. A curious force, and not the least, lay in a little fable Boccaccio slipped into the tales with which his young men and women diverted themselves when the pestilence ravaged Florence.

The *Decameron* tells us that Saladin asked a Jew which religion was the true one: Judaism, Christianity, or Islam. The Jew escaped an embarrassing reply by relating a fable of three rings, and the moral was that just as no one could tell which ring was genuine, so the truth as to religion "still pendeth." Saladin's question was an old one—it can be found in Judah Halevi's *Al Khazari*—but Boccaccio's reply was bold for the fourteenth century. Something we moderns call the Renaissance, a return to that classical world where revealed truths were regarded a bit skeptically, was stirring in Italy. Three hundred years later the three rings will reappear in Lessing's drama, *Nathan the Wise*. And this time, thanks no little to Lessing himself, the civilized part of the world will be ready to agree that the answer "still pendeth."

BOOK THREE

EMANCIPATION

Times change: the only things eternal
are stupidity and wickedness.—*Mommsen.*

10

REUCHLIN AND SOME OBSCURE MEN

THE Renaissance, heralded by Boccaccio and Petrarch, is a vague term denoting a new state of mind not altogether new and at best hard to describe. But the Revival of Learning —or Humanism—which accompanied the Renaissance is more tangible. The literature of the ancient world, while never wholly neglected, was ravenously exhumed from monastic dust and read, studied, glossed, and disseminated in the fifteenth and sixteenth centuries as it had not been in the thousand years which had elapsed since Christian zealots burned the library of Alexandria.

In giving scrupulous and critical care to the restoration and commentary of the classical texts, the Humanists reawakened the scientific spirit of the West, dormant since it had exhausted itself in the stratosphere of theology. And the revived and rekindled words of ancient poets, historians, and philosophers lighted the road back from heaven to earth, from divinity to humanity. Once again man began to be the measure of all things.

Until the invention of printing the Revival was largely the delight of the few scholars who could pluck its fruits and the pride of the few princes who could buy them. But in the last quarter of the fifteenth century, when the presses went into full swing, classical learning came into the hands, and some glint of its spirit into the heads, of everyone who fashioned public opinion. Monks and priests, doctors and lawyers, ambitious merchants and back-country noblemen mouthed it, mangled it, damned or praised it, in any case spread its vogue. And, like all of Western Europe, Germany went "ancient" too. Was it not the Holy Roman Empire and was there not Erasmus the Dutchman?

Scholars in Italy and Germany soon discovered that the ancient world had embraced Palestine, and its literature had included Hebrew. The thirst aroused by Pierian springs turned to the waters of Siloah. Jewish scholars were drafted by the literati to teach them another grammar.

While Erasmus rested content with the Greeks and Romans, his fellow luminary, Johannes Reuchlin—the "phoenix of Germany" and its most distinguished Humanist—pressed on to wrestle with the Bible and Cabala. Jacob Loans, a German Jew and physician to the Emperor, and Obadiah Sforno, an Italian Jew and likewise a physician, undertook his Hebrew education.

Jewish physicians, it should be remarked, were frequent in the princely courts of Germany during the fifteenth century—a sign no less auspicious than their presence in Moslem courts five hundred years before. Loans and Reuchlin cultivated a friendship pregnant for the future of their people. Jews, to be sure, had been seen at court as physicians or financiers from time to time throughout the Middle Ages; but Jew and Christian, in a medieval German court, had little to share or impart. Whereas between Jew and Humanist there was much to say.

Grammar and Cabala furnished a bond where theology and ritual had built a wall.

In his enthusiasm Reuchlin wrote a dialogue, *De Mirifico Verbo* (1494), wherein he praised the wondrous beauties of Hebrew—"the language in which God, angels, and men spoke together, not through the ambiguous murmur of a Castalian spring, Typhonian cave or Dordonian wood, but as friends talk face to face." He followed this eulogy with one of the first Hebrew grammars and dictionaries (1506) in a Western tongue, that is to say in Latin, the universal medium of scholar and cleric.

But Reuchlin soon made another discovery. Although Hebrew was a dead language in the same incorrect sense that Latin and Greek were dead—all three had been spoken uninterruptedly through the centuries—its people, the Jews, were far from dead. On the contrary, their living presence in Reuchlin's Germany turned his innocent studies into one of the burning issues of his day.

The burnings under Capistrano had not consumed the interest of the Dominicans in the Jews. In fact it was, if anything, heightened by the dearth of Hussites, by the recent successful riddance of the Jews in Spain, and by the hope that since most of the German Jews had already been banished or otherwise eliminated, the few remaining communities could be readily dealt the same fate. This interest now took the form of an attack upon the Talmud.

One Johannes Pfefferkorn, a baptized Jew with a shady past and an attractive wife, was encouraged by the Dominicans of Cologne to publish a number of inflammatory pamphlets, the contents of which, revealing the supposed secrets of the Talmud, are sufficiently characterized by their titles: *The Mirror of the Jews, The Enemy of the Jews, How the Blind Jews Observe Their Easter, The Jewish Confessional.* In crass and filthy terms, typical of learned polemic in the sixteenth century and of anti-Jewish polemic in any century, Pfefferkorn demanded the "combustion" and suppression of the Talmud as a storehouse of blasphemies against Christ, the Virgin, and the Apostles; this to be followed by either the mass-conversion or the mass-expulsion of the Jews.

Behind Pfefferkorn, behind even the Jew-hatred professional to the Dominicans as watch-dogs of the Church, lay a shrewd suspicion that the Humanists, in flirting with Hebrew, were verging on a critical and therefore dangerous study of the Bible. Small harm was done when these Humanist sleuths ferreted out spurious lines in Homer and Virgil—though there had been a pretty mess when Lorenzo Valla exposed the forgery of the Constantine donation. But, so it seemed to the Dominicans—and so it proved when Luther put their fears to the test some ten years later—the unity of the Church and the preservation of medieval Christianity, the only Christianity they knew, depended on keeping the Hebrew key to the Bible a dark and forbidden secret.

Through Dominican recommendations Pfefferkorn won the ear of Emperor Maximilian. The latter ordered the seizure and examination of all Hebrew books in Germany and the destruction of such as proved hostile to the true faith. Over one thousand volumes were confiscated in and around Frankfort. Then the Jews got the Emperor's ear, and even elicited a courageous protest from the Archbishop of Mayence; and the whole matter was placed in charge of a commission. Among its members were Pfefferkorn, Victor von Karben, another baptized Jew (both of whom passed as savants in Hebrew), Jacob von Hochstraten, dean and chief-inquisitor of the Cologne Dominicans, and finally Reuchlin—one of the rare uncircumcised Christians in Western Europe who knew an *aleph* from a *beth*.

The Dominicans welcomed the participation of Reuchlin. They had, as a matter of fact, been angling for him in the assurance that with his expert opinion to back them up, their plans were bound to succeed, and, moreover, future Hebraists would be given the proper cue and example. Their confidence in Reuchlin had plausible grounds. The year before he published his Hebrew grammar, he had paid his respects to the living Jews in a published "missive" redolent with the prejudices of the day—laying their woes to their own hard hearts and stiff necks and berating the anti-Christian bias of certain of their writings. To be sure he nowhere proposed to amend their perversities by the use of force—but the Dominicans would take care of that. Altogether he seemed fit for their project which, as revealed in the verdicts of other members of the commission and by pronouncements from sundry theological faculties, proposed to class the Jews as heretics and consign them to the customary rack and fagot.

Formally the commission was asked to decide "if the burning of Jewish literature were godly, laudable, and beneficial to the Christian faith." And knowing that not only their books but their lives were at stake, the Jews trembled for the answer.

Reuchlin rendered his opinion in 1510. He maintained that Hebrew commentaries on the Bible could be of service to Christians. Cabalistic writings, he found, supported and indeed elucidated Christian doctrine. Prayer books and devotional works must not be molested since Church and State recognized the right of the Jews to practice their cult. If these books denied the divinity of Christ, he remarked, they did no worse than the Jews who read them and whom nevertheless the Church had protected. When it came to insults—he added —did not the Christians solemnly proclaim on every Good Friday that the Jews were a "perfidious" people? He went further: in the traditional and authoritative view of the Church, Jews could not be considered or treated as heretics. And still further: Jews were entitled to protection from Christians because they were fellow-citizens of the German Reich— a claim which later he had great difficulty in proving and which nearly cost him his honor, his place in Christian society, and his eternal salvation. As to the Talmud, he confessed he had never read it and knew practically nothing about it. But he added that the same could be said of many others who nevertheless condemned it and who—with a shot at Pfefferkorn—did not blush to carry their braying against it to the Emperor and thereby showed themselves, even as they brayed, "an ass." Finally, he proposed that every German university should establish courses in Hebrew: in this way the Christians would gain a better understanding of Christianity and could more easily persuade the Jews of its truth.

The fat was in the fire. Smarting under the insults—"ass" was one of the least—Pfefferkorn, aided by what skill the Dominicans could muster, wrote a blast (entitled *Handspiegel —Hand-mirror*) against the Jews, their books, and Reuchlin —the latter, it was plainly hinted, had been bought by Jewish gold. Reuchlin retorted in a counterblast (*Augenspiegel— Eye-glasses*). He disposed of Pfefferkorn as a liar, a knave, and a refugee from justice—a little affair of assault and robbery. Then he not only denied ever receiving a penny from the Jews, but accused his antagonists of staging the whole performance as a means of blackmailing the Jewish communities. As a last straw he defended his own friendly intercourse with Jews by reminding the world that, according to Church law, "a Christian must love a Jew as his fellow-man and neighbor."

Reuchlin's restatement of the *Augenspiegel* in German swept the Reich—ghetto traders bought it by the hundreds at the Frankfort Fair; and the original Latin text swept the rest of Europe. For the first time since no one could remember when, a man of repute—a scholar of continental fame, a judge and councilor of high rank—dared publish a friendly word for the Jews.

Reuchlin's peers among the elder Humanists shrank in cautious repugnance. Erasmus wrote Pirkheimer that Pfefferkorn was bound to triumph since he had stupidity and slander on his side. Pirkheimer sighed to think that Reuchlin was bestowing immortality on a scoundrel. Mutianus regretted that Reuchlin had carried a purely scholarly matter to the ears of the common people, and had thereby sullied the dignity of the Empire, the Church, and the Republic of Letters. As to the Dominicans, a contemporary (of whom we shall hear more) wrote, "Whenever anything displeases them, they wrinkle their brows, squint their eyes, stick their noses in the air, and scream 'To the fire with it, to the fire!' "

To the fire it was. Carefully feeling their way—Reuchlin after all was no ghetto-dog or a *relapso* of Spain—the Dominicans of Cologne let him know that unless he publicly explained the *Augenspiegel* to their satisfaction, they proposed to bring him to trial for heresy—the heresy consisting of the moral support and encouragement he gave the Jews and his defense of their literature, both implying a traitorous attitude toward the Church. Reuchlin was old and weary; his honors in this world and hopes for the next were dear to him; and, when all was said, he had given his heart to the "wondrous" Hebrew tongue and not to a parcel of Frankfort money-changers. He sparred for time. Through one of the Dominican brethren, who posed as his friend, the Order slowly pressed him into a corner. And there he threw down his glove.

"Let me whisper in your ear," he wrote the Dominican friend, "I am not without powerful backing. You may find the fight is easier to begin than to end. Can you picture the commotion in all ranks of society if I am forced to tell the whole story of this dirty business? And behind my mighty protectors stand poets and historians, a great band who honor me as their teacher—it is they who will brand your College with eternal shame and immortalize my innocence."

War was declared—the preliminary campaign of the Reformation. The "great band" of young Humanists—scholars, poets, university students—men quickened by fresh horizons, rallied to Reuchlin as the champion of the New Learning and to the defense of the Talmud of which they could not read a word. The liberal scholar and cardinal, Egidio of Viterbo, who had followed Reuchlin's example and procured himself a Hebrew teacher, expressed the mind of this "troop of Minerva" when he wrote its leader: "The Law was revealed in fire, and now you have snatched it again from the flames and rescued us from eternal darkness. In fighting for your cause we are defending not you but the Law, not the Talmud but the Church." On the other side, the clerics and scholastic pettifoggers, the sanctimonious and the timid, closed ranks behind Inquisitor Hochstraten, bent on damning Reuchlin, banishing the Jews, and burying Hebrew once and for all under an official curse.

Four years the battle raged from ecclesiastic tribunals and faculty conclaves to the imperial throne and the papal chair. The Emperor ordered the confiscation of the *Augenspiegel*, and Reuchlin wrote an apology for the pamphlet and himself. In summing up "the whole story" he minced no words. "Jackasses, swine, and quack-theologians of Cologne, who has given you the right to threaten me with the shepherd's staff? . . . Allow them, O my Emperor, to rifle the Jews and pocket the spoils, and they will leave me in peace." The church court of Mayence condemned Reuchlin, and the archbishop of Spires exonerated him and fined Hochstraten. The theological faculty of the University of Paris, followed by lesser faculties in Germany, upheld the Dominicans. Meanwhile, both parties appealed to the Pope (1513).

Leo X, the son of Lorenzo de' Medici, was a Humanist— "Everyone knows," he is quoted as saying, "how advantageously we and our kind have exploited the fable of Christ"— but, more than that, he was a cool and practical politician. Reuchlin, therefore, left no string unpulled. He enlisted the Pope's physician (Bonet de Lates—a Jew) and the amateurs of poetry and the arts among the princes of the church. He won back the Emperor. And he published a garland of commendatory letters from the leading scholars and notables of Europe, not omitting a bouquet in classic Hebrew.

But Hochstraten had the one argument that prevailed in Rome—money. Money bought delay. With the Dominican treasury behind him, Hochstraten had only to pay for postponement until Reuchlin's recommendations were forgotten and his slender purse exhausted; and victory was certain.

Reuchlin would be condemned, and the Dominican treasury reimbursed by looting the Jews.

But neither Dominican gold nor Reuchlin's scholarship nor Jewish pleas nor even papal justice had the last word. Instead, a classic piece of horse-play—the old bladder and snort of Aristophanes—blew the whole affair to the winds.

A coterie of wits, headed by the fiery young knight Ulrich von Hutten, decided that they too would compose a garland of letters. They fabricated and published the *Letters of Obscure Men* (1515 and 1517)—two volumes of gossip, queries, plaints, protests, and naive confessions purported to be written by rank-and-file Dominicans to their superiors in the College of Cologne. In a bombastic hog-Latin which murdered the grammar and committed criminal perversities upon the vocabulary of the classic tongue, the earnest monklets wrote up to Cologne everything dear to their hearts or weighing on their minds; and in every line wrote themselves down, along with their superiors, as greedy, lascivious, and pretentious blockheads.

Was it a mortal sin, they asked with poignant anxiety, to raise your hat to a Jew through mistaking him for a long-robed doctor of theology? Are baptized Jews, on the sounding of the Last Trump, resurrected *whole*? Squinting their eyes and sticking their noses in the air, they cried: "To the fire with Reuchlin and the Talmud! . . . even the housewives, when we go begging at their doors, won't give us so much as a piece of cheese." And how dares the world defame our beloved Dom Pfefferkorn! "He is a good and zealous Christian if ever there was one in Cologne. When he attends Mass and the priest raises the Host he never casts his eyes to the ground—as his slanderers claim—except, of course, to spit. To be sure, he spits very often—a touch of catarrh. As to his winning the favor of our burgomasters and ecclesiastical bigwigs through the pulchritude of his wife—nonsense! Our burgomasters have their own pretty mistresses. And our bigwigs of the Church do not care a straw about women—have you ever in your life heard of one who did? Moreover, Frau Pfefferkorn is as virtuous a woman as you will find in the city." And Master Main-Street (Hoch-straten), what of him? "He is in Rome paying court to the Apostolic Chair—successfully too—for he has the wherewithal to pay . . . besides, it is proved by Holy Scripture that no matter what a man says he can't lie when he pleads in behalf of the Catholic Faith. . . . Reuchlin, we are told, is running short of cash, and thus theology will triumph."

All Europe that had a smattering of Latin read the *Letters* and laughed. Thomas More noted the cream of the jest when he wrote: "Not in a hundred years will these imbeciles [the monks] fully tumble to the trick that's been played on them." Erasmus—the story goes—laughed so heartily he burst a boil on his neck and so cured himself without a doctor bill. Franz von Sickingen laughed and sharpened his sword. Martin Luther laughed and cleaned his pen. Not till Rabelais and Doctor Akakia were men to laugh like that again.

Dominican pressure for a general expulsion of the Jews reached its height in 1516, when a widely-attended conference of princes debated its feasibility; but, upon command of Maximilian, the project was dropped. The atmosphere, already laden with the sarcasms of Von Hutten, was hardly propitious. The first volume of the *Letters of Obscure Men* had of course been promptly suppressed. That, too, hardly mattered: the second volume soon appeared, more outrageous than the first—"How little you know Von Hutten!" boasted the young knight. In the course of time Reuchlin was vindicated by the papal council, and then condemned. But neither action created a stir. For in October 1517 Luther had caught the ear of Europe by hammering his theses to the door of the castle church in Wittenberg.

11

THE REFORMATION

THE Reformation—at least in its immediate occasions—had certain curious roots and shoots in Jewish soil. The scandalous exploitation of the otherwise legitimate sale of indulgences—which provoked Luther's initial assault—was in a measure due to the elimination of the Jews from the financial assets of Germany. Jews or no Jews, Rome still needed money—and more than ever now that St. Peter's was being rebuilt on a colossal scale of architecture and even more colossal scale of graft. So the Fuggers of Augsburg stepped into the shoes of the Jews; but, being Christian bankers on excellent social and political footing, not without first securing ample guarantees from powerful princes of the church. When the Fugger loans came due, they could not be liquidated, like Jewish loans, in a *Blutbad*. They had to be paid. Swallowing, therefore, any qualms of conscience, the Church and its princes permitted the unscrupulous traffic in sin—or, rather, in the wages of sin—and for their pains found themselves compelled to read and refute ninety-five points of theology. One point every German could and did grasp. "Since the pope is as rich as Croesus," it ran, "why doesn't he build St. Peter's with his own money, instead of taking the pennies of the poor?"

Then, again, Reuchlin's fight on behalf of Jewish literature and his consequent feud with the Dominicans smoothed the way for Luther. "Without your knowing it," he wrote Reuchlin in 1518, "you have served as an instrument of Divine Providence." At the outset the battle of the Humanists for Hebrew and of the Reformers against Rome led them to join forces. Upon the persuasion of Von Hutten, the quixotic Franz von Sickingen offered Reuchlin and Luther the protection of his castle—and incidentally settled the Hochstraten matter at the point of his sword.

The Hebrew language, brought into fashion by Reuchlin and brilliantly advertized by the struggle over the Talmud, opened many doors to the Reformers in their search for biblical truth. The Latin version was checked against its Hebrew original and, in many points, was discovered wanting, garbled, or contradicted. The medieval Jewish commentators, Rashi, Ibn Ezra, and Kimhi, were utilized in making the vernacular translations of the Old Testament which—not only in Luther's Germany, but in England, France, and Poland—served as a powerful weapon for the Reformation. Chairs in Hebrew—the dream of Reuchlin—became a reality in both Protestant and Catholic universities. The "Hebrew word" gushed from the presses of Italy, France, and Germany—even the Talmud, under the handsome patronage of Leo X.

In returning, moreover, to the Christianity of the Gospels, the Reformers exposed themselves—much as the early Christians were exposed—to the living tradition of Judaism. Discarding the pagan and medieval elements in Catholic ritual and art, the Protestant churches physically and spiritually took on something of the air of a synagogue. The very names of the worshipers who sat in their pews tell the story. Enamored of the classics, the Humanists had translated their names into Latin or Greek: Rudolph Bauer, the Petrarch of Germany, had become Agricola; Reuchlin called himself Capnio, which in Greek came about as close to "smoke" as *Reuch* in German; and his young relative Schwartzerd—Black Earth—is known to history as Melanchthon. Under the spell of old Hebrew the next generation began, in the phrase of Montaigne, "to populate the world with Methuselahs, Ezekiels, and Malachis, names which smell more of the faith." The adoption of Old Testament names, which quickly became a fad and then a custom, meant the adoption of what passed for Old Testament ideas—in religion, in morality, and, as the Pilgrim Fathers may remind us, in politics.

Early in his career against the Church Luther took up cudgels for the Jews. "Absurd theologians," he wrote in 1519, "defend Jew-hatred by claiming that the race are thralls of Christendom and the Emperor. . . . What Jew would consent to enter our ranks when he sees the cruelty and enmity we wreck upon them—that, in our behavior toward them, we less resemble Christians than beasts!"

In 1523 he published a pamphlet the title of which—"Jesus Was Born A Jew"—was calculated to set theologian teeth on edge. "Our fools and jackasses, these priests, bishops, sophists, and monks," he wrote, "have treated the Jews in such a fashion that if a man wanted to be a true Christian he might better become a Jew"—a phrase which plays a variant on the popular witticism of Erasmus, "If it is the mark of a good Christian to hate the Jews, what excellent Christians all of us are!"

"Were I a Jew," Luther continued, "and saw what blockheads and wind-bags rule and guide Christendom, I would rather become a sow than a Christian. For they have treated the Jews more like dogs than men. Yet the Jews are kith and kin and brothers-in-blood of our Savior. If we are going to boast about the virtues of race, Christ belongs more to them than to us. To no other people has God shown such favor, in entrusting them with his Holy Word."

His conclusions echo the humane sentiments of Reuchlin. "My advice, therefore, is to deal decently with this people. So long as we resort to violence and lies and slanders—saying that they need Christian blood to keep from stinking, and heaven knows what other idiotic rubbish—and so long as we forbid them to work and trade and mingle at our side, thereby forcing them into usury, how can we expect to win them or better them? If we wish to help them, we must employ not papist law but Christian love—we must give them a friendly hand, letting them work and thrive in our midst, in order that they may have reason and occasion to become of us and with us."

Luther, however, had more in mind than Reuchlin's humanity or Erasmus' irony. He used the Synagogue as a stick to beat the Church. By defending the Jews he annoyed the Catholics; and crying up Jewish wrongs gave him a chance—which he never neglected—to cry down the priests. Two centuries later Voltaire employed the same technique, though he turned it inside-out; throwing stones at the Jews he hit the Christians, and mocking the Old Testament he undermined the New.

Furthermore, Luther entertained high hopes of converting the Jews. By stripping Christianity of its centuries of Catholic accretions he felt he was making it attractive and acceptable to the members of the Old Faith. Unfortunately for both parties, while he thought he was bringing the Jews nearer to the church, they thought he was approaching the synagogue. A few Jews even waited on Luther to persuade him to take the final step. It must have been an interview memorable for its misunderstandings.

But as the Protestant movement matured, Luther's attitude changed. He grew embittered to discover that the Jews were as deaf to Martin of Eisleben as they had been to Paul of Tarsus. He became alarmed to find among the sects which sprouted like mushrooms in the fertile soil of Protestant revolt a dangerous tendency to revert to Jewish type; to deny the Trinity, to look upon Jesus as a prophet rather than a deity, to observe the seventh day as the Sabbath, and to take the Old Testament with a literalness embarrassing to the New—in short, to go "Jewish" as the Humanists had gone "ancient." His reactions to the Anabaptists and their sub-sects differed little from the Catholic reaction to the Judaizing heretics of the thirteenth century: the integrity of the Protestant movement must be preserved at any cost, and let the Jews pay.

His experience with the peasants likewise taught him to moderate his sympathies. The ground-swell of the Reformation—already in motion, as we saw, at the time of the Black Death—was the discontent born of the oppression of the urban and rural masses. In the turmoil of the religious revolution which Luther set on foot, a body of princes, headed by the Elector of Saxony, proposed to exploit this popular discontent in order to seize what they could of Church power and property. A Franz von Sickingen proposed to use these means to pillage the Church with the romantic aim of reviving knighthood. Von Hutten, who died before he had time to compromise himself, as romantically hoped to channel the same discontent into a force that would free Germany from Rome and create a reborn united Reich. Altogether, the overlords proposed, for various ends, to employ the masses in a spoliation of the Church much as they and the Church together had, a century before, employed the masses against the Jews.

At this stage Luther, no doubt as unconscious of social forces as the princes and knights, gave voice and comfort to the woes of the poor. "With a hundred gulden," he exclaimed, "anyone can gobble up a peasant a year." He turned his magnificent gift for vituperation upon the feudal lords and denounced them as hangmen whose only trade was to swindle the poor—"such fellows were formerly called scoundrels, but now we must call them Christian and revered princes," whereas "they are generally either the biggest fools or worst rogues on earth."

But the peasants, meanwhile, were inflamed with Anabaptist socialism taken direct from the Old Testament and Gospels, without any toning down by rabbinical or church commentators. Had not God Himself said, "The land is Mine . . . and shall not be sold in perpetuity"? If the land belongs to God, obviously it cannot belong to the landlords. They heard, too, about the Year of Jubilee and the freeing of serfs and the redemption of all that are bound. And encouraged by Luther's language, which must have heartened them as his words on Jesus heartened the Jews, the peasants and town workers resolved to use their discontent not to further the aims of princes, knights, or patriots, but for their own benefit—which is against all the rules that govern society. They rose in bloody revolt (1525). Throughout the South German countryside, castles and their lords and ladies perished in flame. In the towns—where the revolt culminated in the seizure of Münster (1535) and the cry of John Bockelson, "The King of Zion cometh!"—patricians and burghers fell before the popular wrath.

Luther immediately proved that he was conscious enough of social forces to know on which side the bread of his religious reforms was buttered. He attacked the peasants as vehemently as he had hitherto defended them, and incited the nobility to pitiless revenge. "Show no mercy on the poor," he advised, "stab, smite, throttle, who can!" One hundred thousand peasants, it is reckoned, were thereupon smitten and stabbed. After this blood-letting, the Lutheran movement became a Reformation for the overlords and not for the people, who, as the Peace of Augsburg frankly revealed, were now the religious pawns of the princes as they had previously been of the bishops. In his about-face Luther, although the son of a peasant, showed himself to be primarily a conscientious theologian who set his dogmas above any worldly consideration—fighting the great Catholic hierarchy when these dogmas were enunciated and allying himself with the feudal hierarchy when they were endangered. The peasants never understood this. They simply called him "Doctor Liar."

The Jews, too, were slow in understanding him. When the Elector of Saxony proposed, in 1537, to expel them from his domains, Josel of Rosheim—the "advocate of Jewry"—sought Luther's intervention. Luther refused to see him. "I once had the intention," he wrote Josel, "of aiding your people; but they have so misused my services and behaved in such an intolerable manner, I have lost all desire to help them. They must be made to realize they cannot use my goodwill to fortify themselves in their errors and make themselves worse than they are."

How bad he thought they were began to appear, the next year, in his attack on a sect of Sabbath-observing Anabaptists. And it was not long before he had completely reverted to the tradition of orthodox theologians. Nothing written in the Middle Ages surpassed in calumny, hatred, and violence his last pamphlets on the Jews—*Concerning the Jews and Their Lies* and *On the Shem Hamphoras*, both published in 1543. Credulous as the stupidest monks he had once derided, he repeated and endorsed the "idiotic rubbish" of ritual murder, well-poisoning, and black magic. Jewish usurers sucked the blood and Jewish physicians poisoned the bodies of the German people. "How dare the Jews complain of their bitter captivity among us . . . for three hundred years now they have persecuted and martyred us Christians, and even today we do not altogether know what deviltry they have brought into our land."

The measures he proposed against this damned race, who are nothing but "a burden, a plague, and an evil," made the Dominican watch-dogs look like lambs. Synagogues, he urged, must be burned, all Hebrew books—even prayer books and Bibles—destroyed, the ghettos razed and their inhabitants compelled to dwell like gypsies in the fields, Jewish commerce—especially the poisonous occupation of Jewish physicians—uprooted, all work denied them except forced labor of the most degrading type. "I would threaten to tear their tongues from their throats if they do not accept the Christian proof that God is three and not one." If all this did not attune their ears to the glad-tidings of the Gospels, they were to be hounded "like wild-beasts" from the land.

"Never before," complained Josel to the Catholic magistrates of Strasbourg, "has a *Gelehrter*, a scholar, advocated such tyrannical and outrageous treatment of our poor people." The peasants mistook Luther for a social reformer; Josel mistook him for a scholar. But again he proved himself to be a conscientious theologian, sacrificing his humanity to his dogmas and giving of his last strength—he died in 1546—to uphold Erasmus' bitter definition of an "excellent Christian."

ii

The Jews soon learned that nothing in the theory of Protestantism tended to lighten their lot. A renewed acquaintance with St. Paul, while it brought closer contacts with the Jewish tradition, only reëmphasized the Pauline antagonism to the Jews. That every man was now theoretically free to judge the Scriptures for himself and that the Scriptures were in many men's hands could not help the Jews so long as the Protestants believed, which as Christians they were obliged to do, that the New Testament had supplanted the Old. For that matter Protestants were quick to exploit their knowledge of the Old Testament itself against the Jews. Clever theologians in Hessia, for example, quoted Israel's intolerance of idolatry (Deut. 13.17) to justify a proposed expulsion of Israel's descendants. If anything, the Lutheran doctrine of salvation through faith strengthened the conviction that the "faithless" Jews were damned; and their damnation was even less likely to arouse pity if, as the Calvinists believed, God had prearranged it.

In practice the Protestants had merely substituted the Scriptures for the Church as an absolute authority, transferred their uncritical allegiance from priests to pastors, and abandoned images and saints for a no less superstitious worship of the biblical word. New dogmas, canons, synods, and hierarchies supplanted the old; and the minds of men remained as bound and blinded as before.

In both theory and practice the Protestants showed as little love or understanding of tolerance as the Catholics. The rare Reformer such as Zwingli, who believed that righteous men of all creeds will enter the "assembly of the saints," left a precious heritage to humanity, but in this respect little or no influence on his contemporaries. Sebastian Castalio (1515-63), who had sense enough to find predestination absurd and heart enough to proclaim the doctrine of religious tolerance for probably the first time in Christendom, was hounded to starvation and death by the Calvinists. Altogether, the Protestant record of persecution is as black, even if it is not as long, as the Catholic.

Nevertheless, in the course of time Protestantism indirectly proved a blessing to the Jews and other minorities. Once the Protestants won princes and states to their cause, the rage for persecution common to both camps provoked such universal and prolonged warfare—forty years on French and then thirty years on German soil—that little energy was left for molesting obscure groups like the Jews. Moreover, the wars turned out to be so devastating and—what was worse—indecisive that sheer weariness and anemia induced the world to listen to the voice of reason, charity, and good-will. Men were compelled to admit that in order to live themselves, others might be pardoned for presuming to do likewise.

Then, too, the growth and persistence of minor sects in the Protestant lands gradually accustomed the populace, the authorities, and even the theologians, to the presence of men and women who held heterodox ideas about God. Experience showed these ideas to be harmless to society, or at least less harmful than continual warfare. And out of this experience sprang the germs of religious indifference, germs of doubt and perplexity, which corroded the already battered and futile sword of would-be crusaders. God still undoubtedly willed the extermination of the unbeliever, but God could wait. Finally, indifference toward religious differences was fostered by the spread of popular education, already marked before the Protestant revolt and now further encouraged by Protestant theory and endeavor. To be a Protestant, a man had to read the Scriptures. But having learned to read, it was impossible to keep him within the covers of one book. And with reading and writing more prevalent than ever before in Christian lands, and with whole new worlds to study and appropriate, the very schools Protestantism used as a bulwark of the faith enabled its pupils to abandon theology for larger and freer fields.

The drift toward tolerance, however, was as slow as the advance of a glacier, and the work—as we shall see—of many forces besides Protestantism. Up till the respite afforded them by the Thirty Years War, the Jews continued their medieval experience, the butt and pawn of a travailing world which played with their lives and fortunes without affecting their destiny. Whatever strength they could muster was devoted to struggling for immediate rights and privileges. Right instead of rights and equality instead of privilege were still undreamed of; and the occasional grant of these rights threw into only greater relief the perpetuation of their wrongs.

iii

These struggles can best be observed in following the career of Josel of Rosheim whose activities touched on most facets of sixteenth-century Jewry, its high-lights and shadows.

In one sense Josel was the product of a new spirit. He stands out as the first German Jew, certainly the first layman, whom we can clothe with flesh and personality. It may be a stroke of luck that his memoirs have survived, thus enabling us to see a man behind a name. But it was likely no accident that he was impelled to write—however sketchily—this autobiographical account. The Renaissance and the Reformation with their accent on the individual were knocking at the ghetto gates.

Josel neglects to tell us where and when he was born—apparently Alsace about 1478—feeling no doubt that he has more exciting details to relate. His family originally lived in Endigen across the Swiss border; and eight years before he was born, a charge of ritual murder was brought against its Jewry. "The enemy," he writes, "tortured my father's three uncles until they were forced to confess falsely concerning the bastard [Christian corpse] found in the unclean vineyard [church]; and they were burned for the sanctification of the Holy Name. My father saved himself with great difficulty and God's help."

The lucky man found refuge in Obernai. But in 1477 misfortune again overtook him. Charles the Bald was fighting for the possession of Lorraine, and Swiss mercenaries wrought the usual havoc. "My father told me that he and his mother, together with their friends and children, had to abandon Obernai. They took shelter in the castles of Barr and Lützelstein," and hiding in cellars and caves beneath the vine-clad slopes of Ste-Odile, "they suffered hunger and thirst for a whole year."

Eventually the family settled in Mittelbergheim just south of Barr. When Josel was a lad of five or six, his father died. "I stayed in Hagenau with my pious uncle, Reb Elia, who afterwards left for the holy city of Jerusalem and wanted to take me with him."

Josel, however, returned to the profane town of Mittelbergheim. He received a good education, Jewish fashion; and then took up money-lending as a livelihood. This did not prevent him—likewise a Jewish fashion—from pursuing his studies; for, later in life, we find him writing apologetics and, significant of his era, admonitions against traitors, excursions into Cabala, and pious rules for enduring martyrdom.

At the age of twenty-five his business was prosperous enough to incur disaster. "In the years 1503-05," he relates, "many nations fought under our Emperor Maximilian against the Duke of Heidelberg until they overthrew him by reducing numerous towns and castles . . . and I had nothing left but a handful of pawns and such few debts as were owing me by honorable debtors. I also managed to save 101 gulden from the teeth of the spoilers."

He contrived to repair his fortune, extending his operations to Strasbourg. A document of 1512 tells us that "Josel, Jew of Mittelbergheim," was fined by the City Council because he and his wife entered Strasbourg "on many occasions without permission or without paying the body-guard tax." Permis-

sion, of course, was something a Jew should have bought;
and the body-guard tax was a sum exacted from Jewish travelers—and all traders had to travel—for an armed escort they
seldom or never received.

Ten years later his schooling in sixteenth-century life was
resumed. Eight Jews of Mittelbergheim, including Josel, were
accused of desecrating a wafer of the Host. "They thrust us
into two prisons in Obernai; and twice seven weeks passed
over our heads before our innocence came to light." After
that Josel removed to Rosheim.

Meanwhile his public career was well under way. Of the
year 1510 he writes, "I was elected and designated chief and
leader [*parnas* and *manhig*] of the Jews of Hagenau and
other places" in Lower Alsace. His services won him ever
wider recognition and more imposing titles: Chief Rabbi of
Bohemia and Germany, Leader—Commander—Governor—
of All Jewry of the Empire. These titles were neither official
nor permanent, yet they were not mere compliments. The
Jews needed a leader and advocate; Josel led and pled in
their behalf—and if a name helped, they gladly let him take
it. Charles V, it is true, demurred; as emperor he had grounds
for considering himself the "governor" of German Jewry.
But Josel gave him to understand that "governor" on Jewish
lips was used in the Hebraic sense which, it appeared, resembled the Pickwickian.

As *shtadlan*—advocate, intercessor, spokesman—Josel filled
a rôle almost as old as Jewish history. A weak and small people usually living at the mercy of powerful neighbors or masters, Israel has time and again employed the aid and thereupon submitted to the moral leadership of its rare sons who
have enjoyed high favor or position among the Gentiles.

The line of *shtadlanim* includes such august figures as Joseph, Moses, Mordecai, Nehemiah, and Philo. In the Middle Ages these advocates were generally the treasurers, ministers, or physicians of kings and princes. Of the entire line Josel is probably the first to wield influence without the help of rank, office, or kin. By sheer force of character, energy, and wit he became, for the rulers of the Reich, its "representative" Jew. Advocates were to come and go in pomp during the next century, but as a man who made character do the work of "pull," his like will not be met till the days of Moses Montefiore.

Josel's task was manifold. For one thing, he strove to maintain order, discretion, and harmony among his own people and—in view of their dwindling numbers and the overwhelming competition of the Fuggers and other great German bankers—to regulate Jewish business practices. In 1530, while the Protestants and Catholics were trying to compose their religious differences at the Diet of Augsburg, Josel persuaded the leaders of Jewry to agree upon a financial code which limited interest rates, forbade obnoxious loans, and curbed aggressive methods of collecting debts—a code which took no few journeys and parleys to enforce.

Two years later, at the Diet of Regensburg, Josel met Solomon Molcho, the Portuguese who "had the strange notion of leading Jewry in battle against the Turks." Molcho came hoping to win the Emperor's support; Josel knew that such political adventuring, drenched as it was with Messianic dreams, could only harm the Jews. "When I grasped his plan, I warned him by letter of its dangers and took care to leave Regensburg so the Emperor could not say I had a hand in it. As soon as Solomon reached the Emperor, he was laden with chains, taken to Bologna, and burned . . . his soul reposes in Paradise."

Or again—as one case among many—in 1534 Josel was in Bohemia settling a dispute between the communities of Prague and Horowitz. "A man named Sheftel tried to have me murdered" . . . and twice Josel was compelled to flee to the fortress of Prague. Keeping peace in Israel was no child's play.

But it eased Josel's main task, which was to secure protection, redress, and justice from the Christian authorities. "For we too," he once wrote, "are human beings created by God to dwell on this earth and live and deal with our fellowmen."

He began this work while still in his twenties and close to home. Thanks to his flair for negotiation, friends or neighboring communities received permits to trade or live in a profitable town and were sometimes even repaid for damages inflicted on them. In 1525 he used diplomacy and cash to save not only the Jewish but the Christian populace in and around Rosheim from the ravages of the peasant revolt. "Josel," applauded the city councilors, "you and your children will reap the reward of your services." Years later, however, when a mob of Rosheim citizens attacked his house, the councilors did not raise a finger.

In 1530 Josel bagged bigger game. "With God's help I secured from the Emperor Charles a renewal of the privileges of Sigismund." Twice later he procured further renewal of these privileges for all German Jewry. Thrice he negotiated with King Ferdinand, brother of Charles, on behalf of the Bohemian Jews. At the Diet of 1541 he managed to block a decree which would have excluded Jews from the money-lending trade—almost their only source of livelihood. Indeed, three years later at the Diet of Spires, he elicited for them a general privilege to charge higher interest rates than the Christians as an indemnity for paying higher taxes, and—not dissociated from these taxes—induced the Emperor to denounce the calumny of ritual murder. When the Schmalkaldic War broke upon Germany (1546), Josel obtained an imperial order to the army and a mandate to the people designed to spare the Jews from the consequences of a religious quarrel to which they were no party.

With it all he was continuously engaged in redressing individual wrongs and grievances—extortions, expulsions, ransoms, imprisonments, and tortures—that kept him on the highways from Brabant to the Polish border. One case must have struck home with reminiscent force. Five Jews in Würzburg—a man, three women, and a girl—were imprisoned on the charge of ritual murder; the girl had been tortured for thirty-two weeks. Josel won their release, but "it took more than a month and much money."

Josel, it must be surmised, did not gain his ends by charm, miracle, or hypnotism. He often played power against power —local debts against imperial privileges or the Protestant revolt against Charles' need for peace behind the Catholic ranks. Through Jewish informants he once saved Charles' life. But he usually paid cash. The renewal of the general privileges in 1544 was bought by Jewish contributions to the war against France: Josel collected some 5,000 gulden for the Imperial army-chest. In return for the protection during the Schmalkaldic War, the Jews obligated themselves to provision the Imperial forces.

Finally, the task of winning both discipline and rights demanded an unrelenting campaign of defense—vindicating the name of Israel against lies and insults, turning out pamphlets, briefs, and books, pleading in private and debating in public, playing lawyer, politician, journalist, lobbyist, theologian, and moralist all in one person. At the same Diet of Augsburg where he won the first renewal of the general privileges, Josel defended the Jews before the Reichstag and Imperial Court against the charge of having instigated the whole Lutheran movement. As the Turks advanced into Europe, Josel was impelled to write a book proving that the Jews had not instigated the Turks—a book sent personally to Charles and Ferdinand and which, says Josel, "found favor in their eyes." Later, after vainly seeking Luther's aid, he pled before the Elector of Saxony to avert the expulsion of the Jews from that realm because they were presumably the instigators of all Christian troubles. When Hessia proposed a similar expulsion (1537) and Protestant theologians backed the proposal by quoting the Old Testament, Josel out-quoted them at the Diet of Frankfort and convinced not only the Hessians, but the princes of Saxony and Brandenburg, that the measure was both unbiblical and impolitic.

The effort to keep pace with the stream of anti-Jewish pamphlets born of the general religious ferment and the low cost of printing meant the ceaseless use of his tongue and pen. Margarita, the apostate upon whom the mantle of Pfefferkorn had fallen; Butzer, the Hessian theologian; the redoubtable Luther—each were taken on in turn. Luther's refusal to grant him a hearing earned a pointed rebuke. "A Jew," wrote Josel, "deserves an answer, no matter who he is"; and he referred the translator of the Bible to Abraham's interview with God in behalf even of Sodom. As to Luther's pamphlets—again playing sect against sect—he managed to prevent their publication or circulation in Catholic Alsace.

Yet Josel's work unlike his name was writ in water. He died in 1554. Not long before, Bavaria and Württemberg had expelled their Jews. The year after his death, while the Christians celebrated the religious peace of Augsburg, the Jews were driven from the Palatinate. Two decades later (1573) Brandenburg meted them similar treatment, seizing as a favorable moment the execution of Lippold, a Jewish mintmaster, in Berlin. When David Gans of Prague published his Jewish history in 1592—a landmark in the revival of Hebrew letters—he could have recorded little of Germany. Its communities had shrunk to insignificance in number, wealth, and culture.

In their few ghettos and village lanes the German Jews, lost to the rich and growing age—the age of Merchant Adventurers, of Montaigne, Bacon, and Shakespeare—continued no doubt to whisper the words of Josel and Shylock: "We too are human beings." But it was to take revolutions and catastrophes for the world to believe them.

12

GRAND DUKES IN JEWRY

IN ONE and the same year—1612—a mob began rioting against the ghetto of Frankfort, and the authorities of Hamburg recognized the settlement of a handful of Portuguese Jews in their hitherto exclusively Christian city.

The two events are not unrelated. Though in themselves trivial—except to the parties concerned—they throw vivid light on a revolution which had the lion's share in creating the modern world and thereby altering the lot of Jewry. Like two scales of a balance they signified the sinking fortunes of inland Germany together with its medieval economy, and the concomitant rise of sea-ports and a new way of doing business.

For more than a century European business had been pushing through its medieval walls—a veritable ghetto of fixed prices, forbidden usury, poor highways, stifling traditional methods of production, small capital, high local tariffs, and a line of customers limited chiefly to extravagant bishops and princes.

The search for new sources of wealth led to opening sea-routes to India and the discovery of America. The new wealth streaming back to Europe created new spending-power in new pockets. This, in turn, led to further wealth-producing inventions in machinery and methods of work as a response to the increased means of buying goods.

For the first time on a large scale, men with money on hand could lend it to borrowers who did not merely spend it on unproductive luxuries but who could invest it in enterprises that would make more goods—more power—more money, that would in short make a profit for both themselves and their creditors. Wealth was no longer to be gained solely by taking it from someone else—taking his land, his purse, or his person. Wealth was now to be made out of wealth itself by taking it from the silver mines of Tyrol and Potosi, the spice-fields of India, and the mulberry-trees of China, and with it setting to work new resources of European land, mines, water-falls, wind-mills, and new methods of labor.

The masters of this new wealth-breeding wealth—the financiers—had few theories, dogmas, or ideals. They did not orate, write books, or tack up theses on church doors. But they dissolved the Middle Ages. From their magic cornucopia rolled a flood of new comforts and new ambitions which gradually drowned out the pettifogging rules of guilds and canon law and turned a backward tongue of land—a straggly outcropping of Asia—into the mistress of the world. From it, too, rolled a morality which gradually but surely extinguished the old medieval habits, prejudices, and values.

It was nothing new, this business morality. Despite Christianity it had operated back stage throughout the Middle Ages, as the experience of the Jew has shown. The novelty lay in its growing predominance. By the seventeenth century the Catholics had quietly forgotten that money-lending was a crime; and, when practiced by God-fearing gentlemen under the right circumstances, the Protestants began to praise it as the eighth virtue—the virtue of Thrift.

Slowly, but likewise inevitably, the rewards of thrift—that is, of business—made it profitable not to look a gift-horse in the mouth. Long before our department-stores took up the slogan, Europe discovered that the customer is always right: his heart might be heretic, but his purse was orthodox. Travel and travelers' tales, merchant adventuring and the morals of their adventures, likewise helped to break the crust of provincial smugness and dogmatism. Tolerance was born not in a cottage in Rijnsburg or an inkwell of Bayle, but a hundred years before on the bourse of Antwerp and the docks of Amsterdam.

However, unlike the tolerance preached by Spinoza, Bayle, and Voltaire, business tolerance was a fair-weather virtue. When times were good or promising, even competitors were acceptable and orthodox, for they added to the breadth and profits of the market. But when times were bad, woe unto the competitor, workman, and consumer who could be damned as a foreigner or unbeliever! No less than in the Middle Ages they stood at the mercy of bookkeeping. When the ledgers showed red, the outlook for minorities was black.

In the early sixteenth century the Fuggers and their compeers had been the German masters of this new business. In Augsburg and Nuremberg, commanding the highways between the North Sea and the Mediterranean, they had created vast monopolies of mining, banking, and commerce. The money for their banks came from their mines and it was multiplied in their commerce—a web which stretched from Peru to India. Their affluence and power, combined with a genius for monopoly, had swept away all but vestiges of the old Jewish money-trade. Bankruptcy no less than persecution sent its hundreds of Jewish victims to seek fresh opportunities in Bohemia, Moravia, and Poland.

Then, in the last half of the century, the new methods of business which they had themselves promoted did for the Fuggers and Welsers too. Because of its very growth and consequent dependence on sea-traffic, business had shifted its centers to northern and southern ports—above all, to Antwerp, London, Lisbon, and Venice. Augsburg, Nuremberg, and their like were left high and dry. Moreover, the very increase of wealth gave states and monarchs bigger and better ways of destroying men, labor, and money on pleasure-ground and battle-field—ways they were quick to use. The result for inland Germany is familiar—a depression, which beginning in 1575 ruined most of Fuggers' rivals and led to the eventual collapse of the Fuggers as well.

The Catholic city of Frankfort early tried to stem the tide by opening its gates to French Protestant refugees who brought with them capital and manufacturing skill. When this hospitable move proved of no avail, the French bankers and weavers were discovered to be heretics and foreigners, and harassed from the town. And when the depression nevertheless persisted, the Jews were slated as the next victims.

Partly owing to the flicker of prosperity illumined by the Protestants, the Frankfort ghetto had attracted the largest Jewish population in Germany—nearly three thousand inhabitants—giving it a moral leadership not to be disputed till the eve of the nineteenth century. Trouble broke out in 1612, a miniature social revolution engineered by Vincent Fettmilch, a disappointed lawyer and practicing pastry-cook. The usual medieval calumnies were trotted across the boards; and they culminated in a general sack of the ghetto in 1614. Similar outbreaks occurred in Worms. In both cases the ringleaders were severely punished and the Jewries rewarded with new charters on onerous, but for the Jews customary, terms. Significant of a new spirit, not a life was lost. And a certain uneasy conscience was revealed by the quantity of topical poetry, broadsides, satires, and other literature turned out to justify what a century before would have been the merest police incidents.

Meanwhile Protestant Hamburg—on the upswinging scale of German economy—cherished hopes of rivaling Antwerp or at least Amsterdam. At about the turn of the century a few Portuguese Jews—more accurately, Crypto-Jews or Marranos—who shared these hopes slipped into the German port under the color of Christians, as they had previously slipped into Amsterdam. Their trade connections with Lisbon and the Indies as well as their capital—and the further capital they could tap among the friends they left behind in persecution-ridden Portugal—made them welcome. But undeniably they were Jews, the first to set foot in proud Hanseatic Hamburg.

The city Senate went into anxious consultation with the theological faculties of Jena and Frankfort-on-the-Oder. The new morality locked horns with the old: if—it argued—Amsterdam can tolerate a new synagogue and the dikes still hold, a few Jews along the Dreckwall will likely do no harm. So the Senate solved its moral perplexities by drawing up elaborate rules for the public behavior and private worship of the newcomers, and a few years later (1619) even permitted them to subscribe money to the founding of the Hamburg Bank.

The Portuguese were soon followed by German Jews, who settled first in the adjoining city of Altona (at that time under Danish rule) and then in Hamburg itself. Although the pastors recurrently complained and the populace rioted, the Senate had no reason to regret its decision. In the course of the century the Jews helped build up trade with Sweden, Poland, the Barbary States, and the Indies and set Hamburg on its way to becoming one of the chief ports of the world.

ii

Meanwhile the Thirty Years War (1618-48) brought German history to an almost fatal pause and painfully illustrated the profound change that was overtaking European economy. It was the most destructive war the continent had known, if only because in former protracted struggles—the Hundred Years War and the religious wars of sixteenth-century France—weapons, technique, and resources were incapable of the havoc now loosed upon Germany.

Towns and villages disappeared by the score. In some regions the population was reduced to one-half, one-third—or less. Augsburg, pride of the Fuggers, sank from eighty to sixteen thousand inhabitants; the state of Württemberg from about a half-million to hardly fifty thousand. Whole countrysides lay deserted of men and barren of crops. Starvation and pestilence made off with such poor devils as the soldiers and freebooters overlooked.

The Jews naturally suffered together with the Christians, though without the consolation of believing they had a principle at stake. They groaned beneath their share and more of taxes, levies, and forced loans. It scarcely repaid them to know that in some cities—Frankfort and Prague as examples—they were permitted to share in the defense of wall and gate. Or that occasional Jewish soldiers were heard of—a Colonel Eremita for one—who behaved no worse than the Christians.

Yet Jewry reaped certain advantages. The Protestants and Catholics were too busy destroying themselves to give any religious thought to the Jews, who for a whole generation could therefore suffer hardship without persecution—perhaps the only generation since the First Crusade. On the contrary, the need for funds and war-supplies often led the authorities in Catholic cities and states—where the Jews largely dwelt— to encourage Jewish finance and trade, protect the ghettos from pillage (as in Prague), and lift the old medieval restrictions from the shoulders of some of the wealthier class. Moreover, a matter of pure luck, the ravages of war fell less heavily on the few cities where they lived in numbers: Frankfort, Worms, Bamberg, and Fürth. Finally, when the last stages of the war inevitably led to a commercial debauch— "corners" in commodities, profiteering, depreciation of currency—the Jew, thanks to his exclusion from the peasantry, the workers, and the professional classes who as usual in these circumstances paid the ultimate bill, managed to salvage a little more than the average Christian.

Peace found the country close to literal ruin. The terms of the treaty admitted Calvinism to the list of recognized faiths, but did nothing to advance the general idea of tolerance. Politically, the power of the Empire was as good as banished in the three-hundred-odd states of Germany. Each state now enjoyed the right to make its own war and peace. Each— except the Free Cities—turned itself into a midget replica of the absolute monarchism popularized by France, each becoming an absolute sovereignty ruled by a prince, duke, or elector instead of a full-sized king. Each was soon recruiting that post-war novelty, a standing-army and, a little later, in imitation of Louis XIV, conducting a baby Versailles. And most of these German Versailles were soon displaying, among their indispensable equipment, a court Jew.

Commercial ruin, absolute monarchism, palace pomp, standing-armies: together they produced those picturesque figures, the court Jews, who dominated our scene until Napoleon crushed the monarchlets and the Rothschilds introduced a new scale of banking.

Literally a court Jew—a *Hof-Jude*—was a Jew (or Jewess) taken under the direct protection of a princely court and freed from the medieval chains burdening his race. He was free to trade, travel, and live as he pleased, and dress—without Jew-badge or other outward sign—as his tailor pleased. His immediate family, his domestics and private employes—his *Gesinde*—shared his privileges. Actually a *Hof-Jude* was a sort of functionary attached to the court. Just as every court possessed a court brewer (*Hofbrauer*), a court janitor (chamberlain), a court preacher, and a court jester, so it possessed a court Jew.

His function—whence his privileges—was to furnish loans to the rulers, direction to their finances, and supplies to their new standing-armies. Often, too, he was purveyor to their highnesses for jewelry, *objets d'art,* and similar necessities of Versailles life. He was able to fulfill his function because in the slow recovery following the thirty years of ruination he had a running start over his Christian competitors, due either to the capital he had saved from the wreckage, to his wider business connections, or to his superior moral stamina. Undoubtedly, too, he was willing to work at a lower rate of profit, content with less because of the privileges he acquired and which cost nothing for his master to grant.

Jews with somewhat similar functions, such as the financial directors of thirteenth-century Trèves, and with something of the same privileges, such as Josel of Rosheim procured for himself and his family, cropped up like "sports" throughout the Middle Ages. But the first to be called court Jews and to turn their calling into a recognized profession appeared in Vienna and Prague when the Thirty Years War was making its huge demands for money and supplies. With their dependents they created a substantial community in Vienna; and while the Spanish Hapsburgs were burning the secret Jews of Spain and Portugal, the Austrian Hapsburgs permitted a synagogue to open its doors in the imperial capital.

One court Jew of Prague provided the emperor so much to spend and the army so much to eat that he was granted a title of nobility (1622). Born Jacob ben Samuel, he died Bassevi von Treuenburg, his crest with its lion and eight stars on his tomb—while Berthold of Regensburg, Martin of Eisleben, and battalions of crusaders turned in their graves. But it was only natural that the new order of economy should produce a new order of knights.

Indeed, as the new aristocracy ripened in the succeeding centuries, the Jews who were elevated to its ranks made up a Round Table which Heine alone could have properly sung: Don Manuele de Belmonte, diplomat and poet and, in 1693, a count of the Palatinate; Freiherr von Sonnenfels, i.e. Lipmann Perlin, court Jew to the house of Dietrichstein, then baptized and knighted in 1746, and at last rising to be a professor of Semitics at the University of Vienna; Sir Hönig von Hönigsberg—Honey of Honeymount—and Baron d'Aguilar, both court tobacconists in eighteenth-century Prague and Vienna; the "chevalier" Simon de Geldern who, if he wasn't a chevalier, was indubitably a sheik of a bedouin tribe and the grand-uncle of Heine; Baron Jacob von Hirsch who rose from talmud *bahur* to court banker at Munich— along with Baron von Eichthal—during the Napoleonic Wars; Freiherr (and later Baron) Bernard von Eskeles whose tourney-field, or *salon*, rivaled that of his brother-in-law, Baron von Arnstein, when the intellectual knights of Europe flocked to the Congress of Vienna; they and the dozens more that could be culled from the heraldic annals of Germany and Austria all bore the same device—however they worded it—as the French-Jewish banker and minister of state, Achille Fould: *"Aide toi, Dieu t'aidera*—God helps those who help themselves."

iii

In Germany proper the court Jews—who were as likely to end in disgrace as in the peerage—did not emerge in force till the late seventeenth century. A generation was needed to recuperate from the great war. From ghetto to ghetto the Jews slowly respun the web of shattered commerce. And be- cause of their confinement to trade as well as of their exten- sive connections—in Poland, Italy, Holland, England, and the Indies—they contributed a share to the recovery far out of proportion to their numbers.

Freytag, the writer of historical romances, was hardly romancing when he wrote: "Jewish peddlers became trust- worthy couriers between Prague, Frankfort, and Amsterdam, transmitting jewels and bills-of-exchange in their packs . . . the Jews bought laces and embroideries for church princes, and smuggled arms and supplies for war-lords, and fetched leather and fur from the depths of Russia . . . they had friends and protectors at the Imperial court, the Sultan's palace, and the Papal chair." On a smaller scale they did for the broken German world what their ancestors had done for the broken Roman world a thousand years before.

A Jewess of Hamburg, Glückel of Hameln (1646-1714), the daughter and wife of merchants and herself a merchant, tells the story of this generation in her simple and moving *Memoirs*. Her father and husband, like most of their business associates, began at the bottom of the ladder. We see them move from village ghettos to larger centers—Hamburg, Frankfort, Hanover, Fürth, and Berlin—and deal in petty loans, second-hand jewelry, Dutch and English wares (such as ribbons, cutlery, and pottery) or in scattered crumbs from the big Gentile bankers and brokers.

Elsewhere we learn of their retail trade in cattle, horses, feathers, old clothes, and bedding (Mayence 1662) and something of grain-buying (South Germany), tobacco-monopolies (Mecklenburg) and commerce in textiles (Frankfort). Besides trade they go into small manufacturing and home industries, such as knitting, embroidery, and lace-making. In such crafts as the guilds did not dominate, we hear of Jewish seal-engravers, lens-grinders, miniature-painters, musicians, and diamond-cutters.

Bit by bit the fortunes of the luckier ones improved. They bought (like the Hamelns) in Danzig, Amsterdam, Hamburg, and other manufacturing or importing centers and sold in the leading German fairs—Leipzig, the two Frankforts, and Brunswick. They undertook contracts for delivering silver to the mints established by many of the petty states. They dealt in bills-of-exchange on a scale that approached banking.

In 1648 massacres in the Ukraine drove large numbers of Polish Jews back to Germany, their original homeland, and enriched the cultural and trade relations between German Jewry and Eastern Europe. An expulsion of the Jews from Vienna in 1670 sent a new wave of talent and capital into the land, turning Fürth into a rival of Frankfort and creating the nucleus for the modern Jewish community of Berlin. Meanwhile the Empire plunged into continual warfare—against the Turks, French, and Swedes—which stimulated fresh demands for arms and supplies.

As their trade grew to wholesale magnitude, favored Jews managed to secure the best customers of the day: counts, dukes, princes, electors, or even kings and emperors. A court Jew in embryo such as Mordecai Gumperts of Cleves (one of whose sons married Glückel's sister) began as purveyor to Brandenburg. The profits were then invested in the form of loans to the same good customer; and Mordecai's son, Elias Cleve, became banker to the Great Elector. From banker it was a step to financial agent (such as Glückel's brother-in-law, Leffmann Behrens, at the court of Hanover), diplomatic adviser (again Elias Cleve), or minister of finance (such as Glückel's step-son, Samuel Lévy, at the court of Lorraine).

Occasionally a fortunate man ran the whole gamut in a single life-time. Joseph Süss Oppenheimer (1698-1738)—the hero of Feuchtwanger's novel, *Power*—was the son of a strolling play-actor; he rose to be Privy Financial Councilor to the Duke of Württemberg. A poor lad, Jost Liebmann

(d. 1701) came to Glückel's husband with a bit of amber as his sole capital; and he ended—after routing one rival and marrying the widow of another—court jeweler and financial agent to Frederick I of Prussia. Samuel Oppenheimer (d. 1703) began his public career as financial agent to a mere Elector of the Palatinate; before he was done, he had equipped two Imperial armies, made himself the leading financier of Austria, reopened Vienna to the settlement of "privileged" Jews, and died court factor and purveyor-general to Emperor Leopold I.

These court Jews plied a dangerous profession. Their tenure of office was governed entirely by the rules of business tolerance, i.e. expediency. The complots of Jewish rivals, the pressure of Christian competitors, the intrigues of courtiers, the occasion of a bad harvest or business set-back, the discontent of the populace who paid for the whole game with huge taxes and a miserable scale of living—all were liable to earn them dismissal, bankruptcy, imprisonment, or worse.

Samuel Oppenheimer lived to see his mansion sacked and himself jailed; when he died, the Imperial treasury owed him millions which remained unpaid. Max Model, court Jew of Ansbach, after twenty-five years of service (1691-1716), was extinguished upon the charge of defrauding public revenues. His rival Elkanan Fränkel, fell from favor into prison. Samuel Lévy, finance minister to Lorraine, as well as the two sons of Samson Baiersdorf, court Jew of Kulmbach-Bayreuth, likewise met their ruin behind bars. However, after the horrible execution of financial adviser Lippold in Berlin, 1573, the profession proved fatal to only one of its practitioners—Joseph Süss Oppenheimer. He made the social error of conducting himself as an equal among his fellow-courtiers. A

cabal conspired against him, the oppressed populace was encouraged to demand his head, and he was hanged to death in
an iron-cage suspended from a thirty-five foot gallows—most
unjustly. That is to say, if justice had been done, and if the
Württembergers had been French, and if it had been fifty
years later, he would not have hung alone.

iv

But the court Jews were more than acute business-men or
picturesque gamblers. Their influence upon the fortunes of
Jewry was manifold.

First and foremost, their privileged status enabled them to
act as pioneers reopening territory closed to the Jews for a
century or longer. Under cover of the favor earned at court
by these bankers and purveyors, the race filtered once again
into Brandenburg, Mecklenburg, and Saxony across the north,
and into Württemberg and several smaller states in the south;
they moved from village to town in Brunswick-Lüneburg,
Hessia, and along the Rhine in Cleves, the Palatinate, and
Baden. Relatively important communities were founded in
Hanover (ca. 1650), Halberstadt (1650), Mannheim (1660),
Berlin (1671), Dessau (1672), Dresden (1700), Breslau
(1710), and similar centers. And the older communities grew
apace.

The new communities, no less than the old, lived at a constant risk. On the one hand the Great Elector, whose acquisi-
tions were creating modern Prussia, could say: "The Jews
and their commerce, far from being a detriment to the land,
are a decided benefit." Behind his approval lay the benefits he
derived from his court Jews: a Behrend Levi of Bonn, an

Elias Cleve of Cleves, an Israel Aaron of Berlin. On the other hand, the mere prospect of the Halberstadt Jews opening "a cursed synagogue where our Savior is blasphemed daily" threw the guilds and Christian merchants into a rage. The very sight—to say nothing of the success—of the Jews at the fair in Frankfort-on-the-Oder provoked the theological faculty and the merchant guilds of that city to draw up a protest giving eighteen reasons why such "Christ-haters" and "cheating traders" should be barred from the land.

Or again, in 1705 the magistrates of Dresden discovered to their horror the presence of fifteen Jewish families within its walls. And they were not slow in apprising the Elector of Saxony that the "damnable superstition" of the Jews endangered the Protestant purity of the land and that their commercial activities threatened the livelihood of its citizens. But the Elector, Frederick August the Strong, recently crowned king of Poland, was of a different mind. He knew how much the Jews had benefited Poland economically and how much the "important services" of his court Jew, Behrend Lehman, had benefited him, and roundly declared that expulsion was not to be considered.

Everywhere—as in Frankfort and Hamburg before the Thirty Years War—new business clashed with old habits. Accordingly, the status of the Jews rested on a shaky compromise. The monarchs welcomed them for what they brought. But the merchants and artisans feared them for what they gained. And all classes hated them for their Christ-denying faith. Indeed, after six hundred years of unremitting practice in it, the Germans had included this hatred as a standard accessory to their mental equipment.

The general policy, therefore, which prevailed until Napoleon led the French across the Rhine, was to "tolerate" the Jews in return for inflicting upon them endless payments and restrictions. Quite in the medieval style a Jew paid to enter a city, pass the night behind its walls, reside there, obtain a letter-of-protection or "privilege" without which few occupations were open to him and further travel impossible; and he paid to marry and sometimes—as Glückel of Hameln tells us —to die. Other payments were exacted from the community as a whole in order to exist, to open a synagogue, to possess a cemetery, and to meet the varied demands of the higher spheres, running from the need of a margrave for blankets in his new hunting-lodge to outfitting regiments or feathering a king's dowry.

The restrictions were calculated to limit the nature and conditions of Jewish trade so as to minimize competition with Christians, to discourage public worship (which was felt to be an affront to Christian decency), and to keep the Jewish population at a low and stationary figure. Many baroque touches were added to the medieval character of these restrictions. At the Leipzig Fair—as in Mayence and Berlin—no Jew could open a shop facing the street. Synagogues, too, were, if permitted at all, compelled to hide away in courtyards; and when Berlin finally permitted public worship (1712), city officials were detailed to listen regularly through the services in order to make sure that the worshipers did not slip into the *Alenu* prayer, with its reference to idolaters, a Hebrew curse or two against Christianity. The methods employed to limit the population were ingenious. In Berlin, for example, the size of the community was fixed by law and the cost of obtaining a "privilege" steadily boosted. But this still left the processes of nature untrammeled. It was consequently decreed that in any family only one son or daughter was free to marry—free, that is, upon payment of annual marriage-dues. Other children could marry only if their possessions reached a stipulated sum, higher for the third child than the second—and upon payment of proportionately larger annual dues.

The system can hardly be recommended to modern advocates of birth-control or restricted immigration. Despite taxes and obstacles the Jewish population steadily increased. In Dresden the fifteen families of 1705 grew to about two hundred by 1763; and in 1777 the menace of further growth was averted by a general expulsion from Saxony, effective till well into the nineteenth century. In 1671 Prussia harbored only a handful of Jews; by 1728 their number had risen to about six thousand.

These increases, and their like elsewhere, were in part due to the efforts and devotion of the court Jews. Acting as mediators—*shtadlanim*—between their people and the authorities, they were, as a whole, tireless in whittling away at restrictions, dispelling dangers, and bargaining for rights and privileges. Monuments to their work may be seen in the synagogues they secured permission to open and gave the funds to build: Behrend Lehman in Halberstadt, Samson Baiersdorf in Baiersdorf, Leffmann Behrens in Hanover, Alexander David in Brunswick, Mordecai Meisel in Prague—to name but a few.

Their power in Jewry sprang from another and related source. The state used its court Jews as a medium for controlling and mulcting the communities. It encouraged the

Jews to group themselves in a district or provincial body headed by a district-rabbi or a committee of *parnasim*. The court Jews naturally headed these committees; or their appointees, usually relatives, served as the district-rabbis; or, on occasion, they held the office themselves. As a result, they often played the absolute monarch in their own small way. Something like democratic revolts on the part of the unprivileged rank-and-file—the mere common unpropertied Jews—are recorded in Prague and Frankfort; but, in sum, Jewry was constrained to depend on the whims and arbitrary grace of self-constituted leaders until close upon today.

Finally, through no fault or rather no intention of their own, the court Jews and their successors—the barons and bankers of the nineteenth century—cost Jewry whatever they were worth, and more. If they rose in the world, all Jewry was held to be as rich as an Oppenheimer and the village peddler and old clothes' man tasted the edge of Christian jealousy. If they fell in disgrace, the peddler and tailor received the blow of their fall. When "Jew Süss" hung in his iron-cage, the hearts of Württemberg cattle-dealers and horse-traders hung in their throats, and rightly so; for his execution led to their banishment till the last century. The Dutch Jews who bought up the grain harvests of South Germany in 1699 doubtless made a pretty penny and earned themselves an influential place among the *parnasim* of Amsterdam, whence they could shower benefits and philanthropies upon their people. But thirty-six Jewries in the bishopric of Bamberg paid for the ensuing dearth when hungry mobs cried, "On to the *Judengasse!*" and battered and plundered their humble homes.

V

Like all magnificos the court Jews set their hand to culture. Samuel Oppenheimer began to collect Hebraica and Judaica; and his nephew, David Oppenheimer (1664-1736), created a redoubtable library—over 4,000 items—now a proud possession of the Bodleian at Oxford. Alexander David (1687-1765), court Jew of Brunswick, the first collector known to itch for menorahs, spice-boxes, pulpit embroideries, and other objects of Jewish ritual art, founded the earliest Jewish museum. Moving, even if on the outskirts, of the "best" Christian circles, these court figures likewise did something toward familiarizing the German aristocrat with Jewish manners—it became a fad for courtiers to attend the *magnifiques* (as Glückel called them) weddings of rich Jews—and toward introducing Gentile culture into the ghetto homes.

There was further interchange of undoubted importance. The Germans began to wonder what the Jews, who had now passed at least thirteen centuries in their midst, were really like and what they believed and practiced. In 1714-17 Johann Jacob Schudt, a German antiquarian and Orientalist, published his volumes of *Jüdische Merkwürdigkeiten* ("Jewish Curiosities") which, despite their unfriendly tone, told much of contemporary Jewish life, particularly in Frankfort. This work was followed by detailed accounts of Jewish ritual and observance in Paul Christian Kirchner's *Jüdisches Ceremoniel* (1720?) and Johann Christian Bodenschatz' *Kirchliche Verfassung der heutigen Juden* ("Religious System of the Jews of Today," 1748). In their many copper-plates all three give valuable glimpses of costumes and customs, synagogue and home interiors, and ghetto courts and streets. On the other hand—for the first time in German history—a university opened its doors to the *Judengasse*. Beginning in 1672 under the auspices of the Great Elector, an occasional Jewish youth was admitted to the University of Frankfort-on-the-Oder and, other professions being closed, was graduated in medicine.

But on the whole—except for crumbs of etiquette dropped from princely tables and an array of French words which the Jews wove into their Yiddish—the Germans had little to offer. German culture was, indeed, at its lowest ebb. Literature and science were throttled for over a century.

As for literature, turn, if you will, to the *Oxford Book of German Verse*. Between Hans Sachs who died in 1576 and Klopstock who was born in 1724 you will find nothing—apart from Grimmelshausen—but a few pages of nonentities. And if you will read Grimmelshausen's picaresque novel, *Simplicissimus,* which depicts the ravages of the Thirty Years War, you will learn the reason for this blight. The war left a scar on German genius which was slow, if ever, to heal.

As for science and philosophy, the one first-class German thinker the seventeenth century produced, Leibnitz, lived in intellectual isolation so far as Germany was concerned. He roundly scolded his generation for its neglect of the German language and its consequent decay; but he took care, in order to assure himself of an intelligent audience, to write his chief philosophical works in French. In fact, among the learned, German had sunk to a jargon of Latin, French, and local barbarisms which would have made Luther blush for shame.

Yet—to take the measure of Germany's decline—this was the *grand siècle* in France, the century of Corneille, Racine, and Molière in literature; of Descartes, Gassendi, and Pascal in philosophy; of Poussin, Lorraine, and Mansard in the fine arts; of all the glorious names which march like a crusading army of the spirit across the pages of Voltaire's history of Louis XIV. In England it was the century which began with Shakespeare and Bacon and ended with Dryden and Locke, which saw Drake navigate the seas and Newton the heavens. While German genius almost lost the use of its mother-tongue, Rembrandt was giving a new idiom to Holland and the world, and Galileo—on the scent Kepler pursued in Bohemia—was reading the secret language of the planets.

In its cultural decline the Germans first gave way to a moral debauch which set a record unsurpassed until the aftermath of our own world war. The Jews, too, caught something of its fever, though on a different plane. The claims of the messianic pretender, Sabbatai Zebi, and his successor, Jacob Frank, went to their heads, and at spasmodic intervals brought normal life to a standstill. As the Germans sought relief from their intolerable plight in dissipation, the Jews tried to find it in dreams.

Eventually the Germans regained their customary aplomb in a stolid consumption of beer and sausage—dull draughts of theology and platters of medieval superstitious wurst. Magic, divination, and fortune-telling spawned a voluminous literature. Witch-burning reached its height. It was hardly unnatural, therefore, that in 1682 three Berlin Jews went to a fiery death for "buying" a Christian child, presumably to sacrifice it for magic or ritual purposes. This was the very year Bayle published his *Pensées diverses sur la Comète*: one of the first guns to roar in a triumphant battle for tolerance, free inquiry, and sanity. Voltaire was soon to explain these witch-burnings and Jew-burnings, and indeed most of our history, in his single remark: "As long as people believe absurdities, they will continue to commit atrocities."

Meanwhile, absurdities continued to flood the popular mind. In writing the Latin work *Tela Ignea Satanae* (with the subtitle, "The Horrible Attacks of the Jews upon Christ, God, and the Christian Faith," 1681), Wagenseil supplied the learned world not only with a number of notable Jewish polemics against Christianity, but with a mine of hatred dug from obscure Jewish lodes—all the slander and vituperation distilled by the Jews, through a millennium of persecution, in their very human hearts. What Wagenseil did for the scholars, Eisenmenger did for the rabble. His *Entdecktes Judenthum* ("Judaism Unmasked," 1700; republished 1893)—which court Jews, the emperor, and the Church vainly endeavored to suppress and which the Court of Brandenburg allowed to appear in print—is still an arsenal for anti-Semites, with its distortions, misinterpretations, and forgeries of talmudic and other ancient sources. As to satires, broadsides, pamphlets, dramatic skits, and caricatures against the Jews, it would take a volume to catalogue and describe this output of dubious wit, a further reflection and measure of Germany's degradation.

Under such circumstances the output of Jewish culture was no less banal, even if it was, through it all, harmless and comparatively humane. A living culture flourished in Poland, Bohemia, and Moravia: the best of Jewish youth were despatched to these lands for their education, and, when possible, they remained there. On the other hand the best of the German rabbinate came from or received their training in these Eastern centers. Among German Jewry itself, pietistic screeds continued to be as popular as ever. Tireless commentators upon tiresome commentaries, snappers-up of rabbinical trifles, were the rule. The one exception—the only person in the century who wrote with a fresh pen and who can therefore be called an author—was the woman Glückel of Hameln, and her memoirs remained unpublished until 1896.

The nadir was probably reached by two rabbis, Jonathan Eybeschütz and Jacob Emden, both learned and intelligent men. From 1750 to 1756 they carried on a controversy over the former's imputed adherence to the messianic pretensions of Sabbatai Zebi, over amulets and magic, that raged in the Senate, Bourse, synagogues, and even the graveyards of Hamburg. The depths are not revealed by the controversy itself, which could have been matched in sane German circles and among the lunatic fringe in France and England, but by the ease with which it enlisted the leading brains of Jewry. A volley of bans and counter-bans riddled what little authority the rabbinate still possessed.

Surveying the scene in 1750, surely no prophet could have foretold that Germany stood on the eve of its greatest achievements—giving the world, among a host of lesser gifts, Goethe and Beethoven. Or that German Jewry was about to create the richest renaissance in Jewish history since the peak in Moslem Spain; that, reaching beyond Jewry, it would help in astounding measure to create modern Germany and, reaching farther still, transform modern society and thought; that it would give Mendelssohn, Zunz, and Herzl to the Jews, Heine, Boerne, and Lassalle to the Germans, Marx, Freud, and Einstein to the world.

Still, a prophet might have guessed that a new ferment was at last stirring across the Rhine. In 1749 Lessing produced his playlet *The Jews*—in which already lay the germ of *Nathan the Wise*.

13

THE AGE OF REASON

LESSING'S little play *Die Juden* told about a traveler who
saved the life of a baron and refused any and every
reward—even marriage with the baron's lovely daughter.
When pressed to explain his mad refusal the traveler stammered, "But I am a—Jew." Upon recovering from the shock
the baron exclaimed, "How we would respect them if all
Jews were like you!" "And if all Christians were like you,"
exclaimed the traveler in turn, "how lovable they would be!"
The traveler's servant, who now learned for the first time the
race and faith of his master, capped the general bewilderment
with a puzzled confession: "There are, it seems, Jews who are
not Jews at all."

A theologian of Göttingen, Professor Johann Michaelis,
doubted the servant's discovery. He reflected the consensus of
opinion on the play when he questioned whether a decent
Jew—a Jew who was therefore not a Jew—could be considered a probable or even plausible character. The remark came
to the ears of a Jewish youth who was studying philosophy in
a Berlin garret. Without doubting the existence of Christians
who were not Christian but decent and humane—the Christian who wrote the play proved they did exist—the lad poured

his bitter indignation into a memorable letter. "Is it not enough," he wrote, "that we must suffer Christian hate? They are tireless in oppressing us, in depriving us of every means to enjoy a free and peaceable life, nay, in making us the butt and laughing-stock of the world. Must they likewise deny us the one consolation remaining to any victim: his virtue?"

A few years later (1754) the young student met the equally young playwright over a chess-board. Moses Mendelssohn had found the Christian who could be loved and Gotthold Ephraim Lessing the Jew who could be honored. They played chess together, and in the garden of the St. Nicholas church talked philosophy. Surely a reasonable and hardly momentous thing to do. Yet Jew and Gentile had not walked and talked like this since the Renaissance. It meant for Germany and its Jews the dawn of the Age of Reason.

Two streams had belatedly met, the economic evolution heralded by the Fuggers and the humanism incarnate in Reuchlin—both long obstructed by religious strife and ferocious warfare. The waters had nevertheless been accumulating; and when the dam broke with a suddenness seldom paralleled in history, Germany rose on an intellectual tide which lifted her to unsurpassed heights.

With giant stride Frederick II carried out the work of the Great Elector. By the conquest of Silesia (confirmed in 1745) Frederick's military genius made Prussia one of the great powers of Europe: it was centuries since as much could be said of a German state.

Again following the Elector's footsteps, Frederick set about to win the surname "Great" by developing agriculture, reviving commerce, and advancing industry. He reclaimed wastelands and peopled them with villages. In his West Prussian domains he abolished serfdom—a precedent to be adopted some while later by a few smaller states. Among crafts and trades he abolished many of the restrictions inherited from the medieval guilds. He did away with numerous local tariffs. He built factories and stimulated the production of textiles, paper, and porcelain. Jews had reason to remember his efforts in industry: for aside from being occasionally permitted to assume the risks of a new enterprise, they were obliged, upon marriage, to buy a set of porcelain from the royal potteries *pour encourager les autres.* Mendelssohn's home was thus, perforce, decorated with a dozen life-size porcelain apes.

Fortified by political and economic prosperity Frederick sought to foster arts, sciences, and the amenities—in French fashion. He entertained French philosophers, scientists, and poets in his palace and drafted them into the Academy of Berlin. As for himself he wrote French verse, played the lute, composed music, and talked philosophy passably well. A Frenchman who had opportunity to observe this transformation wrote: "Berlin grew rapidly and began to taste the sweets of life. Some of its inhabitants acquired furniture. Most of them even wore shirts—under the preceding reign they had been content with dickies tied with strings. Things changed under your very eyes. Sparta became Athens." In 1750 this observer, M. de Voltaire, moved from Paris to Potsdam.

But it was not the first time Reason had crossed the German frontiers. The previous century had imported French styles and English hardware at its peril. Along with a vocabulary for dress, cookery, and table manners there had drifted over the Rhine words pregnant with new meaning: *bel-esprit, bon sens, raison.* The British had shipped across the channel not only bales of cloth and crates of cutlery but Hobbes'

Leviathan and Locke's *Essay on the Human Understanding.*
From Holland the wares of Spinoza were, as heretical contra-
band, more or less smuggled into the German mind.

Under this influence German pioneers like Christian
Thomasius (d. 1728) opposed persecution for witchcraft and
heresy, and the use of torture. This same Thomasius who
thought "superstition worse than atheism" inaugurated another novelty when he delivered his lectures at Leipzig University in the despised German tongue. A Dippel and an
Edelmann carried the attack directly against the Bible, its
miracles, and the Protestant idolatry of the printed page;
while Wolff popularized Leibnitz in German and thereby at
least enriched and purified this instrument of thought. As for
Leibnitz' intolerable optimism, didn't young Goethe encounter an old gentleman who complained that he "found defects
even in God"? The waters had been accumulating when
Lessing broke the dam.

This is hardly the place to do justice to Lessing—*"ein
ganzer Mann*—every inch a man" Heine called him. Yet
everything he put his hand to affected Jewish destiny. To
begin with, he freed Germany from her servitude to foreign
culture, and by criticism and example recreated German literature and its language. And characteristic of his humanism
—the old but aborted humanism of Reuchlin—he brought
Mendelssohn (and therewith Jewry) into this reborn world.

ii

Mendelssohn too fell heir to a long-thwarted tradition.
Born in Dessau (1729), the son of a penniless Torah scribe,
he had the rare luck to be taught his Bible and Talmud by

a man who, in addition, guided him to the treasures of Maimonides—the same Maimonides who had quickened Rabbi Judah Löw and Spinoza. Day and night the boy studied the master of Jewish rationalism until he had literally crippled his frail physique. "Maimonides gave me my deformity," he used to tell of his humped back, "but I love him nevertheless; if he has weakened my body, has he not atoned for it by strengthening my soul?" Maimonides did more for him than that; he inspired him to become another guide to the perplexed and once again try to marry Judaism and Reason.

At fourteen, driven by his thirst for secular knowledge, Mendelssohn tramped to Berlin. The new spirit was already abroad in its *Judengasse*. One Abraham Posner had the audacity to discard his beard; a youth was discovered in the possession of a German book. To be sure, Posner was compelled to grow his beard again—though the community had to induce Frederick to issue a royal command for the purpose —and the youth was expelled, bookless, from the city.

More significant, Mendelssohn found kindred souls among his people, men able and willing to satisfy his thirst. Israel Zamosc, a self-instructed refugee from the bearded ghettos of Poland, opened for him the realm of mathematics. Abraham Kisch, a physician from Prague, taught him the rudiments of Latin; and he was soon struggling with a Latin version of the bible of reason—Locke's *Essay*. Another physician, Aaron Gumpertz (grandchild of the court factor, Elias Cleve, and the first Prussian Jew to be graduated from the University of Frankfort-on-the-Oder), introduced him to German philosophy and literature, and even to the president of the Berlin Academy—and finally to Lessing.

It was apparent that if one moved among the right people of the *Judengasse* there was no need to hide a German book or grow a beard. And that they welcomed and aided a poor devil like Mendelssohn, who was soon happy to earn a pittance as a tutor and then as a bookkeeper, showed the old spirit of Jewry to be likewise alive. For a generation and more —until Jewish schools were founded and Christian classrooms dropped their restrictions—a host of young Jews repeated Mendelssohn's experience, passing from the Talmud to secular learning through their own efforts and the aid of friends a little further along the road. The lively—and pathetic—adventures of many of these youths who in Poland and Germany fought poverty, ignorance, and intolerance, Jewish intolerance no less than Christian, may be read in the vivid *Autobiography* of Solomon Maimon (1754-1800), long available in English.

Under Lessing's encouragement Mendelssohn turned author. His first work, *Philosophische Gespräche* (*Philosophic Discourses,* 1756), won him the respect of academic circles and piqued Frederick with a desire to meet that curiosity— "the young Jew who wrote in German." And despite his business labors—he eventually became a partner of his employer and possessed of a modest fortune—he flung himself at Lessing's side into the regeneration of German thought and taste.

He translated Rousseau's discourse on inequality among men—in which, as a Jew, he had more than a speculative interest. He edited Nikolai's *Bibliotek,* the famous organ of the new movement, and contributed voluminously to its successor, the *Literaturbriefe.* In the latter he dared call Frederick to task for writing his poetry in French and—we are inclined to hope—for publishing what he wrote. Together with Lessing's *Laokoon* his essays on esthetics broke ground for the later harvests of Schiller and Goethe. In 1763 his study on Evidence in Metaphysics captured the prize of the Berlin Academy against even the competition of Kant; and, as a further reward, Frederick made him a "privileged Jew," giving him the right not to be thrown out of Berlin. The story goes that the Marquis d'Argens wrote the King in his behalf: "A philosopher who is a bad Catholic begs a philosopher who is a bad Protestant to grant this privilege to a philosopher who is a bad Jew." Not to be behind royalty, the Berlin Jewry exempted Mendelssohn from all communal taxes.

His fame culminated in the publication of *Phädon* (1767), a little dialogue which tried to prove the immortality of the soul and which succeeded for the first time in clothing philosophy with a German that was a pleasure to read. The public, in fact, read fifteen editions of it; it was widely translated, and the author was acclaimed the "German Socrates." But its greatest service was to tender recognition, likewise for the first time, to a German Jew as a leader in German and European thought.

Though his home was now a center for intellectuals from all lands, when he left its door and strolled the streets with his family he quickly lost his "privileges." "Papa!" cried his children, "why do the boys throw stones at us—why do they chase us and scream, 'Jews, Jews!' Is it a crime to be a Jew?" Then he would drop his eyes and, as he relates, sigh to himself, "Men, men—what have you let yourselves become!"

Somewhat subtler than the street gamins, a Swiss preacher —Lavater—sought to lure him, as a champion of reason, into either refuting Christianity or embracing it. But Mendelssohn refused to walk into the old medieval trap—a public debate with opinion stacked against him—which had cost his people only too dear. In a reply which awoke Germany to an appreciation of human dignity even when it was not Christian, he proved that while he might be a "philosopher" he was far from being a "bad Jew." And thrusting deeper still, he drove home the lesson of the new age: neither reason nor good taste can tolerate a religious quarrel.

But Mendelssohn had not emerged unscathed. Convinced, like all thinkers of the day, that reason and good taste— "*Aufklärung*—Enlightenment" the Germans called it—were enough to insure mankind justice and amity, he realized that the Jews likewise needed enlightening. The Germans were suffering from a cultural lag due to the Thirty Years War; and the Jews, because of ghetto stagnation, were lagging behind the Germans. A few sallies at playing *shtadlan*—interceding for his people in Switzerland and Saxony—sharpened this conviction. Christian prejudice, he felt, was matched by Jewish obscurantism; together they built the common party wall which kept the ghetto intact. Tearing down one side of the wall would automatically bring down the other. The way to win equality was to make one's self an equal. The key to reason and taste—as Mendelssohn could show from his own experience—lay in abandoning Yiddish, purifying Hebrew, and learning German.

To furnish this key to his fellow-Jews he launched upon his most enduring achievement: the translation of the Torah —the Pentateuch—into German (1778-83). Its volumes contained both the Hebrew original and the German version— the latter written with Mendelssohnian simplicity and grace and, to ease the reader's task, printed in Hebrew characters.

The original text was supplied with a clear Hebrew commentary—the work of learned friends inspired with the new spirit—which avoided talmudic embroidery and sought merely to resolve grammatical and logical difficulties. Through the original and its commentaries the reader could learn to think and write in a correct Hebrew, and through the translation to turn his Yiddish into a pure German.

The work won instant acclaim. A few rabbis thundered impotent bans, a few copies were burned in pious bon-fires; but the mass of Jews, long prepared and eager to break from the narrow horizon of the ghetto, took the book to their heart. A generation of youth used it as a stepping-stone to a larger life. It became the symbol if not the actual tool of an inner emancipation.

iii

Meanwhile Lessing was undermining the Christian side of the wall. He published the famous *Wolfenbüttel Fragments* (1774-78)—the posthumous work of Reimarus—which offered an historical rather than supernatural account of Jesus, denied the miracles of the Bible, especially the Resurrection, in typical deist style, and opposed to official Christianity a "religion of reason." In the controversy which followed, he wrote a masterly plea for freedom of thought and belief. When the Brunswick government, which employed him as court librarian, confiscated the *Fragments* and ordered him to desist from the fight, he resolved, as he said, to see whether "they would let me preach undisturbed from my old pulpit —the stage." And he composed *Nathan the Wise* (1779).

Nathan was more than a vindication of the Jews—more

than a dramatic portrait of Mendelssohn. It made clear that only by rendering justice to the Jew could a Christian do justice to himself. And cutting under both religions it maintained—in the parable of the three rings—the fallibility of all human faith. To claim to possess "the best God" was "pious nonsense." The beliefs of other men must be tolerated not out of a spirit of indulgence and charity, but because the beliefs of no men were sure. As Boccaccio had said centuries ago—"the truth still pendeth." Naturally *Nathan* was banned from the stage for long years. Mendelssohn and Lessing had destroyed the wall, but merely—as yet—between themselves, and between the few *Philosophen* and *Schöngeister* who made the "Berlin religion" a stench in orthodox nostrils.

The following year Lessing closed his life's work with a pamphlet on *The Education of the Human Race*. A slight thing in itself, it belonged to another stream of thought— imported from France—which was to help change the inner character and outer conditions of Jewish life. History, it claimed, was a progress of ideas (Lessing thought, of religious ideas). Herder, Kant, Hegel and other speculators were to play variations on the theme until in the nineteenth century Progress—with a capital P—became practically synonymous with civilization, virtue, and reason. To be unprogressive was as good as being damned.

Lessing had barely laid down his pen when, as though to illustrate what Progress was now in the air, a monograph appeared with the title *On the Civil Amelioration of the Jews* (1781). Its author, Christian Wilhelm Dohm, was state archivist of Prussia and a student of Jewish history. He had fallen in with Mendelssohn, Nikolai and their advanced circle; and Mendelssohn—with an eye to helping the Alsatian

Jews who were under French rule already advanced enough to demand amelioration—had urged him to drop the Jewish past and consider the present. Dohm demonstrated—as Montesquieu had done some forty years before—that the misery of Israel was the work of Christendom. Tied to money-lending and petty trade, the Jews were inevitably degraded. He therefore asked nothing less than the immediate abolition of all restrictions which kept them from crafts, industry, professions, and the land. And in the measure that this freedom "improved" their condition he proposed their gradual enfranchisement as full and equal citizens of the state. He spent little ink on philosophic or humanitarian argument: as a hard-headed Prussian he based his plea on the old appeal of "utility" brought up to date. Not only the Jews but society and the state would benefit from this emancipation.

The plea created wide debate, though nothing was done about it. Not even when, less than a year later, Emperor Joseph II issued for the Austrian Jews an Edict of Toleration which—quite independently—put the first elements of Dohm's proposal into effect.

True, the debate as to whether German Jews could or should be "improved" drew some caustic words from Mendelssohn, and the questions which the mere thought of emancipation provoked on the relation between a Christian state and Jewish citizens led him to write his last considerable work: *Jerusalem* (1783). In this, his final philosophy of Judaism, he disclosed the conflict between faith and reason, between tradition and modernity, which was to rack the coming generations. For himself he resolved the dilemma by embracing both horns. A devout observer, heir and defender of every jot and tittle of the ancient discipline, he laid on his phylacteries; a deist, a man who grounded his faith on reason, he believed in the God of Leibnitz and Wolff—thus content with satisfying his conscience as a Jew and his mind as a philosopher.

Still, Dohm's effort was not without fruit. In 1786 a Count Mirabeau met the man in the *salon* of Henriette Herz and took the book back to France. He even wrote a pamphlet of his own on the subject. Three years later when he was elected deputy to the French States-General (which turned out to be the National Assembly), a Jewish friend asked him, as all young politicians are asked, what he proposed to do. He replied, "I will make you a human being."

iv

A picture of German Jewry on the eve of this revolution reveals profound contrasts. At the top of society a small group of merchants, manufacturers and court bankers—basking in Frederick's favor—enjoyed wealth, "privileges," and the blessings of Enlightenment. A traveler in the Prussia of 1779 writes: "There are very rich Jews in Berlin; [Daniel] Itzig and the Ephraims rank as the wealthiest. Some possess factories, though most of them are in commerce. Their deportment, especially those who have enjoyed a good education, is refined and pleasing: they have long discarded the gross, clumsy and servile manners to which their nation is addicted. Many of them dress their hair like Christians and clothe themselves as we do. Their upper class, or those who have been raised upon enlightened principles, associate freely with Christians and share our amusements—above all the theater, where on Saturday nights they occupy most of the parterre.

More than ever they are given to reading, and theater and magazines have developed among them a love of belles-lettres as well as literary talent. Their women-folk devour the latest novels: indeed their fair sex—and what beauty they can boast! —play a great rôle in Berlin."

Enlightenment, moreover, was not confined to perukes and theater seats. Our traveler would have been just in time to visit the newly-opened Jewish Free School—founded by Daniel Itzig's son-in-law, David Friedländer, and the first school to give Jewish children a primary education in German as well as the elements of Hebrew grammar. Together with its numerous imitators it doomed the traditional *heder* where the Bible was learned by rote and secular knowledge remained a closed book. In 1784 the older generation rubbed their eyes over a secular magazine in Hebrew. The *Meassef* ("Collector") gathered its contributors from German and Polish Jews who were inspired by Mendelssohn to translate modern thought and create modern letters in the age-old language of Israel. In truth the little paper—ten volumes appeared—was big with a rebirth comparable to the renaissance that once flamed in Moslem Spain. To its pages may be traced the achievements of nineteenth-century Jewry in creating for itself a new history and science in Germany, a new literature in Poland and Russia, and a living Hebrew speech in Palestine.

So much for one side of the picture. Over the other, which covered most of the canvas, lay poverty, oppression, and night. Of the Jewish population—which has been placed at 200,000—the lot of the overwhelming majority is adequately described by Dohm. "In many of our states," he reports, "they are denied residence and their presence permitted, upon pay-

ment, only for a brief stay—often for merely one night.
Where they are indeed permitted to reside, their numbers are
severely limited and their taxes huge. For the mass of them,
therefore, our city gates and the frontiers of our states are
virtually shut." In the year 1776—a date with other associations for Americans—Mendelssohn, then at the height of his
fame as a European philosopher, had to pay at the gate of
Dresden an entry-tax, a "head-tax," which, as he remarked,
was set at the same figure as for a "Polish cow."

"Agriculture, our chief occupation," Dohm continues, "is
forbidden them. Every craft and trades guild would feel itself
dishonored if it admitted a circumcised worker to its ranks.
The few available professions are surveying, natural science,
and medicine—and these only to men of exceptional talent
under the favor of an exceptional prince. Nothing, consequently, is left to this unfortunate people but commerce. Yet
in commerce itself they are handicapped by stringent restrictions and onerous taxes, so that none but a lucky few can rise
to become wholesalers. For the most part they remain tied to
peddling and petty trade, and even then under trammels and
prohibitions which allow them but the barest livelihood. The
profits are so meager they can attract only the poor wretch
who must choose misery or death."

Something like statistics existed by the dawn of the nineteenth century. They bear out Dohm's general statements and
paint a situation which was certainly no better than when he
wrote his indictment. Two-thirds of the Jewish population
were petty tradesmen and peddlers; 10% were domestics; 8%
were handworkers. In all, at least 84% were of the poorest
classes. We say "at least" because the number of beggars are
unknown. In the year 1800 the Frankfort community—which

continued to be the largest in Germany—numbered from 650 to 700 families. About 10% of them owned about 50% of its total Jewish wealth; three families (in the Speyer house) owned 10% of the total. And this was when the Rothschild house stood eleventh in the ranks of the rich.

The Jews of Mendelssohn's Berlin or in the world port of Hamburg were hardly the Jews of Germany. In these cities the majority were poor enough, but elsewhere they had more than poverty to bear. To return, for example, to Frankfort, we can learn from Ludwig Boerne—who was born in its *Judengasse* in 1786—something of the life they led in a typical ghetto. Goethe, also Frankfort-born, had already likened it to a "prison" the "confinement, filth, and crowding" of which had "depressed his youth."

"They dwelt," writes Boerne out of his boyhood memories, "in their own little street, without doubt the most thickly populated dot on the face of the earth. There they rejoiced in the tender watchful care of the government. On Sundays they were prohibited from leaving the ghetto lane, to spare them from being beaten up by drunkards. Before the age of twenty-five they were forbidden to marry, in order that their off-spring prove sound and sturdy. On public holidays they had to reënter the ghetto gate by sharp six in the evening, lest over-exposure to the sun ruin their complexions. They were forbidden to stroll in the fields beyond the city wall, so as to run no risk of being attracted to the life of a farmer. When a Jew walked the city streets and a Christian cried *Mach Mores, Jud!* ('Your manners, Jew!'), he needs must remove his hat; in this way the proper politeness was maintained between the two faiths. Then, too, a great many of the streets—because their bumpy pavement was bad for the feet—were altogether closed to him."

Boerne's sarcasms inevitably provoke the question: "In an age when the intelligence of a nation favored tolerance, what were the motives that kept streets and fields—as well as workshops, schools, and offices—closed to the Jews?"

Twice—in 1745 and in 1765—enlightened ministers of finance tried to persuade Frederick to relieve the restrictions and taxes burdening the Jews. Their memoranda summarized the charges laid against the race; and while medieval fantasies —ritual murder, well-poisoning, desecration of the Host— had disappeared, new ones supplanted the old.

The first justification for maintaining discrimination springs, says Finance Minister Manitius in 1745, "from religious hatred which originated in the Catholic Church and which is the source of all persecution." And he disposes of the point by reminding Frederick that as men become "daily" more enlightened, it will be hard to find anyone so "simpleminded" as "to deny a whole nation tolerance and humanity."

The second ground for discrimination is the "false economic presumption" that the Jews are "a detriment to the land and especially to the merchant classes." This, too, Minister Manitius refutes by pointing to the republics—he had Holland above all in mind—"where commerce flourishes best and where the Jews have proved to be a decided benefit." And he clinches the argument with a brilliant statement of the economic morality which in commercially developed lands was superseding ecclesiastic ethics. "Business," he concludes, "knows no difference between religions. All it demands is honest dealing. And in that respect we could only wish that Christians were as scrupulous as Jews."

The third and last charge was likewise grounded on expediency. Manitius finds that "in our present military times" the Jews are considered useless to the state inasmuch as they are held "unfit for army service." But he reminds the king that in the previous century "the Jews were to a great extent responsible for the growth and upkeep of the royal army through mustering supplies from every corner of Europe" and that they can do as much again.

Twenty years later Finance Minister d'Asnières repeated the charges and refutations and capped them with an unanswerable fling. "It is remarkable," he told the king, "that men reproach the Jews for being useless when these same men prevent them from being useful."

Frederick, however, remained deaf to his finance ministers and to the divinity he professed to worship—the Goddess of Reason. The most enlightened monarch of Europe, the king whom Voltaire advertized as the "Solomon of the North," not only kept the old restrictions and imposts but increased them. In Old Fritz—as the Germans call him—there still lived the Old Nick.

v

Frederick's conservatism bares the first flaw in the whole movement to free the Jews. Since the Jews of the next century were to enjoy the benefits of this movement—and in civilized lands are still enjoying them—it is necessary to understand, at the outset, the character of the currents responsible for emancipation.

Foremost in the minds of the men who advocated tolerance and equal civil rights was the appeal of reason. At bottom

and in its origins this was an appeal against the entire Christian tradition and harked back, through the Humanist revival, to the philosophers of the pagan world. It was the pagan Platonists, Stoics, Epicureans, and Skeptics who created the discipline of reason and its corollary, tolerance. The moderns who restored this discipline, a Montaigne, Castalio, Spinoza, Locke, Bayle, Toland—all the liberators of human thought—were almost without exception rationalists or skeptics. They were, one and all, aware of their debt to pagan antiquity and conscious of their contemporary enemy. *"Ecrasez l'infâme*
. . . crush the infamous . . ."* wrote Voltaire at the bottom of his letters, and everyone knew whom and what he meant.

Yet the real obstacle to the rule of reason was not an institution but a human failing. The difficulty was—and is—that most men are incapable of reason: they lack not only the will but the brains. Frederick understood this very well when he wrote to Voltaire: "Let us confess the truth: philosophy touches only a handful of men; the great majority—the masses and the common run of nobility—remain as Nature made them, that is to say, wicked beasts." And he proved he was not cynical, but coldly descriptive, by the example of his own behavior.

The second current sweeping toward tolerance sprang not from calculation and reason, but sentiment and faith. The belief in the fatherhood of God and brotherhood of man regardless of creed, which was common to deists and such heretical sects as the Unitarians; the humane "sentimentalism" of a Lawrence Sterne and the democratic mysticism of a Rousseau—who had their vogue in Germany; the rise of Free Masonry and other more obscure societies, like the Rosicrucians of the seventeenth and Weishaupt's Illuminati of the late eighteenth century, which made brotherly love into a secret cult: the whole humanitarian tide owed its emotional source not to pagan but to Christian-Jewish antiquity.

The history of the Church, however, should have been enough to demonstrate the treachery that lurks in faith. The man who believes this year in God may next year believe as plausibly in Satan. The worshiper who burns today a candle to the St. Michael of humanity may tomorrow burn one to the dragon of nationality. The Germans, being men, did precisely this.

But the Jews and other hopeful minorities were blinded to these elementary shortcomings of mankind by the great light of Progress. The world encouraged them to trust—it became the ranking dogma of the nineteenth century—that men and society were irresistibly moving toward a better, saner, fairer life. Politicians, economists, scientists, poets, clergymen and rabbis joined in fervent embrace of this new religion—although, as a glance at their emptying pews would have told them, the rabbis who spoke of the progress of Judaism actually meant its progressive disintegration. Today the idol of Progress is tottering, if it has not altogether fallen; there are even few Jews so poor in mind as to do it homage. Yet it inspired one of the major credos—and illusions—behind emancipation.

The final and probably the decisive impetus was of a totally different character. The economic innovations of the sixteenth century were preparing still greater changes. England was launched on the Industrial Revolution. Her American colonies had broken the chains which bound them to an obsolete mercantilism by bloody revolt—an ominous precedent. And in France the idea took deadly root that philosophizing may be very well, that brotherly love and progress may be excellent things, but that the emancipation of all oppressed classes—which meant the bourgeoisie and the peasants, for the proletariat were as yet negligible—could only be achieved by radically altering the character of social relations and the state. In short, one could liberate the fellows on the bottom of a heap only by plucking off the fellows on top.

The French Revolution destroyed the power of the nobility and clergy who were strangling the superior energies of emergent capitalism. Guilds vanished or were abolished. A free market for manufacture, trade, and labor took their place. Tumbrils carted to oblivion the whole apparatus of church privileges and a sacrosanct social hierarchy. The violence and bloodshed of this revolution, however necessary, were purely incidental. And in 1791, as another necessary incident, the Jews of France were made "human beings"— for the first time in fourteen hundred years full and equal citizens of a European state.

Thereafter, wherever capitalism flourished and whenever church and nobility were curbed and to the extent that the middle class governed the engines of society, the Jews, either as members of this class or as dependents upon a free market for talent and labor, enjoyed liberty and equality. (Fraternity, of course, was always another matter.) But even these were no absolute or eternal rights. Whether they realized it or not, Jewish freedom was as inextricably bound to the general freedom of the middle classes and to the well-being of an unhampered competitive economy as in the Middle Ages Jewish "privileges" had been bound by the prosperity of an overlord or by a bishop's itch for embroidery.

Meanwhile, the Jews in the ghettos along the Rhine, if they had sharp ears, could hear the drums of Valmy and Jemappes.

14

ROMANTICS

THE "thirty-six kings" of Germany, alarmed at the unwillingness of France to put up with even one king, had the poor judgment to undertake crushing the Revolution by force. In September 1792 a German-Austrian army marched into the Republic; Danton raised his immortal defy, *l'audace et toujours de l'audace!* and in less time than it takes to tell the guns at Valmy sent the invaders scampering back to their three-dozen kings. A camp follower of the Germans, privy-councilor Goethe, curious as to the effects of cannon-fire on the ear drums, told his comrades as the barrage died off Valmy ridge: "From this place and this date begins a new era in the world's history, and you can all say you were present at its birth."

Eager to have as many Germans as possible "present" at the new birth, the French, once they got started, kept right on going. Mayence, Spires, Worms, the whole Rhine lands, fell into their hands; and by October they had crossed the river and temporarily captured Frankfort. It was the First Crusade all over again, but with the republic of mankind rather than the kingdom of heaven as its goal.

In Frankfort the Germans stubbornly refused to be made "human beings"; they insisted on remaining as Heine said nature had created them—*Esel.* And its Jewry, even more German than any German *Esel,* likewise refused. When the Prussian forces came to drive out the crusaders—which they shortly succeeded in doing—the Jews shouted, "Long live the King of Prussia! Down with the French!" This enthusiasm did them scant good, for while truce negotiations were in progress the City Council, doubtless to make them realize that patriotism was not included among their "privileges," locked them in the ghetto. But the French understood. "Caged birds," said the French commander, "whistle the tunes that are played to them."

Mayence and other Rhine ghettos showed a similar loyalty. But when the French returned a few years later to hold the Rhine provinces until the fall of Napoleon—time enough for Heine's generation to be born and grow to manhood—the birds sang a different song, one surely struck from the heart.

We may catch its air in Mayence. On September 22, 1798, the city authorities, now turned republican, ordered the demolition of the ghetto gate "with suitable festivities." But the decree came too late. On the preceding day the watchman of the gate, unaware that times had changed, sought to prevent one Moses Cahn and his young wife from moving their household goods through the gate into the free world outside. As they came to blows, a French officer passed by. Godfrey of Bouillon would have shuddered at his words. "Good for you!" he cried to the Jew, "I'll send you help, and away with that old contraption!" No sooner said than done, and the next evening the demolished gate was burned to the accompaniment of music and fireworks.

In Cologne, where the Jews had been banned since 1426, the French Commissioner issued a proclamation: "All traces of slavery are now abolished . . . you shall account to God alone for your religious beliefs, and as to your civil status, all men stand equal before the law." But without waiting for these words—the presence of the Revolutionary army was guarantee enough—the Jews began to return to the city famous in their history.

ii

What music rang and rockets flamed in the breasts of the Rhenish Jews may be surmised by considering the lot of their fellows in Prussia. Frederick and Mendelssohn had died in the same year—1786. Prussian Jewry still lived under Frederick's "*General-Privilegium und Reglement vor die Judenschaft*—'General Privilege and Statute for Jewry' "—which dated, with its subsequent harshening, from 1750 and which Mirabeau described as "a law worthy of a cannibal."

No sooner had Frederick's nephew and successor mounted the throne when Mendelssohn's successors among the enlightened circles of Berlin petitioned for a reform of the old status. Prussian officers, courtiers, intellectuals, and artists were already at home in the drawing rooms of Jewish bankers and the *salon* of Henriette Herz; it was felt to be high time that the Jews should be at home in the Prussian state— or at least the better sort. For the advanced Jews, under the leadership of Friedländer—whom we have met as banker Itzig's son-in-law and founder of the Free School—were conscious of their cultural distinction, and they smarted under the fate which classed them with the "unprivileged" garden variety of the race. In the hope of inducing the world to note their progress, they began calling themselves Deists and

Mosaists. Soon they would be known (on polite tongues) as Hebrews, Israelites, or Members of the Mosaic Faith. As early as 1793 the bankers and more prosperous merchants of Königsberg Jewry brought the government's attention to the unfortunate fact that "the word *Jew* carries a debasing flavor and its use does us great damage."

The new king, Frederick William II, likely had a surfeit of his uncle's parade of reason. He dabbled in Rosicrucian mysteries, and deciding to show that he had a good heart rather than a strong head, he abolished the shameful "body-tax." But the report of his royal commission, which pondered the *Reglement* for two years, shattered the hopes of Jewry. In 1789, while the French Assembly was proclaiming the Rights of Man, the commission recommended a few sops —which the Berlin Jews manfully refused to accept—and, passing to principles, declared that emancipation could be granted only in the measure that the Jews attained a culture "like the Christians" and thereby rendered themselves innocuous to the state. This arduous achievement, they believed, would be consummated "in about three generations, or sixty to seventy years." The commission was mistaken as to Jewish speed in reaching the level of Christendom, but they knew their Germans. It was precisely seventy-two years—if we except the Napoleonic interlude—before the whole of Germany fully emancipated her Jews, even in a formal sense. The history of these years can in fact be summarized as the ingenious efforts of the Jews to provide themselves a culture "like the Christians" and their battle to convince the Germans they had succeeded.

In their first despair a group of Berlin's enlightened set made a flank attempt to win citizenship. Rebuffed by the state, Friedländer addressed himself to the church. He published an anonymous epistle in behalf of "several heads of families of the Jewish Faith" (1799), in which he asked a liberal Protestant clergyman what the minimum requirements might be for the admission of rationalist progressive Jews into the Christian fold. In order, as he frankly admitted, to become citizens, they were prepared to accept the usual Christian rites, such as baptism, provided it was understood that these rites were mere conventionalities and implied no belief in the divinity of Jesus. Naturally the reply of the clergyman—who had heard of Marranos—punctured the trial balloon, and all Berlin laughed at what it termed "dry baptism." In this tragi-comic episode, however, lay the germ of grave changes. Many of the unhappy champions—or victims—of Enlightenment were soon prepared to accept a wet baptism; and Friedländer, together with such as could not bring themselves to this extremity, became convinced that the only alternative was to convert Judaism itself into tasteful conventionalities.

Another trivial incident pointed, on the Christian side, to an ominous shift of opinion. In 1803 a Berlin lawyer named Grattenauer published a pamphlet which created a brief furore. The portent lay in his virulent denunciation of the "elegant" Jews, even of the *salon* leaders who were at that moment the adored hostesses of German culture and fine society—the very Jews who believed that a whole-hearted adoption of all that was best in German life and thought would bring them equality and liberation. "They may talk about Goethe, Schiller, and Schlegel" as they please, but—Grattenauer contended—they remained an "Asiatic alien people"; and the cleft, therefore, between Jew and German was unbridgeable, equal rights could never change Jewish character, and any and all intercourse with them was, from the German standpoint, "highly reprehensible."

The attack was a flash in the pan, yet in the flash keen-eyed Jews might have seen that the issue did not turn solely on religion or on the acquisition of modern manners. The question of nationality—which together with capitalism was to dominate the nineteenth century—had raised its disturbing head. Indeed, the position of the Prussian government, as stated in 1797 and again in the radical concessions of 1812, plainly showed that it aimed to destroy the folkways and internal cohesion of Jewry. Not Jewish dogmas or ceremonies, but Jewish *identity* was the issue.

Napoleon put the matter bluntly before a state session concerned with the Alsatian Jews in 1806. "The government," he said, "can not look with indifference on the exploitation of Alsace by a debased and degraded nation, one capable of every scurvy vice. The Jews must be considered not a sect but a nation. They are a nation within a nation . . . and they must be dealt with not on a civil basis, but politically." True, the Sanhedrin of Jews summoned to Paris in 1806 could in all conscience assure Napoleon that they were Frenchmen first and last. They could, in all honesty, drop Jerusalem from their past and the hope of Zion from their future. They could surrender their language, traditional legislation, and any number of rites, prayers, and beliefs. But they could not— by any sort of physical or spiritual acrobatics—*abolish themselves.*

For three generations the more vocal leaders of German Jewry misunderstood or evaded the issue. They talked and acted on the assumption—in which they were encouraged by "liberal" German opinion—that, on the one hand, the Jews were a sect and by bringing its dogmas and ritual into harmony with the age, Jewish disabilities would vanish; and, on the other hand, that members of this sect, owing to their compulsory ghetto life, had fallen behind the times—had perhaps acquired a number of unpleasant traits—but education and contact with the world would remedy all that. Meanwhile the bulk of the Germans, and probably a majority of their intellectuals, looked on the Jews as a nation—an old-fashioned term which later became "nationality"—and, while conceding that the Jews could modify their manners and their cult, either doubted or denied that a nationality as ancient, persistent, and vital as Israel could ever lose its identity. *Jew* grew to be a pun; on many Jewish lips it designated a creed; on many German lips, a *Volk*—a people, race, and nationality. Though they used the same words Jew and Gentile talked a different language—until Moses Hess explained the dismal joke.

iii

Napoleon's victories, however short-lived, changed the face of Germany. By 1806 Austria and Prussia were crushed. The Holy Roman Empire—the Reich—vanished even as a name. Prussia was reduced to a shadow of its former size. West and South Germany were incorporated into a Confederation of the Rhine which embraced, among smaller states, Saxony and the newly-created kingdoms of Westphalia, Württemberg, and Bavaria. Whether nominally independent or allies, they were one and all captives of the French eagles.

Many survivals of feudalism joined the Reich in oblivion.

In Prussia a beginning was made toward the abolition of serfdom and the monopoly of the guilds. The Napoleonic Code reigned elsewhere—in Westphalia it outlasted the defeat of its author. Where Napoleon did not literally rule, his spirit prevailed; and, with all its despotism, it was a cleansing wind of liberty and modernity blowing over the medieval swamp of German institutions. For the first time in their history the Germans knew what it was not to be a servile *Untertan*; but, unfortunately, the lesson was taught them at the point of French bayonets and not learned by their own will and effort.

The Jews who suffocated with the peasants in the foulest depths of the swamp likewise got their first whiff of freedom. Westphalia liberated them completely; Mecklenburg, Baden, Württemberg, and Bavaria in a respectively lesser degree. Saxony remained obdurate—the "Protestant Spain." Frankfort tried to hold out, with the approval of its native son Goethe; but was finally compelled to yield (1810). Prussia in a desperate burst of liberalism—caught between the pressure of Napoleon's armies from without and its progressive ministers Hardenberg and Humboldt from within—granted full citizenship, barring only the right to hold positions in the state (1812). It was just in time. Hungry for freedom and lured by the liberal neo-Christian mysticism of pastor Schleiermacher, well over one-tenth of the Berlin Jews had, between 1802 and 1810, accepted baptism.

Every side of life was touched with bloom. Finance quickened: in 1807 thirty out of fifty-two Berlin banks were in Jewish hands; a crop of court bankers sprang up in the Rhine states and Bavaria, a few of whom, as we have remarked, landed in the nobility. One of these Rhenish bankers, Mayer

Anshel Rothschild of Frankfort, who died in 1812, had greater luck—he left five sons with the genius to create an empire unrivaled since the Fuggers. A Westphalian court-banker, Israel Jacobsohn, satisfied other ambitions. He founded a boarding-school open to Jewish and Christian children in the hope of bringing the two peoples closer together; he installed an organ in the school synagogue, as daring an innovation in 1801 as wearing long trousers instead of breeches; as head of the Westphalian Jewish consistory, he established schools which provided a secular education, he abolished private synagogues and sprinkled the public worship with hymns, sermons, and prayers in German. Where the law permitted, Jews served on municipal councils (Prussia), entered professions, state offices, and the higher ranks of the army (Westphalia). The mass of Jewry, however, remained as poverty-stricken as before. In 1813—92% of the Prussian Jews were petty retail-dealers or worse: 20% peddlers and 10% beggars. Their one permanent acquisition was surnames. Although family names had not been uncommon among upper class Jews for a century or more, governmental decree and social imitation now made their adoption universal. Most of the new labels were translations or transliterations from the Hebrew (*Hirsch, Loeb*) or place names (*Oppenheim, Lowenthal*).

In Berlin the *salons* sparkled brighter than ever. The beauty and wit of Henriette Herz and the warm sympathy of Dorothea Mendelssohn lured new admirers: philosopher Fichte, statesman Humboldt, his scientist brother, and princes of the royal blood "who" a contemporary remarks "needed no second invitation"; as well as the apostles of the new Romantic movement, William and Frederick Schlegel, and its eloquent heart-crushing preacher, the Reverend Frederick Schleier-macher. On the top floor of her father's house Rachel Levin (1771-1833), ugly as sin and even more attractive, opened a "garret *salon*" where, with Madame de Staël as visitor and ally, she led the fight for Goethe. Perhaps for the very reason that they came from an outcast minority clan, it was easier for these Jewesses—granting the charm, brains, and money— to serve as the magnet of Berlin's intellectual life than for their German sisters. Once breaking with their past, they had less to fetter them in the present. In any case, "to meet the best society without ceremony," said Schleiermacher, "one must be introduced to the *salons* of the Jews." One way or another they became the midwives and nurses of a generation of German culture.

It all ended rather happily too. Upon her husband's death Henriette Herz gave herself—platonically, she assures us—to Schleiermacher; and when her mother died, to Schleier-macher's church. Dorothea Mendelssohn became the mistress of Frederick Schlegel; they each wrote a romantic novel in praise of free love, and then repented by marrying and join-ing the Catholic Church. Indeed four of Mendelssohn's six children, and all his grandsons save one, rejoiced in baptism and a successful career. Perhaps most successful, considering the effort involved, was Abraham Mendelssohn whose fame rested on being the son of Moses the philosopher and the father of Felix the composer.

Rachel Levin married the Prussian diplomat and writer, Varnhagen von Ense, and turned Christian. Her *salon* played the leading rôle in the literary movements of her long day. "She was the first to understand and recognize me," said Goethe. She captivated the "sentimental" Richter and the "romantic" Chamisso and Fouqué. The reactionary "German Christian" Arnim and Brentano could not afford to be absent from her smile. She lived "an old witch or, rather, an aging fairy" to cast a spell on Grillparzer, and years later dominate the youth of Heine, who could never forget "that enigmatic, melancholy, sensible, mystical smile." What was the enigma and whence the melancholy? No one knows. Yet, "I have a feeling," she once said, "as though some unearthly creature had presided at my birth and, when I came into the world, stabbed me with these words: 'You shall be sensitive, you shall be great-hearted and noble, you shall see things as few can see them, if you will . . . but you shall be a Jewess'— and now my whole life is a continual bleeding."

iv

There was much to bleed for, though hardly as Rachel meant. The Romantic movement which flowed through these Jewish *salons* was, unlike its counterpart in England and France, more than a shift in literary taste. The triumph of Reason in the French Revolution shook the social foundations of Germany and, under Napoleon, threatened its corporate existence. The German intellectual therefore fled the contemporary scene in dismay. While Goethe withdrew to Olympus, lesser men—the Schlegels at their head—made their famous retreat to the Middle Ages and the bosom of the Mother Church. "When the Prussians turned their backs on the French at the battle of Jena," said Heine, "they threw themselves into the arms of religion. For such a hopeless defeat no faith, indeed, serves one as well as the Christian. The example of his Savior strengthened and guided the King

of Prussia; for his kingdom too was no longer of this world.
. . . The French instilled spirituality into the remaining German peoples by very material war-taxes and garrisons. . . .
The Germans are right in holding fast to religion: a land
governed by thirty-six kings can't afford to do without Christianity."

In a more realistic spirit Fichte, the leading philosopher of
the moment and in his own inscrutable way a defender of the
right of revolution, loosed the mighty fountains of patriotism.
His *Addresses to the German Nation* (1807-1808), written in
the depths of its despair and humiliation, are still the ultimate
source and expression of German nationalism. No later pane-
gyric of German virtue, no later proclamation of German
superiority, has ever surpassed this "bible of German patriotism." The German language, culture, and soul are exalted
beyond compare. "Only the German," Fichte told this beaten
unhappy race, "really has a people and is entitled to count as
one, and he alone is capable of a real and rational love of his
nation. . . . To have character and to be a German undoubtedly means the same thing." If this paragon of peoples were
destroyed by foreign power or influence—for "all our evils
are of foreign origin"—then indeed "barbarism would over-
take us all, until we were reduced to living in caves like wild
beasts . . . though only a German can see this, of course."
Indeed, "if the Germans were to perish, the whole human
race must perish with them." He likewise preached that worship of the State which was to become the characteristic of
the reborn Reich. "The state," he said, "has a higher object
than securing peace, property, personal freedom, and the life
and well-being of all"—that object being "the devouring flame
of a higher patriotism." A world away, all this, from Lessing

who had defined patriotism as "a heroic weakness which I gladly forego."

Fichte had previously left no doubt that, in his mind, the German nation did not include its Jews. In 1793 he wrote: "There is spread throughout nearly every country of Europe a powerful inimical State which wars continually against all others and often succeeds in bitterly oppressing their peoples —this State is Jewry. . . . The only way I can see to give [the Jews] civil rights is to cut off their heads in a single night and equip them with new ones devoid of every Jewish idea. . . . To protect ourselves against them, again I see no means except to conquer their Promised Land and pack them all off to it."

Moved by these sentiments of religion and patriotism—as well as by the promises of the Prussian king and his liberal ministers for a constitutional government—the Germans flung themselves into the war of liberation (1813-1814) which, with the help of England, Russia, and Austria, was to free them from the French yoke. Unfrightened by the sentiments and inspired by the promises, the Jews fought and died at the side of their fellow-citizens. For the first time in its history, the population of Germany acted as a unit.

When Napoleon had fallen, the Congress of Vienna (1814-1815) prepared a rude awakening for the Germans—Jew and Christian. The kings and the princes had nothing to gain by German unity, the feudal aristocracy everything to lose by any survival of the Rights of Man. As a part of the reactionary policy of the Holy Alliance, all promises were forgotten and most of the newly-won rights withdrawn. Germany was delivered back to its "thirty-six kings"; and any effectual popular government was indefinitely postponed.

At the Congress the Jews enjoyed their first attention as a problem in general European politics; and like the German burgher, peasant, and worker, they learned what it meant to be swindled by modern statesmanship. Jewry, so the Congress provided, was entitled to keep the privileges already granted *by* the German states. The trick lay in the word *by*, which had been substituted for *in* when Hardenberg and Stein were not looking. Since, outside of Prussia and Mecklenburg, emancipation had been granted *by* the French and not *by* the states themselves, the Jews soon found themselves as badly off as when the French first crossed the Rhine.

Indeed, their lot was worse. Germany seethed with a frustrated patriotism. "From every throat," writes Treitschke, "rose the bitter plaint that the blood of Leipzig and Waterloo had been spilled in vain." Father Jahn led his host of gymnasts—the *Turnvereine*—in a crusade against everything foreign. On the summit of the Wartburg students lit a holy bonfire and cast into the flames all the books offending the national soul. The fire that burned elsewhere in patriotic hearts was fueled with hatred of the French and the Jews: the French who had invented Cosmopolitanism and invaded their sacred soil; the Jews who incarnated Cosmopolitanism and who, as born bloodsuckers and money-lenders, had profiteered by the French invasion.

But the French were safely back home, and all the rage of a robbed and betrayed people fell upon Jewish shoulders. "The powerful excitement of the War of Liberation," Treitschke explains, "brought to light all the secrets of the German character; amid the general ferment all the old and profound hostility to everything Judaic once more made itself manifest." The medievalism of the Romantics and the nationalism inflamed by Fichte joined against the Jews in a common hue and cry. For the Romantics they were the traditional "enemies" of the Church; and it was as much the duty of a good medievalist to hate them as to love stained-glass windows. For the patriots, they were—as Grattenauer and Fichte had preached—an "Asiatic alien people . . . who oppressed all others." Christ and the tribal god Teut clasped hands.

v

A "Christian Teutomania" swept the land. It began with slap-stick—a farce caricaturing the Jews (*Unser Verkehr*—"The People We Go With," 1815), which was applauded in all the leading theaters and which still lives, at least by name, in German literature.

It then fell into the hands of the *Gelehrte*. Frederick Rühs, professor of history at the newly-founded University of Berlin, published a pamphlet *On the Claims of the Jews to German Citizenship*, in which the claims were denied. Military service must likewise be denied them—"only Germans are worthy to fight by the side of Germans"—and this, the very year that Jewish privates and officers at Waterloo gave their lives for Prussia. The professor delved into his *Fach*, history, and urged the revival of the Badge of Shame, "so that a German, even if he be deceived by looks, behavior, and speech, can recognize his Hebrew enemy."

Next, J. F. Fries, professor of philosophy at the University of Heidelberg, came out with a popularly written book *On the Menace of the Jews to the Welfare and Character of the Germans* (1816), in which the myth of a "state within a state" served to justify his demand for their total expulsion. "Jewry," he wrote, "is a social pest which owes its rapid spread to money and is accompanied by misery, tyranny, and taxes. . . . Ask any man whether every burgher and peasant does not hate and curse the Jews as robbers of their bread and as the plague of our nation." Fichte, fresh in his grave, would have been proud of his colleagues.

At the height of the pamphleteering, one Hartwig Hundt, not a professor, outlined a solution which would have done credit to Swift. "We should sell the Jewish children," he urged with no thought of irony, "to the English who could work them on their West Indian plantations instead of the blacks. The menfolk in Israel should be castrated and their wives and daughters consigned to our houses of shame." "Still," he concluded in favor of more medieval and therefore fashionable tastes, "outright expulsion would be best." It may be hard to realize that this delving and mining into the past, into the deep recesses of the folk soul, which produced these enormities were at the same time giving to the world Grimm's fairy-tales.

Finally Teutomania descended to the mind of the mob. Old-fashioned folk riots broke out in Franconia and spread to the Rhine and the North (1819). "Hep-hep!" rang the cry in the Jewish streets of Würzburg, Bamberg, Carlsruhe, Heidelberg, Mannheim, Frankfort, and Hamburg. *Hep,* some scholars claim, is an abbreviation of the Latin *Hierosolyma est perdita*—"Jerusalem has fallen." Other scholars believe it derives from the old German *habe*—"give." But scholarship is unnecessary to understand the cry *"Jude verreckel"* which accompanied it and has been revived in our own times. "A dog's death to the Jew!" explained itself in sacked houses, plundered shops, and in the wounded and the dead.

Through it all, a few voices came to the defense of the

victims. Englishmen and Frenchmen expressed their indignation. An aged German pastor, Johann Ewald, living in the memories of the Age of Reason, and a Professor Brendel of Würzburg, who probably ranked Kant above Fichte, appealed to the German sense of honor and decency. Heinrich Paulus, a theologian of Heidelberg, undertook to distinguish between good Jews and bad Jews, and urged that the good ones—that is, those "whose education and behavior were like the Germans"—should be admitted to citizenship.

Among the Jews, the old guard of Enlightenment added their protest from, as it were, the tomb of a buried century. But from the converted Jews who had found the *Judengasse* too narrow and passed into the larger finer world of humanity—not a word. Rachel von Varnhagen, to be sure, wrote privately to her brother: "My grief is boundless. . . . The hypocritical new-born love for Christianity (God forgive me for my sins!), for the Middle Ages with their art, poetry, and horrors, is inciting the people to the one horror it can still summon from the past. . . . It is not the people who have done this . . . the professors Fries and Rühs, and others such as Arnim, Brentano, *unser Verkehr,* and yet higher persons with their prejudices, have launched the cry."

But the mania had its point. In a few states—Hessia, and to a lesser extent Baden and Württemberg—some of the newly-acquired rights were preserved. Prussia, on the other hand, interpreted these rights so as to exclude the Jews from civil appointments, the army, and most professions; and all benefits of emancipation were denied to the annexed province of Posen with its 80,000 Polish Jews. Elsewhere the principles of a "Christian German" state triumphed, and the old conditions—with slight modern trimmings—were revived.

The effect upon the Jews, as Germany dragged the chains of medievalism into the second quarter of the nineteenth century, was mingled determination and despair. Those who despaired saw in baptism the "admission ticket to European civilization"—it was Heine's phrase. Between 1812 and 1846 thousands purchased the ticket, some with cold contempt, like Boerne, and others with bitter pangs, like Heine. The hardier majority determined to enter Europe's civilization without a ticket; and Boerne and Heine pledged their life to ridding Germany of its "thirty-six kings" who demanded the fee.

Perhaps the last word remained with Goethe. Not the aged privy-councilor who in 1823 led the agitation to thrust the Jews of Saxe-Weimar back into their medieval prison. Not the Olympian whom Boerne taunted, casting the poet's own words in his teeth, "I do you honor? Why? Have you ever lifted a finger to lighten the burden of the oppressed?" But Goethe the world spirit, the Goethe who said: "To tolerate is to insult. Tolerance must be only a preparatory sentiment to open the way to mutual acceptance. True liberalism is recognition and understanding."

15

LIBERATORS

WHEN the Teuton maniacs subsided—as they quickly did upon a nod from Metternich—Germany entered a halcyon age. For nearly a half century—from 1820 until Bismarck took the wheel in 1862—it lived in its own and the world's eyes as a nation of thinkers, poets, and dreamers.

During the greater part of this period the thinkers were undisturbed by the noise of power looms, and the dreams unsullied by the smoke of factory chimneys. The large scale use of machinery, the gigantic growth of cities, the rise of a proletariat, did not begin until the forties, and even in 1862 the industrial revolution was still more a promise than a reality. Coal production, which may be taken as the sign of the revolution, was 1½ million metric tons in 1850; by 1862 it had only reached 15 million. The modesty of this figure may be grasped by comparing it with the output in 1906 when Germany attained its industrial maturity and the mines delivered 136 million tons. In 1840, a midway date, the German banking resources were one-seventh those of the United States and one-eleventh those of Great Britain.

The political lag was equally marked. Metternich and the "thirty-six" kings (actually the rulers of the thirty-eight states which made up the German Confederation, including Austria), aided by a strict censorship, spies, and a sturdy police, kept the paternal despotism of the eighteenth century fairly intact. But it suited the popular temperament to receive orders and obey them. Spared both the fever of industrialism and the responsibility of government, the people could devote themselves to pleasanter and higher things.

In the art of life it was the reign of *Gemütlichkeit*—a word as German as *sport* and *gentleman* are English, and quite as untranslatable. To drink Rhine wine out of tall green glasses, but not too much; to smoke a two-foot pipe and contemplate the universe of a barnyard; to weep with Werther and Jean Paul and sing with Schubert; to enter into all the simple and primary joys with gusto, yet with measure and tidiness—that was *Gemütlichkeit*.

Nevertheless, Germany was no backwater of civilization—no Balkans or Turkey which it so closely resembled in its modest standards of life, economic slumber, and political stagnation. By a stroke of fate, perhaps never to be repeated, a modern gifted people had enough worldly means to indulge their mind and not too much to poison it.

In letters, music, pure science, and philosophy, they were abreast, when not ahead, of the world. Instead of, as a century before, living on the alms of alien ideas, they were now enriching the ideas of others. Their exports of textiles and hardware may have been derisory; but they were shipping to all the cultural marts of the globe Kant, Goethe, Schiller, and Beethoven—merchandise whose trade-mark "Made in Germany" feared no competitors. From the American prairies to the Russian steppes foreigners learned to conjugate German verbs and flocked to Heidelberg and Leipzig, not because it was good for business, but good for their hearts to hear Mendelssohn and Schumann, and for their heads to know Hegel, Humboldt, and Ranke, and a little later Schopenhauer and Helmholtz. "It is a blessing," wrote Carlyle in 1838, "there should be one country where abstract Thought can still take shelter; that while the din and frenzy of Catholic Emancipations and Rotten Boroughs and Revolts of Paris deafen every French and every English ear, the German can stand peaceful on his scientific watchtower and tell the Universe, which so often forgets that fact, what o'clock it is."

Gott, war so gut! ach, war so lieb!

ii

Yet Emancipations—Catholic and otherwise—were mining and brewing beneath the comfortable crust of *Gemütlichkeit.* In 1824 a young poet who had just written the *Lorelei* was tramping through the Harz mountains and, sleeping in a forest hut, dreamed another myth for humanity. The forester's daughter, a little child timid with the thought of witches and goblins, sat at the poet's feet and told him her fears. When he laughed at her old wives' tales, she shrank back in doubt if he were an honest Christian.

"My child," he said—but who can render the magic verse? —"when I lay in my mother's lap I believed in God the Father, and when I grew older I believed in the Son, and now that I am a man my heart swells with faith in the Holy Ghost—the Holy Spirit which topples the walled castles of tyranny and breaks the yoke of the serf—the Spirit which retells us that all men are freeborn and noble—the Spirit which lifts the murky fog shrouding us from life and dispels the specters that haunt our waking and our sleep. A thousand well-armed knights are liegemen to this Spirit: their swords flash and banners fly to fulfill His will. Would you like to see such a knight, my child?" "Then," said Heine as the dream faded, "kiss me once and look at me thrice—for I too am a knight of the Holy Spirit."

In the Jewish world which this knight was to forsake but never forget, the spirit of science and freedom had brought together a band of young university men who likewise dedicated themselves to the Holy Spirit—the Hebrew *Shekinah*. They founded in Berlin, 1819, a society for Jewish culture and knowledge (*Verein für Cultur und Wissenschaft der Juden*). The founder and vice-president was Leopold Zunz (1794-1886), a graduate of the University of Berlin and afterwards of Halle, and already immersed in Jewish research. At his side were the young Hegelian, Eduard Gans, as president; the polyhistor and Orientalist, Ludwig Markus, who left a vast work on Abyssinia; the walking encyclopedia, Moses Moser, whom for his wisdom, practical judgment and warm heart Heine called "the epilogue to Nathan the Wise"; and later, among others, Heine himself.

With the "Hep-hep" storm ringing in their ears and deserters flocking to the shelter of the baptismal font, they faced the dilemma Moses Mendelssohn had embodied in his *Jerusalem*. How could Jewish ways be adapted to modernity? How reconcile tradition with reason? The younger generation, it was apparent, would no longer tolerate the discipline which had maintained Jewry these many centuries; the older generation could furnish no philosophy that would hold the young, once the discipline was abandoned; and Christianity, as the sole avenue to citizenship and a share in modernity, invited young and old alike. Obviously the Mendelssohn formula—that Judaism was not a revealed religion but a body of revealed legislation, hence a Jew could believe as reason dictated but he must behave as the Law provides—would not satisfy Hegelian (or any other) trained minds.

Very briefly, the young men proposed to gain freedom through knowledge. Not merely knowledge of the Gentile world to which Mendelssohn had opened the doors, but knowledge of their own world; not Enlightenment from without, but light from within. They felt that familiarity with Jewish history and literature would create a natural and insensible self-respect which would, in turn, preserve the essentials of a Jewish life. On this basis they launched on an ambitious program of studies, schools, and publications. However, its fulfillment depended, first, on an adequate knowledge of Jewish history and literature, and secondly on money. But neither they nor anyone else possessed the knowledge, and the thirty-odd bankers of Berlin refused to give the money.

After a few years of futile struggle, president Gans reported: "The only link which unites the Jews is fear; the only interest for which they are willing to part with some of their worldly goods is charity." And he forthwith retired to the Hegelian Absolute, and eventually to a professorship—at the cost of baptism. Heine paid the same cost in order to practice law, which he never did. Markus died, an exile, in Paris. Vice-president Zunz prophesied: "The Jewry and Judaism we tried to rebuild is a divided house, the prey of barbarians, fools, money-lenders and *parnasim*. For a long time to come we shall see this people as it is today, adrift and without discipline or principles, turning to Christianity because it can turn to nothing else; one section still sunk in the squalor of the past, despised by Europe . . . the other rustling papers in minor Government posts—rich or bankrupt, persecuted or tolerated, in turn."

Yet Zunz remained true to the task. "A man of responsibility and action, he worked and achieved where the others dreamed and fainted by the way," was Heine's tribute.

When he began the labors which—long before his ninety-two years came to an end—won him the title of the Grand Old Man of the new learning, Jewish history and its literature were sealed books. In fact they were ungathered and unwritten books. The experience of Jewry since biblical days was but dimly known, and its significance unplumbed. The documents which preserved this experience were neglected, or "given equal weight as long as they were written by pious hands." No one knew precisely who wrote what, or why and when. Men, events, and ideas drifted in the indiscriminate chaos of the past, unfixed in time or space. "Jewish history," as Graetz, the greatest of Jewish historians, was to remark, "lacked its two eyes: a knowledge of place and date." It likewise lacked the focus of method or system. In short, it lacked science.

Zunz invented the name for this science: *Wissenschaft des Judentums,* and then spent his life creating the thing it named. He meant by the term a research and understanding of the Jewish past, in its parts and totality, as far as it was preserved in literary monuments. He meant philology—which German scholars, spurred by the Romantic vogue for the Middle Ages, were transforming from a mere criticism of texts into a science of history. His teachers, Friedrich August Wolf and August Boeckh, the founders of modern classical philology, gave him the "eyes" to turn on Jewish history. And Hegel gave him the focus to see that history as an evolution of ideas.

Though all of his work was inspired by the needs of his people, his first monumental achievement sprang directly from an immediate crisis. The Prussian government, in one of its despotic whims, temporarily forbade the rabbis to preach in German. Accordingly, in 1832 he published the *Gottesdienstliche Vorträge der Juden*, which proved that the Jews used the vernacular for their sermons in Palestine and the dispersion from time immemorial. But this was a mere detail. Actually he presented a comprehensive study of homiletics and liturgy which, since these embrace everything from folk lore to philosophy, meant nothing less than a two-thousand year panorama of the Jewish mind. "The synagogal services," he found, "were at once the banner of Jewish nationality and the shield of the Jewish faith."

Similarly, his work on Jewish names (*Namen der Juden,* 1837) received its impetus from a governmental decree forbidding Jews to use "Christian" given names. Again it meant a sweeping light thrown across the ages, which illumined the course of the dispersion as well as revealing that Jewish children had borne almost every conceivable "Gentile" name. So too, his studies and translations of synagogal poetry (1855-1865) were prefaced by a famous chapter on "The Sufferings of the Jews" in which the story of the past—accurately placed and dated—was mingled with passion and irony meant to touch the reader of today.

When he had finished his active work in 1872, he had charted the main currents of Jewish literature and thought, indicated their relations to the world stream in which they flowed, and sketched the outlines of their fortunes. Meanwhile Galician and Italian scholars—a Krochmal, Rapoport, and Luzzatto—had fished independently in the same waters. Younger men had followed in his wake and given body to his sketches: Abraham Geiger on the development of religious thought as revealed in the gradual formation of the biblical text (1857), and Heinrich Graetz, whose universal history of the Jews (1853-1870), while rivaled by Dubnow, is still unsurpassed—to name only two of a phalanx of creative scholars. The book of the Jewish past was open for all to read.

Many chapters were missing—and still are. When Zunz was forming his mind, Marx had not yet turned Hegel upside down. Little or nothing of economics, of history as an interplay between social ideas and social means of producing food, shelter, and pleasures, found place in the work of the entire school. Not enough has found a place even today. Finally, it is hard to say whether the combined efforts of these explorers have attained the result which the young hopefuls back in 1819 proposed: to gain freedom through knowledge. But every subsequent battle to win that freedom owed much of its ammunition to Leopold Zunz.

iii

The battle of scholars to liberate the past from oblivion could hardly excite the average man. Moreover, during all this while, a more demonstrative struggle for liberation was besetting the pulpits, thrilling the pews, and dividing the hearts of Jewry.

It began ostensibly as an innocent question of musical taste and linguistic preference. When Israel Jacobsohn moved from Westphalia to Berlin in 1815, he took with him his predilection for organ music and vernacular prayers. That same year he and another banker, Jacob Beer (father of the composer Meyerbeer), each set up private synagogues in which an organ rolled, and hymns were sung and prayers composed in German. The fashion spread; and after the King—whose head was filled not only with political but religious notions of "legitimacy"—closed the Berlin experiments, a similar "temple" was publicly opened in the free port of Hamburg (1818).

Beneath the surface, however, lay more than esthetics. After all, it was of small consequence whether a choir of unintelligible boys chanted Hebrew hymns according to custom; or whether German chorals were sung with equal unintelligibility to the accompaniment of an organ. It hardly mattered whether the cantor intoned the Hebrew prayers in age-old style; or the rabbi droned German translations in the soporific sing-song which, until recent times, was the prerogative of all clergymen.

The point was that the introduction of musical instruments and of German meant a conscious effort to break with the ghetto, achieve identity with the outside world, and create a form of worship sufficiently like the Christian to diminish social antagonism between the two groups as well as stem the tide of conversion. It was a natural device which in animal and plant life is known as protective coloration. "We no longer have the strength," wrote Heine in 1823, "to wear a beard, to fast . . . and to be patient: that is the reason for our Reform movement. Some, who have received their education and enlightenment by sitting in theater seats, want to provide Judaism with new scenic effects and repaint the lobby . . . others want a miniature Protestant Christianity under a Jewish trade-mark, and weave themselves a *tallit* [prayer-shawl] out of the wool of the Lamb."

Deeper yet, the break arose from an effort to aid the struggle for political emancipation. The rejection from the liturgy of many prayers expressing the faith in a messianic return to Palestine was a declaration of loyalty to the German state— the more effective, it was hoped, because, unlike the declarations of the Napoleonic Sanhedrin, it was unquestionably voluntary. It was doubtless considered a master-stroke, when it came to dedicating the Hamburg temple, to choose from a five-thousand-year calendar of heroism and holiness the anniversary of the Battle of Leipzig. To call their place of worship a "temple"—a term which the Jews had hitherto reserved for the fallen sanctuary in Jerusalem and for the restoration of which they had prayed down the centuries—had similar political implication. It meant that Hamburg or any other city which reared such a temple had supplanted the Holy City, and that the Jews—like the Huguenots who also called their church a "temple"—were purely a religious sect. "Stuttgart," said one Reform leader, "is our Jerusalem." Altogether, the innovators felt that once the German people saw that the Jews had abolished most of the differences in customs and manners which had their origin in an unhappy past and looked forward with the Christians to a common German future, equality in citizenship would soon follow community in life.

Underneath it all worked a change which both the Reformers and their opponents were experiencing in daily life, but which they either did not recognize or, because it was so obvious, failed to mention. Ever since the reconstruction of

Germany after the Thirty Years War, Jewry's economic occupation, like Othello's, was gone. The occupation had in fact been fairly wrecked by the revolution associated with the Fuggers in the sixteenth century. Once money-lending had become a general Christian profession and commerce had expanded to a magnitude which rendered the Jewish net-work of trade relations negligible, Jewry as a group lost its economic relevance. Throughout the eighteenth century the form of this group survived by virtue of the anti-Jewish "statutes" of a Frederick and his kind, and by the force of tradition within the group itself—though its bread-and-butter substance was vanishing. Now, however, in the 1820's, the Rothschilds or any other Jewish banker, merchant, and manufacturer might —and did—continue to be an asset to society as an individual in and a part of that society. But the time had long passed when Jewish bankers, acting as part of a Jewish community, could issue loans—when a Jewry could be responsible for the economic activities of its members, a source of protection to its merchants and bankers, or a mine of revenue to the State.

Consequently, the economic need for the old inner discipline had likewise vanished. Behind the theories of cultural liberation, of the progress of religious ideas, of discarding in the name of this progress the outworn husks of talmudic and rabbinic legislation, of concentrating on the pure essence of Mosaic monotheism and Prophetic idealism—behind all this reared a hard fact. Unless he turned Christian, the Jew who left the medieval ghetto and shook off obedience to its laws —which were both a religious bond and a social and economic shield—would have starved. Whereas the Jew who left the nineteenth-century *Judengasse* and disregarded such of the

613 commandments as interfered with the modern conduct of business had more to eat than ever.

Naturally, this break with old forms aroused stubborn opposition. The Jews on the extreme right, who felt that everything traditional was sacred, entrenched themselves in what has become generally known as the Orthodox position. Between the Orthodox and the Reform rose a group, usually called Conservative, who believed that a future could be secured by a minimum renunciation of the past or who, remembering the services rendered by the old discipline in the days gone by, instinctively clung to it as insurance for the days to come.

Two decades after the opening of the Hamburg temple—which had built up a large membership—the battle passed from the realm of trappings to ideas. Zunz and his fellow-workers had begun exhuming the experience of the past. Following this lead, the Reformers and their opponents likewise undertook a research, restatement, and revaluation of Judaism. Books, learned journals, and rabbinical conferences provided the arena, and Germany at large a congenial atmosphere. It was an accident, but a symbol, that in the year 1835 the first train ran on a German railway; David Strauss, the Protestant higher critic, published his rationalist *Life of Jesus*; and Abraham Geiger issued the first number of his *Wissenschaftliche Zeitschrift für jüdische Theologie*—The Scientific Journal of Jewish Theology.

Thereafter—for another two decades—the conflict raged over the authority of the Talmud, the interpretation of the Bible, the maintenance of Hebrew as the medium of divine revelation, the relative value of observance and belief and the application of both to daily living. The Reform position found its most fertile and learned defenders in Geiger and Samuel

Holdheim; the Conservative in Zacharias Frankel; and the Orthodox in Samson Raphael Hirsch.

When a generation or more had passed in debate and sermonics—it was the golden age of sermons—and the smoke of theology rolled away, it revealed marked similarities between the three contending groups. All of them agreed that they were Germans first and last, and only to be distinguished from other Germans by their religious beliefs and practices —however national or not the character of that religion might be. They all approved of secular education. They all realized that times and traditions were out of step, and that it was merely a matter of theoretical emphasis whether to fit their life to the ancient law—as Hirsch had urged—or fit the law to their life. In observances the moderates prevailed. Of the Jews who maintained their religious affiliations in twentieth-century Germany (large numbers did not), the majority were Conservatives. Fidelity to the dietary laws, fairly strict observance of the Sabbath, the use of the standard orthodox Hebrew prayer-book in public worship together with instrumental music (thou hast conquered, O Jacobsohn!) and sermons in German, were the rule. The next largest practicing group was the Orthodox, although feeble enough. And (when last heard from) there were but two Reform congregations in the whole land.

But Reform Judaism rendered valiant service to German Jewry in its day. It banished obscurantism from its opponents' camp and, eventually, much superficial apery from its own. The controversies it set on foot resulted in a clearer formulation of what all Jews—traditionalists, moderates, radicals, and even non-believers—stood for. The need for knowledge, which its challenge evoked, led the champions of all groups to further historical studies, to create a popular and a learned press, and to establish rabbinical seminaries modern in method and approach, however diverse in their aims. And while they died away in Germany, the Reformers who joined the emigration across the Atlantic, found a kinder destiny awaiting them in America.

iv

After this excursion among the theologians it is high time to return to the common people. Emigration to America? The mass of Germans in the early nineteenth century, like the mass of Jews, were neither engrossed in science, history, or metaphysics, nor even possessed of enough goods to indulge their talent for *Gemütlichkeit*. They were impoverished folk suffering from laws that would have shamed a Turk. In Prussia serfdom lingered for unpropertied peasants until 1850. The servile habits of the nation made revolt difficult and, when attempted in 1848, futile. But the fiasco of 1848—in which a parliament of intellectuals and orators offered the government of Germany to its most reactionary state, Prussia, and when the offer was contemptuously refused, put on their hats and went home—stirred the more resolute and liberty-loving spirits to action. Figures tell the story best. From 1820 to 1850 about 600,000 Germans of the Christian persuasion had migrated to America—by 1910 the number totaled five million.

The Jews had reason to bestir themselves sooner. In Posen and the Rhinelands their poverty was extreme, and in Bavaria their political oppression unbearable. Restrictions in occupations, in the right to marry, to travel to one town or reside in another, survived with all the rigor of the eighteenth century. Only Hessia—in 1833—had to a great extent emancipated its Jews.

Ordinary Moses Lümpchen who bore a pack on his back the whole year round found himself incapable of winning freedom with his head, as the professors of Jewish science recommended; or with his heart, as the sermonizers of Reform were promising. He decided to liberate himself with his heels.

The flight to America and freedom began with a trickle in the last half of the eighteenth century. In the 1830's it grew to be a powerful stream—to Italy, France, England, but above all the United States. By 1847—three years before the German Christian flood got under way—about 50,000 German Jews had reached the American shore, chiefly from Posen, the Rhinelands, and Bavaria. It was the first great breaking of ties with the Old World which was to end—when the Russian Jews followed suit—in the largest mass movement in Jewish history.

"On last Sunday, June 16," wrote a local reporter in the Stuttgart *Israelitische Annalen* of 1839, "about fifty men and women of the Mosaic persuasion in Ebenhausen—eight hours from Stuttgart—started on their journey to the United States of North America. Throngs of onlookers poured from far and near to witness their departure. Not an eye remained dry: deep anguish filled every breast. For not merely young people were setting out, as they did some weeks before, but heads of families with their wives and children. It was truly heartrending to see a greybeard of eighty bid a last farewell to all but one of his twelve children and to his fourteen grandchildren—the youngest barely two months old. Ebenhausen has a population of about 500 Israelites: so far 92 have emigrated. The present group carried with them their Torah scroll."

Another reporter stood on the river docks of Mayence, in 1845, and wrote for the *Allgemeine Zeitung des Judentums*: "Over 200 Bavarian Jews took ship here, last week, to seek a new fatherland in America. Their departure throws a cruel light on the situation in Bavaria. Nothing remains to them but misery or flight. One of the emigrants was asked whether he ever intended to return. 'I'll not come back,' he answered, 'until America turns Bavarian.' I find more to weep than laugh at in this jest. When we think of the fortunate circumstances of our Hessian Jews, we can hardly believe that our enlightened duchy borders on a land where no Jew can own a foot of ground, where only the eldest son may marry, and where the rest are condemned to a forced celibacy."

"Consider, my brothers, and hasten your decision!
Then haste you to America,
Haste to greet the land of freedom,
Free from prejudice, hate, and envy,
Free from hangmen and tyrants!
Over there the dawn of a better day
Beckons you, my brothers—think and make haste!"

So sang a Jewish verse-maker in 1884. The stream of hasteners mounted to a flood. By 1880 about 100,000 more of them had found a new fatherland.

V

Flight, however, did nothing to help those who were left behind, and who through it all continued the struggle for liberation. The battle broke out openly in 1830—when the July Revolution in Paris thrilled young hearts in Germany —and it gradually unrolled on four fronts.

The leader in the Jewish ranks was Gabriel Riesser (1806-1863), born in Hamburg, the grandson of its former chief rabbi. Not a generation but a world separated the two men. The grandfather had banned Mendelssohn's translation of the Pentateuch into German as a profanation of the Holy Word; the grandson was a doctor of laws, graduate of Heidelberg, supporter of the Reform movement, and a champion of equal rights for all Germans: the Orthodox who wore prayer-shawls, the Reformers who wore Bolivar hats, and the Christians who wore crosses. He had yearned for a university post, and, although he could name "twenty or more" who had done so, he refused to barter away his religion for a career. In 1830 he issued his call to battle: "All of us, but especially we young men, children of a century whose very breath is freedom, must strive with word and deed for civil emancipation. . . . Belief in the power and victory of right and virtue is *our* messianic faith!"

He directed his fire—in books, memorials, and his journal *Der Jude*—against the prevalent doctrine of a "German Christian" state which served the reactionary interests of the feudal aristocracy and which, not altogether incidentally, kept the Jews in their inferior status. Proponents of the doctrine, such as the theologian Heinrich Paulus, argued that the beliefs and practices of the Jews were national in origin. Hence, as long as the Jews clung to any one of them, they must be treated as a separate nation—tolerated and protected, if you will, but not to be included on a plane of equality with a "German Christian" citizenry. Baptism, he concluded, and a great body of opinion supported him, was the only "guarantee of German nationality."

Riesser eloquently denied that the Jews were a national group. "Where is that other state to which we owe loyalty? What other fatherland calls us to its defense? We have not emigrated to Germany, we have been born here, and either we are Germans or we are men without a country. There is only one baptism that can consecrate a man to a nationality: that is the baptism of blood shed in a common battle for freedom and fatherland."

In this spirit he raised his voice wherever there was an opportunity to further unconditional emancipation. He counseled the Jews of Baden to reject any religious concessions as the price of citizenship (1831-33). He unmasked a murky project of the Prussian government to segregate the Jews in government-controlled "corporations" (1842). During the brief triumph of the Revolution of 1848, he was elected vice-president of the National Assembly, three other Jews served as deputies, and all discriminations against German Jewry were abolished.

But this second emancipation did not last even as long as the first under Napoleon. In 1850 the Assembly vanished; Jewish rights—save the privilege of sitting in powerless legislatures—remained ink and paper; and Riesser, with a host of patriots, went into exile.

Meanwhile, more illustrious knights of the Holy Spirit had been deploying battle on a wider front. Ludwig Boerne (1786-1837) and Heinrich Heine (1797-1856) both departed for Paris in 1830, not merely to enjoy the freedom of Louis Philippe's bourgeois reign, but as virtual refugees from the German police. Surrounded by similar exiles and in touch with kindred spirits in the homeland, they became the inspiration, the propagandists, and the poets of "Young Germany"—the first republican movement in German history. Boerne's *Letters from Paris* still remain the noblest monument to cap the tomb of German freedom; and whether Heine dealt in philosophy, politics, or literature, whether beauty, satire, or wit poured from his pen, a free kingless Germany was written in or between the lines. Both were tireless, too, in using their Jewish blood and the plight of their people as a lash, an insult, or a plea to arouse the Germans to revolt.

Of the two, Boerne was the more strait-laced and relentless in his republicanism. Jewish emancipation, he argued, could not be achieved until the Germans were emancipated—"the Jewish cause must be bound to the general cause of freedom" —and the Germans would never be free until the "thirty-six tyrants" were deposed. "Because you are slaves yourselves," he told the German people, "you insist on enslaving others . . . you are happy to cower a hundred steps beneath your masters as long as you, in turn, can stand one step above [the Jews]. . . . Are you not one and all my coreligionists and brethren in oppression? Is not Germany the ghetto of Europe? Does not every German wear a yellow Badge of Shame?"

Heine, the incorrigible skeptic, could not be carried away even by his own fervor. When the Young German movement assembled 25,000 enthusiasts to light bonfires on the hills around Hambach (1832) he wrote: "I don't believe in a forthcoming German revolution and still less in a German republic. . . . The Germans still believe in authority, the police, and personages."

But his sympathy and vision swept far beyond the purely

German nationalism of Boerne. "The greatest task of our times," he said, "is not merely the emancipation of Irishmen, Greeks, Frankfort Jews, West Indian Negroes, and similarly oppressed peoples, but the emancipation of the whole world that has now found tongue and breaks the iron reins of Privilege."

His sensitivity to every movement of modern life—the sensitivity of a world poet—makes his writings not a part of the history of literature, but *still* literature. The day when in Germany "the Cross of Christ is broken" and "the old savage warriors break forth anew in barbaric fury, Thor brandishing his mighty hammer"; the revolt of the workers—"we are weaving, weaving the triple curse"; the dread nationalist war, "the first act of the drama," to be followed by "the world revolution, the great duel between those who possess nothing and the privileged aristocracy of property-holders"; communism, "so hostile to my interests and my temperament," but before the logic of which "I am powerless"; the cry "Let the old world be smashed where man battens on man, let justice be done, and there will no longer be a question of nationality and religion, but only one Fatherland, the earth, and only one Faith, man's happiness on earth"—all the issues of our day rise in winged words from his pen.

With the same intuition he fixed and rendered imperishable the bitterness and beauty, the problems and hopes, the irony and strength of the nineteenth century Jews—and our own. A complete Anatomy of Jewry could be compiled from his works; and to its unabashed pages could be added the *Hebräische Melodien*—the greatest Jewish poetry that has been written outside the Hebrew tongue. Only one thing would be lacking —not the sentiment but the philosophy of Jewish nationalism.

vi

The year of the luckless German Revolution, Marx and Engels published the *Communist Manifesto*. A third battle front opened, the full impact of which was not to be felt for decades to come. The *Manifesto* and its underlying philosophy contended that ultimate emancipation was not to be won by the removal of civil disabilities based on religious intolerance —as Riesser hoped. Nor by the creation of republican and democratic government—as Boerne believed. But by the elimination of the economically privileged classes who used civil and political equality only so far as it insured their privileges and who, when these privileges were threatened, would make mock of democratic and human rights. Furthermore, it announced the claims of a new class to the control of society: the working class which the Industrial Revolution had already created in England and France and which was coming into being in Germany—a class destined, according to communist doctrine, to abolish all class distinctions, including therefore its own.

The Jews, in their long history, had seen their fate shaped by the economy of Imperial Rome, feudalism, the financial and mercantile revolution of the sixteenth century, and—even as the *Manifesto* went to press—by the rise of industrial capitalism. The struggle to power of each succeeding class—the feudal barons and the bishops, the Fuggers and the merchant adventurers, the manufacturers and their dependent bourgeoisie—had influenced them, now for better and again for worse. What was the challenge of the working-class to unfold?

It was a riddle over which few men—Jews or Gentiles—racked their heads.

In 1848 the *Manifesto* was looked upon—except by dreamers and poets like Heine—as eccentric speculation. Its co-author, Karl Marx (1818-1883), the founder of modern communism, was born a Jew in Trèves and baptized at the age of six. Growing up in a completely Christian environment he acquired as strange notions about the Jews as many Christians have since acquired about his communism. In the only opinions he published on the subject—two essays written when he was twenty-five—he identified the Jews with the money power of the world and looked for their emancipation through the disappearance of this power and themselves along with it.

Many years later his life-long friend, collaborator, and benefactor, Frederick Engels (not a Jew), was to discover that "there are thousands upon thousands of *Jewish proletarians*, and these Jewish workers are in fact the worst exploited and most impoverished of all." Still, it remained a somber irony that Marx saw in the Jews no one but the Rothschilds, who as bankers were totally irrelevant to Judaism, while enemies of communism have seen in it only Marx the Jew, who had no relation, save the accident of birth, to Jewry. We have already remarked how bankers of Jewish birth have in all innocence cost Israel whatever they were worth; so, too, the arch-foe of bankers was in equal innocence to send a heavy bill to his people.

But the irony does not cease here. While Marx was creating communism, another baptized Jew—Friedrich Julius Stahl (1802-1861)—was creating the doctrines of the conservative party of Prussia. Marx the spiritual father of the proletariat;

Stahl the spiritual father of the Junkers: God save us, the Jews might say, from our great men!

The tragedy of their lot lies in such a prayer. No people in normal circumstances need regret their gifted children. It was left to Hess to offer an explanation of the tragedy—and another battle front for its resolution.

Moses Hess (1812-1875) had run the gamut of liberation. He had been, in turn, Spinozist, Hegelian, anarchist, communist—he worked for three years with Marx—and socialist. He took active part in the German Revolution of 1848, and upon its collapse fled into exile and eventually settled in Paris. "Had I not lived in France," he explains, "it never would have entered my head to interest myself in the revival of Jewish nationalism."

The interest arose from many stimulants. The ritual-murder trial in Damascus, 1840, had left a deep, if temporarily-forgotten, shock. The genius of French freedom, even under Napoleon III, touched his spirit. The sight of the French Jews, as "enlightened" at least as any Hamburg Temple rabbi, who enjoyed this freedom without the surrender of Jewish observances or Hebrew prayers, threw the Reform movement into a new light. Mazzini and the Italian struggle for liberty —popular in France—set him dreaming of another Mediterranean people. But, above all, Graetz' *History of the Jews*, as volume after volume appeared, enabled him to relive the experience of his forefathers, not as the theological development of a sect but as the full-blooded life of a nation whose course was not yet done.

"After an estrangement of twenty years, I am back with my people" are the opening words of *Rome and Jerusalem* (1862). They were words to be re-echoed, under varying circumstances, by many another Jew. In the form of discursive passionate letters, spiced with anecdote and satire, Hess' book endeavored to persuade the German Jews that, to begin with, they were arguing from a false premise when they demanded emancipation as a religious sect. "The Jews are a nation, destined to be resurrected with all other civilized nations." Secondly, they were arguing from a damaging premise. "As long as the Jew tries to deny his nationality . . . his false position must become more intolerable . . . and he will never earn the respect of the peoples among whom he dwells." Finally, it was a hopeless premise. "In vain the 'enlightened' Jew hides behind his geographical and philosophic alibis. Mask yourselves a thousand times over, change your name, religion, and manners—it is of no avail . . . the German hates the Jewish religion less than the Jewish race. Neither Reform, conversion, nor emancipation can throw open to the Jew the gates of social life, hence his anxiety to deny his racial descent."

The solution Hess offered is now familiar. Rabbi Hirsch Kalischer of Thorn had just published his plea for colonization in Palestine. Agitation by French journalists and Napoleon III's interest in the Near East made the project appear feasible; and Hess concluded with a proposal to create a Jewish state.

Not all Jews need or would respond. "In highly civilized" countries, he found, persons of any nationality are granted citizenship either as a birthright or as the result of long residence and a pledge to assume all the burdens and discharge all the duties of the state—"but not," he added, "in Germany."

As for Germany, "the race war must first be fought out and definitely settled before humane and social ideas become part and parcel of the German people—just as the Latin peoples, after a long historical process, finally extinguished racial antagonisms . . . a nation that produced Lessing, Herder, Schiller, and many more champions of humanity must certainly rise to these heights."

16

VICTORY

THE German Revolution of 1848 was easy to destroy. Its republicanism was hooted away as a French idea, and its proffer to Prussia of a constitutional Empire was dismissed as blasphemous to the divine right of kings. No authority could be—or ever was—accorded by the people to a German emperor: the emperor, by grace of God, bestowed upon the people whatever authority he saw fit.

However, the Industrial Revolution was different. It, too, was a foreign importation—from England—and it could be feared by the Junkers and despised by conservative gentlemen. But machines which made money and the middle classes who possessed that money wielded a power which, like the divinely graced kings, did not ask for authority but gave it.

In the two decades following 1848, industrialism made irresistible strides. Again one item of statistics. The 1½ million metric tons of coal which we saw mined in 1850, and which became 15 million in 1862, was 30 million in 1871. Behind this production lay, of course, an equivalent increase of factories, railways, and commodities, and a corresponding growth in the power of manufacturers, merchants, bankers, and their liegemen among the politicians, lawyers, and professors.

As a result, the old monarchical order was compelled to compromise with the new business order. The compromise, moreover, was facilitated by the fact that in a vital respect the aims of business coincided with the ambitions of Prussia—the most powerful of the monarchies. For the expansion of their own interests, both demanded a unified Germany.

The business order, which throve on free competition, equal political rights, and the open door to opportunity, championed many of the liberal ideas inherited from the Revolution of '48. It was likewise imbued with a deep patriotic spirit; and its nationalism was none the less genuine because it paid.

Meanwhile, on the side of the old order, which was agrarian, monarchical, militaristic, and reactionary, Bismarck set Germany on the road to unity by annexing Schleswig-Holstein and trouncing Austria (1864-1866)—much to the distaste of his fellow-conservatives who clung to the parochial doctrine of "legitimacy."

With Austria and "legitimacy" out of the way, the old order in the person of Bismarck struck a bargain with the new as represented by the National Liberal Party—an alliance which lasted until 1879. First, the North German Confederation was formed (1867), which unified all Germany north of the Main. Then, following the victory over France, South Germany joined hands with the North; and in the halls of Versailles was born the second German Reich (1871). After centuries of separatism and internal rivalries Germany was a single nation.

To bring this about, the old order sacrificed absolute monarchism and many of its feudal privileges, in return for the fervent support of the middle classes. The new order surrendered republicanism and all but the shadow of democracy, but it gained a vast and more or less unhampered field for industrial expansion, personal freedom, individual talents, and equal —even if limited—civil and political rights. From the outset there existed in no western country such intimate coöperation between industry and the state. And Germany as a whole, embracing the new and old order in a loyal though often troubled unity, entered on a career which made it the leading nation of Europe in all the practical arts. *Gemütlichkeit* gave way to *Geschäft*—business: business in its best sense of efficiency, enlightened selfishness, and productivity.

As a part of the middle classes or their dependents the Jews—though not without a struggle—received their complete formal emancipation. In 1860 the Prussian Parliament, of which two members were Jews, was still able to reject the measure. But in 1862 Baden removed the old disabilities, and Württemberg followed in 1864. The North German Confederation—after the Bismarck-Liberal alliance—granted unconditional equality in 1869. The edict signed by William I and Bismarck read: "All hitherto existing restrictions of civil and political rights, based on religious differences, are hereby abolished." And in 1871 this principle became law throughout the new-born Reich. There were years of delay in making the law effective in all the states and every branch of the administration; but the last vestige of legal discrimination may be said to have disappeared with the abolition of the "Jewish Oath" in 1877—the swine hide and the more blood-curdling phrases of the formula had vanished some decades before.

While the economic and nationalist transformations had furnished a favorable background, emancipation can as little be reduced to one or two broad factors as any other development in history. The radicalism of the forty-eighters and the pugnacity of Riesser; the efforts of Eduard Lasker and Ludwig Bamberger who as leaders in the National Liberal Party stood at Bismarck's side; floods of petitions loosed by the Jewish communities; the Jewish blood shed in the Austrian and Franco-Prussian wars (7,000 Jews served against France); the growing indifference to religion under the diversion furnished by the new industrial and national life as well as through the attacks of science and materialist philosophy—all, from Riesser to Darwin, shared in the victory.

ii

The German government, it should be noted, had granted the Jews equal rights on their own terms—as a religious minority who otherwise were a part and parcel of the German people. The Jews raised no question as to other possible differences that might exist and need recognition and acceptance.

They ignored the forthright assertions of a line of influential writers beginning with Fichte who had, for a century, told the public that the Jews were not only a religious group but a *Volk*—a people, a nationality. They closed their eyes to the significance of governmental policies—in Prussia, Bavaria, Saxony, etc.—which throughout that period indicated that the Jews had been treated or mistreated as a *Volk*. Still less, therefore, could it be expected they should remember that from at least the tenth century, when Jews were classed with "merchants" or distinguished from "foreigners," the government almost invariably had in mind more than religious traits when it protected or exploited Israel. As for their own historic folk institutions, they had foresworn them. And consulting neither the German nor the Jewish past, they remained oblivious to the present.

The Hamburg riots of 1830—a police incident long closed. Richard Wagner's attack in 1850 on the Jewish influence in music, which obviously had nothing to do with the Jewish religion and little enough to do with music—the mere bile of an eccentric genius. Feuerbach's *Essence of Christianity*, in 1851, which denied the entire validity of religion and yet, like its ultimate sources in Hegel and like its many successors, placed the Jew and his *spirit* on a level inferior to the German —it was professorial theorizing. Lassen's *Hindu Antiquities* (1844-61) which particularized this inferiority of the Semites —the work of another professor. Heinrich Naudh's *Die Juden und der deutsche Staat*, in 1861, which discussed the relations between the Jews and the German state on a racial basis— who can take seriously everything that appears in print?

In most cases this blindness did not spring, as Moses Hess believed, from a lack of self-respect. It implied no prejudice, either, against the concept of nationality as such, and no presumption that the Reich would never tolerate the admission to citizenship of a non-German element. Germany embraced —and still embraces—several non-German peoples: Poles, Masurians, Wends, Czechs, Danes, and Lithuanians, many of whom continued—and continue—to maintain their own language and customs. In fact no European nation, except Sweden and Norway, is limited in its population to a single language or nationality group.

No, the explanation lay in Jewish history. Fifteen hundred years of experience in Germany (as elsewhere in Western Europe) had taught the Jews that on whatever grounds they were distinguished, the distinction was always made into a

stigma and a handicap. The mid-nineteenth century Jews
fought the handicap on a religious basis because, in the three
and four generations since the ghettos fell, they had lost from
mind and use everything distinctive in their habits except their
religion. In all the walks of peace they had shed their past
for Germany, and on the fields of battle they had shed their
blood. And now, in the rosy dawn of the new Reich, they
had won official recognition, respect, and, as it were, equal
treatment for the one distinction they cherished beyond all
possibility of surrender—their faith.

iii

They were destined to a quick awakening. For two years
France poured its millions of gold indemnities into Germany,
and for two years Germany speculated—"bankers and cab-
drivers"—in a grand commercial boom. In 1873, partly as a
result of the speculation and partly in consequence of a world-
crisis, the Great Panic (*Der grosse Krach*) ruined not only the
speculators but a large portion of the population. It was Germany's first taste of modern capitalism on a decent scale.

The Jews were immediately accused of the disaster. As the
depression continued, a flood of books, pamphlets, and newspaper articles made increasingly clear that the Jews were considered a race and damned as such. Passing from literature
to politics, the movement created an anti-Semitic party; and
passing from politics to action, it culminated in boycotts, riots,
and looting in 1881. A decade later the movement reached a
new peak in a ritual-murder trial at Xanten on the Rhine
(1891) where, eight hundred years gone by, the Jews had
tasted the Crusaders' swords.

How deep and sweet was the Jewish dream may be gathered from the cry of Berthold Auerbach. One of Germany's most beloved novelists—writer of innumerable stories of German folk life and remembered by English readers for his *On the Heights*—he had dedicated his pen to his fatherland. Indeed, he had roundly condemned his friend Hess as a "firebrand" for evoking the ghost of Jewish nationalism. But in 1880, when on the threshold of his seventieth year the fire of German nationalism turned against the Jew, he brokenheartedly confessed: "*Vergebens gelebt und gearbeitet*—I have lived and worked in vain."

In the next generation, weaker though no less gifted men turned the rebuffs they received from the Germans into griefs against their own people. Oppressed by the steadily thickening atmosphere, they writhed at the very name and sound of Jew. The most memorable victim of this self-hate was Otto Weininger (born 1880), who hardly out of his teens wrote that amazing book, *Sex and Character,* which flayed the Jews in terms only a Jew tormented with shame could devise, and who freed himself from his torments with a pistol-shot at the age of twenty-three—ending his life in the room where Beethoven died. Walter Calé, born a year later than Weininger, found similar surcease at the same age, leaving to the world a thin volume of writings that reveal a joyous and delicate lover of literature and the arts. Max Steiner (born 1884) wrote a book on Free Thought, another on Darwinism, joined the Catholic Church, and waited until he was twenty-six before he poisoned himself. Paul Rée, the friend and fellow-adventurer of Nietzsche, threw himself into an Alpine glacier.

Others, clinging to life, allayed the reproach of living in vain by licking the boots of their enemies. Wagner had no more faithful disciples than Heinrich Porges and Hermann Levi; and it is still a question whether Wagner's own anti-Semitism was not an unhappy birth-mark. Arthur Trebitsch allowed Nietzsche to persuade him that the Jews were a "slave people" and exemplified it by his trumpeting of Aryan superiority. Trebitsch moved in a circle of brilliant Jewish anti-Semites who probably believed, as he did, that Jewish like Roman slaves lost their servile character after the second generation of freedom. For himself, he felt so completely free from the sin of his ancestry that toward the end of his life— he died in 1927—he fell victim to a persecution mania in which his persecutors were *Jews*. Julius Wiesner, the botanist, a converted Jew and whilom rector of the University of Vienna, allowed Houston-Stewart Chamberlain to dedicate to him a masterpiece of anti-Semitism, *The Foundations of the Nineteenth Century*. One Benedict Friedländer achieved both solutions: suicide and lick-spittling. After he killed himself, his will disclosed—to the astonishment of the recipient—a large bequest to Eugen Dühring, the philosopher of Jew-hatred. Sadder than martyrs' are the lives of these men who, as Deuteronomy foretold, sold themselves to their enemies and no man would buy them.

Still others, however, took a manlier road. The "Hep-Hep" cry of 1819 had awakened sturdy-minded men to the need for self-knowledge, a need which created Jewish *Wissenschaft* and Reform Judaism. The "Hep-Hep" cry of the eighties and nineties awakened the same breed of men to the search for self-realization, a search that led to Zion. In Russia, Leo Pinsker lost faith in emancipations which came from the hands of other peoples—Greeks bearing gifts; instead, he demanded the freedom which can come only from a people emancipating themselves. In Vienna, philosopher Dühring's book provoked young Theodor Herzl to concern himself with the Jewish question. Years later, while drinking beer in a cabaret in Mayence, Herzl, now a successful journalist, heard himself insulted for the first time with a stinging "Hep-Hep." And when the Dreyfus trial brought the cry to France, Herzl answered with *Der Judenstaat* (1896), his dream of a Jewish State. "The Jews," he wrote, "have but one way of saving themselves— a return to their own people and an emigration to their own land"; and he told the Jews, "if you will it, it is no dream."

The German Jews, like so many others, did not will it. When Herzl and his Zionists proposed that their first Congress should be held in Munich, the rabbis of the chief communities of Germany published a protest in which they declared that "the endeavor of the so-called Zionists to found a Jewish national state in Palestine is contrary to the messianic hopes of Judaism" and that "Judaism obligates its followers to give all their heart and strength to the land to which they belong." So the historic congress was held in Basel (1897), and Herzl had to content himself with taunting the Protest-Rabbis for implying that they were not free citizens but that they "belong"—*angehören*—to Germany . . . a taunt that now sounds like prophecy.

Nevertheless, after Herzl's death in 1904, the headquarters of the "so-called" Zionists was established in Berlin, partly because the new leader, David Wolffsohn (a Lithuanian Jew), lived in Germany, and partly because the fervid propaganda of East European students in the German universities had made considerable inroad among the German Jewish youth.

Yet it would give an untrue picture of Jewish life in the Second Reich to imagine it obsessed with anti-Semitism or even appreciating its racial issues. As late as 1893 the spokesmen of Jewry created what was to be its most effective organization of defense and the dominant expression of Jewish opinion under the title of the Central Union of German Citizens of the Jewish Faith *(Central Verein deutscher Staatsbürger jüdischen Glaubens)*. Its name was its program and philosophy. Impervious to the growing shift of German thought from religion to race, from *Christentum* to *Germanentum*, the Jewish leaders in 1893 still thought (or talked) in the language of David Friedländer and Israel Jacobsohn, the "progressives" of one hundred years before. In this lay nothing peculiar. History is full of "progressive" movements which, if given time enough to jell, become static and antiquated.

Meanwhile, German life and culture, emancipation and its opportunities, occupied the foreground if not the whole stage of Jewish effort. The Second Reich was like a new cathedral to be raised on the wreck of an outworn past. Jewry was invited to serve among the humble masons as well as among the sculptors, painters, and master-builders; and it threw itself with all its heart into the task, happy if its talents could add an inch to the mounting spires or a pane of color to the storied windows. Save in rare troubled moments, it forgot that underneath the new cathedrals of Europe lie the old crypts where the saints of the past, the primitive shrines of the people, the first and holiest cults, keep dark and tireless guard.

And that we may enter into the spirit of the builders overhead, we too shall forget the crypts—for the space of a chapter.

17

THE FRUITS OF FREEDOM

How many Jewish builders were there in this new, modern, and united Germany? In 1871, when the corner-stone of the Reich was laid at Versailles, the Jews numbered 420,278, or about 1.2% of the total population—a percentage much the same as in the best years of the Middle Ages. In 1925 they numbered 564,379, or about .9%, despite the presence of some 79,000 foreign-born Jews. A moment's elementary arithmetic discloses in these figures an ominous trend. The drop from 1.2% to .9% seems trifling, but it meant that the Jews were—proportionately speaking—a quarter less numerous in the last days of the Republic than in the first days of the Empire. This dwindling proportion was due to a higher birth rate among the Christians, a higher death rate among the Jews (in the twentieth century), as well as to the growth of intermarriage. Between 1906 and 1930 the latter amounted to 27% of all marriages in which Jews were concerned; and mixed marriages generally resulted in 80% of the offspring being lost to Jewry. It would appear that if the Nazis had waited a bit, there would have been no "pure" Jews to torment them.

In surveying the part played by the half-million Jews in Imperial Germany, it must be realized that the invitation—

or permit—to share in German life had strings to it. Emancipation, after all, was merely legal, and no law can change
men's minds or habits. In fact, during the decades of industrial growth before 1871 the Jews had begun to enter many
new fields, despite their lack of equal rights; and in the decades
after they had gained these rights, they continued to be excluded from many old fields. Though given a vastly greater
scope through formal emancipation, the Jews of the second
Reich in the nineteenth and twentieth centuries were limited,
much as were the Jews of the first Reich in the twelfth and
thirteenth centuries, on the one hand by the occupations which
were virtually closed to them and on the other hand by the
occupations for which their previous history had conditioned
them.

On the whole they were barred—in progressive degree as
time and anti-Semitism went on—from all government and
allied services; and they were shut out, likewise in progressive
measure as monopoly and state capitalism developed, from
big business and key industries. By and large they were barred
by their own background—training, interests, and connections
—from field, forest, and mine; from common labor in industry
and, though to a lesser extent, from skilled labor in most crafts
and trades.

As a result, they chiefly engaged in commerce and private
banking, as owners and employees; in comparatively small
manufactures and independent crafts, particularly in the tex-
tile and garment industry; and, for their intellectuals, in the
"free" arts and professions such as literature, drama, journalism,
music, *beaux arts,* pure science, medicine, and law—everywhere
that individual merit or capital could provide a career.

Our purpose, it need hardly be said, in reviewing some of

the major accomplishments in these fields, is not to make a parade of Jewish talent. We merely wish to sketch the scene as it was and indicate that wherever the Jew was given a fair field—and often where he was not—he did as well or as ill by the common weal as his neighbor. What Germany—and hence the world—stands to lose by closing this fair field may be judged by what it gained when, for two generations, the field was open.

To judge the worth of a people, racial or religious "percentages" are meaningless. Yet for such puerile minds as put stock in them, it may be noted at the outset that the German Jews rolled up an overwhelmingly "unfair" percentage in two favorite branches of racial statistics: crime and genius. As to the first, they showed a marked inferiority when it came to competing for records in brutality, violence, and anti-social behavior. Of the 2,174 cases of murder and associated crimes tried in Germany from 1899 to 1917, Jews were involved in four; and from 1910 to 1917 Jews were convicted in none. As to genius—if a medal and a purse be the measure—out of the thirty-eight German citizens who have received the Nobel prize (to 1933) eleven were, according to Nazi specifications, Jews. In major crimes the Jews stood nowhere at all; in the most conspicuous reward for service to the world—granted, it must be confessed, by non-German judges—one "Semite" on the basis of population showed himself the equal of twenty-nine "Aryans."

ii

Leaving criminals and geniuses aside, let us glance at the industrial order which furnished the girders and much of the design for the new structure of German society. When the basic industries were young, their methods untried and risks enormous, a number of Jews, preparing to be gamblers, turned out to be pioneers.

The coal and iron industry of Upper Silesia—the second largest in Germany—was almost the exclusive creation of a handful of Jews. Moritz Friedländer, Simon Levy, and David Löwenfeld built the first foundry in 1840. Out of it has grown the dominant smelting plant of the district, the work of the Caro brothers who, together with Friedländer, likewise inaugurated the coke industry. In 1869 Ludwig Löwe founded one of Berlin's largest industrial concerns, manufacturing (after American methods) tools, engines, and munitions.

Bethel Henry Strousberg—a converted Jew—introduced Germany to another American specialty. During the sixties he built railroads in north Germany, Hungary, and Rumania and, anticipating Ford and Stinnes, acquired all the factories, mines, and other sources of supplies used in his projects, and crashed in a style that Gould would have appreciated. Yet his rise stimulated railroad construction, hitherto neglected in the *gemütliche* era; and his fall—together with the attacks of Eduard Lasker, party chief of the National Liberals, against railroad buccaneering—hastened government ownership.

Emil Rathenau took a chance on acquiring the German rights to the patents of an American, Mr. Edison, and in 1887 founded the *Allgemeine Elektrizitäts-Gesellschaft*—the wonder-working A.E.G.—which electrified the country. As we shall have occasion to learn, his son, Walter Rathenau, took even a greater chance—in fact it proved fatal—when he tried to talk sanity into post-war Germany.

Similar pioneers worked in other basic fields, chemistry,

dyes, shipping—all the world knew Albert Ballin of the Hamburg-American line; but with the growth of trusts, in which Germany led Europe, the initiative and importance of individuals, Jews or otherwise, faded away. It was the old story in new terms of the twelfth-century Jewish merchant overshadowed by the merchant guilds, and the fifteenth-century Jewish money-lender doomed by the monopolies of the Fuggers and Welsers.

In these older fields, banking and commerce, familiar to the Jews for centuries, they were naturally well to the front. Under the Rothschilds, as we have seen, private banking reached a new peak in the early nineteenth century, though the German branch—perhaps due to the competition of other Jewish houses—was relatively unimportant; while, as a whole, the Rothschilds and their competitors as well became mere midgets compared to the Morgans. In Germany the leading private bankers included the Mendelssohns—descendants of the philosopher—whose conversion to Christianity was so complete that the firm acted as the chief financial agent of Russia throughout the period of the pogroms; and the Bleichröders —descendants of the lad whom the Jewish community expelled from Berlin for reading a German book—who were bankers to Emperor William I, Bismarck, and the early industrialists. The Bleichröders too have ceased to be Jewish, except by Nazi definition. Frankfort, the "mother city" of Jewish bankers, where in 1835 over one-third of the Jews who had employment were in the "bank, money, or lottery business," produced its Lazards, Speyers, Sterns, Dreyfuses, and Sulzbachs, as well as sending abroad one Jacob H. Schiff.

Towards the end of the period the house of Warburg—in Hamburg—played an important part not only in the finances but the destinies of Germany. Max Warburg was adviser to the government at the Versailles Peace Conference. Carl J. Melchior, another member of the firm, served as economic expert in the negotiations with Russia and Rumania, headed the financial section of the Armistice Commission in 1918-1919, and was one of the six German delegates to Versailles; thereafter his efforts helped to scale down the German reparations and eventually abolish them.

It was two French Jews who ushered in the twilight of the private bankers. When Isaac and Emile Pereire—in order, above all things, to further utopian socialism—invented the joint-stock type of banking (the Crédit Mobilier, 1852), it did for finance what trusts did for industry. A number of Jews figured in the history of the four great joint-stock banks of Germany: the Solomonsohns in the Disconto-Gesellschaft, the Wassermanns, Paul Wallich, and Max Steinthal in the Deutsche Bank; Eugen Guttmann, Moritz Kleeman, and Henry Nathan in the Dresdner Bank; and Jacob Goldschmidt in the Darmstädter und Nationalbank. But in these vast impersonal organizations, Jewish enterprise, if there is such a distinctive trait, became shadowier than ever. In 1925 statistics showed that out of 236,000 Germans occupied as bankers or brokers, 7,500 or about 3.3% were Jews. The second era of Jewish finance, which opened after the Thirty Years War, was closed.

In retail trade the most conspicuous development of the century was the department store. Two Jews, Oscar and Leonhard Tietz, brought this French-American idea to Germany; and the Tietz chains expanded to 60 stores and 167 auxiliary enterprises throughout the country. If he does not know Tietz, every tourist who has shopped in Berlin knows Wertheim and

Israel. Many non-Jewish concerns entered the field, and the small retailer howled. He did not notice that a department store looms larger on the street than in statistics—that these stores, Jewish and non-Jewish, accounted for not more than 3.99% of the total retail business. The non-Jewish concerns he never noticed at all, but nourished the illusion that department stores were a racial phenomenon, instead of an economic growth as inevitable as trusts and big banks.

Jewry's relation to German commerce as a whole (including banking) underwent the most profound change in its history. In the Prussia of 1813, before either virtual or legal emancipation took effect, 70% of the Jews, we may recall, were engaged in trade. By 1852 the number had dropped to 51.5%; and by 1907, in all Germany, to 49.5%. What became of these immemorial and hereditary traders?

As a result of the abolition of guild monopolies and other economic obstacles, they had gone, for the most part, into industry and manual occupations. In 1907, some 21.5% of the German Jews were manufacturers or employees. By 1925 it was 24.24%. Lost as we have been in the German scene, it is time to point out that only the Jew of Western Europe had ever been confined to commerce and banking. In Poland and the Orient (as later in the United States) a large proportion of Jews—varying from 30% to 60%—were and are artisans: weavers, tailors, shoemakers, glaziers, carpenters, tinsmiths, and the like. In Germany it meant an approach, after a thousand years' interruption, to the Jewish norm.

The return to the norm, however, was far from complete. While in 1925 over one-third of the Jews were white-collar employees or paid officials, only 7.8% were manual workers and another 7.5% employed in home industries.

The departure from trade, great as it was, would have been more pronounced if equal opportunity had existed for the Jews as employees and workmen in the basic industries and in the largest enterprise in Germany—the State. The State, to take the latter first, eventually embraced almost the entire field of transportation (from railroads and shipping to street-cars and airplanes), communication (mail, telegraph, tele-phone, and radio), public utilities, education (including uni-versities), and, naturally, local and national administration, consular and diplomatic service, and—in pre-war days the biggest business of all—the army. On the other hand, the basic industries—even more rapidly than in other lands—dominated business life and determined its habits and tabus.

All these fields were virtually closed to the Jews. No Jew could hold an officer's commission in the army (outside of Bavaria). No Jew ever held a diplomatic post or (save once) a minister's portfolio. Practically no Jews sat on a judge's bench (again, except in Bavaria) or a professor's chair or behind a teacher's humble desk. Few Jews could find a position in the huge network of government service and administration. They were similarly excluded, as technicians or as manual and clerical workers in the nationalized and semi-national-ized domains of transportation, communication, public util-ities, and state banking. And the key industries put up the same invisible bars. By Jews we mean, of course, unconverted Jews. The conception of a German Christian state, inherited from the romantic age, still ruled in the industrial age; and baptism could still do what the edict signed by William I and Bismarck could not do.

This boycott kept many Jews in trade who would other-wise have gone into factories, the civil service, or the schools;

and it confined the Jewish worker, who had abandoned trade, to clerical employment in a narrow range of industry. Its effect on the intellectual was no less marked.

iii

The proportion of Jews who were engaged in the professions had, in the first place, greatly increased since the days when Heine was compelled to accept baptism in order to practice law. Back in the Prussia of 1813 a bare 1% were registered under "professions." By 1852 the 1% had doubled; by 1907 it had become about 6%; and in 1925 it reached 8.52%. Yet even at this peak the Jews furnished only 2.86% of the total number of Germans employed in professional life.

But in two professions, law and medicine, the Jews appeared in unusual numbers. In 1925, out of 13,579 lawyers in Germany, 2,900 were Jews—around 26%. Berlin, the obvious center for legalist enterprise, had in 1933 about 2,000 Jewish lawyers compared to 1,800 "Aryans." The physicians did nearly as well. In 1933 about 15% of the doctors and dentists in Germany were Jews.

It is a bleak commentary on human nature that the Germans (and some other peoples too) have considered such proportions "abnormal." After all, no man in his senses hires a lawyer or a doctor on any ground except to win his case, or cure it. Almost no lawyer, doctor, or dentist can make a living unless he is as good as the next man in his profession, or better. If a sixth or a quarter or a half of the lawyers and physicians in a given country or community are Jews—or Zulus—it is because they are, so far as lawyers and doctors can, satisfying their clients.

The commentary becomes not only bleak but an enigma to anyone unacquainted with German and Jewish history when he learns why the Germans were, comparatively speaking, but a mere majority in these professions, and why the Jews occupied an "abnormally" large place in them. In many German universities the social sciences—economics, political science, sociology—are taught in the Faculty of Law. Its graduates are thereby qualified for the judiciary, civil and diplomatic service, corporative posts, and foreign trade. It was precisely these domains which were open to the Germans and on the whole closed to the Jews. Hence the Germans who did not hang out shingles were successfully employed elsewhere; and the Jews who were shut off from these employments hung out shingles in the sole remaining field— the private practice of law, where nothing but merit could win customers.

Exclusion from many vocations open to educated Germans likewise helped determine Jewish prominence in medicine. But here more than in law—though centuries of arguing talmudic cases might enter a strong claim—the Jew was following his ancient tradition. The Jewish doctors and medical scientists, literally hundreds of them, who were known as masters among their world-wide colleagues as Paul Ehrlich and Jacques Loeb are known to the average man, were one and all carrying on the fame of Sedechias, physician to Charlemagne. "Honor the physician for the uses you may have of him . . . of his works there is no end, and from him is peace over all the earth," wrote Ben Sira when the ancestors of Charlemagne were cracking skulls in the *Ur-Wald*.

In fact, when we turn to science, philosophy, literature, and the arts, the roll of notable Jews would not merely fill a

279

volume,* but their bare enumeration would be almost meaningless. Behind Einstein in physics, Hermann Cohen in philosophy, Karl Marx in economics, Mendelssohn and Meyerbeer in music, Max Liebermann in painting, and two Austrians, Freud and Arthur Schnitzler, in psychology and literature, were an army of creators whose share in shaping German and all modern culture cannot be measured in statistics or weighed in *Who's Who* paragraphs. The lover of comparisons would have to return to Moslem Spain for its like.

Moreover, racial and national qualities in modern arts and sciences as in modern business play an elusive part. Where these distinctions become apparent, they are largely a matter of style. To be sure, when civilization was parochial and communication difficult, as throughout the Middle Ages, local mannerisms due to isolation and inbred social habits were pronounced and significant. We need only think of folk music to realize the world that separated—even in the universal Church—a Spanish *saeta* from an English Christmas-carol. By contrast, modern economy and science have made the Western World a single cultural parish—however quarrelsome, back-biting, and lawless it may be. Racial and national traits have lingered; they probably never will or should disappear. There is a German style even in science, business, and the arts—a way of working which we call *gründlich*—thorough—when we like it, and pedantic when we don't. But it and similar national styles have retreated to a nuance hardly worth the trouble to identify.

* For a comprehensive outline of these contributions, the reader is recommended *The German Jew: His Share in Modern Culture*, by Abraham Myerson and Isaac Goldberg (New York, 1933).

So, no doubt, the Jews of Germany likewise have their style and cast of thought; but so completely had they lost themselves in German and general culture that the nuance became a shadow. For all their similarity, no reader of Berthold and Judah of Regensburg—granting such readers exist—could mistake Berthold for a medieval Jew, and Judah for a medieval German. Yet what can we distinguish, except individual talent, between the novels of Scheffel and Auerbach, between the compositions of Schumann and Mendelssohn, or between the calculations of Planck and Einstein?

These men and their peers belong not to Jewry or Germany, but to the world. Germany's present attempt to draw distinctions where only hair-line shadows exist has indeed proved invidious. It has led the world to discover how much the Jew has wrought, although little of it can be credited to his blood; and how cruel and ungrateful the Germans can behave, though neither cruelty nor ingratitude, and not even social lunacy, are gifts peculiar to the Teutons.

iv

In politics, which is the reflection of group interests, whether the group be the nation as a whole or its conflicting classes, the Jews were swayed by their economic needs and their status as a now covertly and again openly despised minority. Taken as a mass, they shared the political views of the middle classes and their "white collar" dependents, to which they belonged.

In the early days of the Empire their favorite party was the National Liberals, to whom they could attribute their emancipation and who represented the rising industrial order. Later they supported its liberal successors which stood for "progress" through reform, a satisfaction of their traditional idealism by improving the underdog's condition at no expense to their own. As Jews they could not, with rare exception, support the more or less anti-Semitic parties of conservatism, even when it might serve their business interests. When the Socialists (Social Democrats) became a reformist party—in the nineties and after—they attracted the Jewish workers and intellectuals much in the same measure as Germans of the same classes. Before the World War the Communists were insignificant in numbers, and the Jews among them no less so. Altogether, the candidate who counted on the Jewish vote would have been deceived, and even had he received the united ballots of Jewry he would have had little to count: one percent of the electorate.

The services of the Jews in politics were likewise incommensurable with their numbers. This was not, however, because they flocked to a political career—although lawyers seem irresistibly inclined to run for office—but rather as an accident of talent.

In the constitutional movement which reached its climax at the Frankfort Parliament in 1848, Eduard von Simson—cousin to David Friedländer and a convert—was elected president, while, as we have noted, Gabriel Riesser was a vice-president. Both were opposed to a republic. "God be with Germany and her newly-elected Kaiser!" exclaimed Simson when they announced the Parliament's choice to Frederick William IV of Prussia—who is said to have remarked he would not accept the crown "from the gutter."

Meanwhile Johann Jacoby (1805-1877) was striving for the rank republicanism of Boerne. In 1841 he dared ask the King to grant a constitution; he was thereupon charged with high treason and replied, "Yes, I advocate the uttermost opposition to all injustice and untruth"—a reply which did not shorten his two-and-a-half years' sentence to garrison arrest. He too had his word with Frederick William IV in 1848. When a deputation, of which he was a member, demanded the dismissal of the conservative ministry and the King walked out of the room in contemptuous silence, Jacoby called after him: "That is the misfortune of kings—they do not wish to hear the truth." In 1866 he went to prison again for attacking the militarists and Junkers, and once more in 1870 for opposing the annexation of Alsace-Lorraine. Another soldier in Heine's "Liberation war of humanity."

Lasker and Bamberger we have already seen at work in the National Liberal Party which joined with Bismarck to create the Empire. In 1848 Bamberger had fled into exile with a price on his head. Eighteen years later he was pardoned, became an adviser of Bismarck, and eventually helped create the Reichsbank and formulate the finance laws for the Reich. Eduard von Simson lived to see a Prussian king accept the imperial crown; in fact, as leader of the deputation from the parliament of the North German Confederation, he accompanied Bismarck and William I to Versailles and made a speech which, as the crown prince jotted in his note-book, "was a masterpiece that wet every eye."

The most influential organ of liberalism in the years following Bismarck's desertion of his old allies was the *Nation* (1884-1907). Bamberger contributed to it until his death, and his friend Paul Nathan served as its editor for twenty years. A member of the staff, Maximilian Harden, a baptized Jew, founded his own publication, the *Zukunft*, which became the most brilliant political journal of the country. His polemics against the personal government of William II, his defense of Bismarck and imperial policies of blood and iron, his attacks on liberalism, are classics of journalist style.

Among the leaders of the Left—carrying forward the banner of economic revolution—was first and foremost Ferdinand Lassalle (1825-1864). As a Marxist—though bitterly fought by Marx—he opposed the union of Germany under the hegemony of Prussia, and in 1863 founded the first workers' party, the General German Workingmen's Association, out of which grew the Socialist Party (Social Democrats). He offered Bismarck the support of the workers in return for the franchise and social welfare legislation, on the theory that with the ballot the workers could capture the state. Marx denounced the theory as fantastic; and, though the workers got the franchise and the legislation, so it proved. A year after he founded his party, Lassalle died romantically in a duel over a love affair—and deserves to be embalmed by one of the modern biographical school.

From 1878 to 1890 socialism was outlawed in Germany. When it became legal once more—and enormously strengthened by its repression—the Marxist teeth were removed by the dominant moderates. Among their leaders were Eduard Bernstein, the theoretician of socialism as a reformist movement, and Paul Singer, a wealthy cloak manufacturer, who became one of the party's parliamentarian leaders and debaters.

During the entire Imperial régime, even when the National Liberals were in power, the only Jew to hold a portfolio was Moritz Ellstätter, who for a quarter-century was finance minister of Baden. Heinrich Friedberg and Simson who sat in

Bismarck's cabinet, and Rudolph Friedenthal, founder of the Free Conservative Party and five years minister of agriculture, were baptized.

Only Riesser's "baptism of blood" counted, however, when Germany entered the World War. The first member of the Reichstag to fall in battle was the Socialist deputy, Ludwig Frank—a Jewish volunteer. Thanks to Fritz Haber's "Jewish" genius in chemistry, nitrogen was extracted from the air, or else, as a Conservative deputy has declared, "the war would have been lost in three months." One hundred thousand Jews, a sixth of German Jewry, served in the army—10,000 of them as volunteers. About 80,000 were in the front line trenches. More than 12,000 died for their country. (You want percentages in blood? They were tragically alike for Jew and Aryan.) About 35,000 Jewish soldiers were decorated for bravery, 23,000 raised to non-commission rank, and over 2,000 to commissioned officers. Baron Manfred von Richthofen, the red eagle of the German aviators, when he fell bled Jewish blood from his veins. Ernst Lissauer who wrote the *Hymn of Hate* was a full-blooded Jew; and, to relieve the hate, another Jew wrote *Annemarie*, the most popular song behind the German lines.

Not since Jerusalem and Masada fell had there been such a baptism of Jewish blood.

BOOK FOUR

REJECTION

From humanity . . . through nationality
. . . to bestiality.—*Grillparzer.*

18

THE NEW "HEP-HEP"

GERMAN history up till recent years was, for its greater part, a segment of the history of Christendom. In order to appreciate the fortunes of the German Jews we were led, therefore, to sketch at the outset something of Jewish and Christian origins and of the cleavage between the two faiths —origins and a cleavage which preceded the presence of the Jew on German soil and the emergence of a German Christian people.

Today German history stands under the banners of another religion. The sign of the Cross has faded before the sign of the Swastika. And once again to understand the lot of Jewry we must trace the new faith—which like most faiths is really very old—to at least some of its more important sources. Moreover we must try to seize its meaning not only for the Jews but for all men.

Largely through fate and almost without design, the Jew under the old dispensation was the symbol of religious freedom and the measure of man's humanity toward man. When the medieval mob smote the ghetto gates it was not the plunderers alone who gained a victory, but organized fanaticism. If he were at all sensitive to his true danger, every heretic, every man who in any way dared think or act differently from the ruling powers, should have trembled when the Christian cried "Hep-hep" against the Jew. And for a thousand years, so long as the ghetto outlived sack and storm, so long as a Jew consented to raise his head or climb a pyre, a gleam of hope at the sight of that ghetto or in the flame of that pyre remained to light the soul of liberty-loving men. While a single Jewish breast wore the Badge of Shame and "No" resounded from a single stiff-necked throat, freedom still breathed.

Under the present dispensation it is likewise apparent that only the deaf can lull themselves with the illusion that the new "Hep-hep" menaces no one but the Jew. Today as in the past, through accident rather than intent, the German Jew stands as a symbol of every cause that cannot or will not be *gleichgeschaltet*—stifled and absorbed—by a trampling victorious fanaticism. Because he could have said "Yes," the medieval Jew of Nuremberg who said "No" was a hero. The modern Jew of Nuremberg has not even the privilege of saying "Yes." Instead of a hero he is a victim. But in him, no less than centuries ago, have become victimized the free thought, free aspirations, and free behavior of millions of his fellow-beings.

The rise of the new religion is not confined to the fall of Jewry. Its story—to which we shall now turn—tells the defeat of a whole world.

ii

When Moses Hess, in 1862, wrote that "the race war must first be fought out" before Germany could become "humane," probably few of his contemporaries grasped what he meant. His Marxist readers must have laughed at the notion that a race war could ever paralyze the class struggle—though the day was to come when a biological myth obliterated, almost without a blow, the power of millions of class-conscious voters. His liberal readers would have mocked the prediction that scientific charlatans would officially banish science, tolerance, and liberty: everything tainted with the pale cast of thought or the weakness of brotherly love—and this to the applause of university faculties and the "Heils" of the intellectual and professional classes. His Christian readers would have been incredulous if told that a new Crusade—without the Cross—was to take a toll of victims in Brown Houses and concentration-camps only to be rivaled in the dungeons of the Inquisition or on the sacrificial pyramids of Mexico.

His Jewish readers, as a matter of record, despised him. Abraham Geiger, apostle of Reform Judaism, dismissed him as "an alienated Jew gone bankrupt on socialism and similar swindles." That it was the grandchildren of Geiger who were to go into bankruptcy with the theory that they were "only a religious sect" and, worse than bankruptcy, go back to a bleaker ghetto than the Middle Ages ever built—a ghetto *without a gate*—lay beyond the divination of the gloomiest pessimist.

Perhaps Hess himself did not realize how close he was to prophecy. But we know he was formulating his ideas of destiny not by reinterpreting the Bible and synagogue ritual, but by studying anatomy and ethnology and keeping an eye on the revolts in Italy, Hungary, and the Balkans. And, as the luck we call history would have it, the future belonged to laboratory callipers and nationalist pens.

Up to the creation of the Second Reich in 1871, Germany was theoretically a "Christian" state. When at its founding the Reich abolished "all restrictions in civil and political rights, based on religious differences," it became, still in theory, a secular state. Actually, its "Christian" character persisted throughout its career in the form, as we have noted, of discrimination against Jews in nearly every government service.

Throughout the duration of the Empire, however, Christianity was insensibly losing its dominance over the popular mind; and in its place there developed slowly and subtly a new religion—a cult of race which took its creed from the apparatus of science, somewhat as early Christianity had forged its dogmas with the tools of Greek philosophy. The science employed by this new faith was anthropology, as obscure, flexible, and imposing as any Greek metaphysics. Instead of bread and wine, blood and soil were elevated to eternal verities expounded in scientific jargon. The savior of mankind was no longer the pale Galilean whose death and resurrection vaguely recalled the mythological Adonis and Osiris, but a big blue-eyed, long-skulled, golden-haired Teuton—a synthesis of Siegfried, Balder, and Odin. And finally, under the Third Reich, Germany became not a "Christian" but an "Aryan" state.

Since the Jews were destined to be the traditional "witnesses" and "enemies" of the new faith, as they had been of the old, its rise and influence are once more to be gauged by the fate of that peculiar people. Indeed, if a medal were struck to commemorate the new cult, it would bear on one side the verse of Emanuel Geibel:

> *Und es mag am deutschen Wesen*
> *Einmal noch die Welt genesen.*

> (German character once again
> Will redeem the world of men)

And on the other side would appear the folk rhyme which millions of Germans accept as an article of faith:

> *Was der Jude glaubt ist einerlei;*
> *In der Rasse liegt die Schweinerei.*

> (What the Jew believes is nought;
> In his race the filth is wrought.)

Obverse and reverse, the creed like the medal is of one piece.

Evidence of the new faith came to light—we select one item among a score—before the Second Reich was much over a year old. In 1872 Friedrich von Hellwald contributed to the Austrian weekly *Ausland* an article which informed its readers that "the Jews were not merely a separate religious community but—and this is the most important factor—an altogether different race. The European feels instinctively that the Jew is a stranger who migrated from Asia . . . and possesses a certain cleverness which makes him master of the honest Aryan."

This was hardly more than a repetition of what Otto Wigand, erstwhile publisher of Hess, wrote back in 1858, in his *Two Discourses Concerning the Flight from Judaism.* Analyzing the thesis of Geiger that the Jews were purely a religious group, Wigand maintained that "the wall separating Jew and Christian stands unbattered, for the watchman who guards it never sleeps—that watchman which is the race difference between the Jewish and Christian populations. . . . How can the race difference between a German and a Slav or a German and a Dane be compared to the race antagonism between the children of Jacob, who are of Asiatic descent, and the descendants of Teut and Hermann, who have inhabited Europe from time immemorial: between the proud and tall blond Aryan and the short, black-haired, dark-eyed Jew! Races which differ in such degree oppose each other instinctively, and against such opposition reason and good sense are powerless."

That the Jews, though inhabiting Germany since Roman days, were "Asiatic immigrants" in some German eyes we learned from Grattenauer in 1803. Even Wilhelm Dohm, though he meant it kindly, spoke of them as "Asiatic refugees" in 1781. Teut, also, is a familiar figure from the Romantic revival. But Aryan, and blonds and brunettes?

For some while these heraldings of the new cult passed unnoticed. The "powerful excitement," as Treitschke would say, of the victory over the French and the founding of the Reich, diverted popular interest into more customary channels revealing what Treitschke called "the secrets of the German people."

August Rohling, professor of theology, followed the conventional pattern in his widely-read pamphlet, *The Talmud Jew (Der Talmudjude,* 1871), which revamped the eighteenth-century scurrilities of Eisenmenger against the Jewish religion; later editions included the charge of ritual murder and elicited a refutation from the learned Hebraist and Protestant theologian, Franz Delitzsch. When Bismarck opened battle against the Catholic Church in 1872—the *Kulturkampf* —the Church press countered by flaying the Jews as the mentors of the National Liberal Party which endorsed Bismarck's stand, as the evil genius of Bismarck himself, and as the corruptors of the German soul—a counter-attack which did not end until Bismarck realized that liberalism was a greater enemy of "blood and iron" than the Church, and in 1878 abandoned the Liberal Party and made peace with the Vatican. But the Church, too, confined its polemic to the usual Christian *clichés*. The Panic of 1873 provoked a similarly traditional onslaught against Jewish finance. Otto Glagau's revelations of stock-exchange and corporation methods—"swindles" he called them in *Der Börsen- und Gründungsschwindel in Berlin* (1876) and *Der Börsen- und Gründungsschwindel in Deutschland* (1877)—merely put in contemporary terms what every German had felt who lost a cent since the Romans introduced currency in Germania. And Constantin Frantz offered no novelty in his *Nationalliberalismus und die Judenherrschaft* (1874) which credited the Jews with dominating the liberal movement as they had once been credited with spreading French notions of equality and fraternity.

But the depression which followed the panic proved to be the longest and severest capitalism had so far experienced. It lasted until 1879, and in that final year of hardship the glad-tidings of the new gospel gained the general ear. Wilhelm Marr, the son of a Jewish actor, a convert to Christianity, and a sensation-mongering journalist, published his notorious pamphlet *Der Sieg des Judentums über das Germanentum*—"The Victory of Judaism over Germanicism." The Jewish question, he proclaimed, was at bottom a race question. A Semitic tribe, driven from its lair by Rome, had through the centuries bent every effort to subjugate the native European peoples. Bred-in-the-bone materialists, they had developed industry and commerce to achieve world dominion. After their recent emancipation they had fallen, first of all, upon Germany in order to judaize it—much as the Mongols had overwhelmed China. Semitism was on the eve of triumph, and unless the Germans—presumably a non-materialist people except when the stock-market broke—summoned their strength for a final battle, it meant *"finis Germaniae"*—the end of Germany. The same year Marr founded the Anti-Semitic League to "save the German fatherland from being completely Jew-ified." The cash response to an appeal for a "Jew-free" press enabled him, in 1881, to begin publishing the *Zwanglose Antisemitische Hefte* ("Occasional Anti-Semitic Brochures"). And the word *anti-Semitism* was launched on its notable career.

The word may have been new—perhaps Marr was the first to use it—but not the thing. Religious, economic, and social hatred of the Jews, our reader need not be told, was familiar to the Germans since at least the eleventh century, and probably long before. Hatred grounded on the conviction that the Jews were a separate nationality can be traced, implicitly at least, to the days when they were given a distinct political status as "servants" of the Imperial Treasury, and for that matter back to when the Jews had a state of their own. And hatred based on theories of racial traits—which is the nub of anti-Semitism—likewise had a distinguished history by the time Marr founded his League. Anti-Semitism was born with Aryanism. They are twin-offspring of an aberration as curious as can be found in the annals of credulity and—were it not for the tragic consequences—one of the most amusing.

iii

Mankind, it would seem, has always believed that potent virtues reside in blood and ancestry. Of the making of pedigrees there is no end—and likely no beginning. Totem and tribal relationships were the mainsprings of primitive society.

Among the early civilized nations the most notorious addicts to ancestor-worship were the Jews and Greeks, and it is important to observe that the worship was intensified during national crises—great victories or defeats. The Israelites adopted a genealogy which took them back to Adam after Moses led them out of Egypt to freedom and conquest. On their triumphant return from Babylonian exile, almost the first thing the Jews did was to "put away" their alien-blooded wives. To celebrate Marathon, Herodotus tracks the Hellenes back to the *Ur*-Pelasgians; and to preface the story of the Peloponnesian War, Thucydides derives the Greeks from Deucalion—who outrode the Flood. Greek and Barbarian—Jew and Gentile—are the classic terms of race snobism. The caste system of India is its monumental expression.

In the early Middle Ages the barbarian peoples who had fallen heir to Rome—and Virgil's epic—became convinced by their poets and intellectuals that they were descendants of the Trojans. To have fought on the losing side at Troy was as good as coming over in the *Mayflower*. When the Spanish entered their final battle with the Moors in the fifteenth century, racial purity grew to be a fad and then a mania. *Limpieza*—cleanness—meant that an hidalgo's veins were free from the pollution of Moorish or Jewish blood, and many a doubtful case was cleared up in the laboratory experiments of the Inquisition. Stimulated by the civil wars, Milton worked on a History of Britain which—with due skepticism—he traced back to "a certain Samothes or Dis, a fourth or sixth son of Japhet, who about two hundred years after the Flood planted colonies on this island."

Although poets had always kept alive the Teutonic traditions, the first "scientific" interest in the German tribes dates from the Renaissance. At the dawn of the sixteenth century German editors of Tacitus fell with delight and naive faith upon his description of ancient Germania and its inhabitants. They never suspected that this malicious historian was praising the virtues of the barbarians in order to castigate the vices of the Romans; and on the word of Tacitus they began to boast about *Treue* and *Freiheit*—loyalty and freedom—as hereditary virtues, and were soon recalling that the Germans were hereditary conquerors, having given kings to barbarian Spain, Italy, and France.

Frenchmen then took up the tale of Germanic virtues, and quite like modern ethnologists made race the servant of politics. Germanic love of liberty as embalmed in the blood of the Franks served Francis Hotman (1574) in his Protestant attack on the Catholic monarchy. The Count de Boulainvilliers (1727) used the Frankish spirit of conquest to bolster up the claims of the French nobility against the threat of the middle classes. Mably, Sieyès, and Rousseau defended the bourgeoisie as the true heirs of Frankish freedom against the despotism inherited in the Latin blood of the nobility. A touch more of "science" and the French Revolution would have been written down as a race war.

But all of this was small change compared to what followed. In his *Histoire naturelle* (1779-1789) Buffon created our modern concepts of genus and species. Turning to the human species, Camper, a Dutchman, was soon busy with physiognomy and discovered the famous "facial angle" (1791) which has since worn out innumerable callipers. At the same time Blumenbach (1790-1808) started the callipers to work measuring human skulls. Anthropology was born. Yet at the very outset Buffon left a warning when he defined race as a variation produced by climate, food, and habits, and hence subject to continual change. And quite in the French tradition of skepticism he dropped a remark which no scientist would do well to forget. "Species, orders, and classes," he wrote, although he had given his life to their exposition, "exist only in our imagination. They are merely conventions. Nothing really exists but the individual. Nature does not recognize our definitions: she has never classified her work by group and kind."

Meanwhile science had made remarkable discoveries in another field. The relationship between many Eastern languages —Hebrew, Arabic, Syriac, Ethiopian, etc.—had long been recognized, and towards the end of the eighteenth century these tongues received a common name: Semitic. In 1788 Sir William Jones—and again in 1808 Friedrich Schlegel— pointed out similarities between many Western languages and Sanskrit. By 1833 Franz Bopp had proved the existence of fundamental relationships between a great family of languages which stretched across Europe and Central Asia and included—among others—the modern Romance, Germanic, and Slavic tongues, as well as Greek, Latin, Celtic, Armenian, Persian and Sanskrit. It was eventually established as a reasonable hypothesis that they all sprang from a long-vanished speech which the scholars came to call Aryan. The word

Aryan is related to *Aryas*, the name the Sanskrit-speaking peoples gave themselves, and to *Aryana*, an unidentified country mentioned in the Persian Avesta. The word *Semitic* is derived from *Shem*, one of the three sons of Noah and the father of such ancestors as the Israelites were willing to include in their family-tree.

Here science ends and romance begins. Scholars assumed the identity of language and race, forgetting that in the first place race still awaits a sound definition—no one to this day knows precisely what a race is or how to determine its characteristics. Secondly, they forgot that the same language is often spoken by different peoples—as, for example, the Scotch and the American Negroes; and that the same people often speak different languages—as the Italians in Rapallo and in Nice. The Semitic tongues were accordingly, on the mere analogy of language, credited to a single people called Semites. And the hypothetical Aryan tongue was placed in the mouth of an imaginary race called Aryans. The latter race was given a homeland, at first in Central Asia (by F. A. Pott, 1840) and, later, on almost every plain and plateau between the North Sea and the Himalayas. They were endowed, at least by their German creators like Theodor Pösch (*Die Arier,* 1878), with long skulls, blue eyes, pink cheeks, and yellow hair. In order to account for the presence of the many languages derived from Aryan, the blue-eyed people were set on interminable migrations from their ancestral home, wherever it was, and even provided for the journey (by E. B. Tylor in 1881) with special solid-wheeled wagons. The upshot of the vision is that the peoples who once spoke Greek, Latin, Celtic, and Sanskrit, and those who now speak French, Italian, German, English, Russian, Persian, Bengalese, etc., are at bottom race-brothers—blue-eyed blond Aryans under their otherwise variegated skins.

This pundit's phantasy was harmless and would likely have vanished along with the Aryans and Semites themselves—as indeed it has in all scientific thought—had not a Gascon gentleman intervened with the idea that men not only differ in race, but that some races are superior to others. Aryanism as a cult, rather than a romantic speculation, dates from the publication of Count de Gobineau's *Essay on the Inequality of Races* (1853-55).

M. le Comte Joseph Arthur de Gobineau was a gifted poetic crackpot who spent years elaborating a genealogical history in which he claimed descent from a ninth-century Norman pirate. The thesis of his two-volume *Essay* is expressed in one sentence: "Everything great, noble, and fruitful in the works of man comes from a single starting-point; it belongs to one family, the different branches of which have reigned in all civilized countries of the globe." That family is the Aryans, and its most creative branch the Germanic.

The French paid little attention to the Gascon's work—they knew a Gasconade when they saw one; but after 1875 Richard Wagner took up Gobineau, became his warm friend and admirer, and introduced him to Germany, where his ideas made their fortune. Germany was in no mood to remark that Gobineau had distinguished between the Germanic people (*les Germains*) whom he worshiped and the modern Germans (*les Allemands*) who, he thought, "were essentially not Germanic at all" but decidedly inferior to the French in racial purity. The Germans also overlooked his gloomy belief that the reigning white race was in its decline—a notion that appealed to the composer of *The Twilight of the Gods*; but, intoxicated with Sedan, the new Reich, and a billion dollars of indemnity, they heard in Wagner's music the call of their gods and race, and saw in themselves the Aryan masters of humanity.

Other voices, more authoritative than Gobineau if less thrilling than Wagner, had joined their strophes in praise of Aryan superiority. Christian Lassen, a notable scholar, had written in his *Indische Altertumskunde* ("Hindu Antiquities," vol. I, 1844) that "history proves the Semites do not possess the harmony of psychical forces which distinguishes the Aryans." Ernest Renan had announced in his history of Semitic languages (*Histoire des langues sémitiques,* 1855) that "science and philosophy were almost foreign to the Semites" and that "the Semitic race, compared to the Indo-European, represents in reality an inferior composition of human nature." Few remarked that Renan expressly said he was talking of the Semites of three thousand years ago and, even so, in the same book declared that "physically, the Semites and Aryans were but one race, the white race; and intellectually, they are but one family, the family of civilization." Nor did many remember that in his preface he noted "how the Jews of today possess nothing of a Semitic character and are no longer anything but modern men carried away and assimilated by that great force, itself superior to race and destructive of local traits, which we call civilization." Instead, a delusion of racial grandeur took root in the German mind.

By 1878 thwarted business ambitions, unslaked nationalist enthusiasm, and a victory gone sour through panic and depression goaded Germany to take one of the critical turns in her history—a turn celebrated merely in passing by the first outburst of Aryan worship in the form of damning the Jews.

iv

Four major changes in German policy took place in 1878-1879. Bismarck broke with the National Liberal Party and rejoined the Conservatives partly because the Liberals opposed his stand on the tariff and partly because he recognized in the Conservatives the stauncher backers of his new deal which embraced a semi-nationalized industry, a nationalist economic policy, colonial expansion, militarism, and the perpetuation of Junker ascendancy. Secondly, Bismarck introduced the first high tariff in Germany, which soon restored and enhanced the prosperity of industry and which, combined with a tightening alliance between government and business, enabled Germany to undersell England—the old game of "dumping" —and prepared the rivalry which brought on the World War. Behind this policy moved the spirit of Friedrich List, whose *National System of Political Economy* (1840) placed economics on a racial basis and foreshadowed a pan-Germanic empire. Thirdly, Bismarck came to terms with the Catholic Church—a conservative force he could no longer disregard and a dependable ally (as were all Churches in the nineteenth century) of nationalism and, if needs be, of war. His fourth move was the inevitable corollary of the whole process: he outlawed the Socialist (Social Democratic) Party.

In these circumstances the popular response to Marr's anti-Semitism was a small but telling detail of a larger picture. Bismarck was probably not displeased at the appearance of a Jewish red-herring. Marr himself was, in fact, but one of a host of agitators to divert attention from a high tariff, reinforced Junkerdom, disgraced liberals, and outlawed socialists. In the same year 1878—the year Pösch discovered that the Aryans were blond Teutons—Adolf Stöcker, court chaplain to the Emperor, founded the Christian-Socialist Workers' Party, a bid for the workingmen's vote which, deprived of its own political expression, was now invited to substitute the dictatorship of the Aryan Christian for the economic class struggle. It was Stöcker who first employed the slogan *Deutschland erwache!*—Germany, awake!—later to be revived, along with his pseudo-socialism, by the Nazis.

Stöcker was too genuine a Christian to accept wholeheartedly the new doctrines of race war: from the days of Saint Paul, Christianity had cherished quite another doctrine in which "there was no difference between the Jew and the Greek" (Rom. 10.12). We find him, therefore, preaching conversion to the Church as the means of turning wicked Jews into beneficent Germans. On the other hand, the race issue was too effective to renounce. So, when the occasion served, he preached that German blood contains the German soul, and "modern Judaism is a foreign drop of blood in the German body—one with a destructive power." "All immigrants," he concludes, "are finally assimilated by their adopted country, but not the Jews; their rigid Semitism, their unyielding ritual laws, and their enmity toward Christians stand in direct contrast to the German spirit."

The Germany he awoke, however, was not the proletariat, but the same element which was to respond to Hitler: the lower middle-classes—artisans, shop-keepers, petty officials, and clerks who inherited from the last vestiges of the medieval guilds a hatred of the Jew and a romantic dream they called "true socialism," meaning a self-intoxication with socialist phrases and otherwise leaving everything as it is. He skillfully sought to convince these little folk that the Jews were responsible for the two forces they feared most: Big Business which they impotently resented, and Marxian socialism in which they saw their ruin. "Nathan the Wise will one day disappear from our minds behind the figure of Shylock"—so much for the origin of capitalism. The revolt of the masses as a Jewish contrivance was proved by merely mentioning the names of Marx and Lassalle. "The Jews are at one and the same time the pace-setters of capitalism and of revolutionary socialism, thus working from two sides to destroy the present political and social order." Jewry could begin to learn from Stöcker that being tied to the wheel of capitalism, with its warring classes, was not to differ greatly from being tied to feudalism and its fighting orders. But Stöcker could appeal to progress. He pointed with pride at the nationalism which had superseded the cosmopolitan outlook of Lessing: "In the century which separates us from him, we have progressed a little."

In 1881, thanks to the efforts of Marr's League and Stöcker's Christian-Socialist Party—together with the aid of street riots and possibly a slush-fund of Bismarck's—an anti-Semitic petition bearing nearly 300,000 signatures was presented to the government. "The blending of the Semitic with the German element of our population," it read in part, "has proved a failure. We are now faced with the loss of our national superiority through the ascendancy of Judaism, the steadily increasing influence of which springs from racial characteristics which the German nation cannot and must not tolerate unless it wishes to destroy itself." And the conclusion was reached that "the Jewish race was a menace not only to the economic well-being of the German people, but to their culture and religion." The demands of the petitioners were, from our contemporary point of view, rather mild: a curb on the influx of Jewish immigrants; elimination of Jews from responsible state positions, especially in the judiciary; their removal from the teaching profession in the elementary schools and severe limitation of their appointments in the higher schools and the universities. A few years later (1887) the first demand was answered in the expulsion of hundreds of Jewish families, refugees from the Russian pogroms; and the remainder entered into practical effect throughout the life of the second Reich.

New anti-Semitic parties sprang up, free from the weakness of Stöcker's Christianity with its hope of a solution through conversion—Alexander Pinkert's German Reform Party in Saxony, which popularized a phrase to reappear in Hitler's day when it proposed to solve the Jewish question *im deutsch-nationalen Sinne* ("in a national German manner"); Dr. Otto Böckel's Anti-Semitic People's Party in Hessia, which enlisted the peasants; and smaller groups such as the German People's Union and the Social Reich's Union. A World Congress of anti-Semites was held at Dresden in 1882, attended by Germans, Austro-Hungarians, and Russians. A less ambitious but more effective convention of the German groups assembled at Bochum in 1889 and united most of them into the Deutsch-Soziale Partei (German Social Party) which, under the leadership of Böckel, reached its greatest strength in 1893 when a quarter of a million voters sent sixteen deputies (out of 397) to the Reichstag, and which lingered on to rival and then succumb to the Nazis. Stöcker himself had been elected in 1881 and held his seat intermittently throughout the period.

Supporting these political endeavors, a series of demonstrations and excesses broke out in the early eighties—mere child's play to what took place in Russia and Rumania, but enough to promise that, if properly trained, the German populace would make obedient soldiers in a race war. In small towns Jewish shops fell under a boycott. In the universities students mocked and thrashed their Jewish comrades. Restaurants, hotels, and summer resorts advertized themselves as *Judenrein*—free from Jews. The assaults of individuals by anti-Semitic hoodlums, by which term we are to understand the educated as well as the more homespun variety, were common street incidents. Jewish cemeteries were desecrated and funerals interrupted, and Jewish houses spattered with mire. Riots took place in Pomerania and West Prussia; a synagogue was burned in Neustettin. In 1884 an attempt to stage a ritual-murder trial barely failed in the Pomeranian village of Skurz; similar attempts succeeded at Xanten in 1891, and Konitz in 1900.

Stimulating the populace, books and pamphlets, for the most part by ignoble pens, appeared in monotonous succession. The *Judenspiegel* (1883) of Dr. Justus—the pseudonym of a baptized Jew named Aaron Brimann—made a fitting pendant to the work of Rohling. Professor Gustav Adolf Wahrmund put his debasement of Renan's thesis in the title of his work, *Das Gesetz des Nomadentums und die heutige Judenherrschaft*—"The Law of Nomadry and the Present Reign of the Jews" (1887). Hermann Ahlwardt, principal of a Berlin public school, appealed to the use of the Aryan fist in *Der Verzweiflungskampf der arischen Völker mit dem Semitentum*—"The Desperate Battle of the Aryan Peoples with Semitism" (1890). His *Judenflinten* ("Jew Rifles," 1892), in which he accused the Jewish firm of Ludwig Löwe and Company of delivering faulty guns to the army, earned him a brief prison sentence and an election to the Reichstag. A few years later, when Ahlwardt tried to carry on his propaganda in New York and demanded protection, the Commissioner of Police, Theodore Roosevelt, detailed him a body-guard of Jewish policemen. The final product of this pre-war gutter literature was *Wenn ich der Kaiser wär* ("If I Were the Kaiser," 1913), a widely-read book by the pseudonymous Daniel Frymann, who urged that the Jews be barred from citizenship, the army, the legal profession, banking, theaters, journalism, and the right to own land.

Of the entire school Theodor Fritsch alone attained lasting recognition. His *Antisemitic Catechism* (1887) ran through more than twenty editions and appeared in close to a hundred thousand copies. For years he edited the *Anti-Semitic Correspondence*, a "private" news service for party members, and then the battle-sheet, *The Hammerer*. He fought unwearied till his death in 1933 and has now received his reward in a monument erected to his name in a suburb of Berlin. Representatives of the National Socialist party, the city administration, and the army were present at its unveiling in witness of Fritsch's doctrine that "the Jewish question is a fight between everything honorable and honorless."

Jew-baiting was not, however, the exclusive privilege of shop-keepers and back-alley journalists. Some of the more distinguished figures in German thought added the weight of their prestige to the game. Heinrich von Treitschke, to begin at the top, was one of the "professor-prophets" who made German universities not the cloisters but the sounding-boards of their times. Perhaps more than any other individual, Treitschke embodied the intellectual forces behind Bismarck's program. As a publicist he clarified and trumpeted the policies which created the Empire; and, when it was created, served for thirteen years (1871-1884) as deputy in the Reichstag. After he began teaching in the University of Berlin (1874), his lecture hall became the favorite resort of public dignitaries, army officers, professional men, and society leaders, imbued with Prussianism and autocracy. Today his voice can best be heard in his *History of Germany in the Nineteenth Century* (1879-1894), a monument of masterful and brilliant malignancy. His mental clarity could not stomach the cult of the racists. Instead, his religion was Germany, its temple was Prussia, and its holy-of-holies was the Hohenzollerns. Not one phrase in the five volumes of his *History* breathes a generous thought for humanity or the world; every word is calculated to reprobate the outsider, French, English, Slav, or Jew—whatever foreigner had the ill-grace to fall within the orbit of German events; and the whole is a paean to German genius, running from good-natured apology for the *gemütliche* Bavarian to the clash of cymbals for the Prussian kings. The work gave German nationalism an historical justification, compelling in logic and passion.

When the Anti-Semitic Petition was gathering its signatures—the critical moment in the rise of the new race issue—Treitschke, idol of the intellectual patriots, published *Ein Wort über unser Judentum* ("A Word on Our Jewry," 1880), three essays which set the seal of intelligence on the demagoguery of Stöcker and the charlatanism of Marr. With cool objectivity—"undisturbed by the fact that the Jewish press befouls the historical truth"—he demonstrated that anti-Semitism was "a natural reaction of the German national feeling (*des Germanischen Volksgefühles*) against a foreign element which had usurped too large a place in our life." Heine had once called Judaism not a religion but a "misfortune." Treitschke epitomized his thought by cleverly turning the phrase and proclaiming Judaism "our misfortune"—*unser Unglück*. "In the circles," he wrote, "of highly educated Germans, who would indignantly protest against any thought of religious or nationalist intolerance, a single cry is heard: 'The Jews are our misfortune.' " That single cry, *Die Juden sind unser Unglück,* has since reverberated on Nazi bill-boards, banners, hand-bills, labels, and from the iron throats of *Sprech-Chöre*.

While Stöcker expounded the Christianity of Christian Socialism, Adolf Wagner, the eminent economist, built a learned foundation for its socialism. As a *Kathedersozialist*— which might be translated as a class-room rather than a class-conscious socialist—he defended private property in illusory socialistic phrases, became vice-president of Stöcker's party, and ponderously abused the Jews. Towards the end, however, his anti-Semitism lost its orthodox edge. The Jewish menace, he conceded, while no less a menace was a symptom and not the cause of Germany's plight. "Search," he told the German people, "for the root of the evil in yourselves."

Meantime Paul de Lagarde (*né* Bötticher), professor at the University of Göttingen and one of the most distinguished Orientalists of the day, gave an academic standing to anti-Semitism whether he wrote on Hebrew roots or German politics; and he wrote voluminously on both. His *Deutsche Schriften* (1853-1886) did much to swell the German ego, especially by denying the Jews any touch of originality or creative genius. It impressed the German people, especially cultivated circles, to have professorial authority to back their conviction that the Aryans were the delight of the gods, and to have the University of Göttingen's imprint on the dictum: "Our duty with respect to the Jews must be dictated not by our love for a neighbor, but by our hatred toward an enemy" —a dictum supported by Deuteronomy, "Thou mayest not put a foreigner over thee" (17.15), which showed that Professor de Lagarde could give the Devil points on citing Scripture.

Following on Treitschke's heels, Eugen Dühring, a philosopher and economist of some note in his day, preached a straight racist war in *Die Judenfrage als Rassen-, Sitten-, und Culturfrage* ("The Jewish Question as a Problem of Race, Customs, and Culture," 1881) and other writings. That Dühring had recently been removed from the faculty of the University of Berlin for his anti-religious materialism and that Jewish colleagues had joined in voting for his removal divided rather evenly the honors of prejudice. "The origin of the general contempt felt for the Jewish race," wrote philosopher Dühring, "lies in its absolute inferiority in all intellectual fields. Jews show a lack of any scientific spirit, a feeble grasp of philosophy, an inability to create in mathematics, art, and even music. Fidelity and reverence with respect to anything great and noble are alien to them. Therefore, the race is inferior and depraved." The goal of this incapable people was to exploit mankind. Hence "the duty of the Nordic peoples is to exterminate such parasitic races as we exterminate snakes and beasts of prey." The most dangerous Jews, incidentally, were those who became baptized and slipped into the Nordic fold under the guise of Christians. Not that Dühring loved Christians. On the contrary, "the greatest menace lies in absorbing the characteristics of the Jewish race." The proof is

Christianity, which he condemns as the last manifestation of the Semitic mind. "Mankind will never be free from Semitism until it banishes this final aspect of the Hebraic spirit."

Christianity as a Jewish depravation had already been denounced by Schopenhauer. The Christians, he taught, made a fatal mistake in taking from the Jews a personal God—"a God who created this world of tears and then congratulated Himself and called it good: that is too much!" From this standpoint he ranked Judaism "as the lowest religion among civilized peoples" and the Jews themselves, who did not share his own hatred of life, as "the most immoral" of races. Nietzsche, who reversed Schopenhauer's attitude toward the will to live and whose first books began to win attention in the eighties, likewise reproached the Jew for inventing Christianity—though, far from being an anti-Semite, he regarded the modern Jews as a superior people.

It was left to Schopenhauer's disciple, Eduard von Hartmann, whose *Philosophy of the Unconscious* has a niche in textbooks of philosophy, to join Treitschke in the cry against the "tribalism"—philosopher Hartmann's word—of the Jews. Capitalism, socialism, Semitic depravity, Christianity, tribalism—what sin remained to be laid on Jewish heads? In *Das Judentum in Gegenwart und Zukunft* ("Judaism in the Present and Future," 1885) Hartmann revived an old favorite from French Revolutionary days and claimed that the Jews were a branch of the international—hence damnable—Freemasonry. And finally, as the Second Reich drew near its end, Werner Sombart, one of the most prominent of contemporary economists, returned to the first charge in his massive *Die Juden und das Wirtschaftsleben* ("The Jews and Modern Capitalism," 1910). As a faith and a folk, Judaism and the

Jews were guilty, not to be sure of capitalism to which Sombart does homage, but of all its evils.

v

Far from the majority of Germans shared these views. As
yet it was only seed-time; neither the economic nor the political conditions were ready for the harvest. Immediately upon
Treitschke's attack, his fellow-historian Theodor Mommsen
replied with *Another Word on Our Jewry* (1880), in which
he called anti-Semitism "an abortion of nationalism"—though
he urged conversion as the only solution, not because he believed in Christianity but looked on it as the conventional garb
of the modern man. Franz Delitzsch, as we have seen, disposed of Rohling and Justus. When the Anti-Semitic Petition
was circulating, seventy-six distinguished Christians issued a
counter-appeal to wipe out "the national disgrace" and "restore peace and unity to the land." Among the famous signers,
which included scholars, public officials, artists, and industrial
leaders, were the historians Mommsen and Johann Droysen,
the anthropologist and medical scientist Rudolph Virchow,
the astronomer Wilhelm Foerster, the jurist Rudolph von
Gneist, and E. Werner von Siemens, the great rival of
Rathenau in the electrical industry.

Replying to a questionnaire in 1885, the scientists Jacob
Moleschott, Ludwig Büchner, and Karl Vogt spoke for the
general response when they characterized Judeophobia as the
product of the economic struggle—an expression, as Vogt
said, "of the hatred which the incapable feel toward the capable, the poor toward the rich, and the easy-going toward the
energetic." Gustav Freytag, the novelist, called it a "disease of

the popular mind." Max Müller, who helped invent Aryanism which he later derided as an unscientific confusion between language and race, pronounced anti-Semitism "a disaster to society and the state." Ernst von Aster, professor of philosophy, was more explicit when he said that "racial anti-Semitism is nothing but an expression of the German caste-feeling which is to be found in the deep cleavage between our classes and the growth of an arrogant Junkerdom, and is the greatest obstacle to German unity." The Crown Prince—who was to reign for a few weeks as Frederick III—coined a phrase which went round the world: "Anti-Semitism is the shame of the nineteenth century."

In 1890 a Union to Combat Anti-Semitism (*Verein zur Abwehr des Antisemitismus*) was created by and for German Christians. Its founder, Heinrich Rickert, a member of the Reichstag, told Stöcker on the floor of parliament, "I am convinced that three-quarters of the German nation are on my side"; and he was probably modest in his claim. The Union held mass-meetings throughout the country, distributed literature, issued a weekly, and soon numbered 13,000 members. It led the defense in ritual-murder trials, and naturally enlisted the support of the liberal and left-wing parties. Perhaps its most useful publication was the *Antisemitenspiegel* ("Mirror of Anti-Semites," 1892) in which Fritsch's *Catechism* was refuted point by point, and an arsenal of facts and arguments compressed in a brief compass. Its circulation, however, never approached that of the *Catechism*; apologetics, even if factual, is never as attractive as denunciation, no matter how fanciful.

After the Social Democrats were once more legalized, in 1890, they were tireless in preventing anti-Semitism from spreading among the masses. Their leader, August Bebel, coined another pregnant phrase in his *Antisemitismus und Sozialdemokratie* (1894). "Anti-Semitism," he wrote, "is the socialism of fools." It was more than a witticism. In it lay the whole Marxian thesis that capitalist society was self-doomed and that only fools—the learned as well as the other kind— looked for the source of the evil in the Jews, who were their fellow-victims, rather than in the system itself.

But, for the moment, the most effective check on the race war was this self-same capitalism. An era of prosperity postponed, while it prepared, disaster. To this prosperity must be added the measures of state socialism—health and accident insurance, old-age pensions, etc.—with which the government, as a defense against Marxism, gave a modicum of security to the workers and the petty middle-classes.

vi

By 1900 Germany's production of steel surpassed that of every nation save the United States, and her foreign trade every nation save Great Britain. Her dyes and chemicals and the development of her electrical industry led the world. And what with colonies in Africa and the Pacific, a thrust of railways and trade through the Balkans on the fatal road to Bagdad, and a naval power which frightened Britannia—no wonder the delusion of grandeur grew in the professorial and popular mind.

With the muting of the anti-Semitic strings, the Aryan theme rose to shrill crescendos. Leading a whole school of "race-geographers," Friedrich Ratzel in his *Anthropogeographie* (1882-1891) and *Völkerkunde* (1894-1895—translated as

"The History of Mankind") proved that the Germanic peoples were geographically predestined to dominate mankind. Karl Lamprecht in his *Deutsche Geschichte* (1891-1913), together with a phalanx of historians—Ranke, Droysen, Constantin Frantz, Heinrich von Sybel, Ernst Curtius—whether writing on Germany or on ancient Greece and Rome managed to prove that the Germans were historically predestined for the same glorious goal.

If any doubt lingered in the mind of a German, he need only have turned to the race-sociologists, such as Albert Wirth who wrote *Volkstum und Weltmacht in der Weltgeschichte* ("Racehood and World Power in History," 1901); or Karl Wagner whose political-evolutionary-historical examination of war (*Krieg,* etc., 1906) attracted a huge body of readers; or Friedrich Lange with his *Reines Deutschtum* ("Pure Germanhood," 1893-1904) and the rosy promise of eugenics, meaning a ban on marriage between Aryans and Semites. A more specialized treatment was provided by a school of racial economists from old Friedrich List down to contemporary Gustav Schmoller. If art impressed a German more than economics, Julius Langbehn offered *Rembrandt als Erzieher* ("Rembrandt as Teacher," 1890) with its predestination through culture and, as always, race: by 1909 readers had accepted the offer to the tune of forty-nine editions. If literature impressed a man more than art, Adolf Bartels was ready with his *History of German Literature* (1901) and numerous other works to prove that "no other people, compared to the Germans, shows the influence of race on writing" and that, as a result, "German literature is the richest in Europe"—if, that is, we omit the German Jews, particularly Heine, who are "unwholesome," "degenerate," and "un-German." Heinrich

Driessmans packed all the proofs into one work which damned the Celts and bore the incredible title: *The Plastic Force in Art, Science, and Life* (1898).

Finally there remained the anthropologists pure and simple —and not so pure and simple. Otto Ammon, a lusty measurer of skulls and author of *Die Gesellschaftsordnung und ihre natürlichen Grundlagen* ("The Natural Basis of the Social Order," 1895), could always flatter the middle classes with his proof that they were the true Aryans—"born," as he says, "rulers of all other men"—while the proletariat was the débris of pre-historical races. Ludwig Wilser's *Die Germanen* (1903) flattered everybody by proving that not only the first men but the first mammals originated on the shores of the North Sea. Ludwig Woltmann invented a science he called political anthropology (in his *Politische Anthropologie,* 1903) which, so he claimed, "proved that the entire civilization of Europe is the achievement of the Germanic peoples." Otto Schrader sounded the Semitic *motif* in *Die Indogermanen* (1911) which contrasts desert-bred people with forest-bred folk.

But head and shoulders above them all, for the scope if not the strength of his claims, was the naturalized German, Houston-Stewart Chamberlain. His *Foundations of the Nine-teenth Century*, which appeared in its final year, turned Gobineau's dirge for the Aryans into a spring-song for the Teutons. Throughout two stout volumes he alternates between the Semitic minor—"the Jewish race is altogether bas-tardized and its existence is a crime against the holy laws of life"—and the Teutonic major—"Only a shameful mental laziness or a shameless falsification of history can fail to see in the entry of the Germans upon the stage of history anything else but the rescue of agonizing humanity from the claws of eternal beasthood."

Emperor William II lent the book his august approval, installed it in numerous public libraries, and nearly one million German copies have seen the light of day. For Germany the *Foundations of the Nineteenth Century* has become the corner-stone of the twentieth.

That this mass of "science" has no basis in facts is irrelevant to our story. As Tertullian said of another faith, "I believe it because it is impossible." And Frederick the Great warned us on our approach to modernity that few men possess the gift of reason. The Frenchman Gobineau, the Englishman Chamberlain, and one million German readers prove that Frederick can't be wrong.

Still, it may be worth a moment's attention to turn to one of the oldest devotees of the race cult and its new "witness." By the time the Mishna was composed—let us say seventeen hundred years ago—the Jews divined why God had created Adam. "Mankind," reads the Mishna, "was created in the form of a single man in order, for the sake of peace, that no man can say to his fellow, 'My ancestor was greater than yours.'"

19

REPUBLICAN INTERLUDE

For four years Germany carried the burdens of war, including three allies, in a life-and-death struggle against twenty-three nations. Outnumbered, overpowered, and half-starved she turned revolutionary and scuttled the monarchy. In November, 1918, on the eve of the armistice, the Socialists set up a provisional government. The Republic and the Weimar Constitution came into being in August 1919. Its president, Friedrich Ebert, was a Socialist; and it was governed by a coalition ministry in which the Social Democrats had the largest, though not a majority, representation.

But from the outset there was no effective revolution, and the Republic never had enough republicans. *Der Kaiser ging . . . die Generäle blieben*—"The Kaiser went . . . the generals remained." Indeed they proved most useful. The Kaiser's heels had hardly flashed over the Dutch border when Ebert had concluded an arrangement with General Gröner of the High Command "to maintain order"—that is, the existent economic order. "We owe it to Ebert and his associates," said one of the leaders of the Reich Union of German Industry, "that we were able to retain the capitalistic system in 1918."

More generals, under Gustav Noske, socialist Minister of

Home Defense, crushed the Spartacist uprising in 1919—the only genuine attempt at revolution in northern Germany—by slaughtering 15,000 workers. The leaders of the revolt, Karl Liebknecht and Rosa Luxemburg, two idealists who inhabited a world incomprehensively above the mentality of Germany, were shot by their police guards "while attempting to escape." Generals von Oven and von Epp crushed the Bavarian Soviet government—the one serious effort at revolution in the south. Among its leaders Kurt Eisner was assassinated, and Gustav Landauer and Eugen Leviné murdered by the soldiery. Nearly two hundred civilians—men, women, and children—were "accidentally shot" by these valiant warriors. "The generals were the real masters of the situation," writes Ernst Toller who served under Eisner and Landauer.

In March 1919 the generals carried their confidence a step too far. General Kapp, General von Lüttwiz, and other military notables, led an army into Berlin to put an end to the year-old Republic. Throughout the country trade-unions and socialists declared a general strike; open battle swept Leipzig, Hamburg, Dresden, and the Ruhr; and the Kapp "Reich" lasted precisely four days. Thereafter, local uprisings, strikes, and parades intermittently recurred; but despite the clear proof of what they could do if they laid down their tools and took up their guns, the masses never revolted again.

Hugo Haase, founder of the Independent Socialist Party, was fatally shot on the steps of the Reichstag as he was about to bring in a report on the treasonable activities of the army. Reichsminister Matthias Erzberger, Catholic supporter of the Republic, was pumped full of bullets by recruits of the illegal "Black Reichswehr." Scheidemann, the first chancellor of the Republic, barely escaped a shower of prussic acid. Maximilian

Harden was beaten within an inch of his life. As penalty for the Bavarian Soviet revolt, prison sentences were meted out to Left offenders totaling 4092 years; as punishment for the Kapp treason, the Right offenders received four years. The people did not stir.

For twelve years after 1920 the Socialists held a larger number of seats, by far, than any other party in the Reichstag. The Socialists and Communists, if combined, polled almost a third of the votes and controlled more than a third of the parliament. Yet in all this time only one Socialist (1928 to 1930) served as chancellor, and only twice was a Reich portfolio accepted by the party. And the people did not stir. The generals had done their work: the government belonged, as of old, to the industrialists and the Junkers. "The instinct for freedom," Ernst Toller tells us, and he paid for his knowledge with five years in prison, "simply does not exist in Germany."

ii

The capitalism which Ebert enabled Germany to retain was not, however, the same capitalism which had helped create the Reich in 1871 and which gave the Jews their formal freedom. It was no longer a system which demanded for its well-being individual opportunity and political liberty. Instead, it had become a concentrated order of vast monopolies in which privilege and not opportunity, discipline and not liberty, exclusion and not participation, were indispensable for its continued existence.

As far back as 1909 Walter Rathenau had warned the world: "In the impersonal democratic field of economics . . . three hundred men, all of whom know one another, direct the economic destiny of Europe and choose their successors from among themselves." Rathenau was not, of course, speaking with the accuracy of a statistician when he numbered the economic rulers of Europe at three hundred; but as one of the leaders of the German electrical industry, his words outweigh a ton of statistics. It is a horrible irony that the German anti-Semites, their heads filled with the forged "Protocols of Zion" and its imaginary "Elders," dug up Rathenau's warning and changed his words to read "three hundred Jewish bankers" and "three hundred sages of Zion." The point remains that, as he wrote later, "I had in mind the leaders of international business."

How few of these "three hundred" businessmen ruled Germany by 1919 is impossible to say. But during the War, concentration of industry, already far advanced under imperial policies, increased rapidly. After the war, it made giant strides. The loss of industrial areas in the Saar and Upper Silesia, the dwindling of foreign markets due to the creation of the succession states and the world-wide rise of high tariffs, the burden of reparations, the advance in the technical economy of production, all hastened the growth of cartels and trusts. And finally the inflation, which got well under way by 1920, gave a few industrialists and bankers their golden opportunity. By selling abroad coal, iron, and manufactured goods, and keeping the returns deposited in gold among foreign banks, the chief industrialists sped the fall of the mark, the rise of their profits, and the absorption of their weaker competitors. In 1922 Hugo Stinnes banked his first billion dollars. It was not long until the Stinnes group and a handful of others practically owned and literally controlled the industries of Germany.

Moreover, the post-war capitalism of Germany no longer enjoyed "well-being." It was fighting not for prosperity but for life. The factors which hastened monopoly left it with an equipment too great for its markets: thousands of wheels and hundreds of thousands of hands were idle. (After a brief spell of work from 1924 to 1928, the idle hands were to number millions.) While on the one hand inflation brought profits to the favored few, they proved sterile—as sterile as the booty of a medieval *Raubritter*; for, on the other hand, inflation impoverished the middle classes—merchants, rentiers, and the army of officials and intellectuals employed by the government—and wiped out their purchasing power. Further, the workers never received an increase of wages proportionate to the fall of the mark, and a second great interior market was ruined. The peasants, while they might eat, likewise had no cash to buy the output of mines and factories. Monopoly capitalism was choking from its very wealth of equipment and strength of organization.

The peasants, the lower middle-classes, and above all the workers—ruined or underpaid—were more than a dead loss so far as their purchasing power was concerned: they were a living menace. They were hungry. They were battling with the wolf, not at the door but well over the threshold, stripping the larder bare, ravaging the clothes closet and the coal bin, and gnawing out the hearts of men. Indeed, more potent than hunger was despair.

One light alone shone above the horizon. Like the magi who came to Bethlehem, the little men in Germany saw a star in the East. But for the big industrialists it was a star of ill-omen. They could not foresee that, despite a sign from the Russian skies, the German masses would not stir. Even today they still tremble lest it prove the sign and star of a new destiny.

As hunger and despair entered the peasant's cot, the middle-class flat, and the worker's tenement, so fear took its seat at the table of every board of directors. Karl Marx was no longer a dead book-worm: his spirit inflamed a land covering two-thirds of Europe, his manifesto gleamed in the steel of a million bayonets, the shadow of his black beard fell across the ledgers of banks, trusts, and holding-companies. At long last the Industrial Revolution, which once brought the Jews emancipation, had come full turn.

In these circumstances German capitalists could follow only one road. They had to create, not a liberal and so far as possible democratic state as in the days of the Empire, but a government which would insure the regimentation of the masses and their submission to a continually lower standard of living. Without a lowering standard, profits would cease; and, without submission and regimentation, a lowering standard could not be maintained. Again they had to create a defense against communism, and this meant they had to persuade the very classes which communism would benefit that it was their worst enemy. Finally, they had to create a government which would provide sanctions, i.e. guns and prisons, for their monopolist system—a government which would, precisely like their horizontal and vertical trusts, embody and consecrate monopoly.

To accomplish this program, the magnates needed allies. No handful of men can rule either the economy or the politics of a land without broad popular support. The slow accretion of this support was not, it must be understood, the work of plotting and villainy. We are not describing a melodrama

or the machinations of master-minds, but the casual lumber-
ing drift of history in which the lesser powers of society are
generally dragged in the train of the greater. With the Empire gone and its prestige forever vanished, monopoly industry was the most effective power in Germany and it attracted
other forces by its own superior might—and not because
Stinnes was cunning or Thyssen pulled strings.

The immediate and natural allies gravitated to the industrialists of their own accord: the army chiefs, as we have already seen, and the Junker aristocracy. Informal clubs—
probably the best-known was the *Ring* which later became the
Herrenklub—sprang up as early as 1921, in which bankers,
manufacturers, landed gentry, army officers, and aristocratic
intellectuals linked hands and brains. The *Ring*, for example,
and its successor the *Herrenklub*, numbered from time to
time among its members Hugenberg who owned hundreds
of nationalist newspapers, Friedrich Flick the partner of the
steel baron Thyssen, Dr. Luther the erst-while president of
the Reichsbank, Lübbert of the Stahlhelm, Escherich the unsavory captain of the illegal military troop Orgesch, the
equally unsavory Von Papen, and wealthy Junkers like the
Freiherr Heinrich von Gleichen. In 1922 the intellectual mentor of the *Ring*, Moeller van den Bruck, published the anti-
Marxian, anti-liberal, totalitarian program of Big Industry in
a book bearing the prophetic title: *Das Dritte Reich*—"The
Third Reich." When Ludendorff and Hitler made their unsuccessful *Putsch* in 1923, the *Ring* awaited the outcome with
breathless hope: the *Lokal-Anzeiger*, Berlin's leading reactionary newspaper, had prepared a special edition to celebrate
the triumph that did not come till ten years later.

Other allies, not so inevitable, were subsidized and soon put in harness. Germany was overrun with officers without commissions, veterans without jobs, young students eager to renew a war they were born too late to die in, and the dregs of the lower classes, the *Lumpen* proletariat: a motley throng that in America provides our deputy-sheriffs, private police, Vigilantes, strike-breakers, and rank-and-file gangsters. These disgruntled or arduous spirits banded together in an array of nationalist, semi-secret, military orders, interlocking in their membership.

To name but a few, there were the Brigade Ehrhardt, famous for its treasonable work in the Kapp *Putsch* and which later mobilized 10,000 unofficial "police" against the activities of the Communists in Thuringia; the Werwolf clan which reinforced the regular army with 2,000 men in Saxony; the Organization Escherich, better known as the Orgesch, which helped crush the people's revolution in Bavaria; the Blücherbund, Rossbach, Bismarck Order, Frontbann, Treu-Oberland, Deutschvölkischer Schutz- und Trutzbund, Deutschnationaler Jugendbund, Jungdeutscher Orden, Organization Consul, Neudeutscher Bund, Sturmtrupps of the National Socialists, and the Verband Nationalgesinnter Soldaten (Union of Nationalminded Soldiers)—each of which had members guilty of political murders, whose more prominent victims included Erzberger and Rathenau.

All in all, these Vereins and Bunds, with many more, comprised the Black Reichswehr, tolerated and often covertly recognized by the regular army and the government. Their weapons came by devious routes from army barracks and munition factories, their funds from patriotic business men who appreciated their services. These services varied to suit the occasion: defense of Upper Silesia (and its mines and mills) from the Poles, release of German prisoners in French occupied territory, heartening the opposition to the German Republic, terrorizing the Communists, Socialists, and democrats. But however much the immediate objects shifted, one passion united every fighter's heart: hatred of the Jew. They could all join in the marching song of the Brigade Ehrhardt:

> *Wir sind kein Judenknechte,*
> *In Deutschland soll immer nur ganz allein*
> *Ein* Deutscher *unser Führer sein.*
>   (We are no slaves of the Jews,
>   Forever and ever in Germany
>   Shall only a *German* our leader be.)

They could all echo the war-cry of the Deutschnationaler Jugendbund:

> *Schlagt tot den Walter Rathenau,*
> *Die Gottverfluchte Judensau!*
>   (Kill off Walter Rathenau,
>   The God-damned Jewish sow!)

Eventually the more elegant of these disciplined brigands entered the Stahlhelm or furnished the nucleus for Hitler's Black Brigades, while the plebeian element built up the Nazi Brown Battalions. Altogether they served as guerrilla forces in the cowing of the masses by monopoly capitalism and Junkerdom.

How completely the government sympathized with their aims and activities may be judged by a few simple figures. During the years 1919-1922 there were 376 political murders in Germany. Of these, 22 were perpetrated by Left organizations or individuals. Only four of these Left murders re-

mained unpunished, and 10 of the remaining 18 were atoned
for by immediate death. On the other hand, 354 of these political murders were committed by Right organizations or
individuals, and the impressive number of 326 went unpunished. And only one Right murder was expiated by a death
sentence. From January 1, 1923, to July 31, 1931, the murdered
victims among the radical and liberal groups numbered 357,
against 86 murdered nationalists. The prosecution of the
Right murderers was characterized by the German League
for Human Rights as *so gut wie nichts*—"as good as nothing."
It could hardly have been otherwise as long as the Republic
lacked republicans and the industrialists and Junkers consti-
tuted the effective power in society.

The alliance formed with the lower middle-class—the
Kleinbürgertum—was a different story. As early as 1848 Marx
could describe this class as "the real social basis of the existing
order." Since then it had grown enormously. Technical im-
provements in industry had lowered the proportion of workers; while the increased energies devoted to distributing and
selling rather than producing goods, as well as the assumption by the government of constantly wider social enterprises,
had raised the proportion of technicians, professional men,
clerks, salesmen, agents, jobbers, retailers, and government
employees. By 1932 they were estimated to comprise almost
one half (48.13%) of the gainfully-occupied population, ex-
cluding the peasants. And the majority of the land-owning
peasants shared most of their interests and views. It was
among the *Kleinbürgertum* and peasants, if anywhere, that
monopolized industry had to seek the popular support essential to its political control.

These classes, however, had ambiguous interests and loyalties. They were torn between admiration and resentment towards the rich, between snobbery which made them despise the worker and a sense of weakness which made them fear the worker they despised. The post-war economic miseries— inflation, depression, the burden of reparations—fell hardest on their shoulders. The small shopkeeper and the little peasant had no way of raising prices to meet inflation and taxes, and the legally-fixed salaries of the government employees (who alone numbered one-sixth of the gainfully-occupied) lagged far behind the rising cost of living. All the good, safe, non-speculative investments of these classes—preferred stocks, bonds, insurance, mortgages—were rendered worthless. They saw themselves threatened with extinction by the organized power of industry on one side and the organized power of labor on the other. And, worse than economic miseries, as the bulwark of patriotism they felt more bitterly than worker or manufacturer the insults, swindles, and disgrace of the Versailles Treaty. Impoverished in pocket, destitute of organization, besmirched in honor, robbed of their smug happy glorification of Kaiserdom, shorn of a future, they were hungry for a new hope, a new loyalty, and a new grandeur. They needed religion.

Monopoly capitalism could hardly offer what they required: it was not a religion but a business, and one in which they were slated among the victims. Communism, whatever economic security it might promise, offered no balm for their patriotic wounds, no satisfactions for their pride, and no delusions to feed their impotence. So they turned to the faith of their fathers: Father Stöcker, Father Dühring, and Father Fritsch. They turned to Aryanism and its inseparable shadow anti-Semitism.

Here was the perfect faith. It held out the assurance of regeneration through the doctrine of race election and Aryan superiority. It provided the inspiration of a calendar of saints, from St. Hermann of the Teutoburg Forest to St. Otto of Bismarck. It furnished an intoxicating ritual with banners, processions, hymns, fire-worship, holy symbols, and revivalist meetings in which thousands of the faithful could be reborn in the blood of Teut and banish this world of sin and trouble —the world of reparations, Versailles guilt-clauses, lost provinces, worthless bonds, unemployment—in strong draughts of sacred oratory. It pointed the road to a new City of God where there would be bread, work, love, and glory for all the elect. It promulgated the severest discipline, demanding the utmost sacrifices of time, energy, wealth, personality, and freedom on the part of every adept. And best of all, it answered the eternal problem of Evil. Defeat, depression, and the frustration of the Aryan sons of light were the work of the Semitic children of darkness—the work of the Jews.

It is an apparent axiom in human nature that a positive ideal is not enough in itself to call forth the last ounce of human effort, such as was demanded by the conquest of the new City of God—the Third Reich. To this end every love must be accompanied by a hate. Or rather, every love generates a hate. Throughout the ages, love of God expressed itself in hate for the devil. With the ultimate purpose of inspiring love for his ideals, the communist invokes an immediate enemy in his caricature of the capitalist. Just so, nationalist love breeds a hate of the alien. And if nothing alien is at hand, something alien will be manufactured. For the presence of enemies whets our devotion to our friends, and obstacles intensify the expression of our ideals. Admiral von Tirpitz has been pertinently quoted as saying: "The self-expression of every individual, still more of every nation, is a duty; and since we need hatred for our self-assertion, we will instill it into the heart of every German and we will let it flame up in fire on every mountain-top of our Fatherland."

Our readers will, at this late chapter, need no explanation of why the German faith selected the Jew for the object of its hate. He had been traditionally that object. When the Germans were Christians, he had been the killer of Christ. When the Mongols had threatened invasion, he had been the traitor. When princes and bishops robbed the masses, he had been the exploiter. When murders had remained unsolved, he had been the criminal. When pestilence had stricken the land, he had poisoned the wells. When the French Revolution overwhelmed the German states, he had created the revolution. When the stock-market broke, it was he who invented capitalism. When the Germans lost the World War it was the Jew who had "stabbed them in the back." When the masses arose, it was he who devised Bolshevism. The only point to be emphasized is that each old accusation strengthened the new and became an element of it. The tradition grew by accretion: each generation added a coat of paint and with each coat the Jew grew blacker.

Finally, he was more than the traditional foe. With Frenchmen, Englishmen, and Poles armed to the teeth and therefore dangerous to taunt, the Jew was the cheapest and safest enemy. He was at once a scape-goat to bear the sins of the people, and a punching-bag upon which the faithful could exercise their muscles.

This nationalist anti-Semitic cult, with its immediate roots running back to the previous century and its ultimate sources in the very origins of German history, was a growth quite independent of monopoly capitalism. As we shall see, it became in the hands of the National Socialists a power in its own right. The industrialists, of course, welcomed it and subsidized it heavily, for it assured them the popular support which they needed. It is not, however, clear that Hitler is a dupe or tool of Thyssen. They are playing together, but they are each fortified with a stack of chips. It still remains for the cards to tell who is going to clean out whom.

iii

Such were the auspices under which the Jews entered the Republic. Meanwhile they had been sorely tried during the war. In 1916 when Germany realized that the victory she dreamed would never come true and the discontent of the populace became audible, the Prussian Minister of War had taken a census of the Jews to determine their number at the front and their occupations behind the lines. It was a blow which would have shattered the morale of a group less fanatically patriotic than the German Jews. And as the conflict dragged to its close, the High Command—notably Major-General Count von der Schulenberg—suggested that "the report be spread that the Jews have betrayed the country and sold the people to the enemy." The legend of "Jewish defeatism" and of a Jewish "international conspiracy" against Germany which ran like wildfire through the beaten discouraged land was given an official seal by General Ludendorff, when he was still considered sane, in his book *Kriegsführung und Politik* ("War Leadership and Politics," 1922).

But in the enthusiasm for democracy and a republic, the vast majority of Jews disregarded these portents. Few or none realized that democracy had no place in a monopoly capitalism fighting for its life, and that it met no deep response from a people who invented and for generations reveled in the goose-step. Had not Wilson and America made the world safe for democracy?

Moreover, in its early years the Republic democratically welcomed the Jews. It dropped most of the covert bars to office in the government service—in schools and universities, in the judiciary and ministries. The Jews turned to these fields with ardor and devotion, taking joy in helping rebuild German culture and the state on a basis that promised equal opportunity for every citizen. Hugo Haase and Otto Landsberg were two of the six Socialist commissioners who guided the provisional republic through its first stormy months when the Kaiser and the monarchists were showing how fast they could run. Among the 423 delegates at Weimar, nine were Jews and four were of Jewish ancestry. The Weimar Constitution—the first and only democratic constitution Germany ever had—was chiefly the work of Hugo Preuss, a Berlin professor of law. When the Social Democrats had their brief moment before the Republic completely surrendered to the industrialists (1919-1921), Gradnauer—of Jewish origin—was premier of Saxony, Paul Hirsch was premier of Prussia, and Kurt Rosenfeld its Minister of Justice.

Next to the Socialists, the Democratic Party—heir to the liberal parties of the old Reich—was the staunchest supporter of the Republic; and among its founders were Theodor Wolff, editor of democracy's chief organ, the *Berliner Tageblatt*, and

Walter Rathenau. The latter had rendered incalculable services to Germany by marshaling raw materials during the
war. Now, as Minister of Reconstruction and Foreign Minister, he sought to marshal the resources of peace. At the
Wiesbaden Conference (1921), he renewed for the first time
direct contacts with the French; on the occasion of the Genoa
Conference (1922), he concluded a treaty with Russia and
gave Germany her first foreign friend.

The atmosphere of freedom and ferment evoked an astonishing activity in all the arts. Visitors to Germany in those
spring-tide days will still remember the triumphs of the
German theater, of expressionist painting and sculpture, of
modernist architecture and music, and of the literary schools
culminating in Thomas Mann. By inexplicable fate—for who
can explain how and why a people's creative hour is struck?—
the majority of these artists, in every field, were Jews or
half-Jews.

Again we spare our readers a meaningless catalogue. We
will merely suggest how barren the twenties would have
been without Max Reinhardt's stage, without the acting of
Max Pallenberg and Elizabeth Bergner, without the play-
writing of Frank Wedekind and the imprisoned Ernst Toller,
without the paintings and drawings of Paula Modersohn and
George Grosz, without Erich Mendelsohn's daring architecture, without Arnold Schönberg's compositions and the baton
of a Bruno Walter and Otto Klemperer, and without the
books of Jakob Wassermann, Lion Feuchtwanger, Stefan
Zweig, Arnold Zweig, Emil Ludwig *und wie sie alle heissen
mögen*. The German press—as the event has proved—would
have been unreadable without Alfred Kerr, Siegfried Jacob-

sohn, and the five-fold Tucholsky. And in that other art called science, the name of Einstein went round the world.

Never in modern times, and rarely before, was a Jewry as prolific in its contributions to Israel. The level of Jewish culture in Germany, together with German Vienna and Prague, can hardly be hinted at by the brief mention of Martin Buber's exquisite recreation of Hasidic mysticism in his tales of the Baalshem, Rabbi Nahman, and the Great Maggid; Max Brod's philosophic panoramas in *Heidentum, Judentum, Christentum* ("Paganism, Judaism, Christianity") and his historical novels; the poetic dramas of Richard Beer-Hofmann (*Jaakobs Traum*) and Stefan Zweig (*Jeremias*); the etchings of Hermann Struck and Jacob Steinhardt; the typographical achievements of the Soncino Society devoted to the history and art of Hebrew book-making; the voluminous and often beautiful output of a half-dozen Jewish and Hebrew publishers; the completion of a fully illustrated cyclopedia (*Jüdisches Lexikon*) in five stout tomes, and the undertaking of a new Jewish encyclopedia (*Encyclopaedia Judaica*) now abandoned, a giant's torso, in its tenth volume; the creation or enrichment of a dozen Jewish museums of ritual and folk art; the weeklies, monthlies and quarterlies devoted to belles-lettres, philosophy, scholarship, and the arts; the encouragement, financial aid, and loving appreciation given to Jewish learning, arts, and literature by individuals, groups, societies, and the general community.

But something of the cultural level can be gauged by recalling the incredibly small numbers of this public—amounting, with Vienna and Prague, to 800,000. Chicago, Philadelphia, Boston and Cleveland could together furnish an equal, but by how little an equivalent, number of Jews.

iv

On June 24, 1922, Walter Rathenau was shot to death while driving on a public boulevard. Although an industrialist and a democrat, although he had helped save his country once and was striving to save it again, he suffered the fate of Eisner the communist, Haase the socialist, and Erzberger the liberal Catholic. "In Germany shall only a German our leader be," had sung the Ehrhardt Brigade, and two of its members—who subsequently killed themselves to avoid capture—had together with a band of accomplices set the song to action.

The world's appraisal of the deed could be read in the financial news. On June first the dollar was quoted at 273 marks, and on July seventh at 527 marks. *Wie steht der Dollar?* became a front-page headline in every newspaper until, in the fall of the next year, the dollar rose to two and one-half trillion marks. A million German bank accounts were wiped out; American investors in German currency and securities alone lost approximately one billion dollars. New foreign loans, including another two billion dollars from the United States, were to give the country an appearance of solvency and even well-being; but from the day Rathenau was interrupted in his work of salvage, Germany was a virtual bankrupt.

German reaction to the murder showed the mounting tide of nationalism and anti-Semitism. Thousands of workers paraded in indignation; the liberal press protested and the conservative press regretted. But a large and, only too soon, a dominant element of the population and the authorities believed with the murderers that "Rathenau, the international Jew, desired the defeat of Germany" and that the country could be saved only by "a nationally-minded government . . . and the exclusion of the Jews."

The trial of the thirteen accomplices, under a law expressly designed "to protect the Republic," was reported almost verbatim in the press. It exposed the names, interlocking connections, and activities of the clandestine organizations which, along with the Ehrhardt Brigade, were plotting not merely the "exclusion of the Jews" but the death of the Republic. It bared in detail the ramifications of anti-Semitism "which is assiduously cultivated," to quote the prosecuting attorney, "by all these organizations and created an atmosphere favorable to murder" and which had taken root in many circles of society.

Yet not one of the organizations implicated in the crime was subjected to a government investigation. The "atmosphere" was "favorable" enough to prevent even a cursory examination of the leaders of Junkerdom, such as Ludendorff, whose names flitted across the surface of the trial and were immediately lost in darkness. It threw an impenetrable veil over the financial backing of the movement. It stifled the voice of the general press so that while here and there a stray editor could peep, "What's this?" none appeared to find ways or means to provide an answer. It reduced the prison sentences of the offenders to derision. The significance of the Rathenau case lay in the ominous fact that it was not a Dreyfus case. Whereas the latter—in fairly analogous circumstances—gave France the occasion and enthusiasm to rally the republican forces of the nation, the Rathenau trial evoked little more than official rebuke and public apathy. No German dared to be a Zola.

The chief defendant, Ernst Werner Techow, a youth of good family who drove the murder car while one Kern and one Fischer did the shooting, was asked his motives. He informed the judge: "Kern told me that Rathenau belonged to the 'veiled' Bolshevist movement, that he was one of the three hundred Elders of Zion who was seeking to bring the world under the rule of the Jews." The remaining defendants repeated variations on the theme of another youth, Steinbeck, who announced, "We believe that the influence of the Jews in the government is pernicious" and of one of the leading conspirators, Tillesen, who simply declared: "I am racially-minded [*völkisch gesinnt*]; I am no fanatic, but I maintain my racial standpoint chiefly because I've been raised that way."

Here were clues, disregarded by a court sitting to "protect the Republic," which led to a vast literature and propaganda that from the day of the Armistice sought to undermine the government and outlaw the Jews.

Thanks to the assiduity of army officers, nationalist politicians, and the reactionary press, millions were "raised" to believe that the Jews had given Germany a "stab in the back" and thus caused the loss of the war. It was common knowledge for millions who wished to believe it and so exonerate themselves from any responsibility that Jews and Socialists—the "November criminals"—had overthrown the monarchy, established the Republic, and shackled the nation with the Treaty of Versailles. Of the efforts towards a people's revolution, it was only remembered that Rosa Luxemburg, Kurt Eisner, Gustav Landauer, and Eugen Leviné were Jews.

Of the Weimar Constitution it was only recalled that its chief author, Hugo Preuss, was a Jew. Pamphlets such as Walter Lieck's *Der Anteil des Judentums am Zusammenbruch Deutschlands* ("The Jewish Share in the Collapse of Germany," 1919), Dr. Ferdinand Werner's *Der Wahrheit eine Gasse! Eine Abrechnung mit dem Judentum und seinen Helfern* ("A Reckoning with Judaism and Its Helpers," 1919), Hans Lienhardt's *Ein Riesenverbrechen am deutschen Volke* ("A Gigantic Crime against the German People," 1921), Prof. Dr. Langemann's *The German Collapse Due to the Jews,* Wilhelm Michel's *Betrayal of Germanism,* Willehalm's *Jewish Soldier-Councils in Poland: Treasonable Machinations during the German Retreat,* Usthal's *Woe unto You that You are a German*—all appearing by 1922—constitute but a fragment of this education.

The purpose pursued by the Jews in causing the downfall of Germany was the establishment of a world Jewish empire under the thumbs of the Elders of Zion—as everyone could learn by reading the *Protocols of Zion,* in which these Elders conveniently explained their plans. This forgery—first published by a Russian priest in 1905—had a wide but brief vogue in France, England, and America. In Germany, however, it was honored with numerous editors and enormous commentaries; it enjoyed a huge circulation and, far from vanishing into oblivion, has lived to become a textbook in the public schools of the Third Reich.

The first German text, included in a voluminous work *Die Geheimnisse der Weisen von Zion* ("The Secrets of the Sages of Zion"), was published in 1919 by Gottfried zur Beck, alias Captain Müller von Hausen. Prince Otto Salm and Count Behr, the latter a leader in the Conservative Party, raised large sums for its distribution. Gentlemen of the peerage undertook vigorous propaganda in its behalf, especially in the rural districts of which they were the overlords. Prince Joachim Albrecht of Prussia handed out copies to the valets and waiters of the hotels and restaurants he frequented. Ex-Kaiser William II consoled himself by reading chapters from it to his visitors in Doorn. The conservative press used it for endless editorial reflections. It was soon called "the people's Bible" and by the beginning of 1921 it had attracted 120,000 purchasers.

Meanwhile Theodor Fritsch had brought out twenty-one editions of Henry Ford's *International Jew*, which was based on the *Protocols*; and Alfred Rosenberg sold 50,000 copies of his own text and commentary of *Die Protokolle der Weisen von Zion*. In 1919 Karl Rohm published *Was ist jüdischer Geist?* ("What is the Jewish Spirit?")—a reprint of the chapter "The Jewish Cemetery in Prague" from a series of novels called *Biarritz-Rome*, written by Hermann Goedsche under the pseudonym Sir John Retcliffe in the mid-nineteenth century. It was a hair-raising chapter, with blue flames and the Devil, which served as one of the "sources" of the *Protocols*. Richard Kunze—of whom more in our next chapter—edited and published another version of this "source" under the title *Das Geheimnis der jüdischen Weltherrschaft* ("The Secret of the Jewish World Dominion"). The same year saw the publication of Wilhelm Meister's *Judas Schuldbuch* ("Judah's Book of Sins") which soon achieved a circulation of over 150,000 copies. Its present Nazi publishers advertise it as "the principal work on anti-Semitism and indispensable to every National Socialist library." This elaboration of the *Protocols* borrowed Rathenau's phrase concerning the "three hundred men" who ruled Europe's economy and twisted it to read "three hundred sages of Zion"—a phrase which with Techow at the wheel and Kern at the trigger spelled its author's death. In 1921 Otto Hauser, race-scientist, repeated the fatal phrase in his *History of Judaism*, and Councilor A. Klein repeated the whole legend in his *Rise of Jewish World Power*. Professor H. L. Strack, the noted Protestant theologian, exposed its nonsense in his *Jüdische Geheimgesetze?* ("Jewish Secret Laws?", 1921)—but to no avail.

The relation of the Jews to communism was made clear in *Der Bolshewismus von Moses bis Lenin* ("Bolshevism from Moses to Lenin," 1919) by Dietrich Eckart, an elderly play-actor and poetaster of Munich, who took under his intellectual wing a young man named Adolf Hitler. More in the same strain appeared in Walter Lieck's *Der deutsche Arbeiter und das Judentum* ("The German Worker and Judaism," 1920); in Totila's *Das jüdische Paradies* ("The Jewish Paradise," 1922), illustrating with lurid cartoons the experience of a German prisoner-of-war in Soviet Russia; and Horst Halling's *Proletarier, wacht auf!* ("Proletarians, wake up!").

Jewish control over Freemasonry and its nefarious purpose were revealed by Friedrich Wichtl in his *Weltfreimaurerei, Weltrevolution, und Weltrepublik* ("International Freemasonry, World Revolution, and World Republic," 1919), and Alfred Rosenberg, now the genius of Nazi foreign politics, in his *Das Verbrechen der Freimaurerei* ("The Crime of Freemasonry," 1921). The Jewish relation to capitalism was treated by an army of investigators; their findings can be summarized in the title of C. B. Doppler's treatise: *Jewish Economic Dictatorship in Germany*. And Alfred Roth put a fine point on it in his study of the arch-villain: *Rathenau the Candidate of the Foreigners.*

The call for a new religion—to supplant that outmoded Jewish product, Christianity—was sounded by Friedrich Delitzsch, the Assyriologist whose *Babel and Bible* had shocked the pre-war world. In *Die grosse Täuschung* ("The Great Deception," 1920) he found that the ancient Israelites were a horde of robbers and cut-throats, their god a tribal idol, and their literature, commonly known as the Old Testament, largely a plagiary, which they palmed off on the world. In his *Neues Leben* (1919) Gustav Hildebrandt demanded, as his title indicates, a new life: "It is not enough," he wrote, "to cry, Away with Judah; we must go further and cry, Away with Christ and Christianity; neither one nor the other can be separated from Judaism—both are merely subtler and more poisonous forms of Judaism."

The racists, old and new, were at hand to furnish materials for the coming faith. Otto Hauser did himself proud when in *Der blonde Mensch* (1921) he discovered not only, as Chamberlain had suspected, that Jesus was a Nordic, but that Mary was likewise a blonde. It remains to be discovered that Jehovah was a blonde, and the case will be complete. Prof. Dr. Wahrmund's *Law of Nomadry and the Present Reign of the Jews* (1887) was reprinted. And Dr. Hans F. K. Günther —whom the Nazis were to appoint Professor of Social Anthropology at the University of Jena—published his monumental *Rassenkunde des deutschen Volkes* ("Racial Science of the German People," 1922), which indicated that although the Nordics comprised only 6% to 8% of the population they were responsible for 100% of Germany's achievements; the

Jews, in accordance with the new doctrine, were damned in an appendix.

Racial science, moreover, was not confined to books. The man (and woman) on the street in 1922 could have learned its lessons from handbills. One sample may serve. "German Women, German Girls!" it read, "Keep Clear of Jews, Negroes, Russians, Mongolians, and Men of all other Inferior Races!" The text was enlivened with a quaint medievalism. After a warning against any physical contact with the lower races, a contact "which poisons your blood," German womanhood was informed that "the mind creates the body" and hence all non-material contact, such as conversation with the inferior races or reading their books is likewise to be shunned. "For the spiritual emanations streaming from the lower races will damage your bodies and burden your offspring with physical, spiritual, and mental deformities."

Perhaps the most original touch in this search for a new life lay in a brochure entitled *Secessio Judaica* (1922) by Hans Blüher, a copious writer on the German Youth Movement. He evolved the theory that the highest civilization depends on the activities of segregated men creating their art and ideals under the influence of homosexual love: behold the Greek lyceum, the German comitatus, as well as monasteries and knighthood. It was too early to add: behold the Nazi leadership. Even so Blüher concluded that inasmuch as the Jews have shown themselves incapable of this segregated male life, they are incapable of contributing anything to civilization.

Theodor Fritsch continued inexhaustible in his popularizing of anti-Semitism. Besides a host of minor works, his *Handbuch der Judenfrage* ("Handbook of the Jewish Question," 1919), a revamping of his *Catechism*, was to reach 145,000 readers. On this lower plane, if indeed it be lower, countless leaflets, picture postcards, cartoons, and posters repeated the tale. Their content is to be summed up in a single poster. "Who financed the World War, but didn't fight in the trenches? Who is the labor leader, but shuns all manual work? Who says we must curtail, but lives more luxuriously than ever? Who is against the death penalty for usurers and profiteers, but allows hundreds of workmen to be shot? Who preaches free love, but only for Christian girls?" The answer was brief and, so we have learned, convincing: "It is the Jew."

Finally, in addition to a vigorous daily press, there were novels: *The New King,* for example, by Rudolph Leppin, and Otto Kernholz' *From Ghetto to Power,* which sounds like an Alger book for young anti-Semites. The most successful of these racial novelists was Arthur Dinter, who was to take part in the Hitler-Ludendorff "beer-hall *Putsch*." His *Sin Against Love* and *Sin Against the Spirit* have sold their hundred thousand copies, and his masterpiece *The Sin Against the Blood* over a quarter-million copies.

There was, as yet, little violence. The excitement of the Kapp *Putsch* occasioned riots against the Jews in Munich and Breslau. In 1921 the nationalists celebrated their victory in the Prussian elections by invading the Kurfürstendamm, Berlin's most fashionable street. "Hundreds of university and upper-school students were armed with clubs and stones," reads the *New York Times* account, "and hundreds of Jews were attacked and beaten. The police, having been forewarned, arrived in auto-trucks . . . and pulled the victims into the trucks. A score were taken to the hospitals, where two are reported dying." And the next year was Rathenau.

V

The Jewish reaction to these gathering storm-clouds ran a wide gamut. At the very top, in a world apart, the mother of Rathenau wrote to the mother of Techow: "I stretch out my hand to you, the most unfortunate of all women. Tell your son I forgive him in the name and spirit of my assassinated son, as God Almighty will forgive him if he confesses and repents . . ."

University students and the youth, not armed with clubs and stones, began in larger numbers to arm their spirits with the hope of Zion. A few training camps were organized for a life in Palestine. The Zionist movement made its first serious conquests among the German Jews. Troubled intellectuals began to hear ancestral voices, and Martin Buber gained a growing audience for his mystic nationalism. Jakob Wassermann spoke for a generation which was repeating the experience of Berthold Auerbach; *Mein Weg als Deutscher und Jude*—"My Road as German and Jew"—had reached an impasse. Theodor Lessing, converted to Christianity, started on his road back. Maximilian Harden (born Felix Ernst Witkowski) exclaimed at the trial of his would-be murderers: "I was baptized at a time when racial anti-Semitism was unknown, or I should not have accepted it; for it would have been an apostasy. A verdict of acquittal would concede that all these men are right who think vilely of us. . . . No, I have made a slip of the tongue; I will not say of *us*, but of *you*! Since you will have nothing of me because I was born a Jew, then nothing will it be. I often told Rathenau, 'Why do we always write and say, *We Germans*? They do not want to consider us as such; and while I love the German people, I refuse to lick their boots.' "

The majority of the Jews were, on the whole, unaware and unperturbed. Moreover, they too had discovered a scapegoat: the East European Jews. Thousands of these *Ostjuden* had been deported from Lithuania and Poland by the German army during the war; other thousands had lived in Germany for a generation. After the war, the sharp rise of anti-Semitism in Poland and the fall of the German mark brought further thousands of refugees, bread-seekers, and fortune-hunters. Altogether, however, they never numbered more than 79,000 out of Germany's 65 millions. But, thankfully, they were different, obviously alien, and intruders. It was they who were responsible for anti-Semitism; books, clubs, stones, and bullets, though they might glance on German Jewish pates, were aimed at East European beards. German Jewry fed and clothed their brethren from the East, but they shook their heads and solved the whole Jewish question by sighing, *Die Ostjuden!*

And the leadership of Jewry? Dr. Paul Nathan, the veteran of the Central Union of German Citizens of Jewish Faith consoled himself. "Anti-Semitism with us," he said, "is an artificial product. It is a means for keeping reaction alive and leading it to victory. . . . When thrown on its own resources, reaction in Europe is quite feeble. . . . At a time when universal suffrage is the rule, it is unable to attract and hold the masses. . . . The only way the reactionary elements can secure popular support is to deceive the people as to their true interests . . . and that is what they seek to accomplish by Jew-baiting."

The analysis overlooked one point: the capacity of the people for being deceived.

20

THE ROAD TO DOOM

"THE Kaiser Hall of the Rheingold restaurant was packed with party adherents. What figures and what faces! And I had always believed that our comic papers exaggerated in their cartoons of our German philistines. Not a whit! There they sat, arms crossed *à la* Hindenburg, with high stiff biting collars, bristling mustaches, timid foreheads which hardly rising leapt back in the scrubby hair outlining pates which reminded one of an assortment of apples, pears, pumpkins, anything but human heads."

The writer, Heinz Pollak, was describing in the *Weltbühne* of 1923 a mass-meeting of the Deutschsozialisten—the eldest of the anti-Semitic parties, which dated from the days of Stöcker and Böckel. It was now under the leadership of Richard Kunze, better known as Blackjack (*Knüppel*) Kunze, who won his nickname because of his belief in the superiority of *Gummiknüppel* over parliamentarism in the solution of Germany's difficulties. *Gummiknüppel,* or rubber bludgeons, were the northern substitute for Fascist castor oil; and in Italy government by castor oil—which Aristotle would have classified as oleocracy—had already demonstrated its worth.

"Kunze, meanwhile," Pollak continued, "stood behind a

desk on the platform, eyed his audience with cool urbanity, and warded off applause with a deprecatory wave of the hand, knowing well that each time he shrank in modesty the storm of hand-clapping redoubled its thunder. And he has trained his people to cap a period covering any subject under the sun with one long red-faced bellow: 'The Jews!'

"The secret of his success is that he reckons on the stupidity of the rank and file, and therefore fares better than the leaders of the other parties who imagine they are facing an audience of *Gelehrte*. The slogan 'Jew' lures them on and no less the assurance that he desires no violence—a safe gesture, since violence will come of its own accord.

"A small book business was set up in the lobby. It is significant to observe the tremendous increase, lately, in anti-Semitic literature. Hundreds of scientific books, thousands of pamphlets, innumerable novels—an impressive arsenal.

"Before departing I looked back for a moment. Kunze was working up to his final volley. 'We shall reach out for the government, we shall capture the reins, and then! . . . the entire hall blew up in one prolonged *Heil*! Kunze, however, might have been deaf, so nonchalantly he stepped from the platform to his seat in the ranks and began to polish his eye-glasses. He knows our Pappenheimer."

Others knew their Pappenheimer even better—Count Reventlow of the Deutschvölkische Freiheits-partei; Julius Streicher, formerly the leader of the Deutschsozialisten in Nuremberg—and most knowing of all, Adolf Hitler of Munich and the budding Nationalsozialisten.

Week after week meetings of this character, with "long red-faced bellow" carried to town and countryside the gospel of freedom through suppression of the Jews. Wherever local conditions were peculiarly desperate, the Swastika came to offer salvation. *In hoc signo* paradise. Danzig and Upper Silesia afforded excellent arenas. Forbidden the former, Kunze assumed the name of Hinze, inflamed a mass-meeting which turned into a parade and terrorized the Jewish passersby. The Hitlerites permeated into Upper Silesia: part of the harvest was the bombing of a Jewish wedding-party in Branau, leaving four wounded guests and a dead bride. The Ruhr provided an obvious opportunity for trouble. Posters appeared throughout the district, accusing the Jews of complicity with the French; an old Westphalian secret tribunal, the *Vehmgericht*, was resurrected in Ku Klux style and devoted a share of its attentions to the Jews. "The Alliance Israélite Universelle," so the German People's Council of Leipzig described this French-Jewish philanthropic society, "is an instrument of the Allies. It represents, however, neither the real France nor the real England, but International Jewry and the Jewish World-Synagogue, and its object is Jewish World-Control. The means? Occupation of the Ruhr." Deputy Henning took up the cry in the Reichstag and Count Reventlow in his party organ, the *Reichswart*. In Frankfort the Blücherbund arranged to blow up a synagogue, and five of its ringleaders went to jail.

Hitlerites exercised their clubs and canes on Jews and Italians in the streets of Munich, and the police declared that no attacks occurred since they had no record of them on the police-blotters. Plays written by Jews, such as Richard Beer-Hofmann's *Jaakobs Traum*, symphonies by Jewish composers such as Gustav Mahler's *Lied der Erde*, and a film version of Lessing's *Nathan the Wise*, were hissed from the stage. Parades, mass-meetings, and activities—which meant insulting Jews in restaurants, beating up Jewish shop-keepers in small towns and villages, and bill-posting at large—were the order of the day.

As the mark fell, and misery and wrath spread, the scene of these activities quickly covered the entire land, and the Pappenheimers were not slow in their response. In 1923 the present writer, after six-months residence, reported of Berlin, the stronghold of republicanism: "I learned, by frequent iteration, from postmen, street-car conductors, office clerks, petty government officials, small tradesmen and their wives, that the Jews made the war, that they failed to do their share of fighting in it, that they lost the war by stabbing Germany in the back, that they made the peace which was responsible for all of Germany's subsequent troubles, that day by day they have lowered Germany's currency and sent the cost of living skyward, that they are trying to ruin German industry with Bolshevism, that first they 'sold out' Germany and then 'bought it up,' that they are the only class making money— 'Look who lives in Charlottenburg or Halensee!'—that the French are their agents, that they dominate and ruin the theater, music, art, and literature of the Fatherland, and that, taking it anyway you choose, they are an unmitigated curse. *Die Juden sind unser Unglück.* The womenfolk at the markets, as they pay out their unbelievably gigantic sums, *schimpfen* [abuse] the Jews and thereby find their feelings, as well as their purses, are relieved. On the elevated trains and in the public toilets the standard inscription is 'Kill the Jews.' "

Of Munich he reported: "I talked with a number of folks, youths and old men, picked up in beer-halls and hotels. There the accent was on the ruinous wealth of the Jews. 'But aren't some Christians rich?' I ask. 'Oh, perhaps, a few.' 'What of Stinnes?' 'He's a Jew.' 'Thyssen?' 'A Jew.' 'Krupps?' 'They're Jews.' 'The Kaiser?' 'Now you are beginning to talk nonsense.' I thought we had begun long before. The most illuminating remark was that of a woman who complained of the fearfully high prices of her Aryan grocer. 'That robber Schmidt,' she exclaimed, 'he's a *white Jew*!' And the present writer concluded his account with the observation: "A nationalist victory appears plausible, but whether it be swift and decisive is far from certain; in either case the Jews are doomed to suffer a concerted effort to drive them into a new ghetto."

The southern organization, in fact, showed none of the fat and pumpkinheadedness of its northern compeers. Bavaria, as the center of reaction and hostility to the Republic, was the mecca of ex-army officers and ex-soldiers still hungry to fight: a Captain Hermann Goering of the Richthofen Air Squadron, a Lieutenant Gregor Strasser, a Captain Ernst Röhm, and Rudolph Hess "the Egyptian." These and scores like them joined Hitler and gave the National Socialists a military discipline modeled upon the Fascisti.

A German newspaper of 1923 describes their headquarters in the Corneliusstrasse, Munich: "Storm troops keep watch before the door; messengers speed to and fro, on foot and on bicycle. Within are numerous cubicles, separated by beaverboard, each swarming with clerks. Everything has the imprint of iron organization and moves in a great unified rhythm. Their militarism is itself a danger with its saluting, *melden,* and numbering off of squads, all facilitating a rapid mobilization. The leadership is no less competent: almost all the old professional army officers, after traveling about as advertisers for wines and liquors and dreaming of *revanche,* have given their practical experience and talent to the movement. This new army is being properly trained."

In November 1923—when the mark touched its trillions to the dollar—the new army, with Hitler and Ludendorff at the head, put their training to a test and—owing to sabotage and treason from within—failed ignominiously. All republican Germany laughed. Hitler went to prison where he spent his time, as prisoners will, writing a book—the title *My Battle* and the best-seller of the century.

However, the elections of May 1924 proved to be a different test. The National Socialists—who four years before did not have three thousand members—polled 1,918,000 votes and sent 32 deputies to the Reichstag. Altogether, counting Kunze and the Deutschsozialisten, the avowed anti-Semitic parties polled 2,225,000 votes and elected 40 deputies (out of 472). And the German National People's Party—the Hugenberg party— with its 95 deputies was far from pro-Semitic.

After the acceptance of the Dawes plan, August 1924, loans from abroad stemmed the tide. In the elections of December the National Socialists were reduced to 14 deputies, though the Hugenberg party raised their number to 103. But loans could not continue forever, and the factitious recovery which was based on them meant merely a respite. Moreover, Hitler was out of jail and in the trenches by Christmas. In February 1925, the chief Nazi organ, the *Völkischer Beobachter,* resumed publication. The party was reborn, and the Storm Troopers were again on the march toward their victory over democracy, socialism, capitalism, the Versailles Treaty, and the Jews.

ii

"Anti-Semitism," wrote Gottfried Feder, author of the Nazi platform, "is to a certain extent the underlying principle of the National Socialist movement." Determining the "extent" of this principle will therefore throw considerable light on the outer character, appeal, and success of the movement, as well as on the form of the present government and its reorganization of society.

Feder, of course, was not speaking merely for himself. "The salvation of Germany," preached Alfred Rosenberg, whose *Myth of the Twentieth Century* (1930) ranks him as the philosopher of Nazism, "lies in breaking the idols of democracy, plutocracy, and Marxism"—three inventions, as we have learned, of the Jews, and the destruction of which is the corollary of anti-Semitism. In the same philosophic work Rosenberg explained what he meant by idol-breaking: "On every telegraph pole from Munich to Berlin must be stuck the head of a prominent Jew." Dr. Paul Josef Goebbels, the master propagandist of the movement, likewise saw in anti-Semitism the liberation of Germany. "We are enemies of the Jews," he reasoned in *Die Verfluchten Hakenkreuzler* (1931), "because we are fighting for the freedom of Germany. The Jew is the cause and beneficiary of our slavery. . . . He has ruined our race, rotted our morals, corrupted our traditions, and broken our power. We are Jew-haters because we admit we are Germans. *Who thinks German must despise the Jews.* The one implies the other." Hitler received his training in Germanism from two Austrian anti-Semitic movements: the one founded by George von Schönerer, born a Jew, and devoted to pre-war Pan-Germanism; the other, under the leadership of Dr. Karl Lueger, a counterpart of Stöcker's Christian Socialism. It was inevitable that Hitler should believe "the Jew is the great instigator of the complete destruction of Germany."

These underlying beliefs are rooted in the theory and cult of race superiority. The leaders of Nazism each have their own set of rules for working out the theory, but no doubt Hitler's set is to be considered the most authoritative and orthodox. He divides humanity into three classes: founders of civilization (*Kulturbegründer*); transmitters of civilization (*Kulturträger*); and destroyers of civilization (*Kulturzerstörer*). The foremost examples of each class are the Aryans, the Japanese, and the Jews. By intermarriage with a lower race or by absorbing its spiritual characteristics, the Aryans weaken their power of resistance and lose their creative faculties. This is especially true of intercourse with the Jews, whom *My Battle* describes as "true devils . . . with the brain of a monster, not of a man," whose hideous culture "must finally lead to the breakdown of civilization and the devastation of the world." Hence the primary task of the Germans, if they were to rescue themselves from their present horrible plight and assure their future, was "to collect and preserve the most valuable primeval racial elements of this people, which must lead upward, slowly but surely, to a dominating position."

The populace was hardly interested in the metaphysics and finesse of these theories. It was enough that they played upon the racial pride which had been inflamed by two generations of scientists, historians, and skillful popularizers. Houston-Stewart Chamberlain could be content: indeed, he was probably the first well-known figure to join the National Socialist party. And it was more than enough that the leaders, their theories, and the entire apparatus of propaganda evoked the age-old hatred of the Jew—which Dr. Paul Nathan called "artificial," but which Treitschke claimed to be "a natural reaction of the German folk-feeling." Nothing could be more attractive to the Germans than the assurance, reiterated and demonstrated in endless detail, that not they themselves but the Jews were responsible for the national misfortunes—*die Juden sind schuld*—and that men were at hand to set things right by driving the trouble-makers from the land. With conviction and hope they joined in the Brown Shirt chorus:

> *Schlagt dem Judenpack die Schädel ein*
> *Und dann wird die Zukunft gewonnen sein;*
> *Stolz weht die Fahne im Wind*
> *Wenn Judenblut vom Säbel rinnt.*

> (Crush the skulls of the Jewish pack
> And then the future, it is ours and won;
> Proud waves the flag in the wind
> When swords with Jewish blood will run.)

There would be little exaggeration in saying that it was Jew-hatred which made people Nazis, and not the Nazis who made people hate the Jews. In the realm of ideology it was anti-Semitism which "sold" Germany the National Socialist platform.

Of the twenty-five planks in this platform (adopted February 24, 1920), the first three needed neither ideology nor argument. Probably every German except the most intransigent communists demanded a "union of all Germans,"

355

meaning a union with Austria, as well as "land and colonies for the nourishment of our people"; and every German including the communists demanded, as axiomatic, "equality of rights for the German people in its dealings with other nations, and the abolition of the Peace Treaties of Versailles and St. Germain." Of the twenty-two planks which followed, ten were directly aimed against the Jews, and five more were certain to work to their hurt. With one exception, the more important of these planks derived from the philosophy of race.

In considering the platform we are not—as everyone now knows—dealing with the eccentric rubbish of obscure fanatics, but with an historic document. In their three years at the helm of government, the Nazis have made huge strides toward the fulfillment of every plank, except those concerned with agriculture and Aryan industry: an astonishing record unless we remember that National Socialism is not so much a political party as a social faith.

As envisaged by the platform, the State is to be organized for the purpose of preserving and cultivating the "primeval racial elements" which are bound to regenerate the land. Therefore article 4 excludes the Jew from citizenship; article 6 excludes him "from all public offices, of whatever kind"; and article 5 reduces him to the status of a "guest" and "subject to laws for aliens." To quote Hitler's gloss in *My Battle*, the Jews, guests according to the Nazi laws of hospitality, are to be treated as "subjects of the State (*Staatsangehörige*)— who, however, are in a political sense entirely without rights." Automatically, this means an exclusion from the army as well —a service which in Germany ranks as the highest and holiest honor. And article 19, which promised the substitution of

German for Roman law which "serves the materialist world order" has—as the events have shown—excluded the Jew from the benefits of common justice in the courts.

But the full import of the status destined for the Jew is not confined to these restrictions and prohibitions. On the positive side, the platform demanded "unquestioned authority" for the State "over the entire Reich and its organization; and the formation of Chambers for [social] classes and occupations" (art. 25). The morality and philosophy underlying this demand is expressed in the slogan *Gemeinnutz vor Eigennutz* (art. 24)—"the Common Interest before Self-Interest." The citizen of a Western democracy will have difficulty in grasping what this slogan means. It evokes a conception of the State foreign to our thinking, but one which, quite independent of racial theories, roots deep in the German mind.

From the days of Frederick the Great down to William II, the prevalent political dogma, above all in Prussia, was state absolutism. That is to say, the state and not the individual was considered the be-all and end-all of life. The individual, not merely in his political activities, but in his private life, social relations, economic employments, cultural pursuits, and even in his pleasures and recreations, was an *Untertan*—the subject of a higher power and purpose, which was the State. Preached by Fichte, expounded metaphysically by Hegel, interpreted historically by Treitschke, and practiced by Bismarck, state absolutism captured the mind, the loyalty, and the will of a vast number of Germans. Wilhelm Stapel, a Nazi political scientist, brought the theory of this organic state up to date in his *Antisemitismus und Antigermanismus* (1928) and discovered that as inveterate individualists "there was no room in such a state for the Jews."

State absolutism, it should be noted, is irrelevant to the outer form of a government. It can flourish in a democracy, and it is quite another thing from the tyranny of an absolute ruler. "The State belongs to me," said an absolute monarch like Louis XIV. "We belong to the State," said Hegel, Treitschke, et al. They belonged freely and gladly because in the freedom and power of the State they found their own freedom and power—as men did in the democratic absolutism of Pericles' Athens, or as men do in the imperial absolutism of Hiroshito's Japan and the Soviet absolutism of Stalin's Russia.

It was this absolutism—so congenial to Junkerdom in the old days and no less so to monopoly capitalism after the war— which found its ethical justification in the phrase "Common Interest before Self-Interest," its goal in the Totalitarian State, and its means to achieve the goal in the *Gleichschaltung*—the coördination and submission—of every thought, will, and act of the citizenry. To bring these means into play, parliamentarism—a "Jewish invention"—was to be destroyed, and its place taken by a hierarchy in business, society, and government, culminating through a rising scale of leaders in the one leader, *Der Führer,* at the top, whence all direction, decision, power, and glory flowed.

The exclusion of the Jew from citizenship consequently promised more than a refusal to let him vote or hold office or carry a gun—privileges which thousands of citizens in Western democracies voluntarily renounce without living unhappily. It meant, in a totalitarian state such as the Nazis proposed, the exclusion from practically every service and pleasure of existence: at the work bench, in the laboratory, over the counter, behind the school desk, on the tennis-court, or with pen, violin-bow, microscope, cash-register, drawing-board, ferule, hammer, trowel, or spade. It meant a doom, a death-in-life, as fatal as excommunication from the medieval church or synagogue.

In the field of economics the platform reverted to race by subtle detours. Article 11 demanded the abolition of "incomes unearned by work" and the "breaking of the bonds of interest slavery." The first point we can disregard as have the Nazis themselves. The second point, which was heralded with untold oratory, is elucidated by a phrase likewise popularized throughout the land: *Schaffendes vs. Raffendes Kapital*— "Creative vs. Rapacious Capital." "Creative" capital is blessed, and the interest it earns legitimate. "Rapacious" capital, which Feder, the economic genius of the movement, sometimes calls "stock exchange and loan capital," is cursed, and its earnings must be extinguished. The distinction between the two kinds of capital, though it might baffle ordinary economists, was clear to the Nazis and their huge audience. "Creative" capital is Aryan and national; "rapacious" capital is Jewish and international. As Dr. Goebbels explains, "The Jew is uncreative; he deals only with products—with junk, clothes, pictures, gems, grain, stocks and bonds, peoples and states. And he has stolen everything he uses in his commerce."

The articles dealing with the elimination of this "rapacious" capital therefore have their racial logic, though Jew and Semitic are not mentioned. Number 16 demanded the "maintenance of a healthy middle-class" by the "immediate communalization of department stores and their lease at cheap rates to small traders." Department stores are, of course, Jewish. A further demand was made for "extreme consideration for all small purveyors to the State, district authorities, and smaller localities." Such purveyors are, naturally, Aryans and members-in-good-standing of the party; and the Jew is to be excluded from all business contracts with the national and local government. Article 17 demanded a "land-reform suitable to our national requirements." The nature of the reform is described in a party statement issued in 1930: "Only German people [*Volksgenossen, i.e.* Aryans] may be owners of land; the State has the right to expropriate, with reasonable compensation, land which is not in the possession of Germans [*Volksgenossen*]." A previous statement explained that land owned and speculated in by "Jewish companies" could be confiscated without compensation. Article 10 proclaimed that every citizen "must engage in mental or manual work" and that such work must "not clash with the interests of the whole, but be for the general good." Since Jews are by nature unproductive and averse to work—"Who ever saw a Jew work, and not plunder, steal, sponge, or live from the sweat of another's brow?" asked Dr. Goebbels—everything they undertake is bound to damage the "general good" and, by implication, they must be excluded from all occupations, an implication which is rapidly becoming a reality. To leave the matter beyond doubt, article 18 demanded that "common criminals against the nation, usurers, profiteers, etc. must be punished with death, whatever their race or creed." The clause concerning race or creed was superfluous: profiteering capital is by definition Semitic.

The immediate background and emotional source for the drive against "rapacious" capital was the reign of the *Schieber* —profiteers—who sacked Germany during the inflation years. A profiteer, needless to say, is a businessman who rolls up huge and quick profits at a period when most of his competitors are rolling up equally huge and quick losses: the losers contend that the winner is profiting upon the misery of others and accordingly call him bad names. Among the *Schieber* were many Jewish foreigners, many more Christian foreigners, and most German banks; and the king of all *Schieber* was the Aryan German nationalist, Hugo Stinnes. But Stinnes, the Christian foreigners, and the coin-clipping Reichsbank were conveniently forgotten, leaving only the Jew in the popular memory. This is business ethics.

A minor article—minor in the sense that it affected thousands instead of hundreds of thousands of victims—concluded the economic parade. Article 8 demanded a halt to the immigration of non-Germans and the expulsion of all non-German immigrants who had entered Germany after the outbreak of the World War. This demand was aimed at the Jewish immigrants from Eastern Europe—some 39,000 of whom, at the most, had entered the land subsequent to 1914, but who loomed like 40 million in the popular imagination.

Agriculture, rather strangely, received scant mention in the program. But the defect was soon repaired. Walter Darré, representing a large school of theorists, assured the peasants in his *Neuadel aus Blut und Boden* ("A New Nobility from Blood and Soil," 1930) that a peculiar racial virtue derived from close contact with nature. When he became Minister of Agriculture in 1933 his researches, incorporated in a small but fascinating pamphlet, *Das Schwein als Symbol des nordischen Menschen* ("The Pig as Symbol of the Nordic Man"), further assured the peasants that the Jewish inability to eat pork precluded them from ever sharing in the "new nobility" which was to spring from the soil. And by abolishing a free market for foodstuffs in 1934, he presented them with the announcement that the "bonds of interest slavery" were broken, capitalism was conquered, and with it "the Jewish theory that economics is governed by its own laws independent of . . . blood, race, nation, and Fatherland."

The purpose of these economic demands and measures, we need hardly say, was to throw a racial cloak over the class struggle. It is not necessary to requote Bebel on anti-Semitism as the socialism of fools. We have in Hitler perhaps a more persuasive authority. "The true cleft between classes," he wrote, "can exist only between different races. The cleft between the creative class and the non-productive class [*die Nichtstuern*] is essentially the cleft between the Aryan who makes work the foundation of the national community, and the Jew who sees in work only the means of plundering other peoples." It was a skillful and effective cloak. Heine had once said, "What we now call the hatred against the rich was formerly called Jew-hatred." Hitler reversed the formula, and what formerly had been hatred against the rich was now converted into hatred against the Jew.

The cultural activities of a totalitarian State are, as we have noted, likewise subject to governmental coördination and control. And again the Nazi platform and its commentators made clear the close relation of this control to the concept of race. As for the educational system, article 20 declared that "comprehension of the State-idea must be the objective of the schools, beginning with the first dawn of understanding in the pupil." Not that the understanding was to have much play. "The epoch of 'pure reason,' of 'objectivity,' and 'free science' is ended," announced Ernst Krieck in a book on national-political education when, in 1933, the totalitarian school-system came into being. The schools, including uni-

versities, are an "organ of the State" and the State "must see
to it that no . . . member separates itself . . . from the sworn
goal of racial unity and outlook." The Jews, through a racial
defect, were incapacitated for this as for every other cultural
endeavor. "Jews can't live a German life," is the judgment of
Wilhelm Stapel; "they can only imitate it."

Closely allied to education and its objects were athletics
and recreations. Article 21 demanded "obligatory gymnastics
and sports laid down by law and by extensive [State] support
of clubs engaged in the bodily development of the youth"—
which, in the racial constitution of the State, meant the obligatory absence of non-Aryans from these sports and clubs.

The press was honored with the longest article in the platform (No. 23). It declared "legal warfare against conscious
political lying in the press." It demanded that "all editors and
their co-workers on newspapers must be members of the
nation [*Volksgenossen,* i.e. Aryans]; that special permission
from the State shall be necessary before non-German [i.e.
Jewish] newspapers may appear, and they must not be printed
in the German language; and that non-Germans [i.e. Jews]
shall be prohibited from influencing or participating finan-
cially in German newspapers." Except for the language clause,
these provisions have been carried out to the letter.

The same article disposed of culture in general by demanding "legal prosecution of all tendencies in art and literature
likely to disintegrate our life as a nation, and the suppression
of institutions which militate against the aforesaid requirements." The test for determining the tendencies in art and
literature which disintegrate the national life was simpler
than many students of culture might suppose. Hitler formu-
lated it with brevity when he declared, in *My Battle,* that the

Jews "spread an intellectual pestilence worse than the Black Death."

This pestilence was currently described as Cultural Bolshevism. If we are to judge from the accusations collated from numerous sources, Cultural Bolshevism comprised everything which the moralists of *Kleinbürgertum* did not like. It included—so we learn—pacifism and mixed bathing, atheism and dropping the use of capital letters in book titles or advertisements, "French" comedies and nudism, jazz and the personals in big-city newspapers, Einstein's relativity theory and Chaplin's films, project-schools and Mickey Mouse dollar-watches, sensational reporting of divorces and the flat roof-lines of modernist architecture (called Bedouin or Semitic), Emil Ludwig's biographies and Otto Klemperer's tempo in directing Wagner, expressionist paintings and agitation against capital punishment, sexy magazines and Reinhardt stage productions, wise-crackers and psychoanalysis: all this, and the list could be gloriously extended, was due to the rotting influence of Jewry—*zersetzendes Judentum*. Freely paraphrased, the last paragraph of article 23 meant that a stop must be put to the *Verjudung*—the Jew-ifying—of the daily life.

With respect to religion, the Nazi platform accorded full liberty to the Jews as well as to all other denominations that "do not militate against the moral feelings of the German race" (art. 24). Nor, even up to the present date, have any religious qualifications been set upon the exercise of civil and political rights. Religious tolerance is legally almost as complete in the Third Reich as it was in the Second—at least during the years of the *Kulturkampf*. The chief religious curb placed upon the Jews forbids the slaughter of meat in accordance with the traditional ritual. Aside from this, practically everything which German Jewry as a religious body has asked for, from the days of David Friedländer to Dr. Paul Nathan, is still safeguarded. No failure could be more tragic than such a victory. The man whom German Jewish leadership and its philosophy defended—the man who is a Jew only by and in his religion—has gone fairly unscathed, while the Jew whose existence they denied—the Jew with thirty centuries of national history behind him—has been overwhelmed as almost never before in that history. Unfortunately both Jews lived under the same skin; and if degradation, suffering, and exile be the test, it is the second Jew who was the reality.

Although for the most part unmolested, Judaism was hardly tolerated with good grace. And while "the Party stands for positive Christianity," according to article 24, the churches stood only a little higher than the synagogue in the eyes of orthodox Nazis. Hitler set the tone in *My Battle* with the claim that the churches "sin against the image of the Lord" by preaching the doctrine of the "brotherhood of man." Alfred Rosenberg took up the theme in his *Myth of the Twentieth Century*: "We recognize that neither Protestantism nor Catholicism expresses the needs of the Nordic peoples; we must create a German Christianity." A whole literature was devoted to the search for a "positive" Christianity free from the weakness of brotherly love and other Semitic poisons. "There is no such thing as 'universal' Christianity," discovered Prof. D. K. Dietrich Schmidt in *Die Bekenntnisse des Jahres 1933* ("The Credo of the Year 1933"); "Christendom in itself is an abstraction devoid of all reality; for the German there can only be a Christianity rooted in the people."

As we might guess, the conviction prevailed that the racial cult could alone meet Nordic needs. Every public school was to be a religious school for Aryanism. "The entire education and training by the national State must be directed toward burning an instinct for racial sense and feeling into the hearts and brains of the youth," so Hitler outlined the new curriculum; "no boy or girl should leave school without having learned the necessity of pure blood."

Although the Nazi platform merely alludes to "protecting mothers and infants" (art. 21), eugenics was raised from a scientist's dream to a masterstroke of propaganda. By the side of the Deutsches Jungvolk and the Hitler Jugend for boys and young men, spread the Bund Deutscher Mädel for young flappers who could be heard singing through the streets: *"Wir sind deutsche Mädels; wir wollen Kinder kriegen!"*— "We are German girls; we want to bear children!" Pure Nordic children, as befitting Walter Darré's new nobility, *erste Klasse*. Novels, newspapers, pitiless publicity, and pillory on the streets, drove home the horror of the crime against the blood. *Race Defilement,* which meant accepting even the most innocent attentions of a Jew; and *Race Treason*, which meant yielding in marriage to these attentions, became cardinal sins.

A perversion of Nietzsche supplied a new term for non-Aryans (i.e. Jews). In contrast to the Superman toward whom every Nordic strove, they were sub-men—*Untermenschen*— a species akin to animals. Hermann Gauch's *Neue Grundlagen der Rassenforschung* ("New Foundations of Racial Research"), which has become a standard text in schools and universities, divides all mammals into two classes: (1) Nordics (2) Non-Aryans and the remainder of the animal kingdom. The difference between animals and sub-men, who

are in a transitional state, are trivial; but the differentiae
which distinguish both animals and sub-men from the Nordics are enormous. Only the Nordics, for example, can
enunciate "with untroubled clearness; whereas among non-
Nordic men the pronunciation is impurer, the individual
sounds more confused and more like the noises made by
animals." This is because of differences in the bodily structure; the throats of non-Nordic men and of monkeys "are
round and slant upwards." Dr. Gauch likewise raises a perplexing point in eugenics. "If non-Nordics," he asks, "are
more closely allied to monkeys and apes than to Nordics, why
is it possible for them to mate with Nordics and not with
apes?" But he is not feazed. "The answer," he says, "is this:
it has not been proved that non-Nordics cannot mate with
apes."

Thus the words of Voltaire were once again coming true—
"as long as people believe in absurdities they will continue to
commit atrocities." Atrocities against their victims, and no
lesser atrocities against themselves and their own manhood.
With science, propaganda, divine leadership—"Adolf Hitler
is the real Holy Ghost," says Dr. Kerrl, chairman of the Prussian Diet—a sacrosanct platform, and with Big Industry
cheering them on and paying the bills, a nation went to its
doom. *Deutschland, erwache!*—"Germany, awake!"—was the
war-cry. But Germany never did.

21

FROM HINDENBURG TO HITLER

IN APRIL 1925 Marshall von Hindenburg, candidate of the Nationalists, was elected president of the Republic—a three cornered election which gave him less than the majority of votes. Had the Moderates and Communists voted together, he would have been defeated. As it was, the government passed securely into the hands of the Right. Under its benevolent sway, the National Socialists, and the other racist parties who soon consolidated with them, continued their steady growth.

Their labors were neither silent nor invisible. During the ensuing three years (1925-1927), when the Republic enjoyed its nearest approach to stability and calm, Jewish cemeteries were desecrated in increasing numbers and generally with impunity, synagogues were attacked, minor riots against the Jews grew in frequency, anti-Semitic bills were regularly introduced into the state and national legislatures, and at least 700 *völkische*—racist and anti-Semitic—newspapers flourished in town and country.

The attitude of the government was ambiguous, as though it were feeling the popular pulse. On the one hand, anti-Jewish demonstrations were often suppressed when they went beyond legal bounds, and a professor of law at the University of Berlin was suspended by the Prussian Minister of Justice for advocating the expulsion of the Jews. On the other hand, the perpetrators of outrages against cemeteries and synagogues usually managed to elude the arms of justice; and Professor Theodor Lessing, though still a convert to Catholicism, was compelled to resign from the Technical School of Hanover because he ventured to criticize the monarchists— notwithstanding his support by the Minister of Education. Nor was there lack of signs to tell the beat of the popular pulse. The Berlin Jewish Community saw fit to establish a central employment bureau in an effort to counteract the boycott against Jewish employees and workers. At an anniversary celebration of the Battle of Tannenberg—Hindenburg's great victory—the arrangements to have a rabbi participate in the ceremonies were canceled upon pressure from influential anti-Semites. More perhaps than any other group, the Jewish student body felt the pulse rise; for, as might be expected in a land of science and scholarship, university professors and their pupils were a step ahead of shopkeepers in understanding and advocating the philosophy of race. The 1927 conference of "German Students of the Jewish Faith" acknowledged that while the youth of Jewry had done its full duty during the war, "they had lost their Fatherland and must begin all over again the struggle for their rights as citizens." Jewish students of nationalist rather than religious bent had been acknowledging this years before.

The great turning point came in 1928. Stresemann's sedatives in negotiating the Locarno Pact and bringing Germany into the League of Nations began to wear off. A reaction in favor of the Socialists who made a moderate gain in the elections of that year led to the creation of a Center and Left cabinet under the Socialist chancellor, Hermann Müller. This furnished no little fuel to the fears of the industrialists and the propaganda of the Nazis. The flow of American and British loans slackened: the next year it ceased. Reparation bills could not be met; and the Young Plan, which succeeded the Dawes Plan in 1929, hovered in the offing. Living at best on a risky margin, Germany began to show the cracks which, a year later, became an abyss engulfing the world.

The Nazis held twenty thousand meetings during that year 1928—an average of almost sixty a day. The *Stürmer, Westdeutscher Beobachter,* and other racist papers began to specialize, with flaming headlines and obscene cartoons, in ritual murder accusations and in charges of rape and outrage on Christian girls. Posters accompanied the twenty thousand meetings: "German Women and Girls! Jews Are Your Ruin." They were based on impressive authority. "The black-haired Jewish youth," Hitler had written in *My Battle,* "waits for hours, with satanic joy in his eyes, for the innocent German girl, whom he overpowers and attacks." The black-red-and-gold flag of the Republic, though it originated with the Hohenstaufens, was declared a Jewish emblem. Business failures were increasing in number and size: twenty thousand meetings ignored the Gentile failures and drove home the Jewish. More synagogues and cemeteries suffered odious desecration, and Jews were attacked on the streets of several cities (Oppenheim, Hanover, Bremen, etc.). The *Völkischer Beobachter,* Hitler's official and leading newspaper, referred to the Black Death massacres as a "model" for the present generation; and before a year passed Nuremberg was barely prevented from reënacting its performance of 1349. It all took effect. The year's elections in the provinces increased the Nazi vote anywhere from twofold in Thuringia to fivefold in Saxony.

Quite as ominous, the authorities, ears to the ground, began to respond to the Nazi gains. Jewish students were abused in government aviation schools. The official press-bureau of the national government was discovered supplying anti-Semitic news-items to the provincial newspapers. The Prussian Minister of Justice admitted that in many cases the courts and administration were swayed by racial prejudice. "Violent anti-Semitism," a German Jewish scientist reports of the period, "was rampant in the schools and law-courts. In the schools it was part of the children's education in patriotism. The anti-Semitism in the judiciary system was reflected in the huge political trials for cases of fraud whenever the accused was a Jew." In November, 1928, the *C.-V. Zeitung*, organ of the Central Union of German Citizens of the Jewish Faith, displayed public alarm, and with a peculiar sense of diplomacy published a proposal to engage in intensive "silent" work to combat twenty thousand meetings.

The next year was the same story worsened. Hugenberg's party, the German National People's Party which we have noted as purveying a slightly more refined version of the National Socialists' hatred for the Jews, united with the Nazis in organizing a popular referendum to renounce payments in accordance with the Young Plan—heralded as a Jewish device. Six million voters backed Hugenberg and Hitler. Before 1930 boycott was widespread in the smaller towns; Jews were terrorized and in many instances economically ruined. A riot against Jewish students graced the University of Berlin.

And the Jewish leaders? Several hundred prominent Jews signed an advertisement in the *Vossische Zeitung*, the venerable conservative newspaper of Berlin, in which they deplored the anti-Jewish riots—in Palestine. And they hastened to add: "We profess the Jewish religion, but reject any sort of Jewish nationalism. We regard ourselves, along with the overwhelming majority of German Jews, as members of the German, not of the Jewish, people. In the establishment of the National Jewish homeland we see an error which is bound to jeopardize the work of emancipation of the champions of German Judaism, and the ethical-religious task of Judaism for humanity." It would be enlightening—an *Aufklärung*—to know how many of the signers are today safe and sound in the erroneous homeland. The Central Union of German Citizens of the Jewish Faith, though it adopted a similar resolution early in 1930, showed the measure of its political acumen by advising the German Jews, now that the Democratic Party was on the way to extinction, to vote for the Catholic Centrists. Or perhaps it was economic acumen: report has it that Catholic and Jewish banking interests were closely allied against Thyssen. Not, indeed, that it mattered for whom a few hundred thousands Jews might vote.

ii

World panic in 1929 and the world depression which began in 1930 sealed the fate of the German Republic and its Jews. The millstones of capitalism and communism ground with shrill and heightened speed. In the spring of 1930 Hindenburg dismissed the Socialists for good; and Heinrich Brüning, the Catholic Centrist, formed a "bourgeois coalition" cabinet. By summer the cabinet had practically suspended the Weimar constitution, under its own article 48; and thereafter the

Republic, for most of the short span it had to run, was governed by emergency decrees. The Thyssen group opened its battle royal with the Otto Wolff-Deutsche Bank group for the monopolist seizure of demoralized industry. The latter group consisted of Catholic industrialists and bankers, with a sprinkling of Jews, whose policies were comparatively liberal and directed toward a closer understanding with France. The former were uncompromising nationalists who, it may be suspected, saw in a regenerated "strong" Germany an excellent customer for armaments. Thyssen and his Ruhr ally, Emil Kirdorf, an old supporter of the *Führer*, gave Hitler "something like" a quarter of a million dollars. The Nazis were in the money!

As never before Hitler had the means to apply his methods for political conquest. "Hate is more lasting than dislike," he had written in *My Battle*, "and the thrusting power for the mightiest upheavals has at all times come less from scientific conviction than from a fanaticism that fills the souls of the masses and from a forward-driving hysteria—*vorwärtsjagende Hysterie*." Nothing can describe what followed better than hysteria.

"Storm, storm, storm, storm!"

rang the chorus of *Deutschland Erwache!* Thirty-four thousand Nazi meetings filled the souls of the masses with the necessary fanaticism for the coming elections.

But it was an hysteria directed with shrewd and cool calculation. Far from hysteric himself, Hitler took care to conclude a truce with Hugenberg which enabled both parties of the extreme Right to direct their common fire against the republican and Left parties—a stroke of reason lost on the Socialists and Communists who continued to fight one another with perhaps the most unreasoned and misplaced hatred history can record.

Quite as effective as money and hysteria, the Nazis could offer the nation example and proof of salvation. Since January, Wilhelm Frick, leader of the Nazi faction in the Reichstag, held the office of Minister of Interior in Thuringia—an office once held by Goethe; and he gave the populace a sample of Nazism in action.

Socialists and Communists were ruthlessly and illegally suppressed, and house rents raised. Nazis in good standing were given a feast of posts and salaries. Legislation prohibited the slaughter of meat according to Jewish ritual; similar laws were soon passed in Bavaria and elsewhere, working a genuine hardship on the Jewish population and a harbinger of worse to come. In the realm of culture, as befitting a province which boasted of Weimar and Jena, Frick created a chair for Racial Research at the University of Jena and filled it with Dr. Hans Günther whose anti-Semitic science we have had occasion to cite. He appointed Adolf Bartels, the racial literary expert, as lecturer on German literature. He banished from the museum of Weimar the paintings of Picasso and other modernist artists whom he considered "Oriental submen," and denounced "Cultural Bolshevism" with a vituperation unequaled since Luther or Berthold of Regensburg. He introduced in the public schools a prayer asking divine aid against "people of an alien race," meaning, as he admitted in the parliament, "the Jews who have demoralized the German people." On the anniversary of Goethe's death he permitted one Schulze, a secret-society member with murder to his credit, to deliver a political oration in Weimar, in which the authors of the Constitution were branded traitors and criminals. But Goethe dead could still say:

> *Du gleichst dem Geist, den du begreifst,*
> *Nicht mir!*

—which may be hopelessly rendered as "Thou art like what thou canst understand, but not me."

Liberals and sensible men laughed at these antics; but the Babbitts and yokels with their inveterate admiration for everything pseudo, their appetite whetted for posts and salaries, their pulse stimulated by hysteria, applauded Frick to the echo. Professors and professional men caught the flame, for they too began to see a source of preferments and clients. The Communists profited by martyrdom, and as they increased in strength they increased the menace which they embodied in the eyes of their opponents. The issue sharpened all along the line, and for the Nazis nothing gave it greater edge than Jew-baiting. From January 1, 1930, when eight Jews were killed in a Berlin "excess," till the eve of the elections in September, when again in Berlin seventy-eight were wounded, street attacks throughout the country, molestations in cafés and theaters, disturbances of religious services and Jewish defense meetings helped swell the hysteria.

The election returns justified the means.* Instead of 14 seats when last heard of in 1928, the Nazis captured 107. The Communists rose from 54 to 77 seats (mostly at the expense of the Socialists), and indicated the growing might of the two extremist parties. Not little bands of crackpots but giants were struggling for possession of the German future.

---

* Of 35,224,464 votes cast, the Social Democratic Party received 8,575,343, the National Socialist Party 6,404,397, the Communist Party 4,590,178, the Catholic Center 4,322,039, Hugenberg's German National People's Party 2,457,680, the remaining parties considerably less than two million each.

Now second only to the Socialists in their voting strength, the Nazis celebrated. On the day the Reichstag opened, with shouts of *Deutschland erwache, Juda verrecke!*—"Germany awake and death to Judah!"—anti-Jewish riots swept the Leipzigerstrasse and heads were broken. To the casualties must be added Wertheim's thirty-seven plate-glass windows (insured). The riot, or the windows, made a deep impression on Jewry. At private gatherings and in published statements of the leaders, it was pointed out that the unseemly disturbance had in the public eye nullified the effect of the Nazi victory.

It likewise became common talk, of which the truth can hardly be known, that "certain Jewish firms were among the companies subsidizing National Socialism." If so, the explanation is simple. Far-seeing Jews could well believe that Hitler's ultimate triumph was inevitable, they could flatter themselves that a judicious investment in time might repay itself in immunity, they could fear the devil of Nazism less than the deep sea of Communism. Shrewd gamblers who played heads you win and tails I lose.

As the riots persisted through the autumn—Würzburg, Leipzig, Düsseldorf, Frankfort, and again in Berlin, this time in the University halls—more Jews took counsel. The shades of depression were falling fast, and it gave little comfort to be assured by the leaders that "the huge increase of votes for the Nazis"—and of the riots—"did not indicate a corresponding growth of anti-Semitism, but was rather a symptom of despair in the face of depressed economic conditions and unemployment." And less comfort to observe—quite apart from the general crisis—Jewish unemployment increased by discrimination at the hands of business and government, bankruptcies and suicides due to the boycott of small merchants, and the pressure of monopoly, as applied by both the government and big industry, driving even the upper middle class to the wall. As the result of this counsel, the more timid—or braver?—took to flight. "Better too soon," they said, "than too late." The first trickle of emigration had begun. "There was no reason," the leaders pointed out, "for such hysteria."

The following year other counsel was taken in the higher spheres. Unemployment in 1931 mounted from a monthly average of four and one-half million to six million in January 1932. Private industry had been largely "coördinated" in 3,000 cartels; as for government monopoly, the Prussian State alone owned 10% of the coal and potassium output and over 50% of the electric production of all Germany. The Government, moreover, controlled 60% of the country's credit. An obviously rough but significant estimate claimed that by 1931 only 79,000 individuals—about eight persons out of every 6,000 in the population—possessed a minimum fortune of $25,000 (100,000 marks). The great crash of the year, heralded by the failure of the Credit-Anstalt of Vienna and leading to the Hoover Moratorium and the collapse of the Danat Bank, terrorized industry and at the same time gave it the chance for a desperate golden gamble.

The Nazis were the second largest political party, they were the most aggressive foes of labor-unionism and Marxism which ruled the workers, and of liberalism which rendered the middle-class recalcitrant to monopoly. Give Hitler the means, and one push. . . .

But were the Nazis reliable? Did their platform mean what it said when it demanded the breakage of the bonds of interest and the abolition of unearned incomes; did their orators, with their high phrases "social revolution" and "common interest before self-interest," mean pledges or oratory; was National Socialism nationalist or socialist?

The leaders left no room for doubt. Gottfried Feder, who wrote the platform, publicly declared that "National Socialism recognizes private ownership and places it under State protection." Hitler explained that the party "admits the principle of private property." Otto Strasser, a Nazi leader who mistakenly believed the contrary, published in 1930 a disillusioning conversation with the *Führer*. "Socialism," said Hitler, "does not mean that factories *must* be socialized, but only that they *may* be, when they act contrary to the interests of the nation." "If you came into power," asked Strasser, "what would you do with Krupps?" "Nothing," Hitler replied, "do you think I am so senseless as to upset business?"* And he demonstrated his sense by purging Strasser and other social revolutionaries from the party. No, business would not be upset.

Thyssen introduced Hitler to the barons and magnates of the Ruhr and Rhineland. Hindenburg himself consented to meet the reassuring *Führer*. The gamble was taken. Industry put up enormous stakes—Thyssen, alone, three million marks before the presidential election of 1932.

Lesser men of importance in business, industry, the universities and the professions—small fry in the Reich at large but leaders in their immediate circles—began to have "their eyes opened." It became a popular phrase—"to have your eyes opened." It meant seeing the band-wagon, and climbing on.

Such maneuvers likewise reassured many Jews. Hinden-

* Quoted from Frederick L. Schuman: *The Nazi Dictatorship* (New York, 1935), to which I am indebted for many details on this period.

burg, prominent physicians, and learned professors were no fanatics. Big businessmen were, by definition, broadminded, wise, and trustworthy. Above all, they were ineffably powerful: they would put Hitler in their pocket. Even Hitler, now that he had shaken hands with gentlemen of the *Herrenklub*, the Industry Club, and the National Club, was no longer an agitator, but a statesman. His Judeophobia was for mass consumption: once in power, the responsibilities of office would chasten him.

These comfortable calculations overlooked two facts, which a study of history rather than bank-balances could have taught the Jews. Business tolerance, for one thing, has always been a fair-weather tolerance: in a crisis, the motto of business is dog eat dog. So we found it in the Middle Ages, in the sixteenth century, in the nineteenth, and so we find it today. For another thing, Hitler had genuinely aroused the masses; and aroused masses do not follow but guide their leaders. Even if Hitler's anti-Semitism were a pose, which it was not; and even if his business allies were personally more or less free from racial prejudice, and many no doubt were; they had called the tune—the great mass diapason of hate—and not they but the Jews must pay the piper. Someone had written long ago, "Put not thy trust in princes."

Not every Jew shared this confidence. Anti-Semitic rioting continued with undiminished ardor and almost without hindrance. Bill-boards in the cities and barns in the country blossomed with signs: *Meidet die jüdischen Warenhäuser! Deutscher Mann und Deutsche Frau, Kauft nicht bei der Judensau! Wer vom Juden isst, stirbt davon!*—"Avoid Jewish Department Stores! German Men and Women, don't buy from the Jew-Pig! Food bought from a Jew will Poison

You!" In the smaller towns slanderous campaigns, conducted in the press and by means of hand-bills or by word of mouth, were driving Jewish merchants into bankruptcy, out of the community, or to a suicide's grave. "The natural hostility of the peasants against the Jews," read the 1931 instructions of the Nazi party to local officials, "must be worked up to a frenzy." Vandalism of an indescribably disgusting nature was approaching its grand total—by 1932—of 128 polluted cemeteries and 50 desecrated synagogues. Disturbances against Jewish professors and students became a regular feature of university activities; and the authorities showed, on the whole, a good-natured tolerance of these pranks: perhaps they were influenced by the report that two-thirds of the 142,000 organized students of Germany had expressed their solidarity with the Nazi party. Jewish New Year's Day, September 12, 1931, occasioned the most serious outbreak until the Third Reich set a new standard. As the worshipers left the synagogues of Berlin, particularly on the Kurfürstendamm, truckloads of Brown Shirts under the leadership of Count von Helldorf (now the city's Chief of Police) fell upon their victims. The attack was carried out with perfect military system, and the enemy easily identified by their silk hats and holiday attire. An eye-witness described the discipline that prevailed: "While three youths beat an elderly gentleman with their fists and rubber truncheons, five other young men stood around to protect them." With cries of *Heil Hitler! Juden raus!* and *Schlagt die Juden tot!* the martial gangs did their work until the "somewhat belated" arrival of the police.

More and more Jews realized that the Brüning administration, despite official recommendation, was tarred with anti-Semitism or stricken with impotence. Jewish leaders admitted it "had failed to show any whole-hearted opposition to . . . or take any steps" against the Nazi tactics. There was a drift to the Socialists on the part of middle-class Jews who had hitherto been stalwart supporters of the moribund Democratic (now State) Party. Others did not drift; they took flight across the border. Parents began encouraging their young sons to look for a future abroad. Emigration quickened its pace.

The final election for the presidency, on April 10, 1932, warranted Jewish fears. Thanks to the socialists and republicans, Hindenburg, who had owed his post to the nationalists, was given a second term—by 53% of the ballots. The voters could not foresee, of course, that the senile avaricious Junker was to sell his sworn loyalty to the Republic for a parcel of acres in East Prussia. But they did know that the Communist candidate, Ernst Thälmann, rolled up 10.2% of the vote, and that the Nazi vote of about six and one-half million in 1930 had mounted to about thirteen and one-half million ballots for Hitler—36.87% of the total. Communists, Socialists, Liberals, and Jews could think—though they never, unfortunately, thought *together*—of Hitler's words after the victory of 1930: "In three years [the Nazis] will be the strongest party, and in the future thirty-five million of the forty million voters will support us . . . we shall erect a people's tribunal [for] the November criminals, and I frankly predict you shall see their heads rolling in the sand."

When a little later in April the Prussian state elections gave the Nazis over 35% of the ballots and the Brüning cabinet consequently fell, confusion was added to fears. The new cabinet issued a public assurance that the government would safeguard the equal rights of all citizens, irrespective of creed or race; but it was, after all, the "barons'" cabinet of unsavory Von Papen. Only a few days passed before the new Minister of the Interior, Baron Wilhelm von Gayl, habitué of the *Herrenklub*, announced to the Reichsrat: "It seems to me important and necessary that in the field of the composite cultural life of our people . . . there should be . . . the eradication of all alien, un-German influences, which, at times, have astounded large sections of the German people."

Metaphorically, heads began rolling at once. Jewish officials were retired from government posts, and actors and singers dismissed from state theaters and opera-houses. The Communists, with a devotion to "the party line" which brought its reward, had often joined in a "united front" with their mortal enemies, the Nazis. In June both parties again united and thereby passed a bill through the Prussian Diet which instructed the Government to submit the draft of a law confiscating the property of East European Jews who had entered the country since the outbreak of the World War. The Government of Prussia, however, was still in the hands of a Socialist cabinet and took no action on the bill.

Meanwhile, on the edge of the abyss, the Jews were unable to unite—an inability natural in a group which could not agree as to whether it was a people or a sect, or neither or both. The Zionists, who had grown from strength to strength, were less concerned with fighting what they felt was a lost battle than with preparing refuge in the new-old homeland. The German Citizens of the Jewish Faith and their sympathizers won minor victories in a petty court-decisions, and showed their German patriotism by cutting off their annual contribution to a chair of botany founded by Otto Warburg at the Hebrew University in Palestine. The orthodox and the liberals (i.e. religiously conservative) stood at logger-heads.

Efforts to create a general union of all Jewish forces—finally effected after Hitler came into power—were made and failed. A tiny group of super-Teutonic Jews who embraced the ideas of Hitler—the Society of National German Jews led by the war veteran Max Naumann and numbering not a few *Geheimräte, Justizräte,* and intellectuals—regaled this distraught world with its Nazism; its members, so the story goes, opened their meetings with a hearty cry: "Down with ourselves!"

iii

Before the final curtain we may well pause and ask, what could the Jews have done? Certainly nothing against the hallucinations and hysteria that possessed the popular mind.

We have already given the reader a generous and nauseous sampling of the delusions which a great portion of the people, daily growing greater, accepted as simple fact. Every impassioned Nazi, for further example, believed that the Jews control the big banks of England and America, that Judaism allows them to take false oaths, that they possess sinister doctrines in a "secret" language, that they rule the White Slave traffic, and that the German Jews invaded and dominated the German government. If this last charge, a matter of familiar national politics, was refuted *in vain* by a simple count of noses—a count which revealed that out of 260 or more ministers in the twenty cabinets of the Republic, only seven were of Jewish origin, and of these seven only two, Preuss and Rathenau, were professing Jews—a count which revealed that in 1925 only 5,446, or three-tenths of one percent, of the 1,657,022 government officials were Jews—a count which did not prevent Dr. Hans Luther, German ambassador to the United States, from publicly declaring that the Jews numbered nearly 50% of the government officials, which would mean many more Jewish officials than there were Jews in Germany—it could hardly be hoped that the more horrendous and necessarily "secret" machinations and villainies of the Jews could be successfully denied.

The victims were faced with the invincible power of human credulity and stupidity when fed by liars and fanatics and inflamed by misery, injustice, resentment against the world, and refusal to accept the realities of defeat. They were faced by the power which, similarly incited, forged the fate of the Jew in the Middle Ages, and which only an equally fantastic belief in "progress" has induced the world and its Jews to imagine had vanished forever through some mystic virtue in dates. The average "twentieth-century" man is only another name for the average "thirteenth-century" man: the species changes by aeons and not by generations.

We have followed in considerable detail the social forces and their dependent propaganda which, bit by bit, have created Aryanism and Nazism—beginning with imperialist ambitions and scholarly speculation in the last century, and ending with the wreck of empire in the present century and its tens of thousands of mass-meetings and the message of millions of newspapers, pamphlets, books, posters, and radios. The analogous details have disappeared from medieval records, but the growth of today's delusions go far toward picturing how and why the legends of ritual murder and well-poisoning captured the Middle Ages and prepared the ghetto, the Badge of Shame, and the pyres of the Black Death; and, on the other hand, we must return to Innocent

III, Gregory IX, or Martin Luther to match and understand the hysteria and obscenities of the current German blood-myth and the Jewish "poisoning" of German life and culture. Fanaticism, its origins and fruits, is always contemporary.

Nor could the Jews, as we have seen, unite. They were divided not only by their theories of what they were, a people or a sect, but by differences in what they did and how they lived. A Jewish worker did not inhabit the same world as a Jewish banker; an Orthodox cattle-dealer in Bavaria or an Orthodox tailor somewhere *hinter* Berlin led a different life, with other manners and customs, from a Reform bond-dealer in Frankfort or an irreligious manufacturer of textiles in Chemnitz.

Furthermore, there was no common forum or assembly where these disparate classes could meet and in some measure compose their differences in the face of common danger. Such representative bodies as did exist worked, till the last unavailing moment, for their own constituents and, whatever their claims or intentions, not for the whole. Still further, by long tradition from the fifteenth-century *Gemeinde*, through the reign of the seventeenth-century provincial bodies with their Court-Jew *parnasim*, down to the modern Central Verein, the best disciplined, most articulate, and most capable organizations were dominated by wealthy Jews or their associates. It was therefore natural and inevitable that the welfare of Jewry should be viewed, by these comparatively effective organizations, in terms of the welfare of the rich. And taking into account the sycophancy of the not-so-rich, and the snobbery of the altogether poor tradesmen, clerks, and petty professional men who made up the bulk of Jewry, it can be said that the interests of the rich were generally accepted and believed to be the interests of the whole.

Under these circumstances the choice of action was limited. Few Jews could bring themselves to believe that their interests might best be served by the Communists. Not many, at least until the last years of the crisis when it was too late, could see that their interests might lie with the Socialists. Thus, any road toward the Left was blocked by the prevalent belief—it was centuries old—that the welfare of the rich is the welfare of the whole. And whether few or many Jews were prepared to accept the Nazis, the road to the Right was blocked by the fact that the Nazis would not accept the Jews. Finally, the immediate necessities of their imperiled, marginal economic existence dictated for most of Jewry a loyalty to liberalism. Bankers threatened by government monopoly of credit, tradesmen menaced by coöperatives, chain stores and boycott, employees driven from work by the prejudice of Government and Industry, professional men shut out from laboratories, judiciary, and schools, or deserted by clients, all agreed on what they needed: a good old-fashioned, free and flourishing, individualist capitalism.

But such capitalism was gone; and the majority of Jews were as little capable of adjusting themselves to the realities of its departure, as the Germans were to the realities of a lost war and a lost empire. Men who were busy getting their daily bread could not be expected to study the historical reasons why the bread was harder to get and why it came buttered with hate and lies. They could not be expected to relive the eighteenth and nineteenth centuries and see that the forces of free capitalism and its liberal ideas, which had brought the Jews their Emancipation, had run its course; and that Emancipation, now that its economic foundations were gone, had also reached its term.

Their failure to realize and act on the new state of affairs was by no means complete, and did not, as with the Germans, lapse into hysteria and delusions. Somehow—these differences are hard to explain—the Jews, unlike the Germans, acted as though they had literally inherited an experience with thousands of years of crises and change, and a resignation to them. They made certain efforts at adjustment, at diverting the youth and even adults into new occupations—efforts unfortunately too late and therefore hopeless. Many turned their thoughts and energies, likewise belated, to a new world in Palestine. For the rest, they waited with what faith and discipline a century of rationalism and communal disintegration had left them—as their ancestors waited for the crusaders' swords in the episcopal palace of Mayence. During the nine intervening centuries they had even learned the futility of fighting at the palace gate.

With the horizon set for them by their middle-class leaders and their own middle-class mentality, there was—tragically— nothing else to be done. Today, now that they have enriched Jewish experience with their mortal suffering, those who sit safely in other lands can learn to see wider horizons. From this wider view it would, of course, be absurd as well as impertinent to suggest what they might or could have attempted. No one can turn today back into yesterday.

But the wider view does suggest—for such use as it may prove in the future—that since their welfare depended on an economy free and sound enough to give no occasion for racial or religious fanaticism, and since the old liberal economy had vanished, they might have accepted whatever new economy offered a chance of tranquillity and tolerance. Monopoly capitalism in a totalitarian racist State, haunted by the ghosts of medievalism, obviously offered nothing of the sort. A socialized economy, with its broad distribution of goods which would afford everyone at least food, breath, and security, might, it would seem, offer the hope of tolerance and human decency. But did it, on the other hand, offer the equivalent of middle-class ease and pretensions? Most probably not. With liberalism out of the running, the choice then remained: ease and pretensions which in any case were not to be had for the Jews, or equality and tolerance which might be won in a socialized economy.

Yet the few hundred thousand Jewish votes, what effect could they have had? Suppose, however, a different question is put. If the Socialists—a constitutional, democratic, anti-revolutionary party, and therefore plausibly acceptable to the predominant Jewish mentality—could early in the struggle, when they ruled nearly one-third of the total vote, have received a tithe of the wealth which the Jews have since lost, might it have turned the scales?

Or suppose another question. In any one of the elections under the German Republic—except the last—a united front of liberals, Socialists, and Communists would have carried the day. The French, with their political realism, have now learned to band together: middle-classes and workers, liberals and the Left, in one body against monopoly capitalism and monarchism, militarists and the Right. What if the Jews, who stood to gain most, as we shall discover, by such a union, had used their energies and resources to bring it about in Germany while there was still time? It is more than possible that, in view of the intransigence of Communists and Socialists and the prejudices of the liberals, such an effort would have failed; but, even so, it would have been an intelligent effort. For not having made it, the handful of Jews can of course console themselves that they acted no more blindly than sixteen million German Communists, Socialists, Liberals, and Centrists.

Instead of pursuing these idle ifs and buts, World Jewry and all other minorities can at least learn what it cost the German Jews so dearly to teach. During periods of stress and of straitened economy, no one minority can hope, in the long run, to be freer than any other minorities, whether these minorities be racial, religious, or economic. Jewish liberties are bound up with general liberties, and the cause of all oppressed or threatened classes is the Jewish cause. The only effective fight for Jewish emancipation—to win it or to keep it, cost purse or comfort what it will—is, as Heine discovered a century ago, the fight for "the emancipation of the whole world that has now found tongue and breaks the iron reins of Privilege."

iv

The last honest unterrorized election took place November 6, 1932. The Communist vote touched almost six million. The Socialists stood at seven and one-quarter million. And the Nazis reached eleven and three-quarter million. Communists and Socialists, if combined, still held 221 seats against 196 for the Nazis. The entire Left and Center, if combined, still held 353 seats against 279 seats of a united Right.

On January 30, 1933, Hitler accepted, at the hands of Hindenburg, the chancellorship of the Republic. Horrible rumors, and possibly not unfounded, chilled Jewish veins with the threat of a general pogrom—a Saint Bartholomew's Night in which the knives should at last "run with Jewish blood" and in its streams the Brown Shirts cross to the Promised Land. Instead, however, of a baptism of blood, it was a baptism of fire. The 27th of February brought the burning of the Reichstag, and German freedom perished in the flames.

Fear of the Red Menace, such fear as once rose from the Black Death, maddened the middle-classes and the peasants. The entire Communist press of Germany and the Socialist press of Prussia were forcibly silenced. Mass demonstrations of workers and torch-light processions of Nazis—panic, bludgeons, and guns—were the tools of election. On March 5, the final vote to be taken under the Republic lost the Communists a million ballots and gained the Nazis five and one-half million. But even with a total of 17,277,180 votes, the Nazis failed to secure a majority. Despite force and hysteria, 56.1% of the Germans did not embrace the new faith.*

A week later Hindenburg consented to the abolition of the flag of the Republic. On March 21 the rump parliament gathered in the Garrison Church of Potsdam; and while the organ played Brahms,† and Hindenburg laid a wreath on the tomb of Frederick the Great, Chancellor Adolf Hitler led the German people into the Third Reich. The millions on millions of republicans, liberals, trade-unionists, socialists, and communists struck not a single blow—riot, revolt, or general strike—in defense of liberty.

* The Nationalists and Stahlhelm, who combined in a single party, received 8% of the vote. Since they stood very close to the Nazis, the latter might well claim the moral support of 51.9% of the total electorate.

† The government Racial Bureau, not being established as yet, had still to discover that Brahms' grandfather was a Jew.

Among the hymns and paeans that rang through the land, a tragic little group of citizens, a mere fleck in the sixty-five millions, could have added a faint muted verse—a verse from their poet Heine, who like themselves had given his heart to Germany. Heine the exile in Paris and his fellow-Jews now exiles in their own home could sing together:

Ich hatte einst ein schönes Vaterland . . .
Das küsste mich auf deutsch, und sprach auf deutsch
(Man glaubt es kaum
Wie gut es klang) das Wort: "ich liebe dich!"
Es war ein Traum.

Once I had a fair Fatherland . . .
I was kissed in German, in German told
(And, oh, how dear it sounded):
"I love you."
It was a dream.

22

UNDER THE THIRD REICH

THE Nazi Revolution was one of the swiftest on record. Hitler did in three months what Mussolini, Lenin, or their French predecessors took as many years to achieve. And considering its magnitude and scope, it was one of the world's most remarkable revolutions. Nothing is gained, in appraising present-day Germany or its future, by stigmatizing the leaders as gangsters, their procedure as taking their opponents for a ride, and their achievement a spoils-system grounded on ruthless brutality. If true, it simply means that gangsters can be shrewd, systematic, and thorough. It means that German gangsters, as one might expect, were *gründlich*.

In fact, the speed and thoroughness of the revolution revealed a situation which made Nazi brutality one of the most hideous episodes in history. The reign of terror in the French and Bolshevist revolution, however deplorable, was a defense against revolt at home and invasion from abroad. But the Nazis seized and held their power without revolt from within or intervention from without. The rapidity and ease of their victory were due, moreover, to internal factors which rendered violence altogether irrational.

Years of successful propaganda, desperate economic conditions, and the nation's real as well as fancied grievances against the world had won a good half of the population to the Nazi cause. Among the other half, the nationalist groups, who together polled some three and one-half million votes at the final election, were sympathetic. The centrists, liberals, socialists, trade-unionists, and communists were demoralized —psychically paralyzed—after the burning of the Reichstag. As a recent historian and lover of Germany has eloquently written: "When freedom went down into bloody darkness, not one German, not one descendant of Arminius, was taken arms in hand and fighting, except a poor Jewish boy driven crazy by seeing his mother battered into unconsciousness before his eyes."* The only descendants of Arminius who kept their arms in hand, the Reichswehr, were, as befitting a paid army, obedient to their paymasters. And to the circumstances which precluded any effective opposition must be added the traditional submissiveness of the German to authority, the apathy toward political injustice and social welfare characteristic of all peoples, and finally, the conviction among men of culture—and no country possessed a larger number than Germany—that wanton violence and cruelty were impossible in a civilized nation. Faced with a field as clear as this, and a foe as impotent, not even gangsters would have wasted a bullet.

Neither was there an explosion of berserker wrath, so dear to the traditions of German folk-ways. Days in advance, torture chambers in the Brown Houses were thoughtfully equipped with steel-rods, castor oil, and ropes. Dozens, perhaps scores, of concentration camps were made ready. The pattern of arrest, beatings, examination, torture, morale-

* R. T. Clark: *The Fall of the German Republic*. London, 1935.

breaking discipline, and ultimate murder was so uniform as to leave no doubt it was a planned ritual.

For years the Nazi leaders had followed Goebbel's injunction "to organize hate with ice-cold calculation," and had preached a day of boundless vengeance. National Socialism, it had been reiterated for years, was "a movement which meant action"—*eine Bewegung der Tat.* Sadistic dreams had been planted in the minds of the Brown Troopers, many of them psychopathic victims of idleness, frustration, hunger, helplessness, drugs, war-shock, a blank future, and an insatiable grudge against the world. "Just wait, comrades of the Brown Battalions," said District Commissar Gillgasch in 1932, repeating a common refrain, "only a few weeks more, and you will be able to lock up the Jews in the fire-engine houses where they will be packed like herring. Then, a few tons of salt will be thrown among them. The houses will not be opened. And there let them pickle until the blood and sweat which they have sucked from you will be given back." "We need only act brutally enough," echoed Bürger, a member of the Reichstag, "even though a considerable number of Jews will have already disappeared, we need merely seize a few thousand and make an example of them." "We will make the hemp industry prosper," foretold Stöhr, former vice-president of the Reichstag. "We will put the Marxists and Centrists on the gallows to feed the ravens," said Premier Röver of Oldenburg.

Kraft! Kraft! Kraft!—"Power and again Power!"—was hammered into the heads of weaklings. The leaders who wielded the hammers of this propaganda with "ice-cold calculation" did so under the compulsion of a perfect faith in a sacred irrational cause, and vicariously satisfied their own lust for blood without—except in the case of a Streicher, von Killinger, or Heines—splattering a drop on their gentlemanly hands. The Junkers and industrialists who paid for the hammers—and who used finger bowls after every luncheon in the *Herrenklub*—knew the use to which they would be put. The contemplation of a few thousand tortured and murdered communists, socialists, liberals, and Jews, if we are to judge by the fact that no *Freiherr* or "representative" businessman has uttered a syllable of protest, did not spoil the flavor of a single *Herrenklub Wienerschnitzel*. Just so, at an auto-da-fé in Cordova, the year 1683, the nobility and Church dignitaries consumed huge quantities of veal, chicken, truffles, cherries, and jellies while watching the heretics burned alive. 1683 and 1933—appetite and business as usual.

The urge to vengeance, brutality, bloodshed, and a cruel display of power, thus accumulated and incited for years, could not be dammed even if the leaders had so desired. That they incited it and had no desire to dam it, because it marked and sealed their perfect immutable faith in a phantasy, and that businessmen encouraged and paid for this urge and phantasy, is the story of fanaticism in every age. The inhumanity and sadism which swept the land after the burning of the Reichstag and which has made Germany a by-word and a hissing among all decent men—except, of course, those foreigners who have dined with *Der Führer* and found him charming—was the inevitable consequence of fanaticism, as inevitable as the Inquisition or the Ghetto.

The persecution began pianissimo immediately after January 30, 1933, when Hitler took his oath as chancellor to preserve the Republic. Between the burning of the Reichstag on February 27 and the elections of March 5, the horror heightened; and following the Nazi victory it attained such dimensions that by the end of March the world's outcry drove it to cover where, shielded from the eyes of the public and the ears of the press, it still flourishes. "When wood is being planed," said Minister Goering at a public meeting on March 7 during the peak of the atrocities, "there are always shavings."

Strict censorship, a terrorized populace, and the secrecy clothing the entire enterprise have made any attempt to enumerate the victims a rough guess. All impartial estimates agree that thousands of unarmed communists, socialists, liberals, pacifists, and Jews were murdered; and scores of thousands subjected to arrest, torture, and bestialities too nauseous for description. Every reliable clue so far to hand would indicate that, among the victims, one thousand of the murdered and many thousands of the imprisoned and tortured were Jews—tortured and murdered not because of any political affiliation or religious belief, but simply because of their birth. If the Jewish communities have still maintained enough of their old traditions to keep on hand a *Memorbuch*—though such memorial volumes have been gathering dust since the sixteenth century—and if, like their ancestors in the years of the Crusades and the Black Death, they have recorded the names of the maimed, the missing, and the dead, some day the shavings will be numbered and the truth known. An Eternal People has, with the aid of *Memorbücher*, a long memory.

ii

As soon as Hitler became chancellor the first steps were taken toward the real revolution—the creation of a totalitarian state. The secret of Communist and Fascist success in Russia and Italy and of the Socialist failure in Germany of 1918 was not lost on the Nazis. The whole apparatus of the German government was brought into their hands—again throwing a horrid light on the wantonness of Nazi violence. The personnel of the vast civil service and manifold public and semi-public enterprises was overhauled, and all officials and employees of imputed or doubtful loyalty to the Swastika dismissed. Jewish blood was prima facie and soon to be legal evidence of such disloyalty.

The first official head fell the morning after Hitler entered office. Chief Engineer Schäfer of the Reich Broadcasting Company was dismissed. "With this measure," wrote the *Völkischer Beobachter*, "one of the worst fruits of the November System has been eliminated from our radio service . . . it has always been a mystery why its chief engineer had to be a Jew." A few hours later Engineer Schäfer killed himself. He was not to be alone either in his dismissal or his death. The "de-Jewing" had begun.

But the totalitarian state promised by the Nazi program meant, as we have learned, more than a unified one-party government. It meant rigid control over every department of society; and with a loyalty and thoroughness worthy of a better cause, the National Socialists laid plans to execute their promises. *Gleichschaltung*—coördination and submission— became as popular after the elections as "having one's eyes opened" before. Whether it was foreseen or not, the Aryan cult and anti-Semitism proved an incalculable aid in whipping the nation's activities into line. The elimination of the Jew—boycotts, dismissals, exclusions, discriminatory laws— was more than pure devotion to a faith, more than a blow at an arch-enemy, and more than the blind hatred which such Jews as like to nurse the martyrdom of their kind usually see in it. Intoxicated by race enthusiasm and diverted by Jew-baiting (along with the baiting of Communists) the people of a great nation surrendered to partisan control its business, industry, agriculture, professions, schools, and culture—its body and soul—almost unaware of sacrifice or loss. If no Jews had existed in Germany, it would have been worth while to invent them.

The country-wide boycott of April 1, 1933, was a telling example. For days in advance, press, radio, and mass-meetings swept the nation into believing that the violence and atrocities exercised against Israel had been a foul lie manufactured by World Jewry. The German public was convinced that in self-defense it must retaliate with a boycott against its Jewish fellow-citizens, for such the Jews still were. And under the frenzy and delight of the boycott, the *Gleichschaltung* of all citizens was launched. Before the end of May, all the funds and property of the Communist and Socialist Parties, labor unions, labor banks, and Consumers' Coöperative Societies were confiscated. By July, Nazi cells, spies, and managers were installed in every sizable business firm and industrial plant; a Nazi Labor Front, with its pseudo-unionism, had replaced all labor organizations as well as employers' associations; Culture Chambers had put all professional classes and their livelihood under Nazi dictation; all political parties except the National Socialists had been exterminated, parliamentarism and representative government destroyed, the German states—some of them more than a thousand years old—reduced to Nazi departments under Nazi governors (*Staathalter*) and soon to be reorganized or abolished; democracy, civil rights, free speech and free press, pacifism, liberalism, freedom in science and art, and every instrument of criticism and open-minded discussion wiped from the land. Each of these measures or their supplementary rulings struck at Jewry, but this was the blow which disguised their true import and rendered them palatable. The first of April was indeed a day of terror for Israel; but it was something worse for Germany: it was April Fools' Day.

As for the Jews, beginning on that date, a series of laws were passed which before the year was over had practically excluded them from life and the possibility of a livelihood in Germany. By the spring of 1934, with exceptions to be noted, no Jew or half-Jew or quarter-Jew could hold public office; get or keep a post in the civil service; practice law or serve as judge, notary, or juror; teach in the public schools, colleges, technical institutes, or universities; attend any lower school beyond a proportion fixed at one and one-half percent or, with rare exception, enroll in a university; belong to German sports clubs, learned societies, or art circles; practice medicine or dentistry in any public service or hospital (which embraces most of the medical practice in Germany); work in any capacity on a newspaper, journal, or in the publishing business (except it be purely Jewish); engage in any capacity in the theater, opera, concert stage, movies, or radio; become a member of the government-controlled Chambers of Culture, without which membership the practice of architecture, painting, sculpture, music, and authorship was rendered almost impossible. So much for culture.

Business showed little better. No Jew, half-Jew, or quarter-Jew could legally advertize on the radio or in the general press. He could not own, control, or act in any directive capacity in a department or chain store; or own or control any shares in a newspaper, journal, or publishing house (except it be exclusively Jewish). He could not belong to professional and trade organizations, such as the associations of brokers, druggists, or milk-dealers, nor to the employers' division of the Labor Front—membership in which is often prerequisite for the conduct of business. He could not open new retail stores or enlarge old ones, thus preventing the dispossessed professional man from seeking new means of earning a living. No Jew, or fraction thereof, could receive a government contract, national or local; and government contracts, under Nazi coördination, comprise a huge share of the nation's business.

Non-Jewish firms and stores were advised by the Department of Commerce—and advice from the Nazis is equivalent to command—to display special German (i.e. Aryan) signs, thereby making it evident that an enterprise without such sign was Jewish and to be shunned. Commercial and professional directories have been reëdited, and either omit Jewish names or indicate their non-Aryan character. And lest there be any doubt, Jewish store-fronts and office-doors were in the recurrent waves of boycott plastered with warnings: "Jew," "Don't Buy Here," "Let the Jew's Hands Shrivel from Starvation."

In the field of labor, no firm was permitted to employ more than three percent of Jews. No Jew (or fractional Jew) could belong to the Labor Front, which has replaced all labor and employees' organizations and membership in which is the prerequisite for getting a job either as a manual or a white-collar worker or for receiving insurance benefits and unemployment relief. Local courts, such as the Labor Court in

Berlin—where as many Jews as could were flocking from the smaller towns for work or for supposedly greater safety—have decreed that Jewish blood is sufficient ground for dismissal.

By the summer of 1935 most naturalized Jews had been deprived of their citizenship—some 20,000 in Prussia and Westphalia alone. And citizenship had been taken from a few outstanding German Jews, such as Albert Einstein, Lion Feuchtwanger, and Georg Bernhard, and their property confiscated—measures likewise applied to undesirable Aryans of prominence. However, the citizenship of the main body of German Jews, with what few rights it still entailed, had hung in abeyance. And nearly all the discriminatory and naturalization laws carried one important exemption. The status, occupation, employment, and rights of Jews who had served at the front in the World War, or who were the sons of war veterans, or who were in possession of their status or employment before the outbreak of the War, were to be unmolested —an exemption which has progressively become a dead letter.

Then, on September 15, 1935, in the customary blare of a Nazi national convention at Nuremberg, the Reichstag placed all German Jews beyond the pale of citizenship. They were thrust back to the juridical ghetto which had prevailed throughout Europe up to the French Revolution and in Germany till well in the nineteenth century. No longer citizens, they were relegated to the status of subjects (*Staatsangehörige*), defined as "one who enjoys the protection of the Reich and therefore owes allegiance to it." Again Hitler had translated a passage of *My Battle* into literal action. The allusion to "protection" and "obligation" in the light of the record of boycotts, excesses, tax-impositions, blackmailing, extortions, and legalized robbery, of which more anon, is ominously reminiscent of the "protection" and "obligations" which six hundred years ago characterized the *Kammerknecht*—the Jewish servant of the Imperial treasury.

Further laws passed at Nuremberg and the subsequent executive decrees of November 15, 1935, emphasize the medieval character of the new ghetto. They prohibit intermarriage as well as extra-marital relations between Jews and Germans (or persons of racially related stock), upon penalty of imprisonment. They forbid Jews to employ female domestic help of German or related blood, under thirty-five years of age (effective January 1, 1936). They decree the establishment of separate schools for Jewish children (effective in 1936). And they deny Jews the right to display the German flag.

However, Jews may display their own national colors of blue and white. This was a privilege which the medieval state did not grant, for there were no Jewish national colors when, to take their place, the Lateran Council provided the Badge of Shame. What he saw in the Christian world taught many a medieval Jew to wear his yellow ring as a mark of honor; and it is possible that many a modern German Jew, once repugnant to Palestine, will reconcile himself to the colors of Zion and, looking out from his ghetto, agree with Börne that it is the Germans with their red-white-and-black who fly the Badge of Shame.

The definition of a Jew is shaded with genealogical fractions and hair-splitting marital distinctions. First come full-blooded Jews—about 450,000 of whom belong to the Jewish community, and about 300,000 of whom profess the Christian faith or none at all. Then come fractional Jews, numbering perhaps 750,000. Of these, the three-quarter Jews are to be counted as full Jews. Half-Jews are to be classed as full Jews if they belonged to the Jewish community when the Nuremberg laws were passed, if they are married to or marry a full Jew, etc. Yet they may marry Germans or "related peoples" only upon permission of the Minister of the Interior or the Deputy Party Leader of the Reich. Quarter-Jews are to be accepted as Germans and capable of receiving Reich citizenship; but no quarter-Jew may marry another quarter-Jew— lest, no doubt, the marriage produce an irrational fraction.

These incredible distinctions, the product of a eugenic scholasticism, at least save the German Government from continuing to give official expression to an even greater folly. Hereafter the Government can drop from its decrees the name and concept of *Aryan*, so embarrassing to its relations with Japan. "German or related blood" will serve every purpose of legislation and diplomacy, and leave unsatisfied no one but men of science and common sense.

The ghetto, as yet, is only a legal fact; but a statement in *Deutsche Justiz* ("German Justice," the official organ of the Ministry of Justice, August 2, 1935) promises that it will one day be converted into a physical reality. "The former segregation of the Jews," so says *Deutsche Justiz,* "was looked upon by a more enlightened generation and is still regarded by foreign opinion as a relic of medieval times. As a matter of fact, this segregation was a genuinely wise measure, the abandonment of which has harmed all peoples." One feels confident that German justice will take the necessary steps to repair this evil.

Meanwhile the Nuremberg Laws, like much of this anti-Semitic legislation and agitation, contain a joker—and once again the joke is not exclusively on the Jews. For any people toying with discriminations against race, creed, color, or unpopular minorities of whatever nature, both the occasion for passing the Nuremberg decrees and their wording will repay close study.

Press rumors and speculations showed that the measures were contemplated long in advance. On July 15 and 19 anti-Jewish riots, with the customary beatings and broken heads, swept the Kurfürstendamm. Count Wolf von Helldorf, who made his name at leading such riots in the past, was now appointed Chief of Police to insure, no doubt, that thereafter they would be carried out in *Ordnung*. And Julius Streicher of Nuremberg, who specializes in spicing anti-Semitism with pornography, thus making his appeal apparently irresistible, moved his activities to Berlin. The German public was given its usual treat of Jew-baiting.

Then came the *Bremen* incident. Other publics had the poor taste to disrelish Herr Streicher and all his works. On July 26 a crowd of demonstrators at the North German Lloyd pier in New York expressed their contempt for the Swastika flying in a spotlight from the mast of the *Bremen*. A handful of demonstrators mounted on board and tore down the Nazi emblem. A New York magistrate—his blood colored with Judaism—acquitted the offenders of a charge of unlawful assembly; and, in doing so, quoted the opinions of the accused which were highly uncomplimentary to the Nazis and their flag—opinions which the magistrate declared would not have exonerated them if their assembly had been proved illegal.

Press, radio, and mass-meetings were immediately let loose throughout Germany. Hourly bulletins were issued on the weighty developments of the case. And when indignation and furor were at their height, and the bands played and the three rings of the Nuremberg-convention circus were in full swing, and all hearts and eyes turned in wrath on the Jews, the Government decreed the "ghetto" laws. Most Germans rejoiced or regretted to feel that the Jews had been pounced on again. But it was not only Jews, as these same Germans will discover, who are faced with a ghetto.

When the bands stop playing they will have leisure to remark that the Nuremberg law dealing with citizenship first defines a subject of the state (*Staatsangehöriger*), in terms we have already noted, as anyone who enjoys the protection of the Reich and therefore owes allegiance to it. Consequently the subjects of the state include both Jews and non-Jews—the entire body of the populace hitherto considered as citizens. Next they will remark that citizenship is not taken away from the Jews or other non-Aryans. On the contrary, citizenship "is to be acquired by grant of a citizenship deed." And who may receive this deed, without which citizenship is not to be enjoyed? "Only those subjects of the state," reads the law, "who are of German or racially-related blood *and* who prove by their conduct that they are *willing and able to serve loyally* the German people and the Reich may be Reich citizens" (our italics). To be sure, the executive order of November 15 adds that "until further notice" all persons of German or related blood who possessed the right to vote on September 15 shall be regarded as Reich citizens.

But the tragic joker and its intent are clear. Citizenship may—and in many cases doubtless will—be withheld from any present citizen, regardless of the color of his blood, whom the Nazi authorities judge to be "unwilling or unable to serve loyally"—the Nazi movement. Thousands of applauding or indifferent Germans, their cheers or even their disapproval diverted to the damnation of the Jews, may find their own right to citizenship withheld. Emerson remarked in Abolition days that the chains of slavery bind the master no less than the slave. Wherever freedom or privilege is denied a single man, all his fellows are threatened with the same denial.

We have found the German Jew to be a scapegoat and a punching-bag, but that does not exhaust his services. More insidious and ruinous to his oppressors, he is used as a blind. Even as the pack hunts him with hue and cry, it is they who are stripped of their rights and strength. "The German," wrote Hitler in *My Battle* and then deleted the sentence after its eleventh edition, "has not the slightest notion of how a people must be misled if the adherence of the masses is sought." So far as the Jews are concerned, the Nazi program has been fulfilled to the last plank, and more. They are on the road back to the prison of the Middle Ages; but, in the nature of such a journey, they cannot go alone. The Germans are on the same road. And while Israel chants *Ab ha-Rahamim*, the martyrs' dirge written by their ancestors in the Rhinelands, the Germans can raise their own voices in a song from Beethoven's *Fidelio*—the prisoners' chorus.

iii

By the end of 1935 the realities or the prospects of life in the Third Reich have driven nearly 100,000 victims to abandon their homeland. Of these refugees, more than 75,000 are Jews retrudging the ancient road of exile. Several thousands more are Christian non-Aryans, perhaps the more pitiable because the least prepared. When they, or their parents, or in many cases their grandparents, embraced Christianity they had believed that their wanderings, the mark and burden of Israel, had come to an end; but like the Marranos of the sixteenth century they have found it easier to leave the fold than the fate of Jewry.

About 30,000 of the refugees have settled in Palestine. Another 20,000 have been repatriated in the Central and East European countries of their origin. Some 6,000 have found haven in the United States, and 3,000 in South American lands; while 30,000 remain without political security, and often economically destitute, in England, France, Holland, Czechoslovakia, and other countries bordering on Germany. Ten thousand, driven by hunger or despair, had the temerity to return to the Reich, where a good proportion of them have been sent to concentration camps for "reëducation"—a euphemism for slow death.

But the number of refugees falls far short of the total who would take flight if they had the means. By 1935, it has been estimated that 125,000 "full-blooded" Jews have been deprived of their livelihood by decree, boycott, *Gleichschaltung,* and agitation.* This estimate does not include the indeterminate number of Jewish unemployed before the Nazis entered into power, and who, it may be assumed, are still without work. Since the census of 1925 counted the gainfully-employed Jews at 261,000 and their estimated dependents at 233,000, the unemployed and their dependents today may well be reckoned

* Among this number are about 2,000 trained civil servants; 4,000 physicians, of whom 2,000 are now dependent on charity; 4,000 in the legal profession; 10,500 formerly engaged in public health and social service; 800 college and university professors; 800 teachers in elementary and secondary schools; 1,200 journalists, editors, and writers; 2,000 actors, singers, musicians, etc.; and about 30,000 employees in business and industry. A total of 90,000 shopkeepers have applied for aid to Jewish philanthropic and free loan agencies. None of these figures includes the new victims of 1935.

as comprising more than one-half of the Jewish population. The number will grow and their destitution increase as Jewish business firms are progressively forced into liquidation, capital sequestered, the funds available for relief diminished, and the noose of boycott tightened.

Behind these figures lie torments that go far beyond mere unemployment and deprivation. A glance at life in the smaller towns—and civilized stomachs cannot stand for more than a glance—discloses the "cold" pogrom at work, the effort to kill the manhood of a people who until a few years ago were just folks and neighbors.

What, in actual life, is meant by the boycott? A shopkeeper or professional man, the bread-winner of a family, discovers that his customers, clients, or patients no longer dare to cross his threshold. All members of the local Nazi party and their relatives—the modern exponents of German *Treue*—are pledged to do no business with him. The remainder of the townsmen are deterred by a Nazi guard standing at his door with a camera—one step within the portal means that their pictures and names will be pilloried in the local newspapers or on one of the innumerable *Stürmer* bill-boards.

Employees and workmen discovered dealing with a Jew face dismissal; and employers, the withdrawal of government contracts or of their Aryan customers. The unemployed face the loss of their dole and winter-relief. Peasants face the deprivation of government seeds, cattle feed, fertilizer, and exemption from foreclosures. Local campaigns collect long lists of signatures from townsmen and peasants who bind themselves not to buy from Jews, and the lists are posted in bakeries, groceries, on the *Stürmer* kiosks, and other conspicuous places. Few or none refuse to sign . . . after all, one must live.

The Christian—or rather, one should say, the Nazi—children, and all German children are fast becoming such, take a vigorous part in the boycott. They are educated to look upon every Jew as an enemy and every customer of a Jew as a traitor, and they act—with shouts and stones—accordingly. In many towns they have succeeded in closing down every Jewish shop. If the owner attempts to admonish them, it is considered a "provocation" and he is likely to exchange his shop for a concentration camp. The energy of youth equipped with a few pots of paint can be measured by the number of besmirched sidewalks, store fronts, house doors, and even synagogues and cemeteries. Where there is no paint, there are always stones; and it is not uncommon to forbid the repair of broken windows: this, too, is a "provocation." The parents, like the victims, dare not remonstrate. Camps yawn for disloyal parents.

Boycott is also used to secure the dismissal of Jewish employees. The army commissary of the National Socialist Party, now Germany's greatest commercial enterprise, has requested all firms dealing with it to dismiss their Jewish help and agents—a request backed by the threat of lost contracts. Local party leaders and rioters make it their object to force Jewish employers to rid themselves of their Jewish employees. On the other hand, even if faced with bankruptcy, these same employers dare not dismiss their Aryan workers. Their bankruptcy, moreover, is hastened by the extortions of government officials, tax-collectors, and party leaders—a system of blackmail which gets its teeth from the threat of boycott or concentration camp. In numerous towns the banks are calling in demand-money from Jews or hastening foreclosure actions when boycott has headed Jewish business firms into difficulties, and what the boycott in itself may not have accomplished, the banks quickly achieve. Vultures are everywhere at hand to buy up Jewish shops, homes, and other property for a song. The general liquidation of Jewish business, conducted under the auspices of the government, has given many a German competitor the bargain of his life and left the Jewish seller with sequestered marks which he cannot withdraw for his own use or take from the country: it is much the same robbery as the German kings practiced in the Middle Ages.

In trades and industries where the supply of commodities is rationed by the government, as in all branches of agricultural trade, the Jews are either excluded from the rations or allotted a derisory quota. Thanks to this action of the authorities, the Jewish dealers in agricultural products have been ruined almost to a man. The authorities are indeed *gründlich*. Many Jewish judges and lawyers, in a last effort to earn a living, became apartment-house janitors; and Jewish property-owners gladly provided them with these posts. The government, however, has introduced special "schools" for janitors with obligatory attendance, and naturally with obligatory exclusion of the Jewish ex-judges and lawyers.

But this is only one side of the boycott. On the other side, every conceivable effort—and some inconceivable ones—are made to exclude the Jews from the amenities and necessities of life. Parks, hotels, restaurants, beer-halls, theaters, moving-picture houses, public baths, recreation grounds, and summer- and winter-resorts are frequently closed to them. Social gatherings with Germans are out of the question, and even purely Jewish gatherings—a birthday party, a *Kaffee-Klatsch*, or a wedding—are often foregone for fear of giving rise to provocations, denunciations, arrests, and other "misunderstandings."

Denial of permission to enter towns was recently announced by the authorities of a hundred localities, largely in Brandenburg, East Prussia, eastern Westphalia, and around Mayence. The town of Garmisch-Partenkirchen in Bavaria had long banned the Jews—no doubt in preparation for the Olympic Winter Games. Coupled with these denials of entry—which take us directly back to the eighteenth century in Germany— are prohibitions to purchase as well as sell any goods, acquire real-estate, or have any business dealings with the local Jews. The similarity of wording in these decrees makes it logical to assume that they emanate from a central authority.

Where formal decrees are lacking, placards on the highways leading to the towns have the desired effect. "Jews Enter This Place at Their Risk," "Jews Strictly Forbidden in This Town," "Warning to Pickpockets and Jews" are favorites. Poets have been encouraged to make these announcements rhyme with "sow," "garlic," and "stink." Artists have been given an opportunity to depict on the placard the fate of any Jew incautious enough to disregard the warning. These placards are universal throughout Hessia, East Prussia, Pomerania, and Mecklenburg, and can be found in about one-half of the towns elsewhere. (None, however, will be found in such tourist resorts as Baden-Baden, Kissingen, or Nauheim.) Railway stations, government buildings, and all important highways take up the refrain. In the neighborhood of Ludwigshaven, a dangerous bend in the road bears the following advice to motorists: "Drive Carefully, Sharp Curve—Jews, 75 miles an hour!"

In whole districts Jewish salesmen can procure no lodging

for the night. Peddlers are discouraged by signs on farm gates and before the doors of private houses: "Jews Not Admitted." Jewish cattle-dealers are refused admittance to fairs or—as in Leipzig three hundred years ago—huddled in a "Jew Row" of their own.

In an increasing number of towns and villages, Jews are no longer able to purchase the most necessary articles of food. The windows of dairies, butcher shops, bakeries, and grocery stores confront the housewife with a sign: "Jews Not Admitted." The tradesman who might refuse to display this sign will have the pleasure of reading his name in the next morning's paper, or find written on the door of his shop: "Jew Servant." Among other places, in Madgeburg, Köthen, and Dessau—Mendelssohn's Dessau—the pharmacies refuse to sell medicines or drugs to their Jewish customers. In some cases, where desperate families in need of food or other necessities have resorted to telephoning their orders to the local merchants, the dealers who filled such orders have been trapped by Nazi spies, and their name and shame duly published to the community at large. Milk is no longer available for Jewish children in about fifty towns. Once they have the confidence of strangers, Jewish women admit that they cry night after night, and do not leave their home for weeks at a time.

In accordance with Nazi ethics—the same ethics which permitted the torture and murder of defenseless men—the lot of the Jewish child is rendered unbearable. His helplessness and innocence—for even Germans cannot believe him responsible for ills and disasters that took place before he was born— make him the proper prey of fanaticism. When his schoolmates and teachers taunt him in the class-room, and his playmates in the streets—examples are too pitiful for repetition

—we seem to hear the echo of a cry that has come down the ages, the cry of "Christ-killer!" Sitting through lessons on the "Jew Bench" reserved for his breed, listening in the singing hour to such choruses as

"The German land for the German man, the working man,
The Jew may run to Canaan, if run he can,"

hearing his teacher address him as "Marxist bastard," learning from his text-books that he belongs to a race of sub-humans, humiliated in games and sports, chased and stoned in the by-ways, it can be no wonder if his tongue grows silent and his heart breaks. "My wife and I tremble," writes a Jewish father, "when our daughter sets out for school in the morning, and we tremble when she creeps home in the evening. We no longer ask questions, and she no longer tells what happens."

Even exclusively Jewish schools and orphanages have been molested or disbanded by valiant Nazi warriors, and the children deported secretly after dark. And the same can be told of Catholic children's homes. With his Brown Shirts and Black Guards, with his reborn National Army and air-fleets, with his guns and gas-bombs, Adolf Hitler may sleep safe and sound at night; but if a *man* were sleeping in his place, there is one thing he would fear, one thing to set him starting from his pillow: the tears of little children.

iv

Life is a little less cruel and getting a livelihood still a little more likely in Berlin and other big cities. Among their vast populations the identity of a Jew is not so easy to discover, and an air-tight boycott would cost more than the Nazis evidently deem it worth. Besides, the mopping up of the last Jews can well wait until the posture of general affairs needs this diversion. Only these circumstances and the heroic aplomb of the Jews, a dignity and a patience that demand more strength than any protest or revolt, account for their ceaseless efforts at readjustment and for the continuance of a civilized existence.

For the first year or more after the "change"—as the German-Jewish press calls the Nazi Revolution—energies and organizations were devoted to rechanneling the occupations of dispossessed merchants and dismissed intellectuals. Physicians learned how to make candy and engineers to cobble shoes. But the spread of the boycott and the growth of legal restrictions have dimmed even the possibility of turning the twentieth-century Jew back to the cobbling, peddling days of Moses Mendelssohn.

More and more eyes are turning, instead, to Palestine. The *Jüdische Rundschau*, the official Zionist organ of Germany, contains pages of advertisements, offering lessons in modern Hebrew, instruction in trades likely to prove of use in the new land, information with regard to express companies and steamship lines, as well as advertisements of Palestinian banks, business firms, products, and hotels. Detailed articles are devoted to life in Zion and its prospects. An issue of the *Rundschau* would be something for Herzl to read!

Virtual segregation has likewise stimulated cultural life in and for German Jewry, quite apart from hopes of emigration. A new Jewish theater has been developed; and concert artists who can no longer entertain the German public are furnishing their own people the forbidden scores of Mendelssohn, Meyerbeer, and the outlawed moderns. Within six months a revised edition of the *Philo Lexikon*, a cyclopedia of Jewish history, biography, and knowledge, has sold 15,000 copies. On a population basis, this would be equivalent to 400,000 copies among the Jews of the United States—an impressive testimony to the awakened thirst for self-understanding. With such a spirit abroad, it is difficult to believe that the revival may prove to be, as in all likelihood it is, the last flare before the lamp goes out. Certainly it renders incredible the words of a writer in the organ of the Central Union of German Citizens of Jewish Faith: "We want solid ground underneath our feet, but no new ideas."

New ideas, hard as they are, must be accepted. The Era of Emancipation has closed. Moreover, despite our loose similes, history does not run backwards; and leaving behind him the pleasant paths of freedom, the German Jew has not emerged into the Middle Ages. He himself is no longer a medieval man; the world which confronts him differs vastly from the Holy Roman Empire of the German Nation; and his place and use in this world differ no less vastly. While the persecution he is undergoing is less violent than in the heyday of the Middle Ages and the drive to the ghetto is still something of a metaphor, both inner and outer conditions make his survival far more unlikely. If he is to survive at all—if, indeed, he is to escape from Germany with his bare skin—the new conditions must persuade him of the necessity for new ideas.

In the Middle Ages he was steeled with a faith he no longer possesses, and which would take more than a *Philo Lexikon* to restore. Today the Jew of Nuremberg lacks nothing of the courage of his ancestors, his neck is as stiff as ever; but can his heart, like that of the Jew of old, believe that God in infinite wisdom has made him suffer for his sins, and that submission to the Divine Will shall bring him to the peace of Paradise? The faith of the medieval Jew, moreover, was shared, though in different terms, by his enemies; and his own convictions were strengthened and confirmed by the prevalent trust in God and Providence. The two basic charges leveled against him by the Church and the underlying excuse for his persecution—that he denied the divinity of Jesus and the trinity of God—he not only acknowledged, but proudly died to prove. Today the Jew, even as a "witness," cannot on the face of it accept his enemies' contention that his people are inferior, and himself a sub-human to be classed a shade above the apes. The new gods of the racial cult are not, like the Christian Deity, his own under another rubric. Finally, his medieval faith armed him, as we saw, with a communal discipline which in the individualism of modern life and the structure of modern economy is shattered forever.

Modern economy, even more than a change in faith, has wrecked Jewish resistance to persecution; and, so long as present conditions continue, it renders his outlook hopeless. In the Middle Ages the Jews, first as merchants and later as money-lenders, were so essential to German life that however much their absence was desired, their presence could never long be spared. We need only recall that they were valuable enough for an overlord to keep them on hand and, if necessary, defend them for purposes of taxation and extortion; and that, in the absence of a central authority, as fast as one city or state expelled them, another took them in; the "permanent" expulsions after the Black Death, we remember, were followed by a speedy invitation to return. Jewish usefulness again approached major importance in the peculiar circumstances following the Thirty Years War. But thereafter, and progressively through the rise of modern capitalism, and above all since this capitalism and its attendant industry are now verging on monopoly, the usefulness of the Jews as a group—like the usefulness of any minority people—has vanished. However great their services, they are, as individuals or as a community, no longer economically indispensable to Germany as a whole; and where here and there a town may find them too valuable to crush, the welfare of such a locality is disregarded by a totalitarian, monopoly-ruled nation.

The exceptions sadly prove the rule. Private Jewish bankers and their concerns have in general been spared—to date. The reasons should be evident, and, taking us directly back to the fifteenth century, need no talk of bribes or gifts to explain this exceptional immunity. For the present at least, these private banks are needed to help absorb compulsory government loans, extend forced credit to business, and support the general financial structure. And, unlike the Jewish owners of other big enterprises, such as department stores, who have been or are being eliminated, the name and "goodwill" of a private banker is essential to maintaining the credit and confidence of his depositors and customers. Jews have long been dropped from responsible posts in the joint-stock banks; and private bankers of non-Aryan blood can look forward to the same fate as soon as their depositors can be trained not to miss them.

No other Jews are even temporarily indispensable. And nothing in the material circumstances of Germany can be reckoned upon to divert or soften the effort toward extermination.

Nor does hope lie in any imponderable or moral circumstance. Unlike Christianity which dictated the medieval drive against the Jew, Aryanism has no need to preserve the Semite as a "witness" to its philosophy; it has no nonsense about human brotherhood in its doctrines; it counts neither love, mercy, nor justice among its cardinal virtues; and it holds open no door to converts—the outsider is damned at and by his birth. Christianity often writhed in pangs of conscience at its use of the sword, and felt the miseries it provoked to be contrary to its spirit and better nature; whereas Aryanism is a naked appeal to brutality and force—"What we need," writes Hitler in the new bible, *My Battle,* "is pride, spite, hatred, and once more hatred." As we hinted in the first pages of our story, Aryanism is the final word in intolerance, the ultimate return, in the slow retributions of time, of racial pride upon the head of the Jew, setting up a steel wall where the Jew of two thousand years ago planted a hedge. As Stöcker once said of Lessing's day, "we have progressed since then." Science, as it is now understood in Germany, has shown its superiority over the crude mental processes of the barbarian.

Flight, the one alternative to a life of insult and death by starvation, is impossible for the vast majority of the victims. Either they do not have money enough to flee; or, if they do, they cannot take it with them. Pharaoh is happy to let them go, so long as he can despoil them at the border. And if they leave penniless, they face in most lands the same starvation they fled from in Germany.

Western Europe and the well-populated countries of America, even when they erect no barriers of prejudice against them, are too heavily burdened with unemployment—in this world of plenty!—to provide for thousands of new bread-seekers. The thinly populated countries, Canada and South America, were they willing to be hospitable, would take long years to settle the scores of thousands who have, in their race with boycott and hunger, no long years to wait.

Most lands of Central and Eastern Europe—notably Poland, Austria, Hungary, Rumania, and the Baltic states—are beset not only with an economic crisis, but a vigorous anti-Semitism of their own; and where the native product does not suffice, Nazi propaganda—part of Germany's old-new *Drang nach Osten*—is making dangerous inroads. In fact, the dis-emancipation of the German Jew is more than likely to prove the signal for analogous loss of rights elsewhere to the East, much as over a century ago, emancipation in France set an example for granting rights in all lands swept by the spirit of the French and the Industrial revolutions.

Russia, dedicated to the abolition of anti-Semitism as one of the by-products of the class struggle and by the same sign pledged to the future salvation of humanity, has so far shown little inclination to open its gates to the damned of today. The reasons may not be hard to find—its internal difficulties are still huge, and its external enemies alert; but it remains an unhappy fact that the great image of Lenin in the Kremlin Square is as yet no Statue of Liberty that once kindled the hearts of millions of refugees who streamed to her feet.

The sole feasible asylum, Palestine, can accommodate a substantial number of the needy only if England will relax the present restrictions on immigration or permit settlements beyond the Jordan. And this, or any similar action, requires vast financial aid, far beyond the scornfully inadequate sums which Jewry has up till now seen fit to give.

Altogether, the outlook for nearly one million Germans—Jews, their fractions, and their fellow-victims—is as bleak abroad as at home. That the world, including Jewry, will permit the slow starvation of a million Europeans seems barely credible until we recall how little the world has concerned itself with a million no less starving Polish Jews, with the anguish of millions more of other oppressed minorities throughout the Continent, with still further millions of Chinese, with indeed anyone but the Ethiopian who is lucky enough to sit by the headwaters of the Nile and the road to India.

As the German Jew sinks from the stage of history, he leaves in the very process of his demise a heritage richer perhaps than anything his genius or days of vigor achieved. He leaves a lesson for every minority—racial, religious, political, or economic; and since no group boasting of numbers and power today may know whether the morrow will not rob it of both, as it has befallen the Protestants and Catholics of Germany, it is a lesson for all men. While Thyssen and Hitler, monopolized greed and organized hatred, play out their terrible game, with Schacht quaintly trying to lay down the rules and War hovering to pocket the stakes, the world can learn—if it will—that Jewish rights and universal human rights are inseparable.

No land can remain half-bigot and half-tolerant. The fight against fanaticism is one fight, no matter who the victims are. In waging the fight to save himself or his kind, everyone must be prepared to shed his prejudices as well as his blood to save even those whom he feels impelled to despise. Examples do not exist of Jewries who in the long run have saved themselves at the expense of other threatened groups, or of other minorities who have saved themselves at the expense of the Jews. And no majority is free so long as it holds a minority enslaved. The liberty of no individual can rise higher than its source; and this source is the general liberty of man.

Scant choice or time remains. The world, and Germany, has but a few years to decide whether it will choose liberty, or —in battlefields too horrible to contemplate—it must choose death.

SELECTED BIBLIOGRAPHY

A LIST of some of the more important or accessible works which, together with the numerous sources mentioned in the course of the present book, will prove useful to a reader in search of greater detail.

GENERAL

H[einrich] Graetz, Geschichte der Juden von den ältesten Zeiten bis auf die Gegenwart, 11 vols., revised edition, 1900-1909.

——, History of the Jews from the earliest times to the present day [1870], 6 vols., 1891-1895. The English translation lacks the notes of the original and is based on its unrevised form.

Simon Dubnow, Weltgeschichte des jüdischen Volkes, 10 vols., 1925-1929.

Adolph Kohut, Geschichte der deutschen Juden, 1898. Indiscriminate and disorganized, but lavish in detail and profusely illustrated.

Julius Höxter, Quellenlesebuch zur jüdischen Geschichte und Literatur, vols. III, IV, V, 1927, 1928, 1930. Selections of colorful source material.

Jewish Encyclopedia, especially under provinces, cities, and persons mentioned in our text, as well as under *Christianity, Church Councils, Popes,* and *Antisemitism.*

Encyclopaedia Judaica. As above, and particularly *Deutschland, Antisemitismus,* and *Emanzipation.*

THE EARLIEST SETTLEMENTS

S. Levi, "Frühgeschichtliche Spuren der Juden in Deutschland" in Zeitschrift für die Geschichte der Juden in Deutschland, I (1929), 24-33.

SELECTED BIBLIOGRAPHY

A. Altmann, Das Früheste Vorkommen der Juden in Deutschland, 1932. See critical reviews of this book in Zeitschrift für die Geschichte der Juden in Deutschland, IV, 210-213.

S. Eppenstein, "Zur Frühgeschichte der Juden in Deutschland, besonders in literarischer und kultureller Hinsicht" in Monatsschrift für Geschichte und Wissenschaft des Judentums, 63 Jahrg., 1919, pp. 165-186.

TYPICAL LOCAL JEWRIES

A. Freimann and F. Kracauer, Frankfort, 1929 (in English).

Max Grunwald, Vienna, 1936 (in English).

Siegmund Salfeld, Bilder aus der Vergangenheit der jüdischen Gemeinde Mainz, 1903.

Ludwig Geiger, Geschichte der Juden in Berlin, 1871.

THE MIDDLE AGES

Julius Aronius, Regesten zur Geschichte der Juden im fränkischen und deutschen Reiche bis zum Jahre 1273. 1887-1902. A compilation and digest of a large body of source material from 321 to 1273.

Georg Caro, Sozial- und Wirtschaftsgeschichte der Juden im Mittelalter und der Neuzeit, 2 vols., 1908, 1920. This work, never completed, ends with the catastrophe of the Black Death; it is furnished with detailed notes and bibliography and, together with the two following books, is indispensable for a study of economic and political conditions.

Moses Hoffmann, Der Geldhandel der deutschen Juden während des Mittelalters bis 1350. 1910. Contains numerous translations of rabbinic decisions dealing with money-lending, exchange, and commerce.

Ignaz Schipper, Anfänge des Kapitalismus bei den abendländischen Juden im früheren Mittelalter (bis zum Ausgang des XII. Jahrhunderts), 1907.

J. E. Scherer, Die Rechtsverhältnisse der Juden in den deutschoesterreichischen Ländern, 1901.

M[oritz] Güdemann, Geschichte des Erziehungswesens und der Cultur der abendländischen Juden während des Mittelalters und der Neueren Zeit, vols. I and III, 1880, 1888.

———, Quellenschriften zur Geschichte des Unterrichts und der Erziehung bei den deutschen Juden von den ältesten Zeiten bis auf Mendelssohn, 1891. These works are mines of information, brilliantly presented, on social life, the culture of the learned, and the mind of the populace.

Louis Finkelstein, Jewish Self-Government in the Middle Ages, 1924.

Solomon Schechter, Studies in Judaism, III, 1924. "Jewish Saints in Medieval Germany," pp. 1-24.

Nathan Birnbaum and Hugo Herrmann (edit.), Edom: Berichte jüdischer Zeugen und Zeitgenossen über die Judenverfolgungen während der Kreuzzüge, 1919.

Solomon Grayzel, The Church and the Jews in the XIIIth Century, 1933.

Robert Hoeniger, Der Schwarze Tod in Deutschland, 1888.

S. Salfeld, Das Martyrologium des Nürnberger Memorbuches, 1898.

SIXTEENTH-EIGHTEENTH CENTURIES

Ludwig Geiger, Johann Reuchlin, 1871.

S. A. Hirsch, A Book of Essays, 1905. "Johann Reuchlin, the Father of the Study of Hebrew," pp. 116-150; "Johann Pfefferkorn and the battle of the books," pp. 73-115.

R[einhard] Lewin, Luthers Stellung zu den Juden, 1911.

Ludwig Feilchenfeld, Rabbi Josel von Rosheim, 1898.

R. H. Tawney, Religion and the Rise of Capitalism, 1926.

Marvin Lowenthal (trans.), The Memoirs of Glückel of Hameln, 1932.

Selma Stern, Der preussische Staat und die Juden, I, 1925.

———, Jud Süss, 1929.

Felix Priebatsch, "Die Judenpolitik des fürstlichen Absolutismus im 17. und 18. Jahrhundert" in Festschrift Dietrich Schäfer, 1915, pp. 564-651.

M[eyer] Kayserling, Moses Mendelssohn, 1888.

H. Walter, Moses Mendelssohn, 1930 (in English).

M. Samuels, "Memoirs of Moses Mendelssohn" in Jewish Miscellanies, 1845.

Eduard Fuchs, Die Juden in der Karikatur, 1921. Besides its numerous illustrations, this work is valuable for its general survey of the economic conditions underlying the anti-Jewish movements from the sixteenth to the nineteenth century.

Marvin Lowenthal, A World Passed By, 1933. Chapters XV, XVI, and XVII describe the chief relics and antiquities of Jewish life still surviving from the twelfth to the last century.

NINETEENTH CENTURY

Jakob Lestschinsky, Das Wirtschaftliche Schicksal des deutschen Judentums, 1933. Statistical studies on population, emigration, and occupations, from the latter quarter of the eighteenth century to the last days of the German Republic.

Arthur Ruppin, Soziologie der Juden, 2 vols., 1930-1931. Descriptive and statistical survey, particularly from the eighteenth century to the present time. Much of this material is incorporated in *The Jews in the Modern World*, 1934, by the same author.

M[artin] Philippson, Neueste Geschichte des jüdischen Volkes, 3 vols., 1907, 1910, 1911.

Antonina Vallentin, Poet in Exile—The Life of Heinrich Heine, 1924. Vivid details on the political aspects of the Romantic Movement.

The Works of Heinrich Heine, trans. by Charles Godfrey Leland, etc., 12 vols., 1891-1906. The reader is particularly recommended vols. V-VI, entitled *Germany*, which contain the translation of *Zur Geschichte der Religion und Philosophie in Deutschland* and *Die Romantische Schule*.

Heine, Confessio Judaica, ed. by Hugo Bieber, 1925. A fairly complete collection of Heine's writings on Jews and Judaism, taken from his poems, prose, and letters. Nothing keener has ever been said on modern Jewry.

S. Baruch [A. S. Oko], "Leopold Zunz—Humanist," in Menorah Journal, IX, Feb., June, August, 1923.

Solomon Schechter, Studies in Judaism, III, 1924. "Leopold Zunz," pp. 84-142.

Fritz Friedlaender, Das Leben Gabriel Riessers, 1926.

David Philipson, The Reform Movement in Judaism, 1907.

Samson Raphael Hirsch, The Nineteen Letters of Ben Uziel, 1899. A presentation of the philosophy and point of view of traditional Judaism as confronted by modernity.

M[arcus] Brann, Zacharias Frankel, Gedenkblätter, 1901.
Ludwig Marcuse, Revolutionär und Patriot—Das Leben Ludwig Börnes, 1929.
Franz Mehring, Karl Marx—The Story of His Life, 1935.
Karl Marx, Selected Essays, 1926. "On the Jewish Question," pp. 40-97.
Theodor Zlocisti, Moses Hess der Vorkämpfer des Sozialismus und Zionismus, 1921.
Moses Hess, Rome and Jerusalem, 1918, with a brief biographical notice by the translator, Meyer Waxman.
Kurt Zielinziger, Juden in der deutschen Wirtschaft, 1930.
Rudolf Schay, Von Marx bis Rathenau—Deutschlands Weg seit 1815. 1929. A study of the leading Jewish personalities in German politics, with 16 portraits.

ARYANISM AND ANTI-SEMITISM

Frank H. Hankins, The Racial Basis of Civilization, 1931.
Julian S. Huxley and A. C. Haddon, We Europeans, 1935.
Felix von Luschan, Völker, Rassen, Sprachen, 1922.
Louis L. Snyder, From Bismarck to Hitler—The Background of Modern German Nationalism, 1935.
Maurice Fishberg, The Jews—A Study of Race and Environment, 1911.
Fritz Kahn, Die Juden als Rasse und Kulturvolk, 1920.
Theodor Lessing, Der jüdische Selbsthass, 1930.
Kurt Wawrzinek, Die Entstehung der deutschen Antisemitenparteien, 1926.
Encyclopedia Britannica (11th Edition), article "Antisemitism."

POST-WAR GERMANY

Elmar Luehr, The New German Republic, 1929.
Marvin Lowenthal, "The Jew in the European Scene," four articles in Menorah Journal, IX, X (1923-1924).
Gustav Krojanker, Juden in der deutschen Literatur—Essay über zeitgenössiche Schriftsteller, 1922.
Karl Schwarz, Die Juden in der Kunst, 1928.
Arnold Zweig, Juden auf der deutschen Bühne, 1928.
Frederick L. Schuman, The Nazi Dictatorship, 1935.
Konrad Heiden, A History of National Socialism, 1935.

SELECTED BIBLIOGRAPHY

Benjamin W. Segel, The Protocols of the Elders of Zion, 1934. Many details on the fortunes of this forgery in Germany.

Anti-Anti: Tatsachen zur Judenfrage (7th ed.), 1932, compiled and published by the Central Verein der deutschen Staatsbürger jüdischen Glaubens. The best source for studying the accusations levelled against the Jews during the last years of the Republic.

American Jewish Year Book, 1921-1936, for summary of events, and for annual reports on the German situation by the American Jewish Committee.

Pierre van Passen and James Waterman Wise (ed.), Nazism—An Assault on Civilization, 1934. Articles on various aspects of National Socialism in action, by Dorothy Thompson, Stanley High, Bernard S. Deutsch, Werner Hegemann, Alice Hamilton, I. A. Hirschmann, Ludwig Lore, John Haynes Holmes, Ludwig Lewisohn, Max Winkler, Emil Lengyel, Stephen S. Wise, Albert Brandt, Charles H. Tuttle, Miriam Beard, William Green, Samuel Guy Inman, Alfred E. Smith, and the editors.

The Jews in Nazi Germany: A Handbook of Facts Regarding their Present Situation. Compiled and published by the American Jewish Committee (New York), 1935.

Der Gelbe Fleck: Die Ausrottung von 500,000 deutschen Juden; mit einem Vorwort von Lion Feuchtwanger, (Paris) 1936. The most recent account of the situation in Germany.

The New Germany: A Symposium by Adolf Hitler, Franz von Papen, Konstantin von Neurath, Josef Paul Goebbels, Hans Luther, and Other Leaders, 1934.

The Brown Network, 1936. A study of National Socialist activities outside of Germany.

Jacob R. Marcus, The Rise and Destiny of the German Jew, 1934. Particularly useful for its detailed bibliographies covering the nineteenth and twentieth centuries.

FURTHER READING LISTS

See Adolf Kober, "Die Geschichte der deutschen Juden in der historischen Forschung der letzten 35 Jahre" in Zeitschrift für die Geschichte der Juden in Deutschland, I (1929), 13-23; Heinrich Loewe, "Die Juden in Deutschland: Bibliographische Notizen," ibid, I, 337-358; II, 310-332; III, 151-170; IV, 159-172.

INDEX

INDEX

INDEX

in the Third Reich, 398-99, 400, 401, 407, 408-12

Brahe, Tycho, 104

Brahms, Johannes, 390

Branau, 349

Brandenburg, 121, 136, 172, 173, 185, 187, 411

Brant, Sebastian, moralist, 105

Brendel, professor at Würzburg, 233

Brentano, Clemens, author, 227, 233

Bremen, 370

Breslau, 62, 75, 94, 119, 135, 137, 187

Brod, Max, author, 335

Bruck, Moeller van den, political theorist, 325

Brüning, Heinrich, 372, 380-81

Brunswick (city), 185, 190, 192

Brunswick-Lüneburg, 187

Buber, Martin, 335, 345

Büchner, Ludwig, 313

Buffon, Georges-Louis Leclerc de, 298-99

Bürger, Reichstag deputy, 394

Butzer, Martin, theologian, 172

Cahn, Moses, of Mayence, 218

Calé, Walter, victim of "self-hate," 266

Calvin, John, 117

Calvinists, 163, 164, 177, 180, 244

Camper, Pieter, discoverer of the "facial angle," 299

Canada, 418-19

Capitalism, 54, 118; finance capitalism, 174-77, 179; effects of French Revolution on, 216; in modern Germany, 261-62, 265, 305, 315, 359-61, 372, 386; monopoly capitalism, 271, 321-25, 327, 329, 332, 333, 377, 388, 417

Caracalla, emperor, 13

Carlsruhe, 232

Caro brothers, industrialists, 273

Carlyle, Thomas, 237

Castalio, Sebastian, apostle of tolerance, 164, 214

Casimir the Great, 131

Catholic Centrist Party, 372

Central Union of German Citizens of the Jewish Faith, 269, 346, 371, 372, 382, 385, 415

Chamberlain, Houston-Stewart, 267, 317-18, 354-55

Chamisso, Adalbert von, author, 227

Champagne fairs, 17, 19

Chaplin, Charlie, 364

Charlemagne, 14, 17, 18-19, 20, 22

Charles IV, 78, 81, 127, 129

Charles V, 168, 170, 172

Charles the Bald, of France, 166

Chlotar II, 14

Christian Socialism, 304-05, 310, 354

Christianity, 7-9, 15, 16, 119, 135, 146, 156, 215, 291, 292, 304, 365, 418, 420; as a Jewish depravation, 311-12. Also see *Church, Crusades, Martin Luther, Reformation*

Church (Catholic), 9, 14, 20-23, 55-56, 58-59, 75, 77, 82, 83-98, 99-100, 116, 126, 131, 148, 155, 160, 212, 214, 215, 294-95, 303, 320, 413. Also see *Christianity, Dominicans of Cologne*

Church council, of Clermont, 39; Fourth Lateran, 75, 90-91, 95, 402. See *Synods*

Clark, R. T. quoted, 393

Clement III, 53

Cleve, Elias, banker, 185, 188, 201

Cleves, 187

Coblenz, 60, 121

Cohen, Hermann, philosopher, 280

Cologne, 1, 4, 14, 17, 19, 43, 46, 57, 61, 62, 71, 75, 89, 94, 130, 136, 218-19

Commerce, 26, 162; Jewish, in Roman Empire, 2, 3; in Carolingian Age, 16-20; laws on, 31-32; in feudal times, 36-38; 15th-16th centuries, 136-37; 17th century, 180, 183-86, 213; 18th century, 208, 210, 212;

INDEX

East European Jews, 346, 361, 382, 401, 407
Ebenhausen, 249-50
Ebersheim, 59
Ebert, Friedrich, 319, 321
Eckart, Dietrich, National Socialist, 341
Eckhart, Master, mystic, 105
Edelmann, Johann Christian, freethinker, 200
Education, Jewish, 32, 106-07, 109-10, 209, 225
Egidio of Viterbo, humanist, 150
Ehrenfels, 60
Ehrlich, Paul, scientist, 279
Eichthal, Baron von, court banker, 183
Einhard, chronicler, 19
Einstein, Albert, 196, 280, 281, 335, 364, 401
Eisenmenger, Johann Andreas, 195, 294
Eisner, Kurt, communist leader, 320, 336, 338
Ekkehard, chronicler, 40, 41
Eleazar of Mayence, 112
Eleazar ben Judah of Worms, 67, 68-69, 75, 105
Elections during the Republic, 352, 370-71, 375, 381, 388, 389, 390, 393
Eliezer ben Isaac of Worms, *Testament* of, 33-35, 105.
Eliezer ben Nathan of Mayence, 27, 31, 32
Ellstätter, Moritz, 284
Emancipation of Jews, 207, 213-16, 220, 224, 230, 233, 244, 251-52, 253, 254, 255, 258, 262-65, 268-69, 271, 324, 333, 372, 386-87, 398; end of, 401f, 415, 419
Emden, Jacob, 196
Emerson, Ralph Waldo, 406
Emicho, Count, crusader, 43, 44, 47
Endigen, 166
Engels, Frederick, 255, 256

England, 60, 156, 183, 194, 227, 229, 233, 235, 315, 339; money-lending in, 58; crusades, 67; treatment of Jews, 69, 73, 77; expulsion of Jews, 82, 118, 136; Age of Reason, 199-200; Industrial Revolution, 215, 235, 255, 260; emigration to, 249, 407; policy in Palestine, 419
Ensisheim, 122
Ephraim, Veitel-Heine, court banker, 208
Epp, General von, 320
Erasmus, 144, 149, 153, 157, 163
Eremita, Colonel, in Thirty Years War, 180
Erfurt, 62, 75, 128, 130, 136
Erzberger, Matthias, Catholic statesman, 320, 326, 336
Escherich, Captain of the Orgesch, 325
Eskeles, Baron von, court banker, 183
Eugenius III, 67, 68
Everhard, baptized Jew, 87-88
Ewald, Johann, pastor, 233

Fascism, 351, 397
Faulhaber, Cardinal, 72
Feder, Gottfried, 353, 378
Ferdinand I, of Austria, 170, 172
Fettmilch, Vincent, 177-78
Feuchtwanger, Lion, author, 185, 334, 401
Feudalism, 15
Feuerbach, Ludwig, 264
Fichte, Johann Gottlieb, 225, 228-29, 231, 232, 233, 263, 357
Flagellants, 126, 129
Flick, Friedrich, industrialist, 325
Foerster, Wilhelm, astronomer, 313
Ford, Henry, 273, 340
Fould, Achille, minister of state, 183
Fouqué, Friedrich de la Motte, author, 227
France, 60, 156, 222, 227, 233, 251, 255, 257, 261, 265, 275, 334, 339, 373; emigration from, 24; Jewish

433

INDEX

INDEX

INDEX

INDEX

INDEX

INDEX

Nuremberg, 62, 82, 94, 122, 129, 136, 176, 177, 290, 348, 370, 415; Laws of (1935), 401-05; *Memorbuch,* 119, 130

Oath, *more Judaico,* 92, 262
Obernai, 166, 168
Ogdai Khan, 119
Oppenheim, 80, 370
Oppenheimer, David, book-collector, 192
Oppenheimer, Joseph Süss, court Jew, 185, 186-87, 191
Oppenheimer, Samuel, court Jew, 186, 191, 192
Ortenburg, 120
Otto the Great, 23, 71
Otto II, 23, 29, 71
Otto IV, 74
Oven, General von, 320

Padua, 133
Palatinate, 173, 186, 187
Palestine, 3, 6, 24, 27, 30, 40, 67, 122, 209, 258, 268, 345, 372, 382, 387, 402, 407, 414, 419
Pallenberg, Max, actor, 334
Panic of 1873, the, 265, 295, 296, 302
Papen, Franz von, 325, 382
Parnas—im, defined, 112.
Passau, 17, 19, 57, 96, 137
Paul, 84-85, 86, 163, 304
Pauli, Johannes, 106
Paulus, Heinrich, theologian, 233, 251
Peasants War, 160-61, 170
Pereire, Emile and Isaac, 275
Petahiah of Regensburg, traveler, 24
Peter the Hermit, 42
Peter the Venerable, 67
Peter's Kloster, chronicler of, 128
Petrus, doge of Venice, 37
Pfefferkorn, Johannes, 145-46, 148, 152-53
Pforzheim, 120
Philip, bishop of Cologne, 68

Physicians, see *Medicine*
Pine, Samson, translator, 106
Pinsker, Leo, 267-68
Pinkert, Alexander, 306
Pirkheimer, humanist, 149
Pius II, 94
Planck, Max, physicist, 281
Poland, 57, 60, 110, 113, 137, 139, 156, 179, 183, 188, 195, 201, 202, 209, 419, 420; emigration to, 24, 69, 131, 133, 177, 407; emigration from, 185, 346. Also see *East European Jews*
Pollak, Hans, 347-48
Population statistics, 62, 209, 211, 270, 346
Porges, Heinrich, disciple of Wagner, 267
Pösch, Theodor, 300, 304
Posen (city), 135; (state) 233, 248, 249
Posner, Abraham, 201
Pott, August Friedrich, philologist, 300
Prague, 21, 24, 47, 59, 104, 112, 131, 135, 137, 170, 179, 182, 183, 190, 191, 201, 335
Preuss, Hugo, 333, 338, 383
"Privileged" Jews, 189, 203. Also see *Court Jews*
Professions, Jews in, 210, 271, 278-85, 383-84, 399, 407, 414. Also see *Medicine*
Progress, theory of, 206, 215, 305, 384
Protocols of Zion, 322, 338, 339-41
Provence, 57, 60, 125
Prussia, 187, 190, 198-99, 219, 222, 224, 225, 230, 233, 241, 248, 252, 256, 260, 261, 262, 263; in Second Reich, 276, 307, 309; during the Republic, 333, 377, 382; under Third Reich, 401, 411
Purgolt, Johann, 55

Radanites, 19
Rapoport, Judah Loeb, 242
Ranke, Leopold, 237, 316

440

INDEX

Süsskind of Trimberg, minnesinger, 106, 112
Sweden, 179
Switzerland, 125, 204
Synod, of Breslau (1267), 91, 94; of Frankfort (794), 20; of Mayence (906), 20; (1233 and 1259), 91; of Metz (888), 21-22; of Trèves (1227), 75, 90
Synods, Jewish, 28, 138
Sybel, Heinrich von, historian, 316

Tacitus, 298
Tauberbischofsheim, 76
Techow, Ernst Werner, 338, 341, 345
Tertullian, 318
Teutomania movement, 231-33, 235
Thälmann, Ernst, Communist leader, 381
Thietmar, bishop of Merseburg, 23, 29
Thirty Years War, 72, 179-81, 204, 245, 275
Thomas Aquinas, 89, 117
Thomasius, Christian, 200
Thucydides, 296
Thuringia, 326, 371, 374-75
Thyssen, Fritz, 325, 332, 351, 372, 373, 378, 420
Tietz, Leonard and Oscar, merchants, 275
Tirpitz, Admiral von, 331
Titus, emperor, 70, 81
Toland, John, freethinker, 214
Tolerance, among ancient Jews, 7, 8; Christian attitude toward 8-10; in medieval Jewish thought, 115-17; Boccaccio, 139; Zwingli and Castalio, 164; influence of Protestantism on, 164-65; effect of finance capitalism, 175-76, 188-89; Bayle, 194; Mendelssohn and Lessing, 197-208; support and opposition in 18th century, 212-15; Industrialism, 215-16; relation to free capitalism, 216; Goethe

on, 234; under Third Reich, 291, 364-65, 379, 388, 399; alternative to death, 420-21. Also see *Emancipation of Jews*
Toller, Ernst, playwright, 320, 321, 334
Tosafists, 30, 116
Totalitarian State, 357-59, 362, 388, 396-99
Trebitsch, Arthur, 267
Treitschke, Heinrich von, 230, 294, 308-10, 313, 355, 357, 358
Trent, 135-36
Trèves, 1, 3, 42, 46, 60, 62, 71, 182, 256; *Chronicle,* 120
Tucholsky, Kurt, author, 335
Tyler, Wat, 134
Tylor, E. B., anthropologist, 300

Überlingen, 123
Ulm, 1, 3, 136
Unitarians, 214
United States, 215, 235, 248-50, 333, 335, 336, 339, 407
Urban II, 39, 41
Uri ben Joel Halevi, 75
Usury, see *Money-lending*

Valla, Lorenzo, 146
Valmy, battle of, 216, 217
Varnhagen, Rahel, see *Rachel Levin*
Varnhagen von Ense, Karl August, 226
Venice, 17, 19, 37, 133, 177
Verdun, 19
Verein für Cultur u. Wissenschaft der Juden, 238-39
Vienna, 1, 77, 135, 182, 183, 185, 186, 268, 335; Congress of, 183, 229-30
Virchow, Rudolph, 313
Virgil, 297
Vladislav I, 61
Vogt, Karl, 313
Voltaire, 86, 158, 176, 194-95, 199, 213, 214, 367

INDEX

Text set in Granjon type. The book has been printed on Monoplane Antique, and manufactured by the Haddon Craftsmen, Incorporated.